A DOCUMENTARY HISTORY OF ARKANSAS

A Documentary History of Arkansas

SECOND EDITION

Edited by

C. Fred Williams
S. Charles Bolton
Carl Moneyhon
LeRoy T. Williams

The University of Arkansas Press
Fayetteville
2013

ISBN-10: 1-55728-634-5
ISBN-13: 978-1-55728-634-5

17 16 15 14 13   5 4 3 2 1

Designed by Liz Lester

♾ The paper used in this publication meets the minimum requirements of the
American National Standard for Permanence of Paper for Printed Library Materials
Z39.48–1984.

Library of Congress Control Number: 2013942268

This book is dedicated to our students

CONTENTS

PART I: Early Arkansas, to 1836

CHAPTER I: Under Three Flags

CHAPTER II: Arkansas Territory

PART II: Arkansas and the South, 1836 to 1900

CHAPTER III: Antebellum Arkansas, 1836–1860

CHAPTER IV: Arkansas and the
Civil War Crisis, 1860–1874

PART III: Twentieth-Century Arkansas, 1900 to 1954

CHAPTER VI: Arkansas in the Progressive Era

CHAPTER VII: Between the Wars, 1920–1940

CHAPTER VIII: Arkansas during War and Peace, 1941–1954

CHAPTER X: Contemporary Arkansas, since 1985

PREFACE TO THE FIRST EDITION

This collection of documents represents a behind-the-scenes look at Arkansas from earliest times to the present. Collectively, they give a first-hand glimpse at how our state's history was made. Consideration has been given to the social and cultural aspects of Arkansas history, with special attention focused on the role played by women and blacks.

Each chapter is introduced by an original essay that provides an overview for the period in question and a brief explanation of the individual documents, each of which provides insight into a selected aspect of Arkansas history. Collectively, they represent a beginning, a point of reference rather than a final statement on the issues.

Special appreciation is extended to the Little Rock Panel, Inc., a multiethnic group particularly concerned with race relations in the public schools. Members of that organization first approached the editors in 1979 to encourage the publication of materials that present a perspective on minorities and women in Arkansas history more contemporary than found in many of the textbooks currently used. Their interest and support were primary influences in developing this project. Also, special thanks go to Judy Jauss and Peggy Baker for typing the manuscript.

Thanks are due as well to the editors of the publications in which the indicated material originally appeared:

Arkansas Gazette for twenty-four articles from territorial days to the present.

Fortune for the excerpt from "'Selfish' Arkansas Power."
© 1952, Time, Inc., all rights reserved.

The Lawyers' Co-operative Publishing Company for a quotation from *Cases Argued and Decided in the Supreme Court of the United States.*

Nashville Tennessean for a quotation from "New Factories a Thing of the Past in Little Rock."

National Geographic for a quotation from "The Great
Mississippi Flood of 1927" by Frederich Simpich.

New York Times for "Arts in Arkansas." © 1977 by The New
York Times Company. Reprinted by permission.

Special thanks to Orval E. Faubus for permission to reprint
his letter.

C. F. W., Little Rock, May 1983

PREFACE TO THE SECOND EDITION

When the first edition of this book was published in 1984, teaching Arkansas history had largely been abandoned in the state's public schools. A circular argument had developed with teachers making the case that there were too few text materials in print to adequately teach the course; while publishers countered that they could not afford to publish Arkansas materials because not enough districts were offering the state's history. The first *Documentary History of Arkansas* was designed to provide quality content at an affordable price by using primary source materials as the primary vehicle to present the state's history. Thanks to a generous subvention grant provided by the Arkansas chapter of the Panel of American Women, the University of Arkansas Press (then still in its infancy) was able to publish its second book (the first being *Arkansas Governors*) on Arkansas history. Both titles are still in print, and since 1984 the University of Arkansas Press has become a great engine for Arkansas culture by publishing manuscripts on all aspects of Arkansas, including history textbooks for both secondary and collegiate levels. Through the press's efforts over the past quarter century, the state's heritage has been generously offered to both local and national audiences.

Much has happened in the past twenty-five years. Perhaps the most dramatic was the state's forty-second governor, William (Bill) Jefferson Clinton, being elected as the forty-second president of the United States. His eight years in office focused national attention on Arkansas in a dramatic way. The state's identity emerged in the mainstream press, and most Americans became fully aware of where Arkansas was located even as political analysts puzzled over how it was possible for a small, southern state to provide the nation with its chief executive. But, while politics may have become more complex, the same issues that had defined the state for more than a hundred years continued to dominate. No matter the national exposure, Arkansans still primarily concerned themselves with providing their young people with an adequate education, finding new revenue sources without increasing taxes, accommodating the growing diversity of the population, and conserving, if not preserving, the state's environment.

This second edition has added some new documents and a new chapter, "Chapter X: Contemporary Arkansas, since 1985." However, it has retained the same format as the original publication, with essential, primary documents to illustrate basic themes in the state's political, social, economic, educational, and environmental history.

Thanks are due to the editors of the following publications for copyrighted material in the second edition:

Spectrum: The Journal of State and Local History, for an excerpt from "Effects of Term Limits in Arkansas: New Faces and New Ideas," by Win Rockefeller.

The University of Arkansas Press for excerpts from *The Clintons of Arkansas: An Introduction by Those Who Know Them Best.*

Arkansas Democrat-Gazette, for "Code Changes to Reduce Overcrowding," by Jeanni Brosius, published in Arkansas Online, June 6, 2011.

Arkansas Research Alliance, for "Battelle Study Confirms Return on Knowledge-based Initiatives and Underscores Sustainable, Strategic Funding."

Arkansas Family Council for *Q & A Concerning the Proposed Arkansas Lottery Amendment.*

EARTHJUSTICE for "Fact Sheet on Fracking."

Chesapeake Energy for fact sheet on water use in fracking.

Thanks are also due to Sheffield Nelson for permission to use his private letter on the natural gas severance tax.

C. Fred Williams, 2012

GENERAL INTRODUCTION

In 1820 Cephas Washburn, traveling as a missionary to the western Cherokees for the Society for the Propagation of the Gospel, stopped at the small village of Walnut Hills (now Vicksburg) and inquired about the way to Arkansas. To his amazement, he related, "the way to get there was unknown." Washburn's experience was not unique. Although populated by the Woodland and Mississippian Cultures, perhaps ten thousand years ago, the land of the Arkansas remained a mystery to most of the world until a member of the ill-fated expedition of Hernando de Soto described the region in a diary during the fall and winter of 1542–1543.

Sometime prior to the Spanish arrival, migrating Indians, including Tunica, Quapaw, and Caddo, came to settle on the land. It was from these people that Arkansas earned its early identity. De Soto came into contact first with the Tunica near present-day Parkin, Arkansas, before his westward journey was stopped by the Caddo in the Ouachita Mountains west of Hot Springs. One of his lieutenants recorded the first written description of these Native Americans. More than one hundred years after the de Soto expedition, French explorers Father Jacques Marquette and Louis Joliet visited the Quapaw, who arrived sometime after the Spanish entourage and built villages near the confluence of the Arkansas and Mississippi Rivers. Marquette's written account of that meeting led to the naming of this region as *Arkansas*, land of the "downstream people."

The Spanish and French, having both established claim to the region, passed the land of the Arkansas back and forth for more than one hundred years before the United States acquired permanent title at the beginning of the nineteenth century. Only then did Arkansas become an organized political entity, first as a part of Missouri, then as a territory in its own right until admitted into the family of states in 1836.

Ironically, many of the decisions that were to have formative influences on Arkansas's history were shaped prior to it becoming the twenty-fifth state. For example, the United States Congress determined that the region south of 36°30', Arkansas's northernmost boundary, would be

reserved for slavery. Then, as national political leaders struggled to preserve the balance between the number of free and slave states, Arkansas
was paired with Michigan and admitted to the Union prematurely.

Federal officials also decided to designate the area adjacent to
Arkansas's western border as "Indian Territory." This decision created a
barrier to western migration through the state for more than seventy-five
years and had a millpond effect on settlement patterns, with Arkansas
becoming a frontier area in the Mississippi River valley. Isolated and
removed from the primary routes of travel, the state developed outside
the mainstream of western expansion and throughout its history has
remained one of the least known of the fifty states.

In its search for identity, Arkansas evolved through four stages of development. The first may well be called the "Bear State" era, which spanned
from territorial times to World War I. During these formative years the
state was characterized by a rustic, yeoman-farmer society, only occasionally
broken by the estate of a plantation owner. Prior to the Civil War,
Arkansans were basically a frontier people, largely self-sufficient with a
lifestyle patterned to the cycle of nature. Outsiders gained most of their
understanding of the state through travel accounts of foreign visitors and
adventure stories in selected eastern publications. These sources tended to
picture Arkansas as a hunter's paradise, with bear hunting easily the favorite
sport, and its citizens as having a penchant for violence. The most graphic
visual image of the state during this period came to be associated with
Payton Washburn's painting, *The Arkansas Traveler*. The canvas pictured a
backwoodsman, adorned with a coonskin cap and surrounded by his corn-
cob pipe–smoking wife and gaggle of children, in confrontation with a
sophisticated stranger. The accompanying dialogue alternates between the
suave outsider trying repeatedly, and with increasing consternation, to
entice information from the laconic and suspicious frontiersman.

The Civil War and, perhaps more significantly, Reconstruction represented a turning point in Arkansas history. The emotional trauma of
invading armies and the accompanying imposition of a new political system had a galvanizing effect on many Arkansans. Previously content to
remain aloof and independent, Arkansans now were pressured to indus-
trialize and become more integrated into the mainstream of US culture.
New leadership in the political and business communities sought to pull
the state from its rural moorings and fashion a new social and economic

image. Ribbons of steel now pushed across the Arkansas landscape, and a new series of settlements came into view. Previous communities developed along the river systems of the state, but now the railroad drew settlers away from the waterways and into other sections of the state.

Regrettably, for those involved, efforts to mold a "New Arkansas Traveler" never really materialized. Fifty years of relative isolation had had a lasting impact on trade and travel patterns, and the state was never able to assert itself in the new industrial economy. Political factionalism, deteriorating race relations, and growing problems in the prison system also hampered the state's development.

By the end of World War I, state leaders had convened for a new attempt at remaking the state's image. Aided by the boom cycle created by the war, state leaders christened Arkansas as the "Wonder State" and issued bold new challenges for growth and development. The new era was closely tied to the emerging automobile industry, as once again the Arkansas countryside was altered to accommodate a new transportation system. New rights-of-way were surveyed and the landscape was overlaid with still another network of "civilizing" influences.

The new image was not without its costs, however. Lacking adequate capital, state political leaders allowed local communities to form improvement districts, vote bonds, and build their own roads. The results included a multi-million-dollar indebtedness and an incoherent road system. The state's efforts to rescue local governments from bankruptcy by assuming the indebtedness were undermined by monumental floods and a disastrous three-year drought—all of which combined to devastate the state's budget. For a decade Arkansas struggled under the heaviest per capita indebtedness in the nation. The state's embarrassing plight was exposed to a national audience by eastern newspapers, and the long shadow of the Great Depression stretched across the land. The cycle was not broken until military spending for World War II provided a measure of relief.

In the post–World War II era, state leaders worked hard to recast the shattered Wonder State image. The rapid loss in population, which continued for more than a decade, added a sense of urgency to the new mission. After considering a number of alternatives, business and political leaders reached a consensus for promoting the state as the "Land of Opportunity."

The image was framed around three priorities soon to be known as the "Arkansas Plan." First, major steps were taken to sort out the problems of the highway program. Next, the state began a concentrated campaign to attract a variety of industrial firms that would complement Arkansas's revived agricultural industry. Finally, leaders of the movement emphasized the importance of checking the pattern of outward migration that eroded the labor force and deprived the state of its most productive citizens. A decade of hard work paid handsome dividends. The highway department, although brushed by the ripple of scandal, regained its solvency and won national recognition for some of its activities. Industrial growth proceeded at a record pace, and outward migration slowed to a trickle, stopped, and reversed as the state again began to show an increase in population.

Ironically, just as the Arkansas Plan began to demonstrate its effectiveness, the state was rocked by the integration crisis in the Little Rock public school system. The press brought to the nation an image of a taunting, jeering mob of whites and a governor who defied federal authority, who together resisted desegregation in the Land of Opportunity. The troublesome issue sank deep into the fabric of Arkansas society, leaving indelible stains upon the corporate psyche of Arkansans.

The integration controversy had hardly eased before the state was again vaulted into the national limelight with potentially scandalous disclosures about its prison system. Unmarked graves on one institution's grounds were opened in the light of network television cameras to reveal unidentified bodies, previously unaccounted for, but presumably former prisoners murdered by prison officials. The gravesites were later determined to be part of an old cemetery and the bodies identified; however, this information was not nearly as well covered as the initial story.

In the minds of many Arkansans, the integration crisis and prison disclosures were both overblown by the media. The unfavorable publicity was unjust and represented sensationalism created by a minority of the state's people. Even so, the events have left their marks on the minds of many Americans whose only exposure to Arkansas has been an occasional news item of sufficient scope or curiosity to make the national press.

Although disturbing setbacks in education and the prison system proved difficult, they were not insurmountable. By the late 1960s, all indexes on the state's growth were on the increase. Migration patterns, which traditionally worked to Arkansas's disadvantage, now changed to bring population growth. Increasing costs in energy and labor caused many industries to leave the northern "frost belt" in favor of the state's more congenial climate for business as well as weather. The federal government also contributed to the pattern by providing assistance for development on the Arkansas River, refugee resettlement, and aid to cities and counties. The state treasury, long accustomed to a deficit, began to register a surplus, and a new sense of optimism swept over the state. This new mood was perhaps best reflected in the success of the athletic program at the University of Arkansas's Fayetteville campus. Teams representing the institution, beginning with football, then basketball, baseball, and, finally, numerous other sports, achieved national rankings and a winning tradition, becoming a new source of pride for the state's citizens.

One of the best commentaries on the success of the Land of Opportunity promotion can be seen in the opposition to some of its results. Industrial development and agribusiness increased environmental pollution, and the increase in population, particularly in the Ozark upland region, greatly altered the natural landscape—causing a new set of conflicts. Sportsmen and environmentalists vied with promoters and developers over the best use of the land. The former group sought to keep Arkansas as a natural area by emphasizing its scenic rivers, forest-covered mountains, and vast open spaces. The latter group used the same themes to entice population and economic growth to the state. Success by retailers Walmart, Inc., and Tyson, Inc., the world's largest businesses in their respective categories, along with major developments by transportation companies, extended a new image of the state throughout the world. William Jefferson Clinton, the first Arkansan to be elected president of the United States, enhanced that new image. In keeping with this new image, state leaders changed the state's nickname to "The Natural State."

Ironically, even as the new image was being placed in national advertisements and statewide billboards, construction of an interstate highway and an airport capable of hosting the major airlines of the world, coupled with the discovery of natural gas deposits in the central and eastern Ozarks, combined to challenge some the state's most pristine regions. Still, the Natural State is an identity most Arkansans comfortably adopt as representative of their state.

PART I

Early Arkansas, to 1836

S. Charles Bolton

CHAPTER I

Under Three Flags

INTRODUCTION

The land covered by the present state of Arkansas consists of more than fifty thousand square miles lying west of the Mississippi River in the latitude between 33° and 36°30'. It is rather evenly divided into lowland and highland regions, on a diagonal running from the southwest and to the northeast. The lowland consists of the Mississippi delta, an alluvial plain that forms the eastern border of the state, and a coastal plain that extends across the south. The highland regions are the Ouachita Mountains in the west and the Ozark Mountains in the north. The Arkansas River flows across the state, dividing the highland regions and emptying into the Mississippi. The White and the St. Francis Rivers in the north and northeast and the Ouachita and the Red Rivers in the southwest form other important drainage systems.

About one thousand years ago, during the European Middle Ages, Native Americans in Arkansas entered a cultural stage now known as Mississippian, which was common throughout the southeastern part of the United States. They engaged in intensive agriculture based on corn, beans, and squash, lived in permanent villages often surrounded by palisades, built large flat-topped earthen mounds for ceremonial purposes, made pottery, hunted with bows and arrows, were organized into a hierarchical social structures, had complex religious beliefs, and engaged in trade with people living in other regions. By the middle of the sixteenth century, Arkansas was more densely populated than it would be for the next three hundred years. Perhaps the most significant legacy of the De Soto expedition that entered Arkansas in 1541 is the record it provides of Mississippian culture at it its height. After the Spaniards left, the numbers of Native American people in the state dropped precipitously, and their culture lost some of its sophistication. The cause of this demographic catastrophe was probably the damaging effect of European diseases and a series of severe droughts.

French explorers in the last quarter of the seventeenth century found a much different native population. Living near the mouth of the river whose name they bore were the Arkansas or Quapaw Indians, who were of Siouan stock and had migrated from the upper Ohio Valley. They built large, multifamily dwellings covered with bark, practiced successful agriculture, and supplemented their diet by extensive hunting and fishing. Distant relatives but enemies of the Quapaws were the fierce Osages, who regularly hunted in northwestern Arkansas. Caddo Indians from Texas had entered western Arkansas and taken up permanent residence along the Ouachita and Red Rivers. The Caddos built rounded dwellings from saplings and thatched grass on the mounds left by earlier inhabitants, made excellent pottery, and grew corn in abundance.

The Indians of Arkansas first encountered European culture in the sixteenth century when Spanish conquistadores marched through their lands. The expedition led by Hernando de Soto that left Spain in 1539 with six hundred men and two hundred horses was one of several tentative probes into North America. Arriving at Tampa Bay in May, de Soto marched through the southeastern United States and eventually reached the Mississippi River. On June 18, 1541, the expedition crossed into Arkansas somewhere below present-day Memphis. Harassing the Indians, taking their food, and fighting with them on occasion, de Soto moved north, where he remained for a month at a large town on the Mississippi River called Pacaha, located southwest of modern Jonesboro. Continually searching for gold, the Spaniards visited another town called Coligua, probably near Batesville, and then moved south, reaching the Arkansas River near Conway; and following it north, they made their way into the northern Quachita Mountains, where they suffered many casualties at the hands of the buffalo-hunting residents of a region called Tula. De Soto then returned to the Arkansas River and followed it south to a village called Autiamque, located between Little Rock and Pine Bluff, where the expedition rested for the winter. In the spring, the four hundred surviving soldiers with their forty remaining horses marched to the Mississippi River, where de Soto died and was buried. Seeking to reach the Gulf

Coast, his men crossed southern Arkansas and traveled deep into Texas before giving up and returning to the mouth of the Arkansas River, where they were able to make boats and float down the Mississippi River.

In the meantime, France won control of Canada and, in the latter part of the seventeenth century, moved to create an inland empire stretching down the Mississippi River to the Gulf of Mexico. Exploring the Mississippi in 1673, a Jesuit priest named Jacques Marquette and a woodsman named Louis Joliet arrived at the mouth of the Arkansas and enjoyed the hospitality of the Quapaw Indians, who numbered perhaps five thousand people and were the dominant force in the Arkansas River Valley. In 1682, Robert Chevelier, Sieur de La Salle, reached the mouth of the Mississippi and claimed the entire valley for France, naming it Louisiana in honor of his king, Louis XIV. On a later voyage from France, La Salle lost his life in Texas after failing to find the Mississippi, but his lieutenant, Henri de Tonti, founded Arkansas Post in 1686 at a Quapaw village near the mouth of the Arkansas River. This was the first permanent European settlement west of the Mississippi. In the eighteenth century, the French traded with the Indians and continued to explore. John Law, a Scot with influence at the French court, settled colonists on the lower Arkansas in 1718. Linked to a shaky stock scheme known as the Mississippi Bubble, the colony did not survive.

In 1762, having been defeated by the British in the Seven Years' War, France gave up imperial ambitions in North America and transferred Louisiana to Spain. Spanish troops garrisoned Arkansas Post and the government issued land grants, but little settlement occurred throughout the remainder of the eighteenth century. During the American Revolution, the Spanish forces at Arkansas Post helped Americans traveling the Mississippi River, and in 1783 they beat off an attack by a force of British partisans.

Arkansas became part of the United States as a result of the Louisiana Purchase. In 1800 Spain returned Louisiana, defined as the land drained by rivers flowing east to the Mississippi, to France, whose emperor, Napoleon Bonaparte, dreamed of a North American empire. President Thomas Jefferson, however, feared the French would end American trade on the Mississippi, a major blow to the economy of the United States, and sent ministers to France to protect American interests. Jefferson's concern turned to elation when Napoleon, frustrated by a slave uprising in Haiti and faced with a new war in Europe, sold Louisiana to the United States in 1803.

Under the dominion of the United States, Arkansas was part of the Louisiana Territory, which included all of the purchase north of the present Arkansas-Louisiana border. The name of the future state was first used officially in 1806 when the territorial legislature created the District of Arkansas. When Louisiana became a state in 1812, the name of the territory to the north became Missouri Territory. Five counties in what is now Arkansas were formed as part of the Missouri Territory: Arkansas County in 1813; Lawrence County in 1815; and Pulaski, Clark, and Hempstead Counties in 1818, just prior to the creation of Arkansas Territory.

The increasing complexity of local government reflected a growing population. In 1799 the Spanish counted 368 European settlers in Arkansas; in 1810 there were only about one thousand Americans, but after the War of 1812 pioneers began to arrive in large numbers. The government of the United States rewarded veterans with land grants in Arkansas and began a land survey to secure claims. When the New Madrid earthquakes of 1811–1812, the largest in North America, rearranged the geography of the upper St. Francis River and flooded permanently thousands of acres of land, settlers who lost property were compensated with land in Arkansas. By 1819 the population was nearly fourteen thousand. The settlement at Arkansas Post was matched by small communities at Helena, Washington, Little Rock, Ecore a Fabre (now Camden), Cadron (near present Conway), and Hopefield (near West Memphis). At a place called Belle Point on the upper Arkansas River, a detachment of US troops was building Fort Smith to guard the southwestern frontier.

A. EXPLORERS AND INDIANS

Arkansas entered the historic period through the written accounts of European explorers. Interested in the geography, plants, animals, and the Native Americans of Arkansas, the Spanish conquistadores and French voyageurs provided a thorough description of what they found; at the same time, these documents tell a good deal about the men who wrote them.

Spanish Encounters with the Indians

Edward Gaylord Bourne, *Narratives of the Career of Hernando de Soto*, 2 vols. (New York: Allerton Book Co., 1922), 1:123–24, 135–39, 143, 145.

"A Gentleman of Elvas" traveled with Hernando de Soto and wrote an extensive account of the expedition. The following selections describe the advanced economic activity of the Native Americans in Arkansas and their unhappy experiences with the Spanish. Having only recently expelled the Moors from Spain, the Spanish emphasized the religious differences between themselves and the Indians.

On Wednesday, the [twenty-ninth] day of June, the Governor entered Pacaha, and took quarters in the town where the Cacique [chief] was accustomed to reside. It was enclosed and very large. In the towers and the palisade were many loopholes. There was much dry maize, and the new was in great quantity, throughout the fields. At the distance of half a league to a league off were large towns, all of them surrounded with stockades.

Where the Governor stayed was a great lake, near to the enclosure, and the water entered a ditch that well-nigh went around the town. From the River Grande [Mississippi] to the lake was a canal, through which the fish came into it, and where the Chief kept them for his eating and pastime. With nets that were found in the place, as many were taken as need required; and however much might be the casting, there was never any lack of them. In the many other lakes about were also many fish, though the flesh was soft, and none of it so good as that which came from the river. . . .

The Governor tarried a month in the Province of Cayas. In this time the horses fattened and throve more than they had done at other places in a longer time, in consequence of the large quantity of maize there. The blade of it, I think, is the best fodder that grows. The beasts drank so copiously from the very warm and brackish lake, that they came having their bellies swollen with the leaf when they were brought back from watering. To that spot the Christians had wanted salt: they now made a quantity and took it with them. The Indians carry it into other parts, to exchange for skins and shawls.

The salt is made along by a river, which, when the water goes down, leaves it upon the sand. As they cannot gather the salt without a large mixture of sand, it is thrown together in certain baskets they have for the purpose, made large at the mouth and small at the bottom. These are set in the air on a ridge-pole; and water being thrown on, vessels are placed under them wherein it may fall, then, being strained and placed on the fire, it is boiled away, leaving salt at the bottom. . . .

Then the Governor, with cavalry and fifty infantry, directly set out for Tulla, to see if it were such a land as he might pass through with his troops. So soon as it became known that he had reached there, the inhabitants were summoned; and as they gathered by fifteen and twenty at a time, they would come to attack the Christians. Finding that they were sharply handled, and that in running the horses would overtake them, they got upon the housetops, where they endeavored to defend themselves with their bows and arrows. When beaten off from one roof, they would get up on to another; and the Christians while going after some, others would attack them from an opposite direction. The struggle lasted so long that the steeds, becoming tired, could not be made to run. One horse was killed and others were wounded. Of the Indians fifteen were slain, and forty women and boys made prisoners; for to no one who could draw a bow and could be reached was his life spared him.

The Governor determined at once to go back, before the inhabitants should have time to come together. That afternoon he set out, and travelling into the night, he slept on the road to avoid Tulla, and arrived the next day at Cayas. Three days later he marched to Tulla, bringing with him the Cacique, among whose Indians he was unable to find one who spoke the language of that place. He was three days on the way, and at his arrival found the town abandoned, the inhabitants not venturing to remain for him. But no sooner did they know he was in the town, than, at four o'clock on the morning of the first night, they came upon him in two squadrons, from different directions, with bows and arrows and with long staves like pikes. So soon as they were felt, both cavalry and infantry turned out. Some Christians and some horses were injured. Many of the Indians were killed.

Of those made captive, the governor sent six to the Cacique, their right hands and their noses cut off, with the message, that, if he did not come to him to apologize and render obedience, he would go in pursuit, and to him, and as many of his as he might find, would he do as he had done to those he sent. He allowed him three days in which to appear, making himself understood by signs, in the best manner possible, for want of an interpreter. At the end of that time an Indian, bearing a back-load of cow-skins from the Cacique, arrived, weeping with great sobs, and coming to where the Governor was, threw himself at his feet. . . .

[At Autiamque] they found in store much maize, also beans, walnuts, and dried *ameixas* [*sic*] in large quantities. Some Indians were taken while gathering up their clothing, having already carried away their wives. The country was level and very populous. The Governor lodged in the best portion of the town, and ordered a fence immediately to be put up about the encampment, away from the houses, that the Indians without might do no injury with fire. . . .

The Christians stayed three months in Autiamque, enjoying the greatest plenty of maize, beans, walnuts, and dried *ameizas*; also conies [rabbits], which they had never had ingenuity enough to ensnare until the Indians there taught them. The contrivance is a strong spring, that lifts the animal off its feet, a noose being made of a stiff cord to run about the neck, passing through rings of cane, that it may not be gnawed. Many of them were taken in the maize-fields, usually when it was freezing or snowing.

Marquette's Reception by the Quapaws

John Hugh Reynolds, ed., "Marquette's Reception by the Quapaws, 1673," *Publications of the Arkansas Historical Association* 1(1906): 500–502.

By the second half of the seventeenth century, the English held permanent colonies along the coast of North America and the French controlled a fur trading empire in Canada. Indian tales of a mighty inland river stimulated French authorities to send Father Jacques Marquette and Louis Joliet to explore the Mississippi. Leaving Green Bay in June 1673, they followed the Wisconsin River to the Mississippi and then traveled south as far as the mouth of the Arkansas. The conversion of the Indians to Christianity was an important goal of the French, and Marquette was an energetic missionary.

They told us that at the next great village, called Arkansea, eight or ten leagues farther down the river, we could learn all about the sea. They feasted us with sagamite [hominy porridge] and fish, and we passed the night with them, not, however, without some uneasiness. We embarked early next morning with our interpreters and ten Indians who went before us in a canoe. Having arrived about half a league from Arkansea, we saw two canoes coming toward us. The captain of one was standing up holding the calumet [ceremonial pipe] in his hand, with which he made signs, according to the custom of the country. He afterwards joined us, inviting us to smoke, and singing pleasantly. He then gave us some sagamite [corn-based stew] and Indian bread to eat, and going before made signs for us to follow him, which we did, but at some distance. They had in the meantime prepared a kind of scaffold to receive us, adorned with fine mats, upon which we sat down with the old men and warriors. We fortunately found among them a young man who spoke Illinois much better than the interpreter whom we brought with us from Mitchigamea.

We made them some small presents, which they received with great civility, and seemed to admire what I told them about God, the creation of the world, and the mysterious of our holy faith, telling us by the interpreter that they wished us to remain with them for the purpose of instructing them.

We then asked them what they knew of the sea, and they said we were within ten days' journey of it, but we might perform it in five. That they were unacquainted with the nations below, because their enemies had prevented them from visiting them. That the hatchet, knives and beads had been sold to them by the nations of the East, and were in part brought by the Illinois, who lived four days' journey to the West. That the Indians whom we had met with guns were their enemies, who hindered them from trading with the Europeans, and if we persisted in going any farther, we would expose ourselves to other nations who were their enemies. During this conversation they continued all day to feast us with sagamite, dog meat, and roasted corn out of large wooden dishes. These Indians were very courteous, and give freely of what they have, but their provisions are but indifferent, because they are afraid to go a hunting on account of their enemies. They make three crops of Indian corn a year. They roast and boil it in large earthen pots very curiously made. They have also large baked earthen plates, which they use for different purposes. The men go naked and wear their hair short. They pierce their noses and ears, and wear rings of glass beads in them.

The women cover themselves with skins, and divide their hair into two tresses, which they wear behind their back without any ornament. Their feasts are without any ceremony, they serve their meats in large dishes, and every one eats as much as he pleases. Their language is extremely difficult, and although I tried, I never could pronounce a word of it.

Their cabins are made with the bark of trees, and are generally very wide and long. They lie at both ends on mats raised on a platform two feet higher than the floor. They keep their corn in panniers [baskets] made of rushes. They have no beavers and all their commodities are buffalo hides. It never snows in this country, and they have no other winter than continued heavy rains, which make the difference between their summer and winter. They have no other fruit but watermelons, though their soil might produce any other, if they knew how to cultivate it. In the evenings the chiefs held a secret council wherein some proposed to kill us, but the great chief opposed this base design, and sent for us to dance the calumet, which he presented us with to seal our common friendship. M. Joliet and I held council, to deliberate upon what we should do—whether to proceed further, or return to Canada, content with the discoveries we had made.

Having satisfied ourselves that the Gulf of Mexico was in latitude 31°40', and that we could reach it in three or four days' journey from the Arkansea [Arkansas River], and that the Mississippi discharged itself into it, and not to the eastward of the cape of Florida, nor into the California Sea, we resolved to return home.

La Salle Claims Arkansas for France, 1682

Isaac Joslin Cox, ed., *The Journeys of Rene Robert Sieur de La Salle*, 2 vols. (New York: Allerton Book Co., 1922), 1:19–20.

La Salle, the moving force behind French development of inland North America, made his famous voyage down the Mississippi to its mouth in 1682. Like Marquette and Joliet, he spent time with the Quapaw Indians, and at one of their villages he erected the coat of arms of the French king as a sign that France now owned the land. Kappa was one of several Quapaw villages located on the Mississippi. The narrator in this document is La Salle's second in command, Henry de Tonti.

We continued our route as far as the village of Cappa [Kappa], fifty leagues off. We arrived there in foggy weather, and as we heard the sound of the tambour, we crossed over to the other side of the river, where, in less than half an hour, we made a fort. The savages having been informed that we were coming down the river, came in their canoes to look for us. We made them land, and sent two Frenchmen as hostages to their village; the chief visited us with the calumet, and we went to the savages. They regaled us with the best they had, and after having danced the calumet to M. de la Salle, they conducted us to their village of Toyengan, eight leagues from Cappa. They received us there in the same manner, and from thence they went with us to Toriman, two leagues further on, where we met with the same reception. It must be here remarked that these villages, the first of which is Osotonoy, are six leagues to the right descending the river, and are commonly called Arkancas [Arkansas]. The first three villages are situated on the great river. M. de la Salle erected the arms of the King there; they have cabins made with the bark of cedar; they have no other worship than the adoration of all sorts of animals. Their country is very beautiful, having abundance of peach, plum and apple trees, and vines flourish there; buffaloes, deer, stags, bears, turkeys, are very numerous. They have even domestic fowls. They have very little snow during the winter, and the ice is not thicker than a dollar. They gave us guides to conduct us to their allies, the Taencas, six leagues distant.

La Harpe Explores the Arkansas River, 1722

Ralph A. Smith, trans. and ed., "Exploration of the Arkansas River by Bénard de la Harpe, 1721–1722: Extracts from His Journal and Instructions," *Arkansas Historical Quarterly* 10 (1951): 347–48, 350–52, 354, 357.

In the eighteenth century, the French established themselves at the mouth of the Mississippi and gradually moved to control all of what La Salle had called Louisiana. In 1722, Bénard La Harpe left Fort Louis, near modern Biloxi, Mississippi, with sixteen soldiers to explore the Arkansas River, establish French hegemony in the area, and seek opportunities for trade with the Indians. The rocky bluffs at the present capital of Arkansas were the first major landmark seen by travelers as they made their way upriver. A league was probably about two and a half miles, and a pirogue was a canoe made from a hollowed-out tree trunk.

My first evening [March 1] on arriving at this village [a Quapaw community near Arkansas Post] has been to learn from the Savages the course of the river and about the nations that live along it; they know the river only up to the Rock, which they estimate at twenty days journey by the path; seventy leagues beyond by land they know of a fork in the river, the right branch going to the Panis [Pawnees]. From the village . . . they estimate it to be twenty days journey by land to the Osages, a nation which is their ally, and from the Osages to the Panis five days journey. . . .

The 10th, having made calculations of my provisions, I discovered having thirteen barrels of corn, three of beans, and one of rice; after that we set out, making in all twenty-two persons. . . .

The 22nd, the rain kept us at the camp until eight o'clock, when we departed through a very cold north wind. We, during this day made four and a half leagues, which reduced, amounted to only two and a half leagues toward the west, a quarter northwest. We passed this day large sand banks and very fine country; we came upon, ordinarily, a great quantity of vines and plums [*sic*] trees which are in bloom; the lands bear a quantity of white and red morels [mushrooms]. . . .

The 31st, we set out at six in the morning; at ten o'clock, our Savage killed four turkeys and a buffalo for us, which forced us to stop to smoke them this day. The wind has been in the southeast, the weather is very warm. . . .

The 9th [of April] having advanced a league, we found rocks sticking out of the ground, and have reached a league above the rock, which is on the right of the river; we named it the French Rock [Big Rock, in present-day North Little Rock]. It is a bluff of mountainous rock, which forms three very steep peaks, suitable for making lime; it could be 130 feet perpendicular. There are beyond some oaks, walnuts, and pines. One finds there a stone which has a relationship to marble, being very much like jasper; but it is hard as flint; there are also several quarries of slate, but they are not so convenient to work as that which we found at a league below; there are quarries of the most beautiful slate that one may be able to see, very fine, rising through shells, and of so great abundance that they would furnish all the colony.

There is also at this rock very beautiful black stones suitable for construction purposes; they are hewn by nature and of all sizes. We climbed up this mountain and engraved on a tree upon the top the coat of arms of the King. We perceived to the westward several mountains and beautiful country. At the foot of this rock, there is a waterfall which forms a very pleasant basin, whose water is very clear and fresh.

Having advanced a league through the river, our small pirogue, which had taken the lead with our two Savages and four soldiers, has been dashed upon a log by the violence of the current, so that it turned over. The men hung to the log, but all that was in the pirogue has been lost, which consists of eighty-five pickaxes and hatchets, a boiler, three muskets and several other objects, wheat and clothes. We have had much difficulty in pulling the pirogue from beneath the log, after which we resumed the course.

B. THE POST OF ARKANSAS

From 1686, when ten of Henri de Tonti's Frenchmen chose to remain with the Quapaws, down to 1820, when the capital of Arkansas Territory moved to Little Rock, Arkansas Post was the center of European and American activity in Arkansas. Located a few miles above the mouth of the Arkansas River, near the entrance of the White River, Arkansas Post was in a good position to handle the trade of both the Indians and the early settlers. It also served as a military and administrative center. There were never more than about five hundred inhabitants at the Post, however, and their number declined during the territorial period.

Joutel Arrives at the Post, 1687

Henri Joutel, *A Journal of La Salle's Last Voyage* (New York: Corinth Books, 1962), 143–45.

Henri Joutel was a survivor of La Salle's expedition to settle a colony at the mouth of the Mississippi. Having walked from the area of present-day Houston, Texas, through wild and unknown country, Joutel was understandably happy to find Frenchmen living along the banks of the Arkansas River.

July, 1687

We set out again to come to the Village, and by the Way, met with very pleasant Woods, in which, there were Abundance of stately Cedars. Being come to a River, that was between us and the Village, and looking over to the further Side, we discover'd a great Cross, and at a small Distance from it, a House, built after the French Fashion.

It is easy to imagine what inward Joy we conceiv'd at the Sight of that Emblem of our Salvation. We knelt down, lifting up our Hands and Eyes to Heaven, to return Thanks to the Divine Goodness, for having conducted us so happily; for we made no Question of finding *French* on the other side of the River, and of their being Catholics, since they had Crosses.

In short, having halted some Time on the Bank of that River, we spy'd several Canoes making towards us, and two Men cloath'd, coming out of the House we had discover'd, who, the Moment they saw us, fir'd each of them a Shot to salute us. An *Indian* being Chief of the Village, who was with them, had done so before, and we were not backward in returning their Salute, by discharging all our Pieces.

When we had pass'd the river, and were all come together, we soon knew each other to be *French* men. Those we found were the Sieurs *Couture Charpantier* and *de Launay*, both of them of *Roan* [Rouen], whom Monsieur *de Tonty*, Governor of Fort St. *Lewis* among the Islinois, had left at that Post, when he went down the Mississippi to look after Monsr. *de la Sale*; and the Nation we were then with, was call'd Accancea [Arkansas].

It is hard to express the Joy conceiv'd on both Sides; ours was unspeakable, for having at last found, what we had so earnestly desired, and that the Hopes of returning to our dear Country, was in some Measure assured by that happy Discovery. The others were pleased to see such Persons as might bring them News of that Commander, from whom they expected the Performance of what he had promis'd them; but the Account we gave them of Monsr. de la Sale's unfortunate Death, was so afflicting, that it drew Tears from them, and the dismal History of his Troubles and Disasters render'd them almost inconsolable.

We were conducted to the House, whither all our Baggage was honestly carry'd by the Indians. There was a very great Throng of those People, both Men and Women, which being over, we came to the Relation of the particular Circumstances of our Stories. Ours was deliver'd by Monsieur Cavelier, whom we honour'd as our Chief, for being Brother to him, who had been so.

We were inform'd by them, that they had been Six, sent by Monsr. Tonty, when he return'd from the Voyage he had made down the Colbert or Mississippi River, pursuant to the Orders sent him by the late Monsr. de la Sale, at his departure from France, and that the said Sieur Tonty had commanded them to build the aforesaid House. That having never since receiv'd any News from the said Monsr. de la Sale, Four of them were gone back to Monsr. Tonty, at the Fort of the Islinois.

A British Attack on a Spanish Post, 1783

Anna Lewis, trans. and ed., "A British Attack on a Spanish Post, 1783," *Arkansas Historical Quarterly* 2 (1943): 261–64.

Louisiana, and Arkansas Post with it, became Spanish territory after the French withdrew from North America in 1764. During the American Revolution, the Spanish garrison at Arkansas Post—called Fort Charles III by the Spanish—aided Americans moving supplies up the Mississippi. In 1783, James Colbert, a Scot who lived with the Chickasaws in Tennessee and functioned as a British partisan, launched an attack on the Spanish outpost. The Spanish beat off the assault and eventually got back all the prisoners.

Jacobo du Breuil to Estevan Miro
Fort Charles III
May 5, 1783

Very Illustrious Sir:

Since my last letter of March 26, I have noticed nothing more of the pirates, but unfortunately Colbert entered this place on the seventeenth of last month, at 2:30 in the morning, at the time when every one was asleep, and at the head of a hundred whites and fourteen Chickasaws took possession of all the houses, with no obstruction from a party of eight soldiers and a sergeant which forms the garrison of the fort (according to the orders of Your Excellency). They (Colbert's party) seized the

Lieutenant Don Luis de Villars with all his family who had been living a little apart for four days, there having been a violent wind which blew down the house which he occupied in the fort. The four principal men of the settlement with their families got away, escaping to the mountain with six others who were all that made up the village, except the women and children of the hunters (who had come up there about a year ago). These got away and came to my house, not without danger.

As the first shot (I had surrounded all the posts with palisade) was at the Lieutenant's house, with which they had broken the lock on the door, our garrison ran at once to that place and mixed with them, but as they were superior in numbers to us they killed two soldiers, the one belonging to the hunters and the other a negro of the neighborhood. They seized the Point and five other soldiers. The sergeant got away from three of them who were trying to take him, and ran like a rabbit. Then they made no further movement to kill us when they knew that the sergeant had escaped, and then they took all of the people in the place prisoners and embarrassed us more by taking our cannon.

All this happened in less than a half hour, when they decided to strike the fort, which due to its bad location one could approach within pistol shot before being seen even though there were a thousand men.

Then we began again (with cannons and guns) a fight which lasted from 3 o'clock in the morning until 9 o'clock, piercing like a sieve the palisades with carbines, but the bullets penetrated no more than an inch, because of the evergreen oak of which the palisades were made. On seeing this, I decided to make a formal blockade with artillery. I decided that before giving them a chance to form a battery, that it would be a good idea to make a great sally. . . . With the four Arkansas [Quapaws] who were fortunately in this post, this gave me fourteen men in all including the sergeant Alexo Pastor, the man who had just escaped from the hands of the enemy a little while ago. I gave the orders to yell as the Indians do when they attack.

At this time Colbert sent, by a road opposite from the one which had been made the sally, Dona Marie Luisa Villars, wife of the lieutenant prisoner, carrying a flag of truce accompanied by one of his officials, who was shaking with fright as he drew near the fort. As soon as we saw they were carrying the flag, I ordered all firing to cease. Upon receiving the Senora who presented me a paper which Colbert had written in French, as follows; "M. Le Capitaine Colbert is sent by his superiors to take the post of the Arkansas and by this power Sir, he demands that you capitulate. It is his plan to take it with all his forces, having already taken all the inhabitants, together with the Lieut. Luis de Villars and his family, (signed with the red seal April 17, 1783) James Colbert."

Our sally was not stopped by the white flag, great number of our enemy who upon hearing the shouts and at the same time a volley, retired quickly to the place where they had the camp and the guarded prisoners. As they retreated they said in loud voices, "Let's go! Let's go! The Indians are upon us." Being closely followed by us they left the camp and retreated quickly taking their prisoners with them. It wasn't possible for our party to follow because we saw that the enemy was trying to cut us off from the rear guard. I ordered a retreat, and ordered each one of our men to hide himself behind a fallen tree, always yelling and firing which had made the enemy flee at once. A little more than a league from the fort the enemy had some [vessels], which consisted of the "Bato de la Fondt," which was built up in front in such a way that 40 oars, which it had, were protected from the bullets of the guns, and only cannon or catapults [sic] can hurt it. They had also a "bercha" and two "Piroguas" which they had taken the night they had come here. The first boat belonged to Pinot who had come to the village loaded with necessities for the fort, the other boats were the ones which yesterday afternoon loaded with tallow and some packages of beaver hides. Here they had already embarked the women and children telling them that at twelve o'clock they would return to attack us with 500 Chickasaws and with all their fury. Colbert has not kept his word, since our Indians following saw them plant a hatchet in the ground and get on ship, in spite of the heavy swell of the river which lasted all the following day.

Social Life at Arkansas Post, 1820

Ted R. Worley, ed., "A Letter of Governor Miller to His Wife," *Arkansas Historical Quarterly* 13 (1954): 389–90.

James Miller was the first governor of Arkansas Territory. He was appointed because of his military record in the War of 1812, and he accepted because he needed the money. A native of New Hampshire, he came to Arkansas without his family and was generally displeased with what he found. These comments refer to a stop at Arkansas

Post made while making his way up the Arkansas River to Little Rock.

Post Arkansaw March 20th, 1820

My beloved Wife,

. . . This country is very new, and society very uncultivated. They are at this place particularly very fond of Balls and Loo [a card game] parties. Saturday and Sunday nights are the fashionable nights for their parties to meet, and they never disperse until after daylight. The population was originally French, and the Americans who come in fall into their practice. I wish you could see one of these balls. I refused to attend on those nights, and they made one or two on other nights, which I did attend. They have one young lady, a Mamselle Don Carol, the rest of the ladies are married, from twenty to seventy five years of age. The houses generally have two rooms, one room for dancing, the other to play Loo in and beds to lay the young sucking children on, a married woman is almost disqualified to attend a ball without a child, they nurse as unconcerned as at home in their nursery. They have one fiddler who can play one tune they can dance but one figure, which is a kind of reel or cotillion, they commence at dark and hold on until day light, when each of the fair sex saddles her own pony, mounts and trudges home. The men generally hold on longer at the card table. At these card tables I have seen Grandfather, Grand-mother, son and daughter, and grand-daughters all engaged in gambling as eager to make money as if playing with any one else. It is not uncommon to lose 150 or two hundred dollars in a night, or they may win. This appears to be their principal vice and it is a great one—I have discouraged it since I have been here. . . .

Your devoted husband
James Miller

C. FRONTIER SOCIETY

After the Louisiana Purchase, American settlers citizens gradually moved into Arkansas, which had been little changed by a century of European occupation except that the Quapaws had been decimated by European diseases, wars fought with their French allies, and alcoholism. Many early American settlers were subsistence farmers and hunters, but after the war of 1812 immigration from southeast Missouri brought larger numbers of people down the southwest train that crossed the Arkansas near Little Rock and continued on to Red River, many of them settling along the Ouachita River and its tributaries. It was this concentration of people in central Arkansas that led to moving the territorial from Arkansas Post to Little Rock.

An Aged Settler Describes Early Subsistence, 1876

Ted R. Worley, ed., "Letters from an Early Settler," *Arkansas Historical Quarterly* 11 (1952): 327–29.

John Billingsley's account of life in early Arkansas was written many years after the events it describes, when the author was an elderly man. The story seems plausible, however, and an extant tax record shows four Billingsleys, including a John and a John Jr., living in Crawford County in 1821. This description of how Billingsley lived is probably accurate, typifying the lifestyle of other early Arkansas pioneers as well.

My father, with two other families moved from Middle Tennessee—Charles Addams and Samuel Williams—six in each family, made eighteen persons. That was in 1814. We came to the Post of Arkansas in a flatboat. There we found a French and Creole village. The Quapaw Indians lived on the south side of the river. There we exchanged our flatboat for a keel-boat with an old Indian trader. There was nothing like steamboats on the Mississippi river then. We made our way the best we could until we got to the Cadron; there we found one of my father's brothers that had moved from Kentucky in an early day. We stayed there one year. Then there was a treaty made with the Cherokees . . . [and] they moved to Texas and lived in what is called Cherokee Country. Then we moved to Big Mulberry. In 1816 we made up about thirty families and lived there two years in all the luxuries of life that a new country could afford, such as buffalo, bear, deer, and elk and fish and honey; we had pound cake every day, for we beat all the meal we ate in a mortar, and the first year our corn gave out about six weeks before roasting ears came in. Our substitute for bread was venison dried by the fire and then pounded in the mortar and made up in small cakes and fried in bear's oil. That hooped us on until forward irish potatoes came in. We had all things common. We had no doctors nor lawyers those happy days. The frist [sic] Legislature that was held on the territory was held at the Post of Arkansas. . . . We had no tax to pay then but a county tax. The general government paid all the balance. About that time Major Bradford came to Fort Smith and set up that post and we furnished him buffalo meat for the soldiers, and then we got some flour from him which was a great treat to us. All the way that Major Bradford got the mail then was by sending a soldier to the Post of Arkansas in a canoe which took him about three weeks to make the trip. Then the government made another treaty with the Indians and we moved on the south side of the river and commenced settling all along the river from Fort Smith to where the present seat of government is now fixed, some in McClane's Bottom, some at Dardanelle, some on Shoal Creek and we soon got thick enough to hold camp meeting and everybody would go and leave their houses for a week at a time. And when they came back everything was all right. We then generally built our chimneys up to the mantle piece and hung our meat on the outside on the ribs of the house. If any man had had a lock on any of his doors in those days he would have been looked on with suspicion. We about this time began to get some mail contracts and soon after that some lawsuits mixed in. . . .

Well, the way we clothed ourselves—that is, the men and boys—was by dressing bucksuits and wore full suits of the same. The French came up the river in large canoes and supplied us with domestic and checks and earthing ware and calico. We paid them 37 cents for domestic and 50 cents per yard for calico and 75 cents per yards for checks. I paid $4 for the first set of teacups and saucers I ever owned and $2 for a green edged dish worth about 5 cents. We paid 50 cents for all the coffee that we got. This was all paid for in bear skins and deer skins and coon skins and bear oil, some beaver and otter skins and bees wax and that in abundance. For we had honey in any amount.

A Methodist Preacher Finds
Godly Listeners in Arkansas, 1814–1815

Walter N. Vernon, "Beginnings of Methodism in Arkansas," *Arkansas Historical Quarterly* 31 (1972): 358–64.

As a result of the Great Revival that spread across the Southeast in the early years of the nineteenth century, evangelical Christianity became a common cultural bond among southerners. Through the efforts of circuit riders and the institution of the camp meeting, Christianity was carried to the frontier. William Stevenson, a Methodist preacher, was one of the first clergymen to visit the isolated settlements in the Arkansas portion of the Missouri Territory.

In the fall of [1814] while I was living in the township of Bellview, Mo., following farming, by which I was enabled to support my family decently and to labor as a local preacher, my brother, James Stevenson, who then lived on the Ouachita river, now state of Arkansas, Clark county, visited me and remained a few weeks with us; and seeing the great advantage of a preached gospel among the people, he lamented the condition of the wilderness settlements of the Ouachita, Red river and Forte Caddo, where he lived, and also the settlements of White river and many other settlements on the smaller streams of the West. . . . I felt a great desire for the salvation of those destitute people, and was pressed by my brother to go home with him, see the people, and preach to them. He hoped also that I might like the country and move to it. I agreed to accompany him. . . .

At length we arrived in the settlement where my brother lived, but did not reach his home before night, but stayed at the house of Mr. McMahon, who had once been a member of the Baptist Church in Kentucky. He had greatly back-slidden. At the moment I was introduced to him by my brother, he looked wild and somewhat surprised, and said within himself, Is it possible that God has sent a preacher among us? This I learned of him afterwards. He was kind, fed our horses, and his wife also received us cheerfully. All soon became acquainted, conversation free and social; but turning on the subject of religion, he appeared not rightly to understand the gift that had come upon all men unto justification of life. After hearing the word of God read on those points, I saw joy spring up in his eyes; for he had been for several years nearly in despair, and truly it is good news to hear that Christ died for all. Night came on, we proposed to have prayer; all was right and when we kneeled to pray, I felt like God was near, for Mr. McMahon cried aloud for mercy; his wife wept, and some of his children, the oldest in particular. Here the work began in this family; they were evidently the first fruits of my labor in that part now called the state of Arkansas.

Next Sunday I had an appointment at Mr. Cummings, a few miles below on the Forte Caddo, a branch of the Ouachita. . . . While preaching that day to a desirous looking people, the good spirit was among them; some were deeply affected, and cried for mercy. The old widowed mother rejoiced in God her Savior, and there appeared to be a good work beginning. . . .

From this settlement I went westward, visited the settlements, and preached on the Turnwaw [Terre Noir], Wolf Creek, Little Missouri, and Mound Prairie, and was greatly comforted in having reason, from what I saw and heard, to believe that God had called his servants the preachers to spread the gospel through this vast territory now settled and settling fast. The people had made a great many small settlements all through the country from five to twenty miles apart. No wagon roads yet laid out, as they had generally moved on pack horses, nothing but horse-paths, many of them along the buffalo roads or trails, rivers, and large creeks, etc. No ferry boats, except on one or two rivers. We had to cross by canoes or rafts, or on horseback. . . .

[Stevenson returns in 1815]

The work of the Lord had begun on the waters of Ouachita last year; but this year it extended from the Ouachita east to the Current river and west to the Pecan Point on the Texas side. We got up small societies on the rivers and large creeks where the people had found good land, stock range, etc. Most of the rivers were at the time without ferry boats; of course we were compelled to swim our horses by the side of canoes or rafts, with our saddle bags on our shoulders. I had not appointments so many as we had in years following; yet whenever there were hearers I attended as far as in my power, and almost in every place the word found access, for the Lord was present and had given the hearing ear and the understanding heart. The gospel was glad tidings to those people, who were generally honest, humane, industrious and peaceable, and but very few of them had yet learned to be quibblers about foreknowledge, uncon-ditional election and final perseverance. . . . I must say in truth, to the credit of the first settlers of Arkansas, that they as a people in general, would have been no discredit to the better part of the community of the most respectable of the old or new world. And even those who did not unite with us in the church had sound reason and good sense and courage to know and say that the gospel of Christ was the only means which God generally made use of to civilize, moralize, and Christianize a country; therefore, they received us and freely gave us such things as they had. I have never seen harder times than those people had to encounter, while I was traveling and preaching to them. That year provisions were scarce indeed. The drought had ruined their crops; there was not bread for the people in the country; no market near to supply them; no boats then running. But being a firm, resolute, soldierly people, they endured all with patience. Some of them went far up the rivers into the prairies and returned with meat; others, destitute of horses to travel on, hunted about home, lived on deer, fish and such things as they could find; but all these afflictions never prevented them attending the meetings. They came from afar, heard and received the word with joy, and so it was that the preacher and the people suffered and rejoiced together.

FOR FURTHER READING

A good account of the early Native Americans in Arkansas is contained in the early chapters of Jeannie M. Whayne, Thomas A. Deblack, George Sabo III, and Morris S. Arnold, *Arkansas: A Narrative History* (Fayetteville: University of Arkansas Press, 2002). See also George Sabo III, P*aths of Our Children: Historic Indians of Arkansas* (Fayetteville: Arkansas Archeological Survey, 2001). Kathleen Duval, *The Native Ground: Indians and Colonists in the Heart of the Continent* (Philadelphia: University of Pennsylvania Press, 2006), discusses the power of the Quapaws and other Native American tribes in the Arkansas River during the colonial period of Arkansas history. Using records from the archives of France and Spain, Morris S. Arnold has provided us with a detailed history of eighteenth-century Arkansas; see his *Colonial Arkansas, 1686–1804: A Social and Cultural History* (Fayetteville: University of Arkansas Press, 1991) and *The Rumble of a Distant Drum: The Quapaws and Old World Newcomers, 1673–1804* (University of Arkansas Press: Fayetteville, 2000). Arnold's *Unequal Laws unto a Savage Race: European Legal Traditions in Arkansas* (University of Arkansas Press: Fayetteville, 1985) contains an excellent account of the territorial history of Arkansas from 1803 to 1819. For a thoroughly annotated, firsthand account of its subject, see Trey Berry, Pam Beasley, and Jeanne Clements, eds., *The Forgotten Expedition, 1804–1805: The Louisiana Purchase Journals of Dunbar and Hunter.*

CHAPTER II

Arkansas Territory

INTRODUCTION

Arkansas became a separate territory in 1819 after Missouri applied for statehood in 1818 without its five sparsely populated southern counties, which quickly asked for separate territorial status. For a time, the fate of Arkansas was entangled with the politics of slavery and what became known as the Missouri Compromise. When Rep. James Tallmadge moved to limit slavery in the future state of Missouri, his fellow New Yorker, Rep. John W. Taylor, was prompted to take the same action with respect to Arkansas Territory. Congress was on firmer constitutional ground in controlling slavery in a territory than a state, but Arkansas was farther south than Missouri. After a lengthy and emotional debate, the House narrowly defeated the Taylor amendment, and Arkansas Territory remained open to slavery.

President James Monroe appointed James Miller, a hero of the War of 1812, to be the first governor of Arkansas Territory. Miller's commission was delayed, however, and he made a leisurely trip from his home in New Hampshire. Robert Crittenden, a young member of a prominent Kentucky family and newly appointed secretary of Arkansas Territory, arrived ahead of Miller and seized the initiative. As acting governor— but without clear legal authority—Crittenden called an election to choose a territorial assembly and a delegate to Congress. When Governor Miller arrived, James Woodson Bates was on his way to Washington as the delegate from Arkansas. During its first session, in the fall of 1820, the territorial assembly agreed to move the capital the following year from Arkansas Post to Little Rock, a central location where a number of prominent Arkansans, Crittenden among them, owned land. Miller was a competent chief executive but was never happy living in Arkansas and resigned in 1824. His successor, George Izard, a prominent Federalist from South Carolina, served capably until his death in 1828. Crittenden continued as secretary, however, and during this period was the most influential politician in the territory.

The politics of Arkansas Territory changed markedly when Andrew Jackson became president of the United States. Newer settlers in the territory, many of them from Tennessee, were strong supporters of Jackson and of what was becoming the Democratic Party. Following Izard's death, Jackson appointed John Pope of Kentucky as governor and William S. Fulton, a friend and fellow Indian fighter, as secretary. Having lost his influence in Washington, Crittenden also gradually lost his power within the state. Meanwhile, a new political faction, eventually known as "The Family," formed around Henry W. Conway, a native of Tennessee who succeeded Bates as delegate to Congress in 1823. Conway won reelection in 1827, but lost his life to Crittenden in a duel. Conway's cousin, Ambrose H. Sevier, succeeded him, and his brother, James S. Conway, eventually became the first governor of the state of Arkansas. Conway relatives and a few other insiders, such as William E. Woodruff, editor of the *Arkansas Gazette*, and prominent attorney Chester Ashley, created a Democratic machine that governed Arkansas down to the Civil War.

Under the government of Arkansas Territory, the wilderness gradually became frontier. A depressed national economy slowed the westward movement in the 1820s, but the territory continued to grow; the fourteen thousand Americans in 1820 increased to thirty thousand in 1830. Immigration to Arkansas boomed in the 1830s, and the population reached ninety-eight thousand in 1840. An analysis of birth places for pioneer children shows that well over 30 percent of the new settlers came from Tennessee and that more than 10 percent came from the states of Missouri, Mississippi, and Alabama. Black people, almost all of them slaves, accounted for 14 percent of the American population in 1820 and 20 percent in 1840. The increasing number of slaves suggests the growing wealth of white Arkansans and the southern origins of many of them.

To make room for white settlers, the government of the United States removed Indians from Arkansas Territory during the 1820s. In the previous decade the area had been on the verge of becoming a vast reservation. The Monroe administration gave the Cherokees a new homeland in northwestern Arkansas between the Arkansas and the White Rivers in 1817. The following year, the Quapaws were induced to accept a reservation running south of the Arkansas River between Little Rock and Arkansas Post and extending to the Saline River. In 1820, the Choctaws received a vast area between the Arkansas and Red Rivers that extended west into present Oklahoma. White settlers protested these developments, and during the 1820s, the tribes, one by one, were forced to extinguish their newly acquired claims and move further west.

Immigration to Arkansas grew in part because the trip was easier than before. Forests and swamps were formidable obstacles to the first travelers. Early roads, when they existed, lacked bridges and meandered around fallen trees. Much traveling was done by water, but moving a flatboat or keelboat upstream was a slow and arduous process. In 1820, however, the steamboat *Comet* arrived at Arkansas Post, having made the trip from New Orleans in eight days. During the rest of the territorial period, steamboats operated on the Arkansas and White Rivers, carrying commerce, immigrants, and Indians being moved to the west. The federal government provided funds to improve navigation on the rivers of the territory and also to build new roads.

Territorial Arkansas was a turbulent society of growth and change. The presence of the frontier and the newness of institutions encouraged an atmosphere of violence. Men carried guns and knives, and arguments led quickly to fights. Those who believed themselves to be gentlemen fought duels according to a loose code of honor. There was also an impressive amount of crime, involving highwaymen especially, but river pirates and counterfeiters prospered as well. Arkansas Territory was not always attractive, but it was seldom dull.

A. LAND ACQUISITION

In an agricultural society, land was the basis for economic success, and under federal law a clear title was necessary for ownership. One important concern in Arkansas Territory was the validity of land grants made by the governments of France and Spain; another was obtaining a survey of Arkansas that would allow the sale of land in sections according to the system that was standard for American public lands. Finally, there was the question of the conditions of sale and whether they would encourage settlement by family farmers or ownership of vast tracts by speculators.

An Allegation of Land Fraud

Clarence E. Carter, ed., *The Territorial Papers of the United States*, 27 vols. (Washington, DC: G.P.O., 1952), 19:420–22.

Because Arkansas had been part of the Louisiana Purchase, some land was claimed on the basis of Spanish grants. Beginning shortly after the purchase, the US government began to hold hearings to determine the validity of these early claims. Most of the large claims were disposed of by 1819, but a number of small cases remained. The following document is unclear, but Chilo A. Moultier appears to be alleging that land speculators were making fraudulent claims to occupancy prior to the Louisiana Purchase, a situation that would have entitled them to a preemptive right to purchase the land from the federal government. It is impossible to determine the validity of the facts in question, but there was a great deal of fraud involved in the sale of land in early Arkansas. Best known were the Bowie claims: 124 separate claims attested to by the depositions of three men, supported with the forged signatures of two Spanish officials. Among Moultier's villains were two important Arkansas land speculators, William Russell, the St. Louis–based businessman who owned more land than any Arkansan and who played an important role in moving the capital to Little Rock, and Sylvanus Phillips, for whom Phillips County is named and whose daughter Helena gave her name to the Mississippi port city.

[Chilo A. Moultier] to Josiah Meigs [Commissioner of the General Land Office].
[April 10, 1822]

PROTEST.

In behalf of the United States Republick, of which I claim A part, I Protest the issuing of Patents for the privet claims in the Territory of Arkansaw—until A further investigation has been made, for reasons that the Publick will be defrauded out of much property and many individuals out of their rights.—

I shall make A Statement of one instance, and Prove it by depositions, and then proceed to Such circumstances as may offer.—

The first Packet of depositions, will prove, that the first improvement below the mouth of Cache River, and fronting on White River, was made in the year eighteen hundred and eight, by John Maddox, and that the improvement next below, and adjoining, was made in the year eighteen hundred and ten, by William H. Glass, and that the too improvements, were made from an entire willderness.

The Second Packet of depositions, will prove, that Elijah Mckinny, the person in whose name the Settlement right that covers the too above mentioned improvements, was confirmed, made an improvement on Cache River, two and an half miles from those improvements on White river, and six and one forth by the meanders of the River.—and further, that the Said Mckinny contracted with Joseph Taser for the makeing of the improvement.—the Contract was written on or near the twentieth of September eighteen hundred and five,—And that the Said Mckinny compromised with Said Taser, for what was done towards the contract, in the fall of eighteen hundred and Six, and moved immediately out of the country.—I have Produced an attested copy of the Contract to Hartwell Boswell Register of the land office at Lawrence.—

The third Packet of depositions, will prove that William Smith, was not in the country till eighteen hundred and ten, and that James Murphy was not in the country untill eighteen hundred and thirteen.—

Those two persons, Smith and Murphy, together with William H. Glass who made one of the above mentioned improvements were the witnesses who proved the Settlement right to Elijah Mckinny.—We have the names of those persons conveyed to us by a person who gained admition to the record but could not obtain an attested coppy, the Secretary of the Confirming Commissioners alledgeing that his office was not an office of inquiry therefore he would not issue attested Coppies,—We have made repeted attempts to obtain Coppies from this office without Success.—If Publick Functionaries are not concerned in those attrocious Speculations, why Should this record be a Concealed page of Publick agency.—

Would it not be Consistant with the Publick interest, that A transcript of the Privet claims in the Territory of Arkansaw, Should be refered to the Territory, and be kept open for the inspection of any person who may wish to defend his rights or to detect a fraud that may be practised on the Publick.—If so, would it not be proper to rest the Transcript with an Agent

Vested with authority to adjust those claims, A person who would be trew to the charge, and not Betray the Publick Confidence, And not to an Arkansaw Lawyer, Not even the Delligate to Congress, for they are more *or less bought up with fees in favour of those Robers of their country, and might be liable to treat the Publick* confidence as it has been heretofore.—

Having Shown that the above mentioned improvements on White river were not made in time to deserve A Settlement right.—And that the Person in whose name the right was confirmed, was A hireling and not an actual Settler,—And that he never lived on the above mentioned improvements on White River.—And that the three Persons who Proved the Settlement right to Elijah Mckinny, were improper witnesses,—I shall refer you to that concealed record where you will not only find the names and testimony of those Persons, But how many Claims they have proven, which are as false as the witnesses themselves.—

It has been the plan of this bandity to follow the trace where half Breeds and fugitives have traviled and Camped with the Indians, and to make witnesses to prove them claims,—It is easy for A crafty Surveyor to become A crafty land Speculator, and by these miens Mr. Russel has ingraciated himself into the Principal Directorship of the Bandity, and overcum the vigilence of the confirming Commitioners, for it appears that he has got claims confirmed without the knowledge of intersession of those Pretended claimants in whose names they ware confirmed.—Not one of those wandering fugutives out of twenty ever make any improvement.— Yet they are fit Persons to apply to with a little ready money for the purchace of those pretended claims after they are So confirmed.—With these kinds of Claims they have taken in the most valuable improvements made by the Indians in the Cherokee Village on the St. Francis, and those made by the whites in the neighbourhood of Cache River. And besides takeing all the improvements, where from the ignorence of the Settlers they thought to overcum opposition, laid Some of their Settlement rights where there never was any improvement to this day.—

The three above mentioned witnesses were imployed by Silvenus Phillips who lays claime to twenty of those Settlement rights and out of twenty there is not more than one that can Stand the test of Publick Justice.—

The Need for a Resident Surveyor

Clarence E. Carter, ed., *Territorial Papers of the United States*, 27 vols. (Washington, DC: G.P.O., 1952), 19:631–32.

Even while Arkansas was still part of the Missouri Territory, some surveying was done to fix the location of bounty lands granted to veterans of the War of 1812. Surveys proceeded slowly, however, delaying the sale of lands and settlement of the area. One problem was that until 1833 Arkansas land surveys were managed from St. Louis. Another problem was that surveyors were paid a flat fee, regardless of the terrain, and thus they tended to survey areas that were convenient for them rather than those that settlers wished to acquire.

[Governor James Miller, William Bradford, and William Russell to David Barton, Chairman of the Land Committee, US Senate, Washington, DC, March 25, 1824]

. . . A large portion of Arkansas Territory being yet unsurveyed, we believe it important, not only to the government and the present inhabitants of Arkansas, but also to such as may hereafter remove there and even to posterity, that, when the public lands are surveyed, it should be done well and faithfully, and the lines and corners well and permanently established. All of this, we are confident, would be much better ensured, as also the Sale of the public lands facilitated, by the establishment of a Surveyor's office in that Territory. Heretofore, from the best information we have had, the surveying of a large portion of the lands now surveyed in Arkansas, have been badly done, many of the lines badly marked, and corners not well established: much of it has been done by persons not directly responsible for the work, and done too for prices neither sufficient to justify their surveying the cane lands or richest lands of the country, nor sufficient to justify their doing the work permanently well. A large portion of the lands now surveyed in Arkansas being as poor as any there, they being the most easy and expeditious to survey, we are satisfied that the establishment of a Surveyor's office in that territory, where the wishes of the people interested in the faithful surveying of the country would have some influence, and where the persons performing the surveys would be accountable to the office there, would both promote the better establishment of the lines and corners of the surveys, and better ensure the surveying of the best lands first (or such a portion of them as would most probably sell in some short time) and to avoid for a longer time the surveying of large quantities of the poorest lands of the country, while much of the rich lands remains unsurveyed.

Most of the contracts for surveying the lands of Arkansas, heretofore given to persons, who reside there, have been of the most unprofitable sort, while the larger and more profitable contracts have most generally been given to persons resident at or near Saint Louis, not affording to the people of Arkansas the best means of earning money in their own country, which could be done without prejudice to the public interest. They, therefore, consider it an unjust grievance that the establishment of a Surveyor's office there, which would place the subject upon more just principles, should be withheld.

Called upon, as we are, to communicate what information we possess on these subjects, the foregoing, in which we all agree, and which from our own knowledge and the best information we have, we each believe to be true, is respectfully submitted.

By your obedient servants,
JAMES MILLER

Petition for a Liberalized Land Law

Clarence E. Carter, ed., *Territorial Papers of the United States*, 27 vols. (Washington, DC: G.P.O., 1954), 21:853–54.

Between 1821 and 1836, more than a million and a half acres of public land were sold in Arkansas at an average price of just over $1.25 an acre. Preemption laws allowed settlers to select prime sites, improve them, and have first choice at buying when the land came up for sale. Many settlers gained the use of land by squatting on the public domain and simply moving on if the land was sold. In the following document, the territorial assembly petitions Congress for changes in the land policy to favor settlers lacking the cash to purchase land.

November 19, 1833

To the Senate and House of Representatives of the United States of America in Congress assembled.

The memorial of the General Assembly of the Territory of Arkansas respectfully represents, that within the last four years this Territory has nearly doubled its population—that the Emigrants are generally poor, and have expended their all in reaching their new homes, that within that period, large portions of country have been by them opened and thickly populated, which were previously but an unexplored wilderness, that by their enterprise those lands are now esteemed valuable, and are attracting the Speculator and man of wealth, and that some portions of this country having been rapidly surveyed, are expected shortly to be offered for sale, before it has been possible for the hardy enterprise of the Pioneer to acquire the means of securing his home.—Your Memorialists are fully sensible that a postponement of the land sales would neither conduce to their own interest or that of the Government; but they do indulge a hope, that a medium may be found, to reconcile those conflicting interests, by the passage of a law which shall secure the actual settler and cultivator in the possession of his improvement for a limited time, say two years after the land shall be offered for sale, provided there be no bidder at the land sale; thus stimulating their enterprise by offering, as a reward to their industry, a home for their families. Should the settler fail in making his entry within the time asked for, the lands of the Government will still be increased in value by his industry and be entered with avidity by those who are daily emigrating or by the Speculator: or if the Congress of the United States should decline the passage of a law so humane and just in its provisions, your Memorialists would ask for a law, securing the settler a just compensation, for two years after the land sale, for his labor, should his home be entered by another, without his concent. Your Memorialist forbear to enter into a full discussion of this, to them, all-important subject, because they have seen with pleasure, enlightened Members of Congress, who have, from year to year, discussed the subject with views liberal, and, in the opinion of your Memorialists, conclusive, and much more elaborately than could properly be compressed within the limits of a memorial. Your Memorialists are pleading the cause of half their Constituents, who have sacrificed present comfort to a prospect of future Independence, whose brightest hopes must be blasted without some melioration of the present laws. The granting our prayer would fix upon our soil a hardy, enterprising and industrious population.

We earnestly present our petition and as in duty bound will ever pray &c.

> JOHN WILSON
> Speaker of the House of Representatives
> JOHN WILLIAMSON
> President of the Legislative Council
> [Arkansas Territorial Assembly]

B. INDIAN REMOVAL

As American settlers advanced westward, the federal government pushed eastern Indians ahead of them. The removal policy was painful for the Native Americans, particularly for tribes who lived much like other Americans. In Arkansas, Indians were never a menace to white settlers. Feuding between Osages and Cherokees during the 1820s, however, probably did retard the settlement of Arkansas Territory. More important, the white settlers and Arkansas boosters resented the large amount of Arkansas land that was owned by Indian tribes.

Memorial of the Cherokees

Clarence E. Carter, ed., *Territorial Papers of the United States*, 27 vols. (Washington, DC: G.P.O., 1954), 20:331–32.

The Cherokees were among the first American settlers in Arkansas, living first in the St. Francis River Valley and then along the Arkansas River at present-day Russellville. The United States promised the Cherokees a "permanent" home in Arkansas in 1817, and Lovely's Purchase was negotiated to provide a buffer zone between them and the Osage to the west. By a treaty in 1828, however, the Cherokees were forced west into what is now Oklahoma, and the boundary line became the border between Arkansas and that state. The response of the Cherokees is given below. The "Governor Clark" referred to is William Clark of the Lewis and Clark expedition, who was governor of Missouri Territory.

In Council. CHEROKEE NATION. July 24th, 1826—

OUR FRIEND We are much disturbed in mind by what we are told is in the newspapers.—It is said that the man who is sent to Congress by the White People of Arkansas has written to them and said that the President has ordered a Large part of Lovelys purchase to be surveyed and Sold, and that it will, very soon, be settled by the Whites. This makes us very uneasy.—We think there must be some mistake about it. We can not think that the present President would give such an order if he knew and were to think of what other Presidents have said to us. Nor do we think that the present Secretary of War [James Barbour], who we are told is a friend to red people, would advise such an order if he were to look at the words and promises of the Secretary, who was in office four or five years ago [John C. Calhoun]. Between eight and nine years ago when Our Great Father was persuading our people to come here he talked to us in these words. "I have not yet obtained the lands lying up the Arkansaw River, to the West of your Settlement. I will give instructions to Governor Clark [William Clark of the Lewis and Clark expedition] to hold a Treaty, with the Quapaws this Summer in order to purchase them, and when purchased, I will direct them to be laid off for you. It is my wish that you should have *no limits to the west*, So that you may have good Mill Seats, plenty of Game and not be surrounded by the white people."—He said to us. "I will not forget my red Children because they are far off. I will remember you. It is my wish to make you prosperous and happy in your new homes; and if you will at any time make known to me your wishes I will attend to them."—Now we ask you, our friend, to make known our wishes to our Great Father, and tell him we do not wish Lovely's purchase to be settled by white people: That we never Supposed it would be: that we believed the Talk given to us by our Great Father. He told us he would not forget us and we hope his talk will not be forgotten.—

The late Secretary of War told us in a talk given to us four or five years ago, last October, that white people should not be permitted to settle on Lovely's purchase: That it should be kept as an Outlet for us, according to promise.—He told us that although we Should acquire no right to the soil in it, the Government only reserved to itself the right of disposing of the saltsprings upon it.—We were and always have been satisfied with this, but should be very unhappy were we to be "surrounded by the White people" as we should be were the government to allow it to be settled.—We think we should have just cause to say that the promises of our Great Father and the secretary had been broken— We hope we shall never have cause to say so.

The Lands Ceded to the Government have not all been surveyed. When they are, should it turn out, as we think it will, that we have not yet got as many acres as we are entitled to, where shall we get them if Lovelys Purchase, of which we at present have part, shall have been sold to and setled [*sic*] by Whites? It may be said that the Government Could pay us for it;—but we do not wish to sell any of our Land. We have but little and were promised it should be given to us here, and if we do not get it all, then our Treaty as well as the promises of our Great Father and Secretary would be broken.—We can not believe these things will happen, but when we hear from men that are sent to Congress that they will, it makes us very unhappy. We again ask you, our friend, to make known our wishes to our Great Father—

Signed by

JOHN JOLLY. his mark. X	JOHN LOONY his mk. X
BLACK. FOX his mark. X	TOO-TSN-WUH his mk. X
THOS GRAVES his mark X	SPRING FROG his mark X
WALTER WEBBER. his mk—X	TA-HA-TUH his mark. X
YOUNG GLASS HIS MKX	THO MAW—his mark. X

Migrating Indians Pass through Little Rock, 1832–1833

William F. Pope, *Early Days in Arkansas* (Little Rock: F. W. Allsopp, 1895), 135–37.

After all the tribes had been removed from Arkansas, Indians still followed the Trail of Tears through the territory to the Indian Territory. William F. Pope, nephew of Gov. John Pope, saw several of these forced migrations and described them in detail.

About the first of November, 1832, shortly after my arrival in Arkansas, there passed through Little Rock six or seven thousand Choctaw and Chickasaw Indians from North Mississippi and West Tennessee on their way to their new homes in the Indian Territory. The presence of this vast body of Indians, with their household goods, cattle and ponies, made a sight never to be forgotten. These Indians were attended by several United States officers and surgeons.

Two days before this migrating party reached Little Rock, an officer arrived in town and warned the citizens of the thieving propensities of the lower class of Indians, and advised them to close their stores and dwellings while they were passing through. With all the vigilance that could be displayed, many articles of the utmost uselessness to the Indians disappeared from the yards of private residences. This body of Indians was several days in crossing the river, although hurried out of town as rapidly as possible. They had a great desire to loiter and spy around, and had to be driven almost like sheep. Most of the males wore only the breechcloth, leggings and moccasins, the latter were, profusely ornamented with variously colored beads and porcupine quills. They were, for the most part, a fine looking body of men. The women rode ponies, manwise, and had their papooses slung in blankets at their backs.

These two tribes were attended by their principal chiefs, Pittman Colbert, a French-Chickasaw half breed, and Greenwood Le Flore, a French-Choctaw half breed. These men were well educated and had considerable refinement. They were very wealthy and traveled in great style and comfort, having large roomy carriages and numerous baggage wagons and large numbers of negro slaves. Their state and authority resembled that of the patriarch of old. They were looked up to as the fathers of their people, whose word was law.

Greenwood Le Flore became dissatisfied with the country soon after reaching the Indian Territory, and severed his tribal relation. He returned with his family and slaves to Mississippi, and became a citizen of the United States. He afterwards represented his county in the State legislature.

The spring of 1833 witnessed the arrival of another large body of Indians bound for the Nation. These Indians were dreadfully scourged by the ravages of the cholera, which invaded their ranks when they reached the Mississippi River at Memphis. Large numbers of them died on the march, and it was said that their route westward from the Mississippi was strewn thick with graves.

These disease-stricken Indians were not permitted to cross the river at Little Rock, but were compelled to cross several miles below town and go out by way of Fourche, where they struck the military road. As soon as they reached the pine hills southwest of town the disease began to abate.

The Trial of Five Osages Accused of Murder

Arkansas Gazette (Little Rock), October 26, 1824.

During the eighteenth century the Osages lived along the Missouri River but often hunted in Arkansas and occasionally came into conflict with Quapaw and French hunting parties coming from Arkansas Post. In 1808 the Osages entered into a treaty with the United States and came under American jurisdiction; after which they were a problem for Arkansas citizens only because of their ongoing rivalry with the Cherokees. In 1823, however, a small group of Osage warriors, from a large band that had settled on the confluence of the Arkansas and Verdigris Rivers, attacked a group of hunters from Arkansas Post and killed three American citizens. Their trial took place in Little Rock three years after that town became the capital of Arkansas Territory.

At the late term of the Superior Court of the Territory of Arkansas, five Chiefs or Head-Men of the Osage nation of Indians, viz

Cha-to-kah-wa-she-pe-she, (Mad Buffalo)
Wa-ne-sha-shinger, (Little Eagle)
Wa-sha-ba-shinger, (Little Bear)
Sha-ka-shinger, ((Little Rattle Snake),
He-sha-ke-ree, (Caddo Killer),

Were indicted and arraigned for the murder, on November last, of Maj *Curtis Welborn*, a citizen of this Territory, who was engaged in hunting on the De la Blue, or Blue river, a tributary of the Red river, lying west of the Territory of Arkansas, and within the tract of country ceded by the United States to the Choctaw Indians. It was clearly proven on the trial, that the prisoners composed part of the Chiefs or Head-Men of a party of Osage warriors, who started from the north fork of the Canadian, a branch of the Arkansas, with the avowed intention of making war upon the Caddo Indians. That some ten days subsequent to the departure, an attack was made, by a party of Osages on a camp of American, French, and half-breed Quapaw hunters, who were hunting on the De la Blue, a country to which the Osages have no claim. That in that attack, Maj Welborn and three other white men named *Sloan, Lester, and Deterline*, and a negro man named *Ben*, belonging to Mr.

Antoine Baraque, were killed, their heads cut off, and their bodies shockingly mangled and disfigured. That those of the hunting party who escaped, were dispersed, and found their way by different routes to the settlements on the Arkansas. After their return, some of them went up to the trading post in the Osage Nation, for the purposing of recovering the horses that had been taken from them during the attack; and they there found them in the possession of the prisoners, some of whom readily gave them up, while others refused to do so.

It was also proven, that, shortly after the return of the war party to which the prisoners belonged, a Council was held at the camp of Clermont the principal Chief of the Osage, at which Mad Buffalo (the only one of the prisoners who spoke on the subject) admitted that white men had been killed by his party, but said it had been done by mistake, they having been mistaken for Caddoes or other Indians with which they were at war. Little Eagle, also, when the horses that he had taken were demanded of him, stated that he had himself killed a white man.

And it was further shown in evidence, that the usual custom of the Osage Indians, when going into battle, is, for the Chiefs or Head Man of the war party to remain a short distance in the rear where they employ themselves smoking their pipes, and invoking the Great Spirit to give success to their warriors.

Mad Buffalo, as was stated in our last, was tried separate from his companions, and convicted.

The remaining four were tried together on Tuesday last. After the cause was submitted to the Jury, they retired for a short time and returned with a verdict of Guilty, against Little Eagle. The remainder of the prisoners, Little Bear, Little Rattle Snake, and Caddo Killer, were acquitted and accordingly immediately discharged from confinement by the Court.

On Thursday last, Cha-to-kah-wa-she-pe-she, (or Mad Buffalo), and Wa-na-sha-shinger, (or Little Eagle) were again brought into Court, to receive sentence of death, which was pronounced in a very impressive manner, by Judge Johnson. They are to be hanged on Tuesday, the 21st day of December next.

When Mad Buffalo was asked, what cause he had to show, why sentence of death should not be passed upon him? he made a long and sensible speech to the Court; in the course of which, he admitted that he belonged to the party who committed the murder, but denied having any agency in it himself. He said that [he] was some distance off, in a cave, at the time of the attack, and that he had remonstrated against it—that he was friendly to the Americans, and wished to preserve peace and harmony with them.

This Chief appears to be considerable advanced in years, is large and well-proportioned, of fine and commanding mien, and shows from his interesting countenance and manner, that he possesses a superior mind and great intelligence, for one of his race. The sentence of death he received with the greatest composure, and without betraying the slightest emotion of fear. The mode of his death is all that he objects to, and we understand, he declared to the interpreter, that he would kill himself before the day appointed for his execution arrives. Indeed, so determined is he to avoid the ignominious death that awaits him, that, on Friday evening last, he made an attempt on his life, by stabbing himself with a small pen-knife (which had been given to him for the purpose of cutting tobacco) in his left breast, opposite his heart. The blade of the knife, however, was too short to effect the object which he evidently intended and only inflicted a pretty deep wound, which is not considered dangerous.

Little Eagle is also an elderly man, but of less prepossessing appearance than his fellow-prisoner. When asked for his defence [*sic*] previous to receiving sentence, he replied that he was a poor man—meaning, as was explained by the interpreter, that he was no orator, and therefore unable to make a speech in his own defence. He says but little, and received his sentence in sullen silence.

The prosecution was conducted by Sam C. Roane, Esq. U.S. District Attorney, assisted by A. H. Sevier, Esq—and the defence by Robt. C. Oden and T. Dickinson, Esqrs.

C. TRANSPORTATION AND COMMUNICATION

The growth and prosperity of Arkansas depended on a system that would move people, commerce, and information in and out of the territory. Formidable obstacles, however, stood in the way of effective transportation. Forests and swamps inhibited land transportation and required the building of roads that were expensive and time-consuming to construct. A more curious problem was the Red River Raft, a logjam that was hundreds of years old and a hundred miles long. The federal government began to clear the raft in 1828, and the job was substantially done by 1838, bringing a boom to land values and immigration into southwestern Arkansas.

Instructions for Building a Road

Clarence E. Carter, ed., *Territorial Papers of the United States*, 27 vols. (Washington, DC: G.P.O., 1954), 20:187–89.

Most roads in Arkansas Territory were primitive trails cleared through local initiative. The US government did finance and build a road between Memphis and Little Rock beginning in 1826, however. A major obstacle for road builders was the massive swamp that extended almost from Missouri to Arkansas Post along the line of the St. Francis River. Not until 1836 was the road finally finished. Note that the specifications assume that stumps will be left in the roadbed until they rot away.

[January] 27th 1826
LT. F. L. GRIFFITH U.S. A. WASHINGTON D. C.

SIR, You have been selected to superintend the making of a road from a point on the West Bank of the river Mississippi, opposite the town of Memphis in the state of Tennessee, to Little Rock in the Territory of Arkansas, authorized by an act of Congress approved the 31st of January 1824. —Enclosed is a copy of the report of the Commissioners who surveyed the route, with a copy of the plot of the survey.

The road is to be opened in reaches staked out as straight as practicable, keeping a view the general direction of the survey, in the ascent and declivities of hills, and other localities, which cause a necessary deviation from a straight line. It is to be at least twenty four feet wide throughout, and all timber, brushwood, and other rubbish or impediments, are to be removed from it, and all holes within its limits are to be filled with earth. The stumps must be cut as low to the ground as practicable, their height in no instance to exceed two thirds of their diameter, they should be hollowed towards the centre in cutting them to retain the rain and moisture. Marshy or swampy ground must be causewayed with poles or split timber, from five to eight inches in diameter at the smallest end, laid down compactly, side by side, across the direction of the road the causeways to be eighteen feet wide, secured at each side with heavy timbers or riders firmly and securely staked down. Ditches four feet wide and three feet deep are to be dug on each side of the causeways, and the earth and sand taken therefrom to be thrown upon the causeway so as to render it convex or highest in the centre—and if the swamps or other grounds be of such a nature as not to afford earth sufficient to cover the causeways at least eighteen inches in the centre and six inches at the sides, a sufficiency is to brought from other places—At proper distances in long causeways, or through very wet ground, open log bridges are to be constructed to let the water pass freely through. Where any separate causeway shall exceed seventy yards in length, it must be open in the centre or at each distance of seventy yards, to the width of twenty feet.

The hills on the route are to be dug down and wound round in such a manner as to make them practicable for carriages or loaded wagons.

All streams, branches, Creeks, lagoons and rivers, except [   ] are to be bridged in the most substantial manner—if not more than ten feet wide with strong and permanent log abutments for the floor beams to rest upon—if more than ten feet wide with staunch frame bridges built upon trestles or arches none of which are to be more than fourteen feet apart—the main timbers of the bridges are not to be less than twelve by twelve inches, squared & hewed, & where uprights are twenty feet in heighth, measuring from the mudsill to the cap sill, they are to be fourteen by sixteen inches squared and hewed— The mud sills are to be logs not less than two feet in diameter hewed on the upper and lower sides, the bark to be taken off the other two sides, and to extend at least four feet at each end beyond the exterior sides of the uprights—the uprights are to be firmly secured into the mud sills and cap sills by mortices and tenons with two pins in each, and to be firmly braced with timbers of five inches squared and hewed with mortices and tenons pinned in like manner. The floor beams of the bridges are to be four in number, one on each side of the bridge resting at each end on the cap sill, and immediately over the uprights and the others between them equidistant from them and from each other—The flooring of the frame bridges is to be of sawed plank three inches thick or of hewed puncheons from three to five inches thick the other bridges may be covered with split or hewed puncheons of the same thickness—the bridges are to be twelve feet wide in the clear—that is twelve feet measuring from the exterior sides of the cap sill—the planks or puncheons are to be securely pinned to be beams at each end—no timber is to be used in the bridges, either under the water, or exposed to the air, but that which is known to be durable.

The bridges are to be built so high above the water that no part thereof from bank to bank shall ever be exposed to danger from the highest freshets—Good and staunch hand rails are to be affixed to the bridges. Such small streams as are never deep enough in freshets to obstruct carriages in passing, and have firm sandy bottoms, with firm banks, may be dug and left as fords.

Proposed Mail Routes, 1827

Clarence Carter, ed., *Territorial Papers of the United States*, 27 vols. (Washington, DC: G.P.O., 1954), 20:489–91.

As a network of roads did develop, stagecoach travel and mail delivery became increasingly frequent and regular. The following document, nonetheless, gives a schedule that was probably more ideal than real. Aside from providing transportation to territorial travelers, the mail route offers us a useful index to early centers of settlement.

[June 18, 1827]
IN ARKANSAS.
551. From Greenville, Mo. to Batesville, once a week, 124 miles.
Leave Greenville every Friday at 2 pm and arrive at Batesville on Monday by 6 pm.

Leave Batesville every Tuesday at 6 am and arrive at Greenville on Friday by 10 am.

552. From Batesville, by Little Red River, to Little Rock, once a week, 124 miles.

Leave Batesville every Tuesday at 6 am and arrive at Little Rock on Thursday by 4 pm.

Leave Little Rock every Saturday at 8 am and arrive at Batesville on Monday by 6 pm.

553. From Memphis, by [   ] to Arkansas Post, once in two weeks.

Leave Memphis every other Friday at 6 am and arrive at Arkansas Post on Thursday by 6 pm.

Leave Arkansas Post every other Tuesday at 6 am and arrive at Memphis on Thursday by 6 pm.

554. From Little Rock to Arkansas Post, 120 miles, once in two weeks, the mail to travel 45 miles a day.

Leave Little Rock every other Saturday at 6 am and arrive at Arkansas Post on Monday by 6 pm.

Leave Arkansas Post every other Wednesday at 6 am and arrive at Little Rock on Friday by 4 pm. —Proposals will also be received to send the mail once a week between Languil Greek and Arkansas Post, instead of the existing routes, provided No. 561 is carried into effect.

555. From Batesville to Izard c.h. [courthouse] once in two weeks, 50 miles.

Leave Batesville every other Tuesday at 6 am and arrive at Izard c.h. on Wednesday by 9 am.

Leave Izard c.h. every other Wednesday at noon and arrive at Batesville on Thursday by 2 pm.

556. From Little Rock, by Stanley's Mills, Christal Hill, Pecony, Cadron, and Dardanelles, to Crawford c.h. once in two weeks, 145 miles.

Leave Little Rock every other Saturday at 6 am and arrive at Crawford c.h. on the next Tuesday by 10 am.

Leave Crawford c.h. every other Tuesday at 2 pm and arrive at Little Rock on Friday by 6 pm.

557. From Little Rock, by Clark c.h. and Hempstead c.h. to Miller c.h., 215 miles, once in two weeks.

Leave Little Rock every other Saturday at 6 am and arrive at Miller c.h. the next Friday by 6 pm.

Leave Miller c.h. every other Saturday at 6 am and arrive at Little Rock the next Thursday by 6 pm.

558. From Hempstead c.h. by Long Prairie, to Natchitoches, once in two weeks, 250 miles.

Leave Hempstead c.h. every other Monday at 6 am and arrive at Natchitoches the next Sunday by 6 pm.

Leave Natchitoches every other Monday at 6 am and arrive at Hempstead c.h. the next Sunday by 6 pm.

559. From Arkansas, by [   ], to Villemont, once in two weeks, 70 miles.

Leave Arkansas every other Thursday at 6 am and arrive at Villemont on Friday by 6 pm.

Leave Villemont every other Tuesday at 6 am and arrive at Arkansas on Wednesday by 6 pm.

560. From Little Rock, by [   ], to Monroe, La. once a week, [   ] miles.

Leave Little Rock every Wednesday at 6 am and arrive at Monroe the next Tuesday by noon.

Leave Monroe every Wednesday at 6 am and arrive at Little Rock on the next Tuesday by 6 pm. —Proposals are invited for a fortnight mail also.

561. From Little Rock, by Bayou Martal, White River Crossings, Bayou de Veu, Languil Creek, and St. Francis, to Memphis, and back, once a week, 136 miles.

Leave Little Rock every Saturday at 6 am and arrive at Memphis the next Tuesday by noon.

Leave Memphis every Tuesday at 2 pm and arrive at Little Rock on Friday by 6 pm.

The Steamboat Arkansas

Arkansas Gazette (Little Rock), March 14, 1837.

Speedier and more spectacular than stagecoaches, and also more dangerous as a result of collisions and explosions, were the steamboats, eighty-three of which operated on Arkansas waters during the territorial period. The *Arkansas* was larger, faster, and better equipped than most steamboats of the time. The congratulatory note inserted in the *Arkansas Gazette* by the passengers of the *Arkansas* illustrates the excitement of Americans over steam technology and the local pride of territorial citizens who were pleased to have such a useful and modern device at their service.

THE ARKANSAS

The new steamer ARKANSAS made her first appearance in our river, as a regular trader, on Thursday last. She is unquestionably the most splendid boat we have had, and does ample credit to Arkansas enterprise, and capital; having been constructed by the liberality of our capitalists and citizens residing on this river. She was built at Cincinnati, during the past season, under the immediate superintendence of her commander, Capt. HALDERMAN, and of the very best material. She measures 223 tons—

length of keel 130 feet, of deck 153 feet, and 25 feet breadth of beam, with 6½ feet depth of hold. She has 4 double-flue boilers, 42 inches in diameter and 22 feet long, and a 24-inch cylinder with 6 feet 6 inch stroke. Her Cabin is on the upper deck, and combines elegance with convenience and comfort. The Gentlemen's Cabin is 54 feet in length, with state-rooms on each side, 15 in number, with doors each opening into the cabin and to the guards, and is lighted by a skylight from the hurricane roof, 70 feet in length, extending over the Social Hall. The ladies' Cabin, which is large, commodious, and airy, contains 4 staterooms and 8 open double births. She is also provided with a powerful apparatus for hauling in the event of running aground, being a double forward and a single one in the stern.

•   •   •

A CARD.

The cabin passengers of the new steamer ARKANSAS, on her first voyage from New Orleans to Little Rock, feel that they ought not omit making a public acknowledgement to Capt. T. J. Halderman (and the officers generally of the boat), for their unremitted exertions throughout a hazardous trip, for the comfort and safety of his passengers, as well as the cargo shipped by him. The ARKANSAS, will recommend HER SELF to the public patronage by her superior accommodations, and her powerful and splendid model as a boat—but this tribute is given, (not as a matter of course), to one well known in the trade, where he designs to remain, as an evidence of the renewed confidence of his old friends in his industry and skill as a navigator.

Wm. Walker	L. N. Clarke
L. Richards	S. H. Tucker
James S. Jones	J. Conway
H. A. Anderson	T. J. Pew
Wm. Field	N. Phillips
Reuben Dye	Rich'd T. Banks
Albert Peel	Jacob West
William Adkins	R. McCall
J. C. Julian	Andrew Ross
James Anderson	M. Wright
M. Wright	A. B. Anthony
Robert Grimes	W. Green

D. FRONTIER SOCIETY

Arkansas Territory, like most new American societies in the nineteenth century, experienced a great deal of violence wrought by settler against settler. Dueling, a custom that originated among Italian gentlemen of the sixteenth century, was the most genteel form of territorial violence. A number of duels developed out of the heated political conflicts of the time. Sometimes the principals compromised their differences before the fight or after exchanging misses; on occasion men died for what now seem trifling reasons. Violence also occurred in less formal ways; impromptu gun battles, knife fights, and free-for-all brawls were all common in early Arkansas. Meanwhile, however, economic, political, and cultural development was taking place. In the second document in this section, an Englishman deplores the violent and crude aspects of frontier Arkansas but also notes signs of improvement.

The Scott-Selden Duel

Arkansas Gazette (Little Rock), June 1, 1824.

During a game of whist at Arkansas Post in 1824, Judge Selden contradicted a lady player's account of the score. Judge Scott, who was also playing, called for an apology from Selden on behalf of the lady. Selden refused, and the ensuing quarrel resulted in a challenge and an acceptance. The fatal consequences of the event and also the opposition to dueling by William E. Woodruff, editor of the *Arkansas Gazette*, are illustrated in this selection.

The long talked of and much ridiculed DUEL, which has been the topic of conversation in every class throughout our Territory for six weeks past, has at length, contrary to our expectations, resulted in the death of one of the parties! We have received the following particulars of this affair from an eye-witness:

A Duel was fought on the east side of the Mississippi river, (in the state of Mississippi), opposite the town of Helena, on Wednesday last, 26th ult., between ANDREW SCOTT and JOSEPH SELDEN, Esqs., both *Judges of the Superior Court of the Territory of Arkansas*. At the first fire, Judge SELDEN was killed on the spot. The ball of his antagonist entered his body just below his right nipple, passed thro' his heart and lungs, and came out on the opposite side below his left nipple. He expired in a few seconds, without speaking a word, or uttering a groan. Judge SCOTT received no personal injury.

As the laws of this Territory against duelling, are probably as rigorous as those of any state in the Union; and presuming that a legal investigation of this affair—which is a flagrant violation of the laws of God and man; at variance with, and destructive of, every principle of good morals, and an insult to the community at large—will of course take place, we forbear making any further remarks for the present.

We, however, wish it to be distinctly understood, that, in making the foregoing observations, we are actuated only by a sense of duty, and not from any private hostility, or personal animosity, toward either of the gentlemen concerned in this unfortunate and melancholy affair—for both of whom we have hitherto entertained the most sincere sentiments of friendship and respect.

An Attempted Mediation Fails

Lonnie J. White, ed., "The Pope Noland Duel of 1831; An Original Letter of C. F. M. Noland to His Father," *Arkansas Historical Quarterly* 22 (1963): 117–23.

The Pope-Noland duel, subject of the documents below, originated in a newspaper attack on Pope's uncle, Gov. John Pope, written by Noland. Note how much each man valued what he believed to be his honor. The duel ended when Pope received a wound from which he later died.

Little Rock Jany. 16th 1831
[To Mr. C. F. M. Noland]

Sir,

The undersigned have witnessed with sincere regret the progress of an altercation between y. self and Maj. Pope. The respect which we entertain for you both as well as a firm conviction that no just cause of hostility actually existed in the origin of your controversy, has induced our earnest solicitude that (if possible) a compromise or adjustment of the difficulty might be effected. To promote so desirable an end, permit us to tender our mediation and to ask your permission, to make such suggestions to you as in our opinion would conduce on that object—

We confidently indulge the hope, that you will not doubt the sincerity of the declaration that we are prompted by no motive unconnected with your present and future welfare, and that we should consider ourselves dishonored in making any proposition in relation to this subject which would be incompatible with yours. We should be pleased to hear from you on this subject as soon as convenient—

A duplicate of this note will be handed Mr. Pope at the same instant you receive this[.]

Very Respectfully
Ben[jamin] Desha
J[ame]s Woodson Bates
Robt. Crittenden
Williams S. Fulton

• • •

Little Rock Jany 17th 1831
To Messrs. Bates Desha Crittenden & Fulton,

Gentlemen

Yr. note of the 16th. inst. was received last evening[.] I have reflected much on its contents—And al[t]ho. I agree with you, "that no just cause of hostilities existed in the origin" of the controversy between Maj Pope and myself, yet *matters* have gone *so far*, that I fear it will be impossible to adjust amicably our difficulty—I will however hear any suggestions coming from you with pleasure—And for the kind feelings which prompted you to this act of disinterested friendship accept the sincere thanks of one who has the honor to subscribe himself

Very Respectfully
Yr. Obt. Sevt.
C. F. M. Noland

• • •

Little Rock Jany 18th 1831

To Messrs. Desha, Bates, Crittenden & Fulton

Gentlemen

Your note tendering a mediation on the part of yourselves, in the quarrel between Mr. Noland and myself was duly received. The regret expressed therein that any thing of a nature to disturb the harmony of the scene should have occur[r]ed, finds in my bosom a most cordial response. A careful examination of the facts which led to this affair have resulted in an earnest conviction that there is on my own part nothing to *ask hope* or *fear*, and in refusing a request so kindly and liberally urged, I do my feelings a violence which nought could atone for but *conscious rectitude* and a deep sense of *injury* and *insult*. To the motives which prompted your communication I accord all the credit due them, and if it comported with my feelings to submit this quarrel to the arbitrators of any board, I could not select one of which capacity candor and honorable award I entertain so high a sense. I beg leave in conclusion to tender to each and eve[r]y one of you my grateful thanks for the kind expressions of interest in the welfare of one who will always feel proud and happy in saying that he reciprocates those feelings and can not and will not forget your kindness[.]

> With Sentiments of Esteem & gratitude Yours &c
> Wm. Fontaine Pope

Brawling on the Devil's Fork

Leonard Williams, ed., *Cavorting on the Devil's Fork: The Pete Whetstone Letters of C. F. M. Noland* (Memphis: Memphis State University Press, 1979), 60–62.

In addition to being a duelist, Charles Fenton Mercer Noland was also an accomplished writer and humorist whose tales of Arkansas were published for several decades in a New York journal called *The Spirit of the Times*. Noland's accounts of frontier life make enjoyable reading, and they also seem roughly accurate. In the selection that follows, we see the backwoods penchant for fist fighting and its relationship to other amusements such as drinking, gambling, and horse racing.

I just wish you could come to the Devil's Fork. The way I would show you fun, for I have got the best pack of bear dogs, the closest shooting rifle, the fastest swimming horse, and perhaps, the prettiest sister you ever *did* see. Why, those fellows on the Raccoon Fork of the War Eagle, ain't a priming to us boys of the Devil's Fork. They aint monstrous friendly to us, ever since I laid out *Warping Bars*, with the *Bussing Coon*. I tell you, we used them up that hunt—red headed Jim Cole drove home twenty-four of the likliest sort of cows and calves, and Bill Spence walked into a fellow for three good chunks of horses.

I'll tell you how that race was made. Monday evening of the election, I was standing talking to Squire Woods—we were just outside of the Doggery, when I heard somebody cavorting—I stepped right in— There stood big Dan Looney the Raccoon Fork Bully. I said nothing, but stopped right still—Says Dan, "I say it publicly and above board, the Warping Bars can beat any nag from the Gulf of Mexico to the Rocky Mountains, that is now living and above ground, that drinks the waters of the Devil's Fork, one quarter of a mile with any weight, from a gutted snow bird to a stack of fodder!"

Before I had time to say a word after Dan got through, in jumped Jim Cole—says he, "Dan, the Bussing Coon can slam the Warping Bars this day three weeks, one quarter of a mile, with little Bill Allen's weight on each; for fifty dollars in cash, and two hundred in the best sort of truck."

"It is wedding," said Dan, "and give us your hand."

They shook hands and agreed to put up two good horses as forfeits. No sooner was the race made, than the boys commenced drinking and shouting. Dan said Jim Cole owed a treat—Jim Cole said Dan owed a treat. They agreed to leave it to Squire Woods; now Squire Woods is up to snuff and makes no more of belting a quart, than a methodist preacher would of eating a whole chicken, so says he, "boys, taking all things into consideration, I think it but fair that *both* should treat to a gallon, and sugar enough to sweeten it." "Hurrah for Squire Woods," roared every chap except Dan and Jim.

It did'nt take more than twenty minutes to make some of them feel their keeping. I knew what was coming, and you may depend I kept my eye skinned.—Dan soon became uproarious, and made out he was a heap drunker than he was—After a little while he could'nt hold in—

Says he, "I can pick the ticks off of any of you hell-fire boys," (meaning the Devil's Fork chaps)—the words were hardly out of his mouth before Jim Cole cried out, "you are a liar, Dan," and *cherow* he took him just above the burr of the ear—Dan reeled, and 'ere he recovered, several persons rushed between them.—"Come boys," says one, "there is Squire Woods, and have some respect for him." "Damn Squire Woods," says Dan, "a Squire is no more than any other man in a fight!"

The physic was working—there was no chance to control it—coats were shed—hats flung off—shirt collars unbuttoned—but one thing was needed to bring about a general fight—that soon happened, for Bill Spence jumped right upon the table and shouted "hurrah for the Devil's Fork!" Dan answered him by yelling "go it my Coons"—the Doggery was on about half way ground, and the two settlements were about equally represented. The fight commenced—I tell you there was no time to swap knives—I pitched into Dan—'twas just like two studs kicking—we had it so good and so good for a long time—at last Dan was using me up, when Squire Woods (who had got through whipping his man) slipped up and legged for me, and I *rather* think gave Dan a slight kick—Dan *sung out* and the Devil's Fork triumphed.

I reckon there were all sorts of 4th July's cut over the fellows' eyes—and bit noses and fingers were plenty. We started home just about dark, singing Ingen all the way. I did'nt want Daddy to see me that night, so I slipped to the stable loft—next morning I started out bear hunting, the particulars of which I will write you some of these times.

An Englishman Describes Little Rock in 1834

George W. Featherstonhaugh, *Excursion through the Slave States* (New York: Harper and Bros., 1844), 94–100.

George W. Featherstonhaugh was an English geologist who traveled widely in the Missouri River Valley during the 1830s. Like most foreign observers who visited the United States, he was appalled by much of what he saw, particularly in Arkansas. Featherstonhaugh's prejudices, his dislike for democracy, for example, are evident in his comments about Little Rock, and they are exacerbated by his often-humorous sarcasm. Note, however that he says nice things about the new state capitol under construction, which is still standing and now known as the Old State House. Featherstonhaugh makes fun of the American love of newspapers, ignoring the fact that it is a sign of both widespread literacy and a universal interest in public affairs. He also documents Arkansas's contribution to hand-to-hand weaponry.

This territory of Arkansas was on the confines of the United States and Mexico, and, as I had long known, was the occasional residence of many timid and nervous persons, against whom the laws of these respective countries had a grudge. *Gentlemen,* who had taken the liberty to imitate the signatures of other persons; *bankrupts,* who were not disposed to be plundered by their creditors; *homicides, horse-stealers,* and *gamblers,* all admired Arkansas on account of the very gentle and tolerant state of public opinion which prevailed there in regard to such fundamental points as religion, morals, and property. . . .

The town of Little Rock receives its name from being built upon the first rock, a slate, which juts out into the Arkansas, in coming up the river from its mouth in the Mississippi; it is tolerably well laid out, has a few brick houses, and a greater number of indifferently built wooden ones, generally in straggling situations, which admit of their having a piece of ground attached to them. The population at this time was betwixt 500 and 600 inhabitants, a great proportion of them mechanics; lawyers and doctors without number, and abundance of tradesmen going by the name of merchants. . . .

Newspapers are too expensive for the poorer classes in England, and therefore by far the greater part of them are not distracted, enfeebled, and corrupted by *cheap* newspapers. . . . But in Little Rock with a population of 600 people there are no less than *three* cheap newspapers, which are not read but devoured by everybody; for what pleasure can be equal to that which—through the blessings of universal suffrage—those free and enlightened citizens called "the sovereign people" [learn] that the political party which has omitted to purchase their support is composed of scoundrels and liars, and men who want to get into power for no other purpose but to ruin the country? . . .

It was my good fortune to become acquainted with a few respectable and agreeable individuals here. Governor Pope, the governor of the territory, is an unaffected and worthy person. . . . This gentleman has been of great service in various ways, especially in the judicious use he has made of the funds entrusted to him by the general government for the erection of a legislative hall, which is a very handsome building, placed in an advantageous situation, on the brink of the river, and one of the neatest public buildings I have seen in North America. . . . He lives among the inhabitants in an unpretending and plain manner, encouraging them to use no ceremony in talking to him. . . . [I went to visit the governor, and his wife answered the door.] Upon which without mincing the matter, she very frankly told me that "he was gone in the woods to hunt for a sow and pigs belonging to her that were missing." . . .

Mr. Woodruff, the editor of the principal Gazette of the place, and postmaster, was always obliging, and is one of the most indefatigably industrious men of the territory. At his store we used to call to hear the news of the day, which were various and exciting enough; for, with some honourable exceptions, perhaps there never such another population assembled —broken tradesman, refugees from justice, travelling gamblers, and some young bucks and bloods. . . . Quarreling seemed to be their principal occupation, and these puppies, without family, education, or refinement of any kind, were continually resorting to what they called the "Laws of Honour," a part of the code of which, in Little Rock, is to administer justice with your own hand the first convenient opportunity. A common practice with these fellows was to fire at each other with a rifle across the street, and then dodge behind a door. . . .

One of the most respectable inhabitants told me, that he did not suppose there were *twelve* inhabitants of the place who ever went into the streets without—from some motive or another—being armed with pistols or large hunting knives about a foot long and an inch and a half broad, originally intended to skin and cut up animals, but which are now made and ornamented with great care, and kept exceedingly sharp for the purpose of slashing and sticking human beings. These formidable instruments, with their sheaths mounted in silver, are the pride of an Arkansas blood, and got their name of *Bowie* knives from a conspicuous person of this fiery climate. . . .

A traveler, whom I met with at Little Rock, told me that he was lodging at an indifferent tavern there and had been put in a room with four beds in it. There he had slept quietly alone for two nights, when on the third, the day before the legislature convened, the house became suddenly filled with senators and members, several of whom, having come up into his room with their saddlebags, got out a table, ordered some whiskey, and produced cards they had brought with them. The most amusing part of the incident was that they asked him to lend them five dollars until they could get some of their legislative "wages."

What must strike a stranger here, is the apparent indifference to what we call personal comforts. No one seems to think that there is any better thing in the world than little square bits of pork fried in lard, bad coffee, and indifferent bread. To this, without almost any variety, they go regularly three times a day to be fed, just as horses are fed at the livery. Venison, it is true, is abundant, but it is no better than any thing else.

FOR FURTHER READING

S. Charles Bolton's *Territorial Ambition: Land and Society in Arkansas, 1800–1840* (Fayetteville: University of Arkansas Press, 1993) offers a positive view of economic growth in early Arkansas, and his *Arkansas, 1800–1860: Remote and Restless* (Fayetteville: University of Arkansas Press, 1998) provides a survey of its subject. Important specialized studies include Lonnie J. White, *Politics on the Southwestern Frontier: Arkansas Territory, 1818–1836* (Memphis, TN: Memphis State University Press, 1964); Margaret S. Ross, *The Arkansas Gazette* (Little Rock: Arkansas Gazette Foundation, 1969); and Donald P. McNeilly, *The Old South Frontier: Cotton Plantations and the Formation of Arkansas Society, 1819–1861* (Fayetteville: University of Arkansas Press, 2000). A highly useful traveler's account is Thomas Nutall's *Journal of Travels into Arkansas Territory*, ed. Savoie Lottinville (Norman: University of Oklahoma Press, 1980). Details about the Arkansas Cherokees may be gleaned from William G. McLoughlin, *Cherokee Renascence in the New Republic* (Princeton, NJ: Princeton University Press, 1986).

PART II

Arkansas and the South, 1836 to 1900

Carl H. Moneyhon

CHAPTER III

Antebellum Arkansas, 1836–1860

INTRODUCTION

Arkansas Territory became a state on June 15, 1836, when President Andrew Jackson signed the bill that admitted it to the Union. Statehood marked the beginning of a period of rapid growth that continued until the outbreak of the Civil War in 1861. During this time, the population increased by nearly 860 percent, reaching toward half a million by the war. Agricultural productivity climbed to $91 million, and the state's cotton production ranked sixth in the nation. Along with the settlement and expansion of agriculture came growth in the manufacturing areas that provided necessary services for the society: mills, gins, and lumbering. During the 1850s, the state even made advances toward solving its persistent transportation problems with the laying of the first railroad tracks.

Through the entire antebellum period, four major themes provided an identity for Arkansas: the rural nature of its population, its agricultural economy, the slave labor system, and the southern orientation of state politics. Life in the country was an experience shared by over 98 percent of Arkansas's citizens, although by 1860 there were a few towns. Little Rock was the largest, with 3,727 inhabitants, followed by Camden, Fort Smith, Pine Bluff, Van Buren, Fayetteville, and Arkadelphia. Most people lived in the countryside, where their days were regulated by nature's clock.

Agriculture provided Arkansans with their principal source of income throughout these years. Almost every inhabitant of the state, either directly or indirectly, owed his or her livelihood to the farm. Everywhere in the state farmers produced corn and wheat. In the rich river valleys, however, they added cultivation of the most important cash crop, cotton. By 1860, cotton production had increased to 367,393 bales of "white gold." Even when one examines manufacturing, the importance of the agricultural economy can be seen. Almost all of Arkansas's industry focused primarily on processing the state's farm goods for market.

Two major types of agricultural units dominated the landscape—the small, self-sufficient farm and the plantation. Economically, the plantation was the more important and specialized in major cash crops, often to the point that food had to be purchased from outside. These large-scale enterprises varied in size, but generally they contained at least two hundred acres of land actually under cultivation. Unless the planter had this much, plus more acres to put into operation after the older land had played out, it was simply not feasible for him to emphasize a single crop. The census does not provide a clear indication of the number of plantations, but of 33,190 farms in Arkansas in 1860, only 4,607 possessed more than one hundred acres. For the most part, the plantations stood upon lands along the great navigable rivers of the state, where soil richness and the accessibility of transportation made possible the growth of these crops for market.

While the plantation was the most productive agricultural unit, most farmers worked on a much smaller scale, one that required different organization: in particular, emphasis upon self-sufficiency rather than marketable crops. The small farms, nestled amid the plantations in the river valleys, occupied the state's poorer agricultural lands and climbed the mountains of the northwest. Operating with modest resources and leading a life far from luxurious, these Arkansas yeomen were typical of the state's population before the war.

In addition to country life and agriculture, slavery was a major component of the state's prewar identity. This system, binding black people into a role of perpetual bondage, provided the chief source of labor for the large farms and plantations of the state. By 1860, there were 111,115 slaves in Arkansas, over 20 percent of the total population. Most of the slaves were located in the river valley counties, where the cotton was grown; four counties on the Mississippi River and two on the southern border were more than 50 percent black. By contrast, in the mountainous area of the northwest there were few slaves. While only 11,481 white Arkansans were slave owners in 1860, and despite the concentration of slaves in the south and southeast, most Arkansans had some stake in the institution, either real or potential.

Agriculture and slavery caused Arkansas politics to be more closely associated with southern rather than western states. Throughout the antebellum years, the Democratic Party dominated local politics. Its leadership, known as "The Family," controlled local offices from the beginning to the end. While it sometimes faced challenges, including that of Whigs, American Party advocates, and ambitious individual politicians, the Democratic leadership successfully maintained its position throughout the era. The government was successful in large part because its leaders appealed to the interests of the farmers and the slaveholders. Limited taxation and legal institutions supporting slavery earned the hostility of opponents, but no one successfully changed the system. Perhaps no single politician better illustrated the interests and power of the group than Elias N. Conway, or "Dirt Road" Conway, governor from 1852 to 1860, who maintained throughout his administration a policy of limiting taxes and, consequently, delaying the construction of railroads. In the sectional agitation between the North and the South that would take place in the 1840s and 1850s, this leadership would tie itself firmly to the rest of the South—and in the end help to drag Arkansas into the disastrous Civil War.

A. GROWTH AND DEVELOPMENT

Between statehood and the Civil War, Arkansas experienced rapid population growth. With this expansion, the state began to develop a culture. In many ways, this frontier society was similar to that found in the states immediately east of Arkansas. The first wave of immigrants was seen as a particularly unambitious group, content to exploit but not develop the riches of the countryside. Observers noted their unwillingness to put out much work and repeatedly wrote about their drinking and fighting, their lack of manners, and the primitive nature of society. By the Civil War, however, Arkansas achieved the basic institutions of civilized life and was, for the most part, undiscernible from neighboring communities. The following selections document the growth of Arkansas and detail the observations by various authors of the developing cultural life of the state.

A New Orleans Newspaper Assesses Opportunity in Arkansas

Debow's Review 23 (1857): 209–10.

In the antebellum period, *DeBow's Review*, published by agricultural reformer J. B. D. DeBow at New Orleans, was one of the most influential newspapers in the South. DeBow tended to focus on economic opportunities in the South and encourage development, but his assessments of conditions were usually accurate. The following article examines Arkansas in 1857, pointing to the expansion of its population, its economic conditions, and the possibilities of economic success. The article also points to some of the characteristics that outsiders had begun to associate with Arkansans by this time.

All accounts represent that a rapid increase is going on in the settlement and development of Arkansas, for which, it has undoubted advantages. In the last twelve months over a quarter of a million acres of land have been entered by new and enterprising settlers. Population—

	WHITE	FREE COLORED	SLAVE	TOTAL
1820	12,576	59	1,617	14,273 [14,252]
1830	25,671	141	4,516	30,388 [30,328]
1840	77,174	465	19,935	97,574
1850	162,189	608	47,100	209,897

In 1857 the total cannot be short of 300,000 persons. Absolute debt of the State in 1855, $1,506,017; contingent liability, $1,813,579. Eight million acres of swamp land were donated to the State by Congress, much of which may be reclaimed. Taxable property, $55,377,384; State tax, $146,488.

In 1828 the western boundary of Arkansas was changed by the Federal Government, and a very large slice of that territory was added to the Cherokee nation. Mr. Benton, in his "Thirty Years in the Senate," bemoans the act of transfer as equivalent to the conversion of so much slave territory. The fact, however, remains to be proved when the Indian reservation comes to take its place among the States. . . .

A correspondent of one of our Northern journals has thus written in regard to the present state of things in Arkansas:

"Beginning with the northeastern portion, he describes it as one of the best corn, grass, and stock-growing regions in all the Southern country; though, owing to the want of market facilities, it has till lately attracted little notice. It was, also, particularly unfortunate in its early settlers, Ishmaels of old, without means or love for civilized life, the wilderness is their home; they scorn the city and multitude; neither have they house or lands; wherever night overtakes them they pitch their tents and herd their flocks; 'and when the railroad starts, they will start also, to go whither it cannot come,' so strong is their love for semi-civilized life, so great their aversion for improvement of whateverkind.

"Northwest Arkansas is mountainous, the river valley narrow, rarely more than two or three hundred yards wide, the soil, however, is fertile. Admirably adapted to pasturage and general tillage, it makes the most beautiful and productive farms in the Southwest, where peace and joy and contentment dwell. On the highland, too, or more properly the hills, are fertile and well-watered fields, good for raising wheat and other small grains, as well as for general tillage and pasturage. This part of Arkansas has the advantage in health, its waters are clean, pure, and cool, and valuable minerals—marble, slate, and lead—abound. White river and its forks water this whole region; made navigable, as they easily might be, they would soon develop the inexhaustible resources of this portion of the State.

"The cotton-growing region of Arkansas is south of the base line.

"It is true cotton is raised as high as Jacksonport, in White river, but the southern part of the State is justly considered as the region adapted to cotton and for the production of this great staple, the lands of the Mississippi, White, Arkansas, Ouachita, and Red rivers, are not surpassed. Their richness and productiveness are too well known for me to attempt to say anything more in their favor. These streams are rendered navigable in the spring of the year by rains, and the melting of the snows in the mountains above, and not until then the greatest part of the cotton goes to market. But, in order that they may ship their cotton as soon as it is ready, they are building a railroad from Fulton to Red river, to Gaines' Landing, on the Mississippi. And to remove a like difficulty, (to which the Arkansas river is subject;) they have been talking of a road from Little Rock to Napoleon, at the mouth of the Arkansas."

Arkansas as Viewed by an Irish Immigrant

John Kerr to James Kerr, May 25, 1851, Small Manuscripts
Collection, Arkansas History Commission, Little Rock.

John Kerr came to the United States from Ireland in the 1850s and
moved to Arkansas the following year. Settling at Napoleon, on the
mouth of the Arkansas River, Kerr set up business. The following letter, which he wrote to his uncle, gives excellent insights into the
nature of opportunities presented to the individual in the expanding
frontier economy. He also provides useful information concerning
wages, the cost of living, the productivity of farms, and comparative
economic conditions. These allow the reader to reconstruct the general economic scene in antebellum Arkansas. In addition, Kerr's letter
is particularly useful because of the view he presents of local social
customs—intemperance, lack of cleanliness, desire for education, and
contemporary views of medicine.

Napoleon
State of Arkansas
May 25th, 1851

Dear Uncle:

It is now a good while since I wrote you—perhaps too long—but I
depended on Wm. or David to write, altho' I think they have not done
so. . . . I came to this place "Napoleon" in the beginning of April. I was
not doing well at New Orleans, and got an offer of better wages to come
here. It is a small village, situated at the mouth of the Arkansas River,
640 miles above New Orleans. A merchant of N.O., and one of this state
established a house here to do a general business, grocery, Dry Good,
etc., and also for the purpose of re-shipping goods left here by Cincinnati
and New Orleans boats intended for the interior of this state. The concern is a new one, but is doing pretty well. I keep the Books and attend
to things in general. I get $50 per month and room and board, etc., which
is equal to $80 in New Orleans without board, which is considered good
wages there. There are other advantages, however, which make the situation worth more, that is by forming acquaintance and learning something of the country I probably can, before long, get into business in my
own account. A new country presents a much better prospect for that

than a city or an old country. I wish I had come here—to this state rather—instead of going to Pennsylvania and killing myself teaching school for nearly nothing and studying what has been of no pecuniary advantage to me. Why the best wages in Pennsylvania for teaching was $20, in one or two places $25 without board. The other day a planter across the river (Mississippi) offered me $250 for 10 months to teach his family about 4 children, and give board, washing, etc. besides. That would be $25 per month clear. Now James K could get that if he was here just now. I wish he was. Anyhow, if he is getting better or thinks and has any reason to believe he will get better, I would advise him to come out here. I can get him plenty of situations to teach—the schools will be small, perhaps only a family or two and he can do it well. People are anxious to get teachers, many, I might say most of the Planters have to send their children from home 4 or 500 miles and they would much rather employ a teacher at home. If Jas can stand another voyage across the "big pond" and if he desires, let him bundle up his 'duds' and make for New Orleans; then strike for "Napoleon" and he can get employment in a short time. When tired of teaching, he can go home again if he feels unwell—he will have money—or he can get into a store, I think, after a while. This is a fine healthy state, when you get back from the Mississippi. There are many flourishing towns in it and it is settling fast. I expect to settle in some healthy little town on the Arkansas river, bye and bye, and have a share in a store. I have one or two places in view where a store will do well, and when I have about $2,000 capital, I can commence for myself. I do wish I had come to Arkansas 10 years ago.

This place "Napoleon" is but very small, containing about 100 inhabitants. It is not a pleasant place to live. The Mississippi overflows it every year, sometimes twice; this renders it unhealthy. They are going to make a "Levee" (embankment) this year to keep out the water. It has good facilities for trade and many say that in 10 years, it will be a large place. The *people* of the place are not like those of the North. In fact, the Southern Americans are different from the northern a great deal. They are far inferior in intelligence and morality. They have not the same steady, sober, peaceable, persevering and enterprising character possessed by their Northern brethren [*sic*]. Many of them are ignorant (unable to read), rude, filthy in their habits, and intemperate. Those of this town particularly so, especially as to filth and intemperance. Drinking is their principal, I might say only enjoyment. And O! how strong drink degrades a people—turns them from men to imbeciles and demonds [*sic*], by turns. I never was before so strongly impressed with the evil tendency of alcohol on man, as I am now. Its habitual use produces the most melancholy effects; deteriorates the body, stupefies the mind and degrades the soul; besides it almost destroys the moral feelings and blunts all the sensibilities of our nature. The intemporate [*sic*] habits of the people here, form my principal objection to the place. This *county* consumes a vast quantity of "liquor" and it presents a greater amount of mortality, taken from the statistics of the State, than any other county in it. The state of Mississippi lies across the river opposite us. The county in it directly opposite this one is by no means unhealthy, and there is not a glass of liquor sold in it, and very few use it!

The passengers with Sam were very kind to him. He got his leg hurt somehow and an old woman and her daughter cooked for him half way over. The mate was very kind to him. The ship came in about 8 p. O'C. and I was on board about 10. Sam was in bed but someone brought him up. I wouldn't have known him from Adam. Sam is quite childish and a little dull I think, but will brighten, I hope. I don't know where the two young men went, that came with him. One of them got drunk the day after their arrival and some tavern runner blackened his eyes, because he wouldn't got [*sic*] with him. I would have nothing to do with him nor take any interest in him after his being drunk. From what I saw among the passengers the night of their arrival, I could not help thinking that the Irish character presented a feature different from that of any other nation. When I got aboard, the bacchanalian songs and boisterous laughter of about 30, almost drowned every other sound. A number of them were running round the vessel, staggering, swearing, and boasting of how they could fight, etc. There they were, in all their native filth, unwashed and unshaven, swallowing drafts of their country's curse, and as careless of what was to come of them as if they were to take possession of a farm each and be independent tomorrow. Just at a time when they required all the forethought and prudence they possessed, they drowned all in drink. Did ever the lunatic display greater folly than this? I saw many steady, sober, sensible people, but many were drunk,—even the women were staggering under the effects of Whiskey! A newly come Irishman despises the negroes here, but they are more civilized than he.

This part of the United States is almost exclusively a cotton growing country and it is considered the best for that article of any other in the country. Farming is done altogether by negroes; Planters owning from 10 to 100 of these. The land is very rich and planters have done well the last 2 or 3 years, cotton having been high for three seasons. An acre produces, I think, if I remember right, about 500 pounds cotton, which sells for about $50—I believe they raise sometimes 800 pounds. The plant is coming up now; I have not seen it in the field in any other shape. I can tell you what it is like and how raised etc. again October. I frequently visit at a planters across the river—he shows me his farm etc., and I will learn how planting and raising Cotton is performed. So far, the process resembles that of sowing turnips and the plant now is very small and quite a tender one, as much as so any vegetable or flower of the garden—I have but little news to send you. Robt. Thompson and family who lived in New Orleans, went all to California in March last. Francis Henderson is there. In coming from N.O. to Napoleon, I got acquainted with John F. Douglas from near Parkgate; he was clerk on the steamboat I came up on. He had lived in N.O. for the last 3 years but I never saw him. He was well when I saw him last, a few days ago. Tell James that Sam Rainey is married.

David wants Jas. to send him a newspaper—he says he has seen no Belfast paper since he came to this country. Jas. promised to send him some. I hope you are all in good health and trust that Elizabeth still continues well. In my opinion she should take plenty of exercise in the *open air. Avoid close rooms.* Bathe or wash the whole body *frequently* in *cold* water; and with proper precautions in regard to food, she need not fear consumption. I am convinced people bring almost every disease upon themselves, and this among the rest. Close rooms, with the windows always down, and 3 or 4 sleeping in a room, perhaps 2 in a bed, is quite sufficient to create disease. It is almost sure to do so in time. I expect to hear from you soon after the receipt of this. Let me know what Jas. thinks of coming. If he thinks his health will admit, I think he ought to come. When he was returning home, I told him if he wished to come back, I would pay his passage—so I will. I can send a draft to you if you furnish him with money. Let him come when he chooses, anytime will do. The draft Sam brought was paid in New York. I sent it to a merchant there who got it cashed. If I had known no merchant or responsible person there, it would not have been worth a cent. Crawford is a fool if he said that anyone in N. Orleans would pay it. My health is middling. I am troubled with Dyspepsia a little. Write soon; my regards to all—to Uncles David and Samuel.

Yours as of old,
John Kerr

A South Carolina Immigrant Paints a Better Picture

Mrs. Thomas Campbell, ed., "Two Letters of the Meek Family, Union County, 1842–1845," *Arkansas Historical Quarterly* 15 (1956): 260–66.

John Meek moved from his native South Carolina to Union County in the 1840s. By 1850 he would own 560 acres in the county and seven slaves. In this letter he proves to be an ardent booster of Arkansas: particularly noteworthy is his effort to correct pervasive views about the inhabitants of the state. From his observations we can gain a picture that counters the one presented by John Kerr.

John Meek To Dr. Rob't E. [Erskine] Campbell, Newberry District, South Carolina.
Union CT.H. Arksas [*sic*] 20th Sept. 1842

Dr. Son

We are all in health at present (thank God) & have enjoyed fine health this year but if you saw the Christal Springs we have to drink from, & the pure clean undulating Country with tall forests shading it & waving under a delightful breeze from the Rocky Mountains you would not wonder at our health being good, & we have the most fertile soil I ever saw (except the Mississippi swamp which exceeds description). The Banks of that Majestic River is like the streets of a great city with steamboats always in sight & trading constantly, if health could be enjoyed on that river it would be the "Gloria Mundi." The poorest land in our country would beat in Corn, Cotton, Wheat, oats or potatoes, any land in Laurens or New'y, SC.

James Meek will make a bale of 500 lb. cotton to each acre & has noble corn, oats, wheat. Potatoes of every sort grow extra fine. James is well pleased & doing well. He has got open 102 acres of land in fine improvement, good buildings, you would be surprised to see his place.

Such good buildings, fine fences & fruit trees & a first rate wife, well educated and healthy, industrious.

We are building 3 miles from here on a place of good land & extra fine water & beautiful situation. Mr. Hamton's family are well & he is well pleased. He is on first rate land & has a good Crop. We just came from James's, they are well and the Country has enjoyed the best health I ever saw in any country this year.

You have made a great mistake as to our inhabitants, the people composing our community are the enterprising Citizens of Europe and America from the first Citys and Countys of Main[e] & every other state till you reach New Orleans & for urbanity we think we could compare with any country without a blush. The people are a Churchgoing people & they greatly pride in being orderly when at Church, & our Statute Laws are as good as yours and quite like them. Many of our Citizens have been of the unfortunate & came here to get homes and repair their conditions. This many of them will soon do as they are industrious.

I wish you were here, you would be bettered in every way, as well as good land at 1.25cts an acre, better health, better trade as New Orleans is as it were at our Door, & from there a ready access to every port of the Commercial world. At New Orleans I have heard every living tongue and language spoke by the native (almost) in one day, seen almost every kind of fruit in market. As to religion, I think we have pleasing prospects, new Churches are constantly rising, and invitations pressing me daily to preach in every direction. I was yesterday at a meeting at a new Church 30 miles southwest from us on the Line of La. & Arks. & a more interesting meeting I never was at, & there was a Camp meeting near us last week, a very pleasant and encouraging meeting indeed.

The Indians are farther from us here than we every lived from them before (except a few) & the U. States Garrison between us on the Arks. River, & Texas between us and their Indians. We live 100 miles from the Line of Texas and 25 from La. State Line and 200 from the west line of Arks, and 75 miles from the Missippi [*sic*] River, 400 from the Gulf of Mexico.

If you and William were here, I should be well pleased in all respects. Oh, how I desire to see my dear Tabitha and embrace her sweet babes and hear dear Aunt who I love dearly. My dear son, comfort your aunt and raise your children in the nurture & admonition of the Lord & live the life of an humble Christian & be always looking for the call that may be sudden to render up your accounts to God of your Stewardship in this world. I know many obligations rest on you, may an omnipotent God enable you to discharge them all agreeable to His will.

Do not think we are out of the world, 20 days by land would bring a horseback traveler from your place here and it is a good road and good accommodations and no Indians [slight tear here] on the road, but well settled with civil settlers.

A Woman's Perspective on Antebellum Life

Mary Owen Sims Journal, Small Manuscripts Collection, Arkansas History Commission, Little Rock.

Another view of life in Arkansas is provided by Mary Owen Sims. Born in Tennessee in 1830, she married Dr. John D. Sims in 1845. They migrated to Dallas County, where Dr. Sims practiced medicine and attempted to farm. He died in 1855, leaving his twenty-five-year-old widow with children to raise and a small plantation to manage. Mary Sims's journal shows the difficulties facing a young woman alone on the American frontier.

May Saterday 14 1859

My time has been so multifariously imploid that I actually have not had time to write—I have hired out two of my negro men and discharged the oversee and keep one of the men at home and the women and children and farm it myself this year I live quite aloan no white soul on the place save me and the childrn they all grow very fast so I have to devote a good portion of my time to instructing them I feel very solitious for ther future but he aloan who judges in writiousness can tell—as for mysilf I feel, that the sunshine of my days had passed and oh how loanly I do feell, at times I feel as though I was cut off from all sympathy of my kind at least as fare as sympathy and congeniality of feeling is con-serned I feel perfectly isolated—those whom I most looked to for advice and protection have proved false and I am left aloan to strugle with a cold and selfish world oh no one save those who have felt it knows the feelings of a proud spirit bound down by povety—the Eagle taken from its lofty eya and chain to earth does not long to soar in the pure air again and

chafes at its confinement more than the Spiret whose aspiration are so
fare above those whom they are compelled to associate it has often been
a source of regret to me that my daughters were not sons a man can
change his station in life but a woman scarsely ever arrives at more exalted
station than the one she is born in if we acept those whose minds are
mascaline enough to cope with men—there are very few of our great
women who are not in some degree difisient in those feminine qualities
that makes woman lovable—but a woman whose mind is supirior and
whose feelings have been cast in a more equisit mould to be compell to
associate with *courser* minds who can not understand her is compill to
feel loanly ya almost writehed at times for the want of some kindred
nature to meet and mingle with her own but what am I compared to the
many millions who now live and breathe here whose wishes and expectations hopes haps and disapointments is as much to thim as mine are
to me—when I vew they wonderous works oh Lord my soul is lost in
wonder and I am dum with astonishment that what is man that thou
are mindful of him.

B. AGRICULTURE

As already indicated, agriculture was the principal source of wealth in
antebellum Arkansas. The great planters dominated the economic scene
with their production of cotton on the plantations in the southeastern
and southern sections of the state. Elsewhere, however, the countryside
was covered with small farms and farmers struggling to achieve self-
sufficiency by producing corn and raising livestock, looking toward the
day when they could put together enough land, and perhaps acquire sufficient labor, to grow their first cotton. The vast majority of Arkansans
were among these small farmers, some owning their lands, more leasing,
renting, farming on shares, or even "squatting" until the land's actual
owner might force them off. For all except the great planters, farm life
was a difficult struggle for survival.

A Plantation in Southern Arkansas

Dorothy Stanley, ed., *The Autobiography of Sir Henry Morton
Stanley* (New York: Houghton Mifflin Company, 1909), 148–50.

Unlike older southern states, Arkansas had few observers to chronicle life on its grander plantations. Perhaps the best is that of Henry
Morton Stanley, the English adventurer and explorer, who came to
Arkansas in 1860 hoping to establish a business. He came into the
state by riverboat, traveling first up the Ouachita River, then the
Saline River. He stayed for a time on the plantation of a Major
Ingham above Long View Landing in Ashley County. Because his
autobiography was written long after this visit, much may be
embellished to make his points, but Stanley's view of life on a large
Arkansas plantation remains one of the very few that we possess. It
is worth noting how, except for the presence of slaves, life for the
Inghams was not much different from that of Saint, a small farmer
in the next reading.

In September of 1860, we met a tall and spruce gentleman, of the
name of Major Ingham, on board of a steam bound to New Orleans.
From what I gathered, he was a South Carolinian by birth, but, some
few years since, had removed to Saline County, Arkansas, and had established a plantation not far from Warren. . . . Before reaching New
Orleans, we had become so intimate that he extended an invitation to
me to spend a month with him on his Arkansas plantation. . . .

Soon after, Major Ingham started on his return home in a stern-
wheeler bound for the Washita and Saline Rivers. The Washita, next to
the Arkansas, is the most important river which passes through the state
of Arkansas—pronounced "Arkansaw." The Saline is one of its feeders,
and has a navigable course of only about one hundred and twenty-five
miles. The Washita in its turn empties into the Red River, and the latter
into the Mississippi.

On, or about, the seventh day from New Orleans, the steamer
entered the Saline, and a few miles above Long View we landed on the
right bank, and, mounting into a well-worn buggy, were driven a few
miles inland to Ingham's plantation.

I am unaware of the real status of my host among his neighbours,
as I am of the size of his domain. It then appeared in my eyes immense,
but was mostly a pine forest, in the midst of which some few score of
black men had cleared a large space for planting. The house was of solid
pine logs, roughly squared, and but slightly stained by weather, and
neatly chinked without with plaster, and lined within with planed boards,
new and unpainted—it had an air of domestic comfort.

My welcome from Mrs. Ingham left nothing to be desired. The slaves of the house thronged in her train, and curtsied and bobbed, with every token of genuine gladness, to the "massa," as they called him, and then were good enough to include me in their bountiful joy. The supper which had been got ready was something of a banquet, for it was to celebrate the return of the planter, and was calculated to prove to him that, though New Orleans hotels might furnish more variety, home, after all, had its attractions in pure, clean, well-cooked viands. When the hearth-logs began to crackle, and the firelight danced joyfully on the family circle, I began to feel the influence of the charm, and was ready to view my stay in the western woods with interest and content.

But there was one person in the family that caused a doubt in my mind, and that was the overseer. He joined us after supper, and, almost immediately, I contracted a dislike for him. His vulgarity and coarseness revived recollections of levee men. His garb was offensive; the pantaloons stuffed into his boots, the big hat, the slouch of his carriage, his rough boisterousness, were all objectionable, and more than all his accents and the manner of his half-patronising familiarity I set him down at once as one of those men who haunt liquor saloons, and are proud to claim acquaintance with bar-tenders. Something in me, perhaps my offishness, may probably have struck him with equal repulsion. Under pretence of weariness I sought my bed, for the circle had lost its charm.

The next day the diet was not so sumptuous. The breakfast at seven, the dinner at noon, and the supper at six, consisted of pretty much the same kind of dishes, except that there was good coffee at the first meal, and plenty of good milk for the last. The rest mainly consisted of boiled, or fried, pork and beans, and corn scones. The pork had an excess of fat over the lean, and was followed by a plate full of mush and molasses. I was never very particular as to my diet, but as day after day followed, the want of variety caused it to pall on the palate. Provided other things had not tended to make me critical, I might have gratefully endured it, but what affected me principally were the encomiums lavished upon this style of cookery by the overseer, who, whether with the view of currying favour with Mrs. Ingham, or to exasperate my suppressed squeamishness, would bawl out, "I guess you can't beat this, howsumdever you crack up New Or-lee-ans. Give me a raal western pot-luck, to your darned fixin's in them 'ar Mississippi towns."

With such society and fare, I could not help feeling depressed, but the tall pine forest, with its mysterious lights and shades, had its compensations. As, in process of time, the planter intended to extend his clearing and raise more cotton, every tree felled assisted in widening the cultivable land. On learning this, I asked and obtained permission to cut down as many trees as I liked, and, like a ruthless youth with latent destructive propensities, I found an extraordinary pleasure in laying low with a keen axe the broad pines. I welcomed with a savage delight the apparent agony, the portentous shiver which ran from root to topmost plume, the thunderous fall, and the wild recoil of its neighbours, as it rebounded and quivered before it lay its still length. After about a score of the pine monarchs had been levelled, the negroes at work presented new features of interest. On the outskirts of the clearing they were chopping up timber into portable or rollable logs, some were "toting" logs to the blazing piles, others rolled them hand over hand to the fires, and each gang chanted heartily as it toiled. As they appeared to enjoy it, I became infected with their spirit and assisted at the log rolling, or lent a hand at the toting, and championed my side against the opposite. I waxed so enthusiastic over this manly work, which demanded the exertion of every ounce of muscle, that it is a marvel I did not suffer from the strain; its fierce joy was more to my taste than felling timber by myself. The atmosphere, laden with the scent of burning resin, the roaring fires, the dance of the lively flames, the excitement of the gangs while holding on, with grim resolve and in honour bound, to the bearing-spikes, had a real fascination to me. For a week, I rose with the darkies at the sound of the overseer's horn, greeted the revivifying sunrise with anticipating spirits, sat down to breakfast with a glow which made the Major and his wife cheerier, and then strode off to join in the war against the pines with a springy pace.

How long this toil would have retained its sportive aspect for me I know not, but I owed it to the overseer that I ceased to love it. He was a compound of a Legree and Nelson, with an admixture of mannerism peculiarly his own. It was his duty to oversee all the gangs, the hoers, woodcutters, fire-attendants, log-rollers, and toters. When he approached the gang with which I worked, the men became subdued, and stopped their innocent chaff and play. He had two favourite songs: one was about his "deah Lucindah," and the other about the "chill winds of December," which he hummed in a nasal tone when within speaking distance of men, while the cracks of his "black snake" whip kept time. But, as he sauntered away to other parts, I felt he was often restive at my presence, for it imposed a certain restraint on his nature. One day, however, he was in a worse humour than usual. His face was longer, and malice gleamed in his eyes. When he reached us we missed the usual tunes. He cried out his commands with a more imperious note. A young fellow named Jim was the first victim of his ire, and, as he was carrying a heavy log with myself and others, he could not answer him so politely as he expected. He flicked at his naked shoulders with his whip, and the lash, flying unexpectedly near me, caused us both to drop our spikes. Unassisted by us, the weight of the log was too great for the others, and it fell to the ground crushing the foot of one of them. Meantime, furious at the indignity, I had engaged him in a wordy contest: hot words, even threats, were exchanged, and had it not been for the cries of the wounded man who was held fast by the log, we should probably have fought. The end of it was, I retired from the field, burning with indignation, and disgusted with his abominable brutality.

I sought Major Ingham, whom I found reclining his length at an easychair on the verandah. Not hearing the righteous condemnation I had hoped he would express, and surprised at his want of feeling, I hotly protested against the cruelty of the overseer in attacking a man while all his strength was needed to preserve others from peril, and declaimed against him for using a whip in proximity to my ears, which made the Major smile compassionately at my inexperience in such matters. This was too much for my patience, and I then and there announced my intention to seek the hospitality of Mr. Waring, his neighbour, as I could not be any longer the guest of a man who received my complaint so unsympathetically. On hearing me say this, Mrs. Ingham came out of the house, and expressed so much concern at this sudden rupture of our relations that I regretted having been so hasty, and the Major tried to explain how planters were compelled to leave fieldwork in charge of their overseer; but it was too late. Words had been uttered which left a blister in the mind, personal dignity had been grossly wounded, the Major had not the art of salving sores of this kind, and I doggedly clung to my first intentions. In another quarter of an hour I left the plantation with a small bundle of letters and papers, and was trudging through the woods to Mr. Waring's plantation.

A German Traveler Visits a Small Arkansas Farm

Frederick Gerstaecker, *Wild Sport in the Far West: Translated from the German* (London: G. Routledge & Co., 1854), 134, 136–37, 153–54, 155–56, 164–66, 170.

In 1837, Frederick Gerstaecker left his native Germany for the United States. He hoped to settle in Arkansas, joining with other German settlers and working to bring the territory into the Union as a German-speaking state. By the time he arrived, he found Arkansas already admitted to the Union. From January 1838 until July 1842 he traveled through the state. In 1842, he returned to Germany, where he began to publish books on his journeys. They concern his experiences with a small farmer named Saint, and we can see the lifestyle of the individual producing farm goods only at the subsistence level.

On the evening of the 6th day of May [1838], after a rich feast on the quantities of blackberries which grew by the way, we came to a house belonging to a man of the name of Saint, and decided on staying there to sleep; we found a better set of people than we had expected, and engaged in a long conversation with our host. After supper, to our no small horror we learnt that unless we could swim twenty-eight miles, further progress was not to be thought of, as the whole swamp between this and White river was under water. Uhl and I looked at each other, with long faces, as much as to say, "quid faciamus nos"; but Saint was good enough to invite us to stay with him till the swamp had somewhat dried up, which at latest would be about the middle of July; meantime we could go out shooting, and the game we brought home would well repay him for all our expenses. . . .

Our hosts to all appearances were very religious people, and we had prayers every evening. This evening we went early to bed, being all very tired, so that, as yet, I hardly had time to take much notice of the people we were to live with. We had to be awakened for breakfast; afterwards we strolled about the house and fields to realize our situation. Saint was a man of about forty, with a bright clear eye, and open brow; you were captivated by him at the very first sight. His wife, an Irish-woman, treated us very civilly and kindly, and proved to be an excellent manager. They had no children; but there was another person in the house, who demands a particular description. This was a duodecimo Irish shoemaker, or, as he always insisted—schoolmaster, for such, by his own account, was his former occupation, though now he made shoes. Saint had bought a quantity of leather, and the little Irishman was to work it up, receiving a certain monthly sum. He had red hair, was pockmarked, stood about five feet, but was stout and strongly built, and may have been about fifty years old. . . .

The house was built of logs, roughly cut. It consisted of two ordinary houses, under one roof, with a passage between them open to north and south, a nice cool place to eat or sleep in during summer. Like all block-houses of this sort, it was roofed with rough four-feet planks; there were no windows, but in each house a good fireplace of clay. A field of about five acres was in front of the house, planted with Indian corn, excepting a small portion which was planted with wheat. South-west from the house stood the stable which S. was obliged to build, because he gave 'good accommodation to man and horse,' otherwise it is not much the custom in Arkansas to trouble one's self about stables. A place, called a 'lot,' with a high fence, is used for the horses, hollowed trees serving for mangers. Near at hand was a smaller log-house for the store of Indian corn, and a couple of hundred paces further was a mill which S. had built to grind such corn as he wanted for his own use, and which was worked by one horse.

About a quarter of a mile from the house, through the wood, there was another field of about five acres, also sown with maize. The river L'Anguille flowed close in the rear of the house; another small building at the back of the dwelling was used as a smoking house; near it was a well about thirty-two feet deep. . . .

. . . Hitherto we had always eaten maize bread, because, although S. could grind wheat, he had no means of bolting it; and as it was stacked in the field, he decided on sending it to a mill about fifteen miles distant. The wheat was in sheaves, but there was neither barn nor thrashing floor, neither flail, nor winnowing machine, nothing to clean it from the straw; however, we set to work Arkansas fashion. The weather was bright and dry, the road before the door as hard as a stone, but dusty: a space about thirty feet in diameter was fenced in, and swept as clean as possible; the sheaves were unbound and laid in a circle, every two sheaves with their ears together, one with the straw to the center, the other with the straw outwards; six horses were mounted, and ridden round and round, while two men kept shaking down fresh corn; when it had been well trodden out, it had to be sifted.

I had probably worked rather too hard, caught another attack of ague, and was obliged to lie down till evening. . . .

On August 3rd, I felt better, and decided in the afternoon on driving to the mill: but the grain had first to be cleaned. This, without a machine, was rather a difficult matter, but the sharp Americans know how to manage it. Two of the stoutest fellows hold a blanket by the four corners; a third stands on a chair with a sieve full of grain, which he shakes, not too fast, nor too long at a time, while the two with the blanket make as much wind as they can, by working it up and down; the chaff is blown away, while the wheat falls to the ground, and is at once gathered into the sack, though not quite so clean as it would be with our system.

By two o'clock we were able to start, the cart being drawn by oxen, and, owing to their slow discreet pace, it was pitch dark when we arrived at the mill. At so late an hour grinding was out of the question; we lighted our fire, broiled our supper, and laid down in the wagon to sleep till daylight. But the night was so beautiful, the stars shining so mildly down upon us, the wind blowing so soft and warm through the green branches, that we could not sleep, but went on talking. Both my companions were Americans, one of them a strict Methodist, and there was nothing more natural than that we should talk of the stars, then of Heaven, then of religion; and as we entertained very different views, our conversation degenerated into a hot dispute which was put an end to about midnight by a heavy shower of rain, that forced us to seek shelter for ourselves and our sacks. Next day we began to grind, and slow work it was, for we had to turn the mill with our own oxen, who had no idea of inconveniencing themselves; however, we managed to reach home the same night. The season was now far enough advanced for the leaves of Indian corn to be stripped and laid up as fodder for the winter. This plant, in the southern States, will grow to a height of eleven or twelve feet, and often bears three cobs: the white sort is the best for bread, the yellow, containing more sugar, is best for fodder and for whiskey. . . .

On the 9th, Saint commenced his Indian corn harvest, which lasted till the 11th, and I gave my assistance. The cobs were simply broken away from the stems, and cast into a cart which carried them to the building prepared to receive them. When this work was done, we began another—namely, to clear about half an acre more land, and sow it with turnips.

The western settlers, and particularly those in the southwestern states, are not very fond of hard work; in those wild regions they prefer rearing cattle and shooting, to agriculture, and loth to undertake the hard work of felling trees and clearing land. To make the labour as light as possible, yet still to increase their fields, they generally clear a small space every autumn, and ploughing it very slightly, sow it with turnips, which answer best for the new ground. Next year it is fenced in and added to the field.

When about to make a clearing, the American looks out for the largest and straightest oaks, which he fells and splits into poles, about ten to twelve feet long, for fencing. When he thinks he has enough for this purpose, the rest is cut up and piled; next, the trees which have a diameter of eighteen inches and under are felled, about half a yard from the ground, and cut into lengths, while the larger trees are girdled all round with the axe and very soon die. The shrubs and bushes are then rooted up with a heavy hoe, and, with the help of the neighbours who are invited for the purpose, the whole, except for the poles for the fence, is rolled into a heap and set on fire.

As soon as the land is cleared of all that can be easily removed it is fenced in, and ploughed. This last work is very severe, and gives the ploughman and cattle many a rough shake, as the ploughshare, catching in the roots, has constantly to be lifted out of the ground, or to be moved out of the way of the standing stumps. These stumps give the fields a very extraordinary appearance; it takes from six to ten years before they rot away entirely. It sometimes happens that the trees killed by girdling are blown down amongst the growing crops, and the settler has a great deal of trouble in removing them.

The land about Saint's farm, when not inundated, was very fertile, and required little labour. It produced splendid oaks, black and white hickory, and sassafras. . . .

On the evening of the 18th October, S. came back from Strong's, where he had bought a couple of negro children, and brought them home on a led horse. One was a boy of about fifteen years old, as black as pitch, and with a regular Ethiopian cast of countenance; as he crossed the threshold, he examined every one present, with a rapid glance of his large dark eyes, and then looked unconcernedly at all the furniture, &c., as if all that was of no consequence to him. The other was a little girl of about eleven, who seemed already to have gone through some hard work. When she saw so many strange faces, a tear glittered in her eyes: she had been sold away from her parents, whom she would probably never more behold, and stood an image of suppressed grief. The boy was from Maryland, had been taken by sea to New Orleans, and from thence brought here. He had been told that he had fallen to a kind master, and his countenance seemed to say that was enough, happen what might.

The View of Arkansas from the Bottom

Montgomery Family Papers, Arkansas History Commission, Little Rock.

For Arkansans at even the lowest level of society, their state appeared to be a land of great opportunity during the antebellum period. When Hugh Montgomery moved to Conway County from his native Georgia, he brought with him only a couple of head of cattle. This letter home chronicles his hopes, as well as the uncertainty of a young man with few resources on the frontier.

State of Arkansas   Conway Co.   Nov 29th 1857

Dear Father and Mother

We now take the opportunity of letting you know our whereabouts. We have stopt in Springfield, Conway Co. and has bought a house and three lots and give two hundred and seventy five dollars. We are all well and has stood the trip very well Dock and Quince has stopt about ten miles from heare Quince has boght land has bought one hundred and sixty acres and give his wagon and Steers Buck he died with the murine. Mel and Robert is agoing to work in the Shop blacksmithing is very high here horse Shoing is one dollar and fifty cts and other things in proportion and there is no doubt but what we can get more work than we can do. I think if we keep our health we will make money fast Thare is plenty of cheap land heare up land is worth from 12½ cts to one dollar per acre anyone can do better to look a round a while I am not able to tell you all whether you could better your selves or not but I will tell you more

---

about it after a while tell Jep not to give Arkansas tar o bad a name he might want to come back agane.

What we are is the heltiest looking place I have seen in Arkansas the people looks helthy here Tell Abb thaare the out shootings people here for a pool I ever seen I am about to sell my gun for twenty five dollars I got a dollar aday for house carpentering last week and I think we will get our Shop in blast next week Robert says to tell Bob Wood to come on to burn coal Coal is worth from five to ten cts per bushel Corn is worth from 35 to 40 cts per bushel pork 5 cts per lb

Dec 1th 1857 I will take a new starte I sold Charley yesterday for 20 dollars a bad loss Abb I killed a turkey yesterday lots of game heare but not time to hunt teel Keeler I wont to heare him laff and I would like to see the Conection and friends if Jim is started I wont you to write to me as soon as you heare whare he is write as soon as this comes to hand write how Sick is and whare you are all Sitled and every thing else give my best respects to the Conection and inquiring friends and if you find anything you cant reed let it rip So nothing at more at present but remains your sones and daughter un till deth.

H. P. Montgomery

C. SLAVERY IN ARKANSAS

Slavery was a legal institution that allowed whites to control the labor of black people and that defined the lifestyle of over one-fifth of the state's population. The almost absolute control over blacks given to masters did not, however, define the conditions under which slaves lived. Some masters dealt with their slaves with a degree of human compassion; others were not reluctant to beat and mutilate their property for no reason whatsoever. The only safe generalization to state is that slavery represented almost total limitation of a slave's freedom of choice. In earlier documents, white views of slaves have been apparent. Here we shall see the legal framework of slavery and the institution from a slave's perspective.

The Arkansas Slave Code

Revised Statutes of the State of Arkansas (1838), 730, 733, 736.

When admitted to the Union in 1836, Arkansas entered as a slave
state with a constitution giving sanction to slavery. It was not until
1837, however, that the state's first legislature passed a comprehensive slave code to regulate slaves, slavery, and free blacks. The slave
code incorporated regulations from the territorial period with those
taken from the codes of other southern states into a single set of
laws. This code provided the framework within which slavery
existed. While not the entire code, the following selections provide
something of the flavor of the Arkansas slave laws.

Sec. 1. No person shall knowingly bring or cause to be brought into
this State, or hold, purchase, hire, sell, or otherwise dispose of within the
same; first, any slave who may have committed in any other State,
Territory or district within the United States, or in any foreign country,
any offence, which if committed within this State, would according to
the laws thereof, be a felony or infamous crime; or second, any slave who
shall have been convicted in this State, of any felony or infamous crime,
and ordered to be taken or removed out of the State, according to the
laws thereof; or, third, any slave who shall have actually been removed
out of this State after a conviction of felony or other infamous crime,
although no order of removal shall have been made; or, fourth, any person or the descendant of any person who shall have been imported into
the United States, or any of the Territories thereof, in contravention of
the laws of the United States, and held as a slave.

• • •

Sec. 15. If any slave shall sell, barter or deliver, to any other slave any
vinous or spiritous liquors, he shall be punished by stripes not exceeding
twenty-five, and shall stand committed until he be discharged in the
manner hereinafter directed.

Sec. 16. Every slave charged with the commission of the offence specified in the preceding section, shall be tried and proceeded against in the
circuit court by indictment.

Sec. 17. Upon the conviction of any such slave, he shall after the execution of the sentence be committed to jail, unless his master will pay

the costs and enter into a recognizance in any sum not less than one hundred dollars, conditioned for the good behavior of such slave for one year, and that during that time he will not violate the provisions of the fifteenth section of this act.

Sec. 18. When a slave shall be committed for the act of such recognizance, he may be discharged by the circuit court or the presiding judge of the county court, on the application of the master or owner, and his entering into recognizance as specified in the preceding section, and paying all the costs and expenses.

Sec. 19. If the master or owner of such slave do not appear and comply with the terms specified in the preceding section, on or before the second day of the circuit court next to be held after the commitment, such slave shall be sold, and the proceeds of such sale applied as specified in the thirteenth section of this act.

Sec. 20. Every slave who shall harbor or conceal any slave, who shall have absented or deserted the service of his master, overseer or employer, shall be punished by stripes not exceeding twenty-five, by the order of any justice of the peace.

Sec. 21. If any slave shall go from the premises or tenements of his master or other person with whom he resides, without a pass, or some letter or token, whereby it may appear that he is proceeding by the authority of his master, employer or overseer, he may be apprehended by any person, and being taken before a justice of the peace, shall by order of such justice, be punished with stripes not exceeding twenty-five.

Sec. 22. If any slave shall come and be upon the plantation of any person without permission in writing from his owner, employer or overseer, not being sent upon lawful business, the owner or occupier of such plantation may cause such slave to be punished with stripes not exceeding twenty-five for every such offence.

Sec. 23. Any gun or other offensive or defensive weapon found in the possession of a slave, without having the written permission of his master to carry the same, may be seized by any person, and upon proof of such seizure before a justice of the peace of the county where the same shall have been made, such gun or weapon shall be by the order of such justice, adjudged and forfeited to the seizor for his own use, and such slave shall receive by the order of such justice, any number of stripes not exceeding thirty.

Sec. 24. All riots, routs, unlawful assemblies and seditious speeches of slaves shall be punished with stripes by the order of any justice of the peace, and it shall be lawful for any person without further warrant to apprehend slaves so offending, and take them before some justice of the peace.

Sec. 25. If any master or overseer of a family shall knowingly permit or suffer any slave not belonging to him or under his control, to be and remain on his premises more than four hours at any one time without the consent or permission of the owner, employer, or overseer of such slave, such master or overseer so permitting, shall forfeit and pay to the owner, employer or overseer of such slave, five dollars for every such offence, to be recovered before a justice of the peace, by an action of debt on this statute.

Sec. 26. If any owner or overseer of a plantation shall permit or suffer more than five slaves other than his own to be and remain on his plantation, or in any house attached thereto, at any one time with or without the consent of the master or overseer of such slaves, he shall forfeit and pay to the informer one dollar for every slave that number, to be recovered by an action of debt, unless such slaves may have met together on Sunday at public worship, or on any other day for the purpose of laboring or on some other lawful occasion.

Sec. 27. If any white person, or free negro or mulatto, shall be found in the company of slaves, at any unlawful meeting, or shall harbor or entertain any slave, or shall be found drinking or gaming with any slaves, without the consent of the owner or overseer of such slave, such white person, free negro, or mulatto shall forfeit and pay a sum not exceeding one hundred dollars, and shall receive any number of stripes not exceeding thirty.

Sec. 28. Every justice of the peace, upon his own knowledge of any unlawful meeting of slaves, white men, free negroes and mulattoes, or on information whereof, shall forthwith issue his warrant to apprehend such slaves, white men, free negroes or mulattoes, and cause them to be brought before himself or some other justice of the peace, to be dealt with according to law.

Sec. 29. Sheriffs, coroners and constables, upon a knowledge or on information of any unlawful meeting of slaves, white men, free negroes or mulattoes, or of any riot, rout, or unlawful assembly of slaves, shall suppress the same, and without warrant take the offenders before some justice of the peace of the county, to be dealt with according to law.

Sec. 30. Any sheriff, coroner or constable, who upon knowledge or information, as prescribed in the preceding section, shall neglect or refuse to comply with the requisitions of the foregoing section, shall for every such offence forfeit to the informer ten dollars to be recovered by action of debt.

Sec. 31. Any slave who shall by noise, riotous or disorderly conduct or otherwise, disturb any religious congregation assembled for the purpose of public worship, may be apprehended by any person, and forthwith taken before some justice of the peace of the county, who shall examine into the truth of the charges, and on being satisfied of the truth thereof, shall cause such slave to be punished with any number of stripes not exceeding thirty.

Sec. 32. Any master, commander or owner of any steamboat, or any other vessel, who shall transport or carry any servant or slave out of this State in such steamboat or vessel, without the consent of the person to whom such servant or slave doth of right belong, or who has authority to grant such permission, shall forfeit and pay to the owner of such slave the sum of five hundred dollars, to be recovered by action of debt on this statute, without prejudice to the right of such owner to recover the value of such slave in an action therefor.

Sec. 33. If any person shall buy, sell, or receive of, to, or from a slave any commodity whatever, without the consent of the master, owner or overseer of such slave, first had and obtained, or shall deal with any slave without such consent, such person shall forfeit to the master or overseer of such slave, any sum not less than ten dollars for every such offence, and also the sum of twenty dollars to the county.

Sec. 34. Any person migrating beyond the bounds of this State, who shall have in his possession any slave or other personal property, the absolute title of which is not in such person, may be restrained from removing such slave or other property out of the State, by a writ of injunction.

Sec. 35. The term "master" as used in this act shall be construed to include every person who at the time, shall have the possession and control of a slave, whether he be owner or bailee, or have the general or special property in his own right or in right of another. [Approved February 24, 1838.]

Narrative of a Former Slave

Samuel S. Taylor, interview of Columbus Williams, Ouachita
Co., Ark., in *Slave Narratives* (St. Claire Shores, MI: Scholarly
Press, 1976), vol. 20, pt. 7:154–58.

Columbus Williams was a former slave. In 1937, at the age of
ninety-six, he was interviewed as part of a federal project to capture
the stories of the remaining blacks who had lived during the time
of slavery. Williams was one of the few interviewed who had spent
any of his adult life as a slave; he had been almost twenty-three years
old when he gained his freedom. This makes his narrative particularly valuable for the view it presents of slavery from the slave's perspective. Williams had a particularly harsh master, and his story
shows the reader how bad the slave system could be.

I was born in Union County, Arkansas, in 1841, in Mount Holly.

My mother was named Clara Tookes. My father's name is Jordan
Tookes. Bishop Tookes is supposed to be a distant relative of ours. I don't
know my mother and father's folks. My mother and father were both born
in Georgia. They had eight children, all of them are dead now but me. I
am the only one left.

Old Ben Heard was my master. He came from Mississippi and
brought my mother and father with him. They were in Mississippi as well
as in Georgia, but they were born in Georgia. Ben Heard was a right mean
man. They was all mean 'long about then. Heard whipped his slaves alot.
Some times he would say they wouldn't obey. Some times he would say
they sassed him. Some times he would say they wouldn't work. He would
tie them and stake them out and whip them with a leather whip of some
kind. He would put five hundred licks on them before he would quit. He
would buy the whip he whipped them with out of the store. After he
whipped them, they would put their rags on and go on about their
business. There wouldn't be no such thing as medical attention. What did
he care. He would whip the women the same as he would the men.

Strip 'em to their waist and let their rags hang down from their hips
and tie them down and lash them till the blood ran all down over their
clothers. Yes sir, he'd whip the women the same as he would the men.

Some of the slaves ran away, but they would catch them and bring
them back, you know. Put the dogs after them. The dogs would just run

them up and bay them just like a coon or 'possum. Sometimes the white people would make the dogs bite them. . . .

We didn't have no church no nothing. No Sunday-schools, no nothin'. Worked from Monday morning till Saturday night. On Sunday we didn't do nothin' but set right down there on that big plantation. Couldn't go nowhere. Wouldn't let us go nowhere without a pass. They had the patrollers out all the time. If they caught you without a pass, they would give you twenty-five licks. If you out run them and got home, on your master's plantation, you saved yourself the whipping.

The black people never had no amusement. They would have an old fiddle—something like that. That was all the music I ever seen. Sometimes they would ring up and play 'round the yard. I don't remember the games. Some kind of old reel song. I don't hardly remember the words of any of them songs.

Wouldn't allow none of them to have no books nor read nor nothin'. Nothin' like that. They had corn huskin's in Mississippi and Georgia, but not in Arkansas. Didn't have no quiltin's. Women might quilt some at night. Didn't have nothing to make no quilts out of.

The very first work I did was to nurse babies. After that when I got a little bigger they carried me to the field—choppin' cotton. Then I went to picking cotton. Next thing—pullin' fodder. Then they took me from that and put me to plowin', clearin' land, splittin' rails. I believe that is about all I did. You worked from the time you could see till the time you couldn't see. You worked from before sunrise till after dark. When that horn blows, you better git out of the house, 'cause the overseer is comin' down the line, and he ain't coming with nothin' in his hands.

They weighed the rations out to the slaves. They would give you so many pounds of meat for each working person in the family. The children didn't count, they didn't git none. That would have to last till next Sunday. They would give them three pounds of meat to each workin' person, I think. They would give 'em a little meal too. That is all they'd give 'em. The slaves had to cook for theirselves after they came home from the field. They didn't get no flour nor no sugar nor no coffee, nothin' like that.

They would give the babies a little milk and corn bread or a little molasses and bread when they didn't have the milk. Some old person who didn't have to go to the field would given them somethin' to eat so that they would be out of the way when the folks came out of the field.

The slaves lived in old log houses—one room, one door, one window, one everything. There were plenty windows though. There were windows all round the house. They had cracks that let in more air than the windows could. They had plank floors. Didn't have no furniture. The bed would have two legs and would have a hole bored in the side of the house where the side rail would run through the two legs would be out of the wall. Didn't have no springs and they made out with anything they could get for a mattress.

Marriage wasn't like now. You could court a woman and jus' go on and marry. No license, no nothing. Sometimes you would take up with a woman and go on with her. Didn't have no ceremony at all. I have heard of them stepping over a broom but I never saw it. Far as I saw there was no ceremony at all. . . .

I never went to school. One of the white boys slipped and learned me a little about readin' in slave times. Right after freedom, I was a grown man; so I had to work.

D. POLITICS

Politics in antebellum Arkansas was a vital element of daily life among the adult white male population that possessed the vote. Candidates and issues were common topics of conversation on court days, at church, and even at social gatherings. The state had a two-party system, but it was one in which Democrats greatly outnumbered their opponents. Nonetheless, in the prewar years the Whig Party and then the American Party remained to challenge the dominant Democrats.

Political life existed on several different levels, as the following documents will show. For the common man, elections were social events, with candidates trying to manipulate the voters with rhetoric, propaganda, promises, and alcohol. A frontier state generally sympathized with the symbols and manipulation of the Democrats. For politicians and the economic leaders of Arkansas, however, much more was at stake than control of elected offices—the great number of appointed positions within the control of public officials made elections even more important. Skillful use of political appointments, for example, had allowed one small group, "The Family," to control the Democratic Party from territorial days. For economic leaders, politics was the means for securing help for roads, river clearance, railroads, and even capital. The national context within which local struggles took place, however, was an overwhelming identification with the South—one established at the very beginning.

Whigs and Democrats

Arkansas Gazette (Little Rock), May 13, 1840.

In 1840 the Whig Party ran Gen. William Henry Harrison for president against Martin Van Buren, the incumbent. This document is a Democrat's view of a meeting held in Little Rock on May 13, 1840. He presents a hostile view of the proceedings, but his picture does provide excellent insight into how parties manipulated the common voter during this period and how little campaigns had to do with more serious issues.

ATTENTION WHIGS!
PULASKI COUNTY

The Whigs of Pulaski County are invited to attend a Major Peay's lot on the corner of Cherry and Scott Streets, on Wednesday morning the 13th (rain or shine), at 9 o'clock, to assist in erecting a log cabin and liberty pole, and it is hoped that every true Whig will be present, the pitiful censures of a few Democrats to the contrary notwithstanding.

TIPPECANOE CLUB.

• • •

MR. EDITOR—These are such exciting times, so big with interest to every portion of the community, that when a leisure moment offers itself, I am bound to embrace it, and apply it to the best possible purpose. I said that the times were big with interest to every part of the community. For instance, the conflagration in Little Rock, the threatened overflow of the Arkansas, and the raising of the pine pole and log cabin, are pregnant with interest to the farmer, the mechanic, and the politician. Nothing is necessary to be said of the two former, but I propose saying a few words about the latter.

After publication being made in the Whig papers at this place, and posting up handbills with the cut of a log cabin on which the names of the

Harrison candidates were emblazoned, and after them, of course, (it being mannerly), the names of the two belligerents of this place, the "Times" and "Star," the whole being baited with the enticing cut of a barrel of cider, calling on every [true Whig] in Pulaski county to attend on Wednesday, the 13th of May, and assist in the rearing of a pine pole and log cabin in honor of the immortal Harrison. I say after all this was done, the "true Whigs" assembled on that day, and proceeded to the accomplishment of that, to them important business. I would say, before going further, that if every "true Whig" in Pulaski attended that raising, which was in all probability the case, we have nothing to fear from the "true Whigs" of Pulaski at the next election. There was at no time a very great collection, say not over a hundred persons, and of that number a considerable portion were Democrats, who came as lookers-on.—The first thing was to raise the pole; proclamation was made that when it was raised, the barrel of cider would be tapped. Upon which information, the pole was walked into, and it began slowly and feebly to raise its head. After raising by degrees for a short time, it commenced going slower and slower until at length it caught on the dead centre, and looked like a race horse that had started round the track and had the misfortune to let down on the back stretch. Now was the time for exertion. All the hands had hold, and by the help of the "old tars" who gave the word, they at length succeeded in standing their pole erect. The flag was now raised, after which, they waved their hats, and gave a faint huzza. The order of the day was now hard cider, and I assure you that the enthusiasm which appeared at the raising of the pole to be a negative was now changed to a positive quantity, so close was the barrel hemmed in, and so eager was each to drink before the other. In the crowd you might see the mechanic and laborer mingling with the lawyer and merchant, all aiming at one thing, all aspiring to one place, and that was who should get the first pull at the cider. The Doctors, however, kept a respectful distance, no doubt anticipating a call to attend on several patients the next day, who, from the too free use of hard cider, would doubtless have an attack of the cholera morbus. So the matter proceeded until the log cabin was finished. As near as I can count, it took three barrels of cider to raise the cabin, which I think will be sufficient proof that they are greater enthusiasts at drinking cider than raising cabins, for a dozen men could take a gallon of good Democratic whiskey, which would be a plentiful supply, and raise a better house in less time. The cider barrel commanded a majority of the crowd for the greater part of the day in such a manner as to monopolize their whole attention. 'Tis true you could occasionally see a fellow who had his eyes wide enough open to recognize a Democratic acquaintance sitting in the shade, looking on and laughing at their humbuggery. And all they had to say was that the Democrats had no right to be there.

If there ever was a party who stood in need of more hobbies on which to ride their candidate into office, or a party whose genius was more prolific in inventing hobbies of all sorts, than the Whig party, they have never come under my observation.

The Whigs have said that Gen. Harrison lives in a log cabin; but any person who will take the trouble to examine, will find that he lives in a house which consists of nine large rooms, and out buildings in proportion.

They have said he drinks hard cider; but I have been informed by a gentleman who is well acquainted with him that no man is a better judge of wine or a dearer lover of old brandy than this same Gen. Harrison. Indeed, if any of his miscarriages in the last war are attributed, by those who had the best opportunity of knowing, to an unfortunate habit that he had of turning up his little finger.

They have said that his long service of his country and his poverty justly compare him to Aristides [an Athenian general noted for his honesty], when, by fact, he has a farm worth $100,000, and a salary of $6,000 per annum. Heaven preserve us from such an Aristides.

They have said that if he is elected, he will faithfully discharge the duties of his office without respect to persons; when the last accounts from the North Bend (per Cincinnati paper), confirm the report that he has consigned himself, soul and body, to three conscience keepers, and that he does not even dare to say boo! to a goose without their permission.

They have said that they will elect him President at the ensuing election, and by way of facilitating that object, they have done a day's work raising a big cabin and pine pole; but we will do a day's work on the day of the election, which will throw them and their day's work in the shade; and the dreary little log cabin and the towering pine pole, without bark or foliage, which fain would have reached from earth to heaven, will be a fitting and only memento to his fame—the only land mark by which it can be ascertained, that the name of Harrison was ever heard in Arkansas.

CYRUS.

John Brown's Views on the 1856 Elections

John Brown Diary, Arkansas History Commission, Little Rock.

John Brown was a prominent merchant from Camden and a strong supporter of the Whig Party before its collapse. In 1856, he backed the American Party; in the August general election, his candidates went to defeat. His diary notes the election disaster but also presents a view of how a minor politician saw politics—the kinds of things he thought were at stake.

July 29, 1856. As usual the approaching election begins to excite much interest. A meeting was called tonight to form a Fillmore Club. I was called to the chair after some remarks by myself and others. Meeting adjourned to meet next Tuesday night. Some hopes are now entertained of defeating the Democrats and saving the country.

August 4, 1856. Election day. . . . A good deal of interest and excitement but all peaceable and I think it worthy of notice how that although an intense interest is manifested by persons and parties, and great exertions made, the election passed without any outrage or violence, comparatively quiet. I voted the American ticket, and when there was no Am. candidate for an office I did not vote at all.

August 5. This day mainly engrossed with the subject of the election, news &c. The Aritis as usual have carried the country by about an average majority of one hundred, although the City went for the Americans.— and here is a bad omen for the maintenance of our Institutions. Col. Fowler a firm consistent conservative Union loving man, candidate for Congress, was beaten largely over the district by Col. Warner who has neither patriotism nor talents to do anything as a Statesman—a mere party Hack and blustering pothouse politician.

August 9. Disappointed in the slight hope I had that the elections might go somewhat favorable to an improvement in our public affairs by the sobering cry of Democrat that seems to be sweeping everything before & I see but little hope for the country. I have declined buying any more property till I see some further developments. I am satisfied that if some providential change does not take place, our Union cannot stand five years longer—and whenever the Union is dissolved, there is an end to all safety in the right of property or security for its peaceful possession.

Offices for the Family, 1836

Clarence Carter, ed., *Territorial Papers of the United States*, 27 vols. (Washington, DC: G.P.O., 1954), 21:1207–8.

This letter from Ambrose Sevier, head of the Democratic Party in Arkansas, to President Andrew Jackson shows the behind-the-scenes manipulations that went into the appointment of federal officeholders in the state. Sevier did not consider the qualifications of a new surveyor general, but rather the factor that might influence local politics and keep his faction in power.

WASHINGTON CITY [April] 4th 1836

DEAR GENL. You remember that some months ago I stated to you that Col Conway was a candidate for the office of Governor in Arkansas, and that after the expiration of his present term [as surveyor general], which expires either in June or July next, he did not desire the office— At the same time, I informed you, (and these letters were also of that purport,) that Conway—Fulton, Yell and Judge Johnson, desired that you would appoint Col Wharton Rector as his successor. At the time that these recommendations were made, it was not known that Judge Cross, who is at this time one of our United States judges for Arkansas,— would desire the office—He is a man well qualified for the office, and if he has a single enemy in Arkansas, I dont know him—

I feel under great obligation, to you, for your readiness ever to conform to the wishes of your friends in Arkansas in their efforts to advance the public good—I have conversed fully with Cross upon Arkansas affairs—and he likes Rector and would not hold the office an hour after he returns to Arkansas, if the arrangements about that office is not satisfactory to all of our friends—The reason why I think it best to appoint Cross, in preference to Rector is this—

Col Rector at this time is agent for the Creek Indians—His brother Elias Rector, is now Marshal and will expect a reappointment under our state, as soon as it is admitted—James Conway, who is not the incumbent, is Rector's cousin, and is the democratic candidate for governor— Conway is my relation also—I am thus particular, in order to show you that if Rector is appointed in the place of Conway to the exclusion of Cross, who wants it, the people of Arkansas will consider that there is too much monopoly in the offices of Arkansas by my relatives and intimate friends—And this impression may injure the cause in Arkansas, and on that account, I desire the appointment of Cross—

The only relative I desire office for is for Judge Johnson; Let him be made federal Judge. Elias Rector Marshal—Cross surveyor General, and either Randolph—Childress or Ringo district attorney, and Biscoe register of the land office at Helena, the same I spoke to you about on Friday last, and I pledge myself for a fortunate issue to the administration in the coming contests in Arkansas—

I am authorized by Cross to state, that if Rector himself, or any of our friends are displeased at the arrangement that he will resign the office—I think I can reconcile all our friends to this arrangement without difficulty—

Your friend
A. H. SEVIER

Railroads and the General Assembly

Jesse Turner Papers, Special Collections, Duke University Library, Durham, NC.

While Ambrose Sevier saw politics as a way to office, Jesse Turner and his friends worked political machinery to economic advantage. The following document is a letter from J. H. Haney, secretary of the Little Rock and Fort Smith Railroad Company, to its president, Jesse Turner, a prominent businessman and politician from Van Buren County. The letter shows business and sectional antagonisms and focuses on manipulation of the legislature in an effort to secure state support for internal improvement schemes. Much as today, Haney lobbied to build a coalition favorable to his enterprise.

Little Rock Dec. 13 1860
Jesse Turner Esq.

Dr. Friend

You are perhaps desirous to know what Col. Hays & myself have been doing since our arrival & also what the prospects of success are. The Col. has been in his bed since last Monday evening suffering from a violent attack of winter fever or pneumonia but he is now rapidly convalescing & if he receives no backset will be out in a day or two—so the Doctor says.

He devoted himself the few days he was well to operating upon members of the Senate & seems confident as well as Miller that that body is safe for the measures we desire to carry—Miller seems very zealous in the cause & also Brown & Morton. You will have observed that a Bill granting the 5 per cent fund (some $180,000) to several of the Companies in the State—including the proposed Border R.R. & also the Iron Mountain & Helena R.R. was defeated by a majority of 5 in the House—Duval, Humphreys & Cravens voting *no*. It would have given to our Co. $40,000. It was ridiculed as a "scatteration" Bill and perhaps thus defeated. Clark of Sebastian has a Bill proposing to give R.R. Cos. $5,000 per mile to be devoted strictly to the purchase of iron whenever the Cos have prepared 5 miles of road & deposited for cancellation in the Auditors office $5,000 in the bonds of the State or Real Estate Bank. This is all nonsense as its effect will be to enhance the market value of said bonds nearly to par & thus be only a benefit to speculators in such bonds. Such a Bill would not assist us in the least—so I think. Miller has another Bill appropriating the Swamp Land in the Clarksville District & investing it as stock at the minimum prices now established by law. This is good as far as it goes. But it is not enough.

As to the House of Representatives they passed an Act on Tuesday investing the Swamp Lands in the Champanole District as Stock in the M.O.& R.R. R.R. Co. [Mississippi, Ouachita, and Red River Railroad] our members voting for it having received the pledge of the friends of the measure to vote for a similar Bill for our road. The vote I believe was 44 ayes to 21 noes, Duval Humphrey & Cravens voting *no*. We today had a bill introduced & referred to Com. on Internal Improvements appropriating & investing the Swamp Lands in the Clarksville District & also the money belonging to said District as Stock in our Road. Van Patten of Poinsett chairman of the Committee is our warm friend & will be an able advocate. Cravens' opposition was mollified by the incorporation of a provision that the Co. should sell said lands at the minimum prices now established by law—50 to 75 cts per acre. He seems to be not a little under the influence of Duval with whom he rooms. Hays threatens him with annihilation at home. Louden of Sebastian is understood to be with us as also all of the members from Washington Benton Pope

Johnson Conway Pulaski &c. The northwestern members will perhaps require our Co. to make the survey of the Border R.R. as it has so been limited to Brown & if necessary I shall not hesitate to make that promise in behalf of the Co. I think the Senate will pass the Bill if it passes the House which I have no doubt it will.

We called upon the Governor on Monday & presented copies of the Reports which he promised to examine & transmit to the Assembly with a short message as soon as possible. It has not yet been sent in & if it does not come tomorrow I shall call upon him again & request it to be sent as soon as possible so the Assembly may hear it before the Bill comes up for discussion. The Governor remarked that any measures which the Assembly saw fit to adopt to aid our road he would sanction. So our prospects seem to be very flattering to get the Swamp Lands & the Swamp Land Fund. I doubt very much if any surplus funds of the State will be appropriated to works of internal improvements as there is much anxiety respecting the conditions of national affairs. Members generally are disposed to reserve the financial resources of the State for emergencies which may arise in our federal relations. The Governor sent in a weak message on this subject the day before yesterday. Blue cockades are worn upon the street by a few & yesterday I noticed ladies distributing the colors red white & blue among the members of the Legislature & these colors now far outnumber the melancholy looking blue. There is a strong Union sentiment pervading the halls of legislation & I am inclined to believe that nothing rash or sudden will be done to precipitate matters. Some resolutions on the subject are the special order for to-night. A convention will probably be called but nothing more.

Burrow still lingers but he stands no chance for the Senate at all— Hempstead has lost ground rapidly & Dr. Mitchell now leads with a very fine prospect of success. If no changes occur he will be our next Senator.

It is impossible to tell whether the Legislature will take a recess for the Christmas holidays or not. There is much opposition to it. Should they do so we will probably go home & return but should they not it is probable that we will remain until in January or maybe until the end of the session—just as the interests of the Co. require. If we stay over Christmas we may require more means & should we do so I hope you will be prompt to meet the requisition. Our success may possibly depend upon this.

Allow Ward Scott & the other directors to read this if they desire. Will write again as soon as anything of interest occurs.

I am dear Sir
Very respy Yours
J. H. Haney

Governor Yell Identifies Arkansas's Interest with the South

Gene W. Boyett, ed., "A Letter from Archibald Yell to Henry A. Wise, July 12, 1841," *Arkansas Historical Quarterly* 22 (1973): 338–41.

Although two parties struggled within the state for offices and spoils, on national issues there were no disagreements. By 1841 leading politicians in Arkansas identified their state's interest as southern. In a letter to Henry A. Wise of Virginia, Archibald Yell, governor from 1841 to 1845, notes the interests of Arkansas in national affairs.

Little Rock
12th July/41

Mr Dear Sir

In the language of one of old I can say to you "well done thou good and faithful servt &c" and I have no doubt the same reward will drown your exertion as did that of the Christian spoken of in the Evangelist. We have the proceedings of the Ho[use] of Repr[esentatives] up to the 24th June; on that day the old Mass[achusetts] agitator [John Quincy Adams] showed his hand upon the subject of a Protective tariff as he is pleased to call—the friend of free labour & the friend of slave labour. I was sorry you was not in the precis. Then I see the Ho[use] adjourned without taking a vote & I hope you had a chance at the old felow before the subject was brought to a close or rather before the Gag was applied. You seem to be the old Sinner's "evil Genius" and which I am sure gives you as much pleasure as it tends to elevate and distinguish you. I hope you will not be drawn off in pursuit of smaller game that you can give you no anoyince or elivate you for this distinction, however I need not make those suggestions to you who is so well skilled in the mode of warfare, in which you are engaged. The Republicans everywhere are in doubtful suspinse as to what will be the ultimate course of the [president]. Will he submit to Mr. Clay's system of a protective Tariff, a fifty million [dollar] Bank with an indirect assumption of the state debts. Will he sanction a Distribution of the proceeds of the pub[lic] and with an empty Treasury.

If Mr. Tyler should yeald to all those measures dictated by that Arch Magician from Kentucky "then we may abandon all hope for the future" & content ourselves for the next eight years to battle in the minority for southern principles; for I have no doubt if Clay now succeeds he will be able at the next election to secure his own elevation which is the hight of his ambition. He will not consent for any others of his party suplant him at the next election.

If the President adheres to his former Republican principle he will be taken up by the true Democratic party by acclamation, and we may again see the principle of Mr. Jefferson in full tide of prosperity. He is from the proper region, the "Old Dominion" who has always stood firm to her principle because they are taught in the proper school of politics & who have more regard for principle than for office. . . .

Among our present men for the presidency I have but little choice so that he is a good states rights man. I should prefer Mr. Calhoun to any of our party, but will pledge myself without hesitation or reservation to Mr. Tyler if he is but true to the cause & I pray God he may be. Should we be disappointed there I am for some states rights man South of Mason's & Dickson's line. I am not satisfied to try the best of those "Northern men with Southern feelings." I prefer to take a man who has a stake in the game himself and who can not be driven or coaxed into submission.

[PRIVATE]

If Mr. Tyler is to be the Republican candidate & that you can be informed & will know from the course he will perisue, let me here suggest to you the policy of a causius [cautious] "Reform" in Arkansas. There are some who might be [turned] out without injury either to the country or the [president] and in filling their places he sould assertain who are the applicants. [Clay] has a [clique] in this state who want all his particular friends to fill the offices. Col. [Rector] or [Sevier] may be relied upon for information. There are some Whigs here who are of the "Republican portion" and who would be acceptable to the country and add strength to Mr. Tyler.

I have said this much with the expectation that you would feel a solicitude for the ultimate success of your friends & stand in a relation to him that will allow you to see that he does not weaken his own prospects.

Should I be mistaken in the views of the President or his ultimate position then you will have no need to make any suggestions upon the subject of appointments; for if the Clay Dinasty is to rule I care not who of them are in or out.

You must put me on your [list] & send me all your speeches & write to me when ever you can spare time from your pub[lic] duties.

> I am my Dear sir your
> Sincere friend
> A. Yell
> Hon, H. A. Wise
> H[ouse] of Repr.

FOR FURTHER READING

Several monographs touch on broader aspects of Arkansas history from the territorial period to the Civil War. S. Charles Bolton's *Arkansas, 1800–1860: Remote and Restless* (Fayetteville: University of Arkansas Press, 1998) provides the best overall assessment of the era, including political developments. Donald P. McNeilly's *The Old South Frontier: Cotton Plantations and the Formation of Arkansas Society, 1819–1861* (Fayetteville: University of Arkansas Press, 2000) offers important insights into the evolution of the state's society in the antebellum years.

Several contemporary observers should be used to capture the flavor of the period. These include George W. Featherstonhaugh's *Excursion through the Slave States from Washington to the Potomac* (New York: Harper, 1844); and Frederick Gerstaecker's *Wild Sports in the Far West* (London: G. Routledge & Co., 1854) and *Western Lands and Western Waters* (London: S. O. Benton, 1864). These are available in reprinted editions. Although literary in style, the works of C. F. M. Noland, under the pen name of Pete Whetstone, also provide a view of Arkansas culture before the war. See particularly Leonard Williams's *Cavorting on the Devil's Fork: The Pete Whetstone Letters of C. F. M. Noland* (Memphis: Memphis State University Press, 1979); and Ted Worley and Eugene Nolte's *Pete Whetstone of Devil's Fork* (Van Buren: Press-Argus, 1957).

Various aspects of early Arkansas life have been touched on by scholars. The best examination of slavery in the state remains Orville W. Taylor's *Negro Slavery in Arkansas* (Durham: Duke University Press, 1958), which may be supplemented by the readily available stories told by the slaves themselves in George E. Lankford's *Bearing Witness: Memories of Arkansas Slavery, Narratives from the 1930s WPA Collection*, 2nd ed. (Fayetteville: University of Arkansas Press, 2006). Taylor's study may be supplemented with more recent works, such as Gary Battershell, "The Socioeconomic Role of Slavery in the Arkansas Upcountry," *Arkansas Historical Quarterly* 58 (Spring 1999): 45–60; and Carl H. Moneyhon, "The Slave Family in Arkansas," *Arkansas Historical Quarterly* 58 (Spring 1999): 1–23. Robert Walz examines the settlement of the state in "Migration into Arkansas, 1834–1880" (PhD diss., University of Texas, Austin, 1958). The only look at early economic life is William B. Worthen's *Early Banking in Arkansas* (Little Rock: Democrat Printing Co., 1906). As yet there are few studies of early towns and counties. Among the best available is Ira Don Richards's *Story of a Rivertown: Little Rock in the Nineteenth Century* (Little Rock, 1969).

Politics has attracted the most scholarly attention. D. A. Stokes's "Public Affairs in Arkansas, 1836–1850" (PhD diss., University of Texas, Austin, 1966) provides the best overview of the early political history of the state. *The Whigs of Arkansas,* by Gene W. Boyett, is the best analysis of that party's history (Ann Arbor, MI: Xerox University Microfilms, 1975).

CHAPTER IV

Arkansas and the Civil War Crisis, 1860–1874

INTRODUCTION

During the period between 1860 and 1874, a series of events took place that jolted Arkansas society to the core. Following the election of Abraham Lincoln as president of the United States in 1860, South Carolina withdrew from the Union, to be followed shortly by Mississippi, Florida, Alabama, Georgia, Louisiana, and Texas. The following February, delegates from these states met at Montgomery, Alabama, where they created the Confederate States of America and, for all practical purposes, destroyed the old Union. When inaugurated in March 1861, Lincoln made it clear that he did not believe secession was legal and declared his intention to suppress what he called an insurrection with force, if necessary. The result was a war that lasted for four years, concluding with the collapse of the Confederacy, the restoration of the Union, and the liberation of three million black slaves throughout the South. For the South, Robert E. Lee's surrender did not bring peace, however; for another decade Southerners struggled to define the role of the freedmen in their society and to reconcile the political problems raised by the war.

The secession of Arkansas from the Union on May 6, 1861, marked the state's entry into the war crisis on the side of her Southern sisters. South Carolina's secession had initiated a lengthy debate between those who wanted to follow that state's example and those who argued for maintaining the Union. The events that followed indicated that most Arkansans did not believe that the election of Lincoln alone required secession; at a convention called for March 4, 1861, the Unionists won, preventing withdrawal. As the crisis worsened and conflict between the North and the Southern Confederacy became more likely, the attitude of many Unionists began to change. After Lincoln called for troops to respond to South Carolina's attack upon a Federal post in Charleston harbor, Fort Sumter, Arkansans favoring secession secured their state's withdrawal from the Union to join the Confederacy.

Despite the action of state political leaders, the Civil War did not promote unity among Arkansans, and the war would become as much a struggle among citizens of the state as one between the North and South. Many supported the new Confederacy and joined Arkansas military units sent off to fight in Virginia, Missouri, and elsewhere. In the early days, communities were alive with Confederate volunteers, and Arkansans talked about their holy duty to defeat a wicked North. Many others wanted little to do with the struggle, either because of ideological attachment to the Union or simply because they did not want to fight. Especially in the northwestern counties of the state, Unionist sympathizers promoted resistance to the Confederate government and its agents. No document provides more striking testimony to the Unionist support found among Arkansans than the enlistment of some fifteen thousand white and black men in the Union army to fight against the Confederacy and, often, their neighbors.

The war itself became a costly affair to Arkansans. Military activities in the state were widespread, including several major engagements. Usually these battles meant disaster for the Confederate forces. On March 6, 1862, at Pea Ridge in northwestern Arkansas, a battle that was one of the most important resulted in a Union victory, opening up all of the northern part of the state to Federal troops. The victorious Gen. Samuel A. Curtis went on that May to occupy Batesville and free the White River to Union operations. The next year opened with the capture of the Confederate fortifications at Arkansas Post at the mouth of the Arkansas River, the first step in an advance upriver that ended only nine months later with the fall of Little Rock. While Confederate troops fought valiantly and gained victories, at Prairie Grove and Camden, for example, the combination of manpower shortages, inadequate supplies, and, sometimes, poor leadership prevented them from taking advantage of their few opportunities. By the end of the war, Confederate forces held on in the southwestern corner of the state; Union forces operated practically unrestrained elsewhere.

While we usually think of wars in terms of generals and battles, it is important to realize their tremendous impact upon the lives of the people who actually fought those battles and also upon those who stayed at home. The Civil War in Arkansas claimed a tremendous personal cost, paid in the lives of men lost in both armies and in the injuries sustained. For those who escaped unharmed, life in the camps of nineteenth-century armies would be remembered as, perhaps, almost as horrible as battle. Those at home did not escape untouched, for a stream of Union and Confederate armies crossed and crisscrossed the state, and many communities experienced the sound of marching troops, the movement of wagons loaded with wounded, or the flight of slaves who found their freedom amid the upheaval. Many Arkansans were torn from their homes in the face of these operations by the armies, fleeing to Texas to protect themselves and their property, leading refugee lives that were uncomfortable and often dangerous.

In April 1865, four years of war ended with the Confederacy's defeat. The battles decided once and for all the issue of secession but left unresolved a more difficult problem, the fate of 110,000 black Arkansans who had been freed when the loyal government of Isaac Murphy adopted the Thirteenth Amendment. Although the freedmen were no longer slaves, most whites were unwilling to recognize them as equals—politically, economically, civilly, or socially. The end of slavery disrupted the principal source of labor in the state, and few landowners were willing to let the freedmen go so easily. As a result, Arkansans confronted a continued struggle: blacks, bolstered by the national government through the Freedmen's Bureau and by the local Republican Party, attempted to ensure their freedom, while many whites sought to impose limits. The result of this confrontation was that blacks obtained protection of many of the rights we connect with citizenship: they could vote, be treated as equals in the courts, and gain access to public institutions, including schools. They lost their efforts to achieve economic independence, however, and most entered into a new labor system in which contracts to labor as tenants or to farm on shares fixed them as closely to the land of the old planters as they had been before the war.

Politically, the decade after the Civil War also saw a continued struggle. Unionists created a government under Isaac Murphy in 1864 and wrote a new constitution. While recognized by President Lincoln, the senators and representatives elected under that constitution were never allowed by Congress to take their seats in Washington. The Murphy government continued to operate as the practical government of Arkansas, however, until March 1867, when Congress passed laws for a new program of restoring the Confederate states to the Union. Under the Reconstruction Acts of 1867, Congress placed Arkansas in the Fourth Military District under the supervision of Gen. Edward O. C. Ord, who directed the organization of a new constitutional convention in which blacks, for the first time, were allowed to vote for delegates and to serve in the convention. A new constitution that ensured civil rights for blacks resulted. Afterward, an election ratified the constitution and chose a new government, headed by Republican Powell Clayton. On June 22, Congress accepted the new constitution and the results of the election and readmitted Arkansas to the Union.

From 1868 to 1874, although the state had reestablished normal relations with the national government, politics at home remained unstable. Many whites believed that Gov. Powell Clayton's government had taken power unfairly and attacked it and its programs. While Clayton encouraged railroad construction, immigration, and education, his Democratic opponents focused on the taxes and corruption of his administration in their attacks on him. In 1872, after Clayton moved on to Washington and the Senate, a complex struggle took place between factions within the Republican Party, a conflict encouraged by their opponents among the Democrats. The result of the struggle between Joseph Brooks and Elisha Baxter was the return to power of the Democratic Party. Baxter, originally a supporter of Powell Clayton, became governor and then supported the Democrats as they did away with many of the programs of the Clayton administration and wrote a new constitution that ended Baxter's term two years before it was supposed to expire. The election of Democrat Augustus H. Garland as governor in 1874 finally ended the political upheaval of Reconstruction and allowed Arkansans to leave behind the crisis that had begun with their secession in 1861.

A. SECESSION: PRO AND CON

The course that Arkansas should take following the election of Abraham Lincoln as president of the United States was not clear. The rise of the

Republican Party in the 1850s was seen by most Southerners as a threat to slavery, their unique institution. In the campaign of 1860, Lincoln had indicated that he did not believe slavery should be allowed to expand further; for people in the South, a limit to the expansion of the institution was seen as only the first step toward its total abolition. Following his election, however, Lincoln tried to reconcile the South to his presidency and insisted that he had no intention of interfering with slavery where it already existed. Southerners were presented with a crisis in which their fears were weighed against the newly elected president's pledge to follow a course of moderation. The following documents indicate how Arkansans reacted to the election.

Gazette Argues for Moderation

Arkansas Gazette (Little Rock), November 17, 1860.

Most Arkansans were not radical secessionists. In central and north-western counties in particular, political leaders urged that the state wait, rather than rush into disunion. Throughout the 1850s, the *Arkansas Gazette* had been one of the foremost means through which Unionist sentiment was expressed. While expressing caution, however, this editorial also indicates the existence of limits to Arkansas Unionism in the crisis of 1860.

The Condition of the Country and the Duty of Patriots.—The election is over, and Lincoln, the representative of the Black Republicans, is elected. The first announcement of this fact struck horror into many bold hearts, for the same wires that brought it, brought also the intelligence that South Carolina had seceded from the Union. That report, however, has been contradicted and it is now hoped that the President elect will govern the whole people for the time for which he has been constitutionally chosen to serve.

In this emergency it is proper that our people should act upon wise and discreet counsels, and do nothing rashly or inconsiderately. Lincoln is elected in the manner prescribed by law, and by the majority required by the Constitution. Let him be inaugurated, and let no steps be taken against this administration until he has committed an overt act which can not be remedied by legal and Constitutional means. Then the people have the remedy in their own hands, for revolution is a sacred and an inherent right in all.

Governor Rector's Plea for Secession

Arkansas Gazette (Little Rock), December 22, 1860.

Elected governor as a Unionist in 1860, Henry M. Rector, upon taking office, became the state's foremost secessionist. In his inaugural address that November, he urged the General Assembly to consider secession. He continued his agitation, and this address of December 21, 1860, shows the argument of those who believed secession was necessary. Within it Rector touches upon the fears that had built among Southerners for decades and that made them reluctant to wait for Lincoln's inauguration. The "Helper Book" referred to is *Impending Crisis* by Hinton R. Helper (1859).

Special Message of the Governor.—

TO THE HOUSE OF REPRESENTATIVES:

The election of Abraham Lincoln to the Presidency of the United States, having been ascertained but a few hours preceding the delivery of my Inaugural Address to the General Assembly; and the attitude which some of the Southern States, would, in consequence assume, being then in doubt and uncertainty, I designed only to lay down in that Address, as briefly as possible, my convictions, touching the abstract legal right of a State to secede from the Federal Union, coupling with that assertion of right, the opinion, that notwithstanding there was a clear legal right, and cumulative moral wrong on the part of the North, the exercise of this right. Still, so long as there was even a remote hope that by compromise and concessions made by the Northern States the Union could be preserved and held together that it was the duty of every patriot in the land, every functionary of the Government, every citizen, rich or poor, slave holder or non-slave holder, the son and daughter, with the parent, the parent with the child, to labor for, and conserve their course and conduct to this end.

The Providence of nations and the destinies of the world seem to will it otherwise.

The wisest and best government that has ever been allotted by man, has fallen prey to the madness and fanaticism of its own children, for I am convinced, that the Union of these States, in this moment is practically severed, and gone forever. It seems to be impossible, upon casual reflection, that it can be so, and we realize it only by the stern inflexibility of facts patent and palpable as when the mantle of death spreads itself upon the fair form and features of some beloved one of earth preparatory to an eternal farewell, never, never again to return.

I utter these sentiments in tones of solemn reverence, for I feel that I am chronicling events portentous of a gloomy future for my countrymen —for the rising generation—many of whom cluster around my own fireside.

My duty prompts me to announce to you, what I conceive to be, "the State of the Government"—which is, I repeat, that the Union of the States, may no longer be regarded as an existing fact—making it imperatively necessary, that Arkansas should girdle her loins for the conflict and put her house in order. . . .

That we must . . . seek an alliance, as a necessity, with a Confederacy of Southern States, is, as plain to my mind, as the sun at noon-day. To do this it is necessary as every one must see, to put the country in a thorough state of military preparation. That the separation will be peaceful, should it occur before the inauguration of Abraham Lincoln, is guaranteed by the Message of President Buchanan recently delivered to the Congress now in session. . . .

No Constitutional barrier, however, will stay the arm of Mr. Lincoln, elected and led on by the aggressive and vile fanaticism of the North, the chief embodiment of the "irrepressible conflict" doctrine, and staunch endorser of the "Helper Book," need not be counted upon because of the lack of constitutional authority; but he may be impeached. Who is to do it? Will a Black Republican Congress impeach a Black Republican President? Never. But the power and forces of the Federal Government, as possible, we may well calculate will be by him levied and brought to bear against any and all States attempting separation from the General Government. Contemplating these events as I do to my mind, it is highly important, that an appropriation be made at once adequate in its amount for arming the militia with approved modern arms and ammunition to be stored at convenient points along the North-west border of the State and at the seat of government. . . .

I am not for war, but I am in favor of preparing for war in time of peace, and recommend to you who have authority to provide the means necessary for the defense of our citizens.

B. UNIONISM VERSUS THE CONFEDERACY

Most Arkansans in the spring of 1861 took the advice of the *Gazette* and adopted a wait-and-see attitude. Elsewhere, however, the state's sisters in the South were withdrawing from the Union. In February 1861, delegates from six of the Deep South states met in Montgomery, Alabama, and formed the Confederate States of America. Arkansas tended to support the Union as the crisis deepened, but Unionism had limits. While Arkansans did not want to leave the Union, they believed the South had legitimate grievances that had to be resolved before the crisis could be ended. Moreover, they were not ready to support any effort that might be made to end secession through military action. When President Lincoln called upon state governors on April 15, 1861, to provide seventy-five thousand militiamen to suppress secession, the attitudes of many Arkansans changed. On May 6, 1861, a convention at Little Rock took the fateful step that pushed the state into the war.

David Walker's Dilemma

David Walker to W. W. Mansfield, March 3, 1861, W. W.
Mansfield Collection, Arkansas History Commission, Little Rock.

In February 1861, Arkansans voted for delegates to a convention to consider the crisis precipitated by the secession of the Deep South states. Candidates who supported the Union drew 23,620 votes to only 17,927 for the secessionists. The majority of delegates were for union. Judge David Walker of Fayetteville was elected convention president. The following letter from him explains conditions in the convention; it also shows the depth of Unionist sentiment in Arkansas. More ominously, however, it shows clearly that Arkansas Unionists would not sustain the Union at any cost.

Ozark Arks.
March 3rd, 1861
Hon. W. W. Mansfield

Dear Sir:
     I set my self down today, Sunday as it is, to drop you a hasty line.
. . . Well tomorrow is the ominous day. It will possibly be a day long to

be remembered by the people of Arkansas and by the people of the United States. In the language of the Roman Ancient, the *ides* of March have *come,* but not passed. It is befeared that an attempt may be made to prevent the inauguration of Lincoln. This could do no *good,* but might be productive of very much *harm.* From the returns which we have received, I presume there is little doubt but that a majority of the delegates will be *Conservative.* And if the convention should think proper to pass an ordinance of secession, it will be referred back to the people for their approval or disapproval. We have no late news here as to what the Border State Convention has done. There were some slight intimations in a slip from Fort Smith papers, that an adjustment had been made, that was thought to be satisfactory to the border states; but we have not had any news on the subject since. So we remain in ignorance (not blissful I hope) of what is going on in the capital. You will of course, be posted up every day with the very latest news from Washington. It is to be feared that from Lincoln's line of policy that he will attempt to collect the revenue at Charleston and other southern ports. This will, in my opinion, be looked upon, and treated by the southern states as equivalent to a declaration of war. And there will no doubt be a measuring of arms between the South Carolinians and the federal troops at Fort Sumpter [*sic*] if it is not given up [to] the authorities of South Carolina. I think that any attempt to blockade the ports of the southern states, will be crossing the Rubicon. Although I am willing to acknowledge that South Carolina has acted hastily and it may be to some extent wrong; yet I have too much southern blood in my veins to sit quietly down and see her contending with the abolition hordes of the North and not wish her God-speed. I have but little doubt but that General Davis, the newly elected President of the Confederacy, will demand in language strong and emphatic, the surrender of Fort Sumter; and if his request be not complied with, an attempt will be made to *take* it by force of *arms.* We are living in the midst of trying times. Great events are so continually transpiring that we do not appreciate them. One unlucky spark would now touch off the whole magazine and build up a gulf wider than that which existed between the rich man and Lazarus. But we must try to prevent that calamity from taking place and it is to be hoped that every person in the government will realize that *he* is responsible at least to some extent, for the way in which the ship of state, and the glorious old Union, are to be conducted in the future. I must confess that I have not as much confidence in my own judgment as I have usually had. When I look at the blessings the Union has conferred on us, I feel like it would be almost sacrilege to even think of seeing it dissolved, again, when I look at the wrongs and indignities that have been heaped upon me in newspapers, pamphlets and even stereotyped in books, I can hardly maintain my conservative position. I am afraid that having once divided it will be easy to get up new divisions, until we will be like the little Republics of South America. I shall wait with much impatience and anxiety, the inaugural address of Lincoln. It will, in my opinion, either inspire new confidence, and give us new and strong hopes of an equitable adjustment of our difficulties, or otherwise, it will destroy all that is left, and place us in a condition to know what we may rely on. In a word, I think that *war,* with all its horrors, that send a chill to the very heart; or *peace,* and restored confidence, which will cause one shout of joy to go from each and every true patriot in the land, to the great dispose of human events. But, I have already trespassed on your patience. Nothing has transpired since you left worth telling. The river is getting down again, and I fear that there will not be much boating going on for some time.

Drop me a line and let me know what your Convention is doing.

Very truly,
Your Abdt. Servt.
D. W.

Preparation for War

C. C. Danley to W. W. Mansfield, April 23, 1861, W. W. Mansfield Collection, Arkansas History Commission, Little Rock.

C. C. Danley, editor of the *Arkansas Gazette,* had been a prominent Little Rock Unionist. As had the others, he supported moderation and careful consideration of the situation before secession. Following the Confederate attack upon Fort Sumter and President Lincoln's call upon Governor Rector for troops to suppress the insurrection, however, Danley went for secession. His letter to W. W. Mansfield shows the conversion to war by this particular Unionist.

Steamboat Tahlequah
April 23, 1861
Hon. W. W. Mansfield

Dear Sir:

Enclosed I send a slip by which you will see that Judge Walker has called the convention in the 6th of May. I hope to be at home by that time. I think the conservative men of the convention should take charge of the affairs of the state and prevent the wild secessionists from sending us to the Devil.

Lincoln's administration has committed the overt act and I am now for war. We are going to attack Fort Smith, if it will not surrender without an attack. We have a battery of eight pieces of artillery and when our force concentrates, expect to have about 500 men. The party is under the command of Major Borland, the only man in the state that I know to be fit to command such an expedition. A reinforcement of 9 companies is expected at Fort Smith. If that happens, now, we will have to cut off their supplies and call for more help from the adjoining counties. In that view of the case, our friends at Ozark, who desire to do so, might form a company and await a call for their services. The war has commenced. You know that, from the first, I was for the Union. Now that the "overt act" has been committed we should I think draw the sword, and not sheathe it until we can have a guaranty of all our rights, or such standards as will be honorable in the South.

Let me urge you to go to the convention, I think it[']s of vast importance that conservative men should continue to control its action.

C. C. Danley

P.S. The Union men whom I have met are all for war. I think in our parts there is a majority of Union men or those who were Union a few days ago.

Ordinance of Secession, May 6, 1861

Arkansas Gazette (Little Rock), May 11, 1861.

On May 6, 1861, the Arkansas convention elected to consider secession reconvened. The Unionist majority had collapsed, as men like

Danley believed war was now necessary. Unionists who still hoped to avoid secession attempted to have a popular vote on secession, but the secessionists prevented delay. The convention then voted for secession by a vote of sixty-five to five. The ordinance chronicled grievances with the Federal government and spelled out the reasons that had finally led the majority of Arkansans to believe they could not continue in the Union.

An Ordinance to dissolve the Union now existing between the State of Arkansas and the other states united with her under the compact entitled "The Constitution of the United States of America."

WHEREAS, in addition to the well founded causes of complaint set forth by this convention, in resolutions adopted on the 11th March, A.D. 1861, against the sectional party now in power at Washington city, headed by Abraham Lincoln, he has, in the face of resolutions passed by this convention, pledging the State of Arkansas, to resist to the last extremity, any attempt on the part of such power to coerce any state that had seceded from the old Union, proclaimed to the world that war should be waged against such states, until they should be compelled to submit to their rule, and large forces to accomplish this having been marshalled to carry out this inhuman design; and to longer submit to such rule, or remain in the old Union of the United States, would be disgraceful and ruinous to the State of Arkansas.

Therefore, we the people of the State of Arkansas, in convention assembled, do hereby declare and ordain, and it is hereby declared and ordained, that the "ordinance and acceptance of compact," passed and approved by the General Assembly of the State of Arkansas, on the 18th day of October, A.D. 1836, whereby it was, by said General Assembly, ordained that, by virtue of the authority vested in said General Assembly, by the provisions of an ordinance adopted by the convention of delegates assembled at Little Rock, for the purpose of forming a constitution and system of government for said state, the propositions set forth in "an act of supplementary to an act entitled an act for the admission of the State of Arkansas into the Union, and to provide for the due execution of the laws of the United States within the same, and for other purposes, were freely accepted, ratified and irrevocably confirmed articles of compact and union between the State of Arkansas and the United States," and all other laws, and every other law and ordinance, whereby the State of Arkansas became a member of the federal union, be, and the same are hereby, in all respects, and for every purpose herewith consistent, repealed, abrogated and fully, set aside; and the union now subsisting between the State of Arkansas and the other states, under the name of the United States of America, is hereby forever dissolved.

And we do further hereby declare and ordain, that the State of Arkansas hereby resumes to herself all rights and powers heretofore delegated to the government of the United States of America—that her citizens are absolved from all allegiance to said government of the United States, and that she is in full possession and exercise of all the rights and sovereignty which appertain to a free and independent state.

We do further ordain and declare, that all rights acquired and vested under the constitution of the United States of America, or of any act or acts of Congress, or treaty, or under any law of this state, and not incompatible with this ordinance, shall remain in full force and effect, in no wise altered or impaired, and have the same effect as if this ordinance had not been passed.

Adopted and passed in open convention on the 6th day of May, Anno Domini 1861.

Elias C. Boudinot
Secretary of the Arkansas State Convention

C. PATRIOTISM AND DISSENT WITHIN CONFEDERATE ARKANSAS

Once Arkansas had withdrawn from the Union and joined the Confederacy, the debate over the course of action that had been taken continued. Many Arkansans actively worked against the Confederate state government's attempts to recruit men and prepare for war. The following documents indicate the lack of cohesion among Arkansans concerning the war.

Confederate Volunteers

William E. Woodruff Papers, Arkansas History Commission, Little Rock.

With secession, a war spirit swept across much of Arkansas. Young men rushed off to join military units organizing throughout the state. J. W. Felts of Arkansas County reports on this military fever in his locale. While reporting the war excitement, however, Felts also notes that from the very beginning the coming war disrupted the state's economy—the result of which would be long-term problems for Arkansas and its citizens.

Homestead, Arkansas Co., Arks.
May 24, 1861
Wm. E. Woodruff Sr. Esqr.

Dear Sir

Yours of 19th Inst came to hand yesterday evening. I was glad to hear that you were all well, Addie included. Since sending you the draft I have had unfavorable news from New Orleans. The last shipment of my cotton out of the proceeds of which I expected the draft to be paid had not at last accounts been sold, and my Merchants refused to pay anything on it until sold. I would therefore say to you if you have not disposed of the draft you will please not do so, and I will either send or bring you the money the first safe opportunity, as under the circumstances I fear the draft will not be paid.

The war spirit does not seem to abate in the least as there is companies organizing in every direction in this part of the State. There has two companies gone from this country to Virginia[;] there is now two companies of Cavalry organized and one of them ready to leave if not gone from our frontier. The Capt. of the other company is now gone to Little Rock to tender his company to the Governor for his reception and direction. There is also a company of cavalry in Desha County to start to Little Rock in a day or two from thence to the frontier. We have found companies of home Guards all along the River and are drilling once a week, to be ready for any emergency. The report here is that Major McCullock has been appointed to the command of our frontier. My prayer is that the Lord may crown him with success and that he may be able to achieve a complete and glorious victory over Montgomery, Lane, or any other blackhearted abolitionist that may dare to set foot in Arks for the purpose of invading its soil, and that our Arks boys may crown themselves with honors that can never be effaced. This leaves us all well and crops promising.

Yours truly
J. W. Felts

Confederate Patriotism

William E. Woodruff Papers, Arkansas History Commission,
Little Rock.

By September 1861, Arkansas was into the war. On August 10,
Arkansas troops had participated in the Confederate victory at
Wilson's Creek in Missouri. This only fanned the fire of military
spirit. The letter of Mrs. M. B. Eskridge expresses this spirit and
the early willingness to sacrifice for the war effort. Mrs. Eskridge
shows how many Southerners believed that they could change their
lives—to win the war.

Wapannoka, Ark. Sept 9th 1861
Mr. William E. Woodruff

Kind Friend—

Amongst many present calls, I have regretted that day after day I
have been denied the pleasure of congratulating yourself and your wife
on the safety and heroism of your son! As we are informed through the
newspapers, in reading which I have rejoiced for the anxious parents who
have given him up "to do his duty" confident that he would not perish
in the hour of danger, as you said in your last letter. In this time of trial
and impressment for our people I trust that—while the Roman virtues
of self-denial, patriotism and courage are being revived and cultivated
amongst our soldiers—that of gratitude and generosity, in doing "honor
to whom honor is due" will be nourished by us at home. I have but one
cause of dissatisfaction—with our remote, isolated location here—it has
been this—that I have but one son, one dependence for us here at home
in establishing a new plantation—or one—to go into the war. We find
that we cannot in this have all wishes gratified & the infliction seems
needed—to my son—to stay *at home*—for the time—all has been against
his leaving. If I had a hundred under my control and keeping solely they
should go—to resist the *fiends*, who assail us, & the embodiment, the
impersonation, of evil. I consider that man Fremont—he was the *fire-
brand*, the poison first resorted to by the Black Republicans, in 1856, &
his late proclamation in Missouri shows how ripe they feel for their
wicked purposes. Our confidence, I trust, is not like theirs, for in our
right will be our *might*. I am confident, —and in these our fiery days of

trial, as a people, we will learn to practice virtues to enoble us. The tone of our newspapers gratifies me very much—& I like the Gazette and Democrat too for they speak to the common sense and virtue of the reader, & they animate us in our retired homes to industry, management and economy & as we have never before tried at home (but were *wanderers* and *idlers*). We experience each day—how many new lessons we have to learn in domestic management as farmers—only regretting that we are unorganized and unfurnished with means—of much avail—for the times of war. I must beg your indulgence—when on these subjects—I am apt to tax my friends.

Please present me most kindly to your wife and daughters. When times become easier, I hope our families may become personally acquainted. I have never ceased to remember with the kindest feelings all those whom I knew in Little Rock and Batesville, and have so far been glad to bring my children once more to their native state.

Truly and respectfully yours
M. B. Eskridge

Antiwar Sentiment in Carroll County

J. R. H. Soolt Papers, Special Collections, University of Arkansas at Little Rock.

While the previous letters expressed patriotic sentiment, the next document indicates that many Arkansans carried their prewar Unionism into the war itself. Confederate Capt. John R. Homer Scott had been sent to northern Arkansas to halt an invasion. Instead of Yankees, he found himself confronting a hostile and reluctant population. His arrests began a truly civil war within the state. The hatred engendered by a war of Arkansans against Arkansans would continue into the postwar years.

Headquarters Battallion
Arks. Cavalry Volunteers
Camp Culloden
Carroll County Arks
Decr. 3rd 1861

General,

I have under arrest (and daily making more) some thirty five or Forty men positively proven to belong to a secret society held together by secret signs tokens pass words and under the penalty of *"death"* should one of their members reveal the same.

I have been enabled from their own confessions upon each other to obtain their oaths signs, tokens & words & c.

I conceive the organization to be of Northern origin having in view the subjugation of the South!

It breathes Treason and insurrection of the most conclusive and positive nature.

Some of the most important signs, tokens & c. are given thus (from their own statements).

A member when leaving home was to suspend from his door or window a piece of *"yellow ribbon, calico* or *paper"* to distinguish them as members and as a token "that if a friend or the Northern Army came along that his property & family would not be molested by seeing and finding *this sign* at his door.

Another token was to say *"secession"* which if recognized by a member would be answered by saying "In the Southern Confederacy."

•   •   •

This society was called by some of them a "peace party or peace society" or to unite the friends of "peace."

•   •   •

This Society or organization numbers several hundred and extends through Fulton, Izard, Searcy, Newton, Van Buren parts of Conway, Pope, Marion & Carroll Counties. There has been nearly one hundred arrested in Clinton, Van Buren Coy Berryville in Searcy County, and I have arrested thirty five or forty in Marion, Searcy, Newton & Carroll Counties. All around my camps and are daily making them. It seems almost universal in certain localities.

. . . We need not go north to find our enemies[;] they are all around me bound together by solemn secret oathes &c. Some of the prisoners have stated it was an understanding that if the Northern Army did drive your command before them that this Squadron would have been attacked or that they "*laid such hints*" & if I made or attempted to arrest persons in certain places (after I commenced making them & their plans &c. were detected) that they would "give me a fight" &c.

I think it would be advisable to station some of the companies of my command in Wiley's Cove Searcy County. There is a camp meeting ground with some good buildings a very large Harbor and near or in midst of this secret-society &c. I think Capt. Boon is in the vicinity or county of the same kind of men, but fear not able to procure Winter Quarters convenient. I am in hopes I may be permitted to Station the companies, if found necessary *separately* in the most disaffected and unloyal localities or adjoining counties within reach or days ride from my head qts. It will be better in giting [*sic*] the use of buildings in part now erected at certain points by religious societies & in neighborhoods where protection would be needed &c.

I am sir very Respectfully
Your obt. Servant
Jno. R. Homer Scott Capt.

Lukewarm Support for the War

Kie-Oldham Collection, Arkansas History Commission, Little Rock.

The presence of Unionists provoked pro-Southern Arkansans into an all-out effort to suppress such sentiments. Governor Rector received reports of Unionist activities from ready informers throughout the state. In Camden, a mob ran several merchants believed sympathetic to the Union out of town. Sam Leslie of Wiley's Cove in Searcy County tried to defend the people of his county against charges of inadequate patriotism. Nonetheless, he recognized that his county had long been a source of pro-Union sentiment.

Wiley's Cove Arks Oct 21 1861
H. M. Rector
Gov of Ark

Dear Sir
Your letter of the 16th Inst is now before me and contents notised.

You say it has been reported to the Military Board there are One Hundred Good fighting men in Cove Township, Searcy Co that has not nor will not volunteer thir servicis in behalf of the South.

What would prompt aney one to attempt to cast such a stigma upon the people of this Township I am not able to comprehend, ware your informant a citizen of Searcy Co I might have some Ida of the cause, this Township (Cove) has not turned out as many volunteers as she might have done, this county has about 300 men in service of the Confederate States though we are only represented by two companies[;] the rest of our men Joined companies in the adjoining counties and those counties is receiving the credit. Cove Township has about 60 able bodied men subject to military duty all told[,] only five out of that number single men and Eight volunteers[,] which will leave 52 now subject to duty[;] the Great bulk of our men now in service has been furnished by three Townships, there is other Townships in the County that has done but little better than Cove, and they pass unnoticed. I will say to you that the citizens of Cove Township is as Law abiding a people as lives and the records of our corts will bear me out in the assursion, which may account in some degree for their not being more ready to volunteer[;] there is other causes, so many Missourians running off and leaving the State, has had its influence[.] I know this county has had a bad name[;] at a distance we have been called Black Republicans and Abolitionists &c but we have never had any of thos characters amongst us.

It is true the citizens of this county war [were] union men as long as there was aney hope of the Union and perhaps a little longer, but all Ida [idea] of the Union as it onst [once] was is banished[;] the time has passed for the North and South to live together in pease and harmoney and we must be loyal to the government we live under[;] this is the fealings of the people of this Co so fare as I have any knollege and when you hear men call the people of Searcy Co. by hard names rest assured they are willfully lying of uninformed with the character of our people. I write you this letter Gov. in order to plase the Good people of Searcy Co write before you I feel it is a duty I owe to them to do so.

I hope Cove Township will yet give a Good account of hir self that you may have no reason to complain.

Respectfully your friend

Sam Leslie

P.S. You will please commission Saml Boyd as 2 Lieut Cove Township Searcy Co 45 Reg Ark Militia Cap S. L. Redwines Co

S. L.

D. THE COMMON PEOPLE AND THE WAR

Arkansas left the Union to protect state rights and prevent interference with slavery. For most people, the concept of state rights was an illusive idea with little pertinence to their day-to-day lives. Similarly, most people had little direct interest in slavery. It would be the very people for whom the issues that brought on the war had so little relevance, however, who would carry the greatest burden of fighting. The letters and diaries of Arkansans during the war years indicate how deeply the conflict affected the lives of the state's common folks.

War and Business in Camden

C. F. Kellam Journal, Arkansas History Commission, Little Rock.

Almost as soon as war broke out, it had an impact on the home front. C. F. Kellam, a merchant at Camden, kept a daily journal during the war. From the journal it is apparent that the war produced economic difficulties perhaps unforeseen at the outset.

Friday, October 4, 1861

Business almost none in consequence of low stocks. Our country women making up goods, at home with the spinning wheel & loom. Coffee selling at 25 to 40¢ here & in N.O. Salt selling at 5 to $7.50 per sack.

November 2, 1861

One day this past week we stopped all customers from buying on credit. Adopted strictly cash & posted it up in the store. Goods nearly gone in a cr. & country friends & customers will not let us have any provisions without the naked cash.

November 28, 1861

Dull-little doing—great complaint & dissatisfaction in all kind of business. Farmers grumble at the rise of groceries. Won't sell their produce, say that they will retaliate & have big prices too. Won't pay any debts not even where they owe—this makes all parties growl & grumble. Heretofore the planters would pay off their dues in any and all kind of provisions.

Life in the Field

D. D. McBrien, ed., "Letters of an Arkansas Confederate Soldier," *Arkansas Historical Quarterly* 2 (1943): 270–71.

By 1863, the tide of war had turned against Confederate Arkansas. Losses at Pea Ridge, Prairie Grove, and Helena and the surrender of Little Rock relegated the Confederate army and state government chiefly to areas in the southwest. Federal foraging parties roamed at will. For the Confederate army times were hard. W. W. Garner of Quitman, who was with a home guard cavalry unit (Tenth Regiment), wrote of the conditions with the army at this time.

Tulip, Dallas County, Ark, Sept. 24, 1863
Mrs. Elvira Ellington

My Dear Sister
Captain Morgan of our Regt starts for home tomarrow [*sic*] morning. He lives near Batesville and will be apt to pass through out [our] neighborhood. I have invited him to call on you. He is a gentleman. I will write you a few lines although if you get all I have written you in the last few days it will be enough to worry your patience for it is a repetition of the same thing, as nothing new, or I hear nothing to write you. I write often because I don't know that you get what I write. There is danger of all being captured. I have not seen or heard of any person crossing the Arkansas River since I did. Have not heard a word from the north side of the river since I left. A great many of our officers have gone home to try to get the men back to the Command but I think the men and most of the officers will stay on this side of the Arkansas River. Col. Shaver started north a few days ago with a wagon, ammunition, and some thirty men. The report is

the wagon and most of the men are captured. Lt. Thompson started home the 23rd inst. in company with Lawler, Lt. Barnes, and one or two others. I send by Lt. Thompson $700.00. I also send Willoughby's pay account and will send the affidavit that has to go with it by Capt. Morgan. Charley has gone home with one of the Lts. It is reported here that the Feds are at Benton advancing this way. I hope they may go somewhere else than Van Buren County. I do hope that our country may escape their scourges. I am yet in the Commissary dept. and am getting along well. I am well. My leg is improving and I think will be well in a few days. Our Regt is nearly broke up and if something is not done or some change takes place I don't think it will be in existence long. I wish I knew if any of our men were coming back to their command. I believe we have seventeen men in our company and about 250 or 275 men in the Regt. all told. Last April we had 900 men in the Regt. Captain Rollow has got well. He is low down. I think he will be home before long. I live in hopes that something may turn in favor of our Confederacy to bring this unholy unnatural war to a close. For a soldier's life is a hard one. Live on blue beef, flour and grease to go into it. Once in a while a little sugar or molasses. Worse still, a man's family is a home with no comforts, his wife killing herself to make clothing and doing the drudgery of the family.

I will close my letter and put on the blue beef to cook for supper. I have no idea when I will be at home.

A Woman's View of the War

From the Diary of Mrs. Virginia Davis Gray, typescript in Special Collections, University of Arkansas at Little Rock.

At home in Princeton, Dallas County, Virginia Gray had thought the war far off. Her husband, Capt. Oliver Gray, was fighting with the Third Arkansas Cavalry in Tennessee and Georgia. By December 1863, the Federal troops in Arkansas had begun to penetrate the southwestern counties. Her diary notes one such Federal raid. The Federals came looking for provisions and Rebel sympathizers. As they left, however, they precipitated a mass exodus of slaves, who would follow them to Little Rock in search of freedom.

December 23, 1863

A few days ago we were all sitting quietly by the fire sewing, Hannah with us, knitting when Tildy rushed in to say the Federals are coming. We doubted, as usual, but Hannah went home. Soon they came close after our pickets—who were retreating reluctantly, fighting as they went. Some stopped in town, arrested all the citizens and guarded them all day at the hospital. The others followed the pickets and came upon their camp near Mr. Pope's there were about seventy men. Only a few fought, as they were in their very usual unfortunate condition, with only a little ammunition, but those fought like Spartans—about thirty against one thousand. They carried away fifteen prisoners—but none of our men were killed. They deny that they lost any but we have reason to believe that not less than thirteen were killed. They left one wounded man and a nurse at our hospital. All day we had to watch them but at night we had a guard and then went to sleep—even Berta came down from Sam. She had sat on him half a day to keep him. One told her she knew how to keep a horse. She said she was obligated to do so, if she got down one minute they would steal him. They left in the morning, very much fearing that Marmaduke would follow them. At some places they were very rude—at others very civil, as they were to us. Dr. Hitchcock had just gone to carry Molly to Miss, when they came. By riding fast, they escaped being overtaken. Mr. Anderson took "old Pete" and also escaped but leaving his cares and anxieties in Princeton—he look back like Lot's wife and was consequently compelled to wade Tulip Creek. We were better off without men. In the morning when the Feds left, a strange panorama began to move. First was Mrs. Harley's old "Uncle Jerry" limping once in five or six steps,—Mr. Hayes' lame Reuben, and Mrs. Holme's old Edmund.—After then Mr. Lindsay's Bill—one-legged, Maj. Harley's Rush, lame—and Mr. Lea's old lame Nathan—then old women—young women, children and babies innumerable: Mr. Lea told a Fed. they were doing us a favor. "We thank you, sir" he said. "Such as that is our greatest tax—we are indebted to you for taking them away." The man tried to frown but it was *too-funny*. Poor things! I wonder what kind of fate they will meet. Mr. Ben Holmes has not a servant, horse or mule left.

E. THE STRUGGLE FOR FREEDOM FOR BLACKS

When the Civil War began, few white people had believed that it would bring about an end to slavery. Emancipation, however, turned out to be one of the major consequences of the war. Although the war and passage of the Thirteenth Amendment ended slavery, many whites continued to believe that blacks needed somehow to be controlled—economically, politically, and socially. For black people the period after the Civil War would become an era of terrible struggle in which they would attempt to secure for themselves complete liberty. The documents that follow indicate the opposition they encountered and the result of their efforts.

Four Labor Contracts

Ted R. Worley, "Tenant and Labor Contracts, Calhoun County, 1869–1871, *Arkansas Historical Quarterly* 13 (1954): 102–6.

The first question among white planters after the war was whether blacks would continue to work as they had before the war. Most blacks wanted instead to farm their own land rather than to work for their previous owners. They found it almost impossible to obtain property. To survive, most turned to contractual arrangements with landowners—farming for shares or wages. Generally, these arrangements condemned blacks to lives of perpetual labor as tenant farmers. The following documents illustrate such arrangements. These four are between various individuals and J. C. Barrow, a planter in Calhoun County.

State of Arkansas
County of Calhoun

This contract entered into by and between James Blanset of the first part and J. C. Barrow of the second part. Witnesseth the said James Blanset of the first part, agrees to rent a west portion of the bottom field, some twenty acres from said Barrow on the said Barrow's farm, and agrees to pay him for the rent thereof, one third of the corn, and one fourth of the cotton, and one fourth of the Sweet potatoes raised during the year 1870 and house the same at the usual time, then haul the seed cotton to some near gin, with Barrows wagon and mules, have it ginned; and the said Barrow agrees to furnish the said Blanset the necessary supplies to make said crop, and the said Blanset agrees to pay the said Barrow for them out of his portion of said crop and the said Barrow agree to not seize upon the said crop unless the said Blanset attempts to deceive or defraud the said Barrow, and that we will consult each other before setting upon the subject of selling the same.

This January 25th 1870   J. C. Barrow
Witness   J. W. Blanset

           his
Lewis x Haines   her
      mark   Lucrecia x Haines
Mr. J. Barrow   mark

•   •   •

State of Arkansas
County of Calhoun

This contract entered into this day by James W. Blanset of the first part and John C. Barrow of the second part both of said County and State are as follows: To wit: to rent the south west portion of the ditch said ditch running through the bottom field, or all the land lying west of said ditch, and the field lying between Barrow's house and said Blansets house which he now occupys. The said Blanset agrees to keep up said fences around said fields and that said Barrow shall be at no expense whatever about any thing only paying the taxes on it. That Blanset will keep up the place which he occupies, for his comfort without any charge or expense to the said Barrow. And the said Barrow hereby agrees to take by the first day of December (1871) Eighteen hundred and seventy one ($72) seventy two dollars for the rent of said (and the said Blanset agrees to give it) lands and premises.

This January 9th 1871
J. C. Barrow Seal
J. W. Blanset Seal

Witness
Lafayette Barrow
James Barrow

•   •   •

State of Arkansas
County of Calhoun

This contract entered in between Dick Smith of the first part and J. C. Barrow of the second part are as follows, to wit—The said Dick Smith agrees to live with the said J. C. Barrow and to do anything necessary to be done by or for the said Barrow, to either work on a Bayou Bartholomew farm or work here on his Calhoun County farm or stay and work at the Monticello place, and to work with Lafayette Barrow or with James Barrow that the said Dick Smith here by agrees to take $120, one hundred and twenty dollars for his services or work for this year of eighteen hundred and seventy one, payable one half of the amount each month which is five dollars, (his wages being ten dollars per month, or $120.00 dollars per year) and the said Dick Smith hereby agrees that if he quits, or leaves before the expiration of said year that he will forfeit the one half of his labor, or wages at the end of the year. (And the) said J. C. Barrow agrees to (give to the said) Dick Smith one hundred and twenty dollars for the years work payable one half at the end of each month, and the other half at the end, or expiration of this year. The said Barrow is to give said Dick Smith his rations for said year.

Witness his
Signed   Dick x Smith
                mark

Hampton, Ark. Jany 13th 1871
J. C. Barrow

•   •   •

An article of agreement made and entered into this 11 day of March 1871 between J. S. Howard of the first part and Aaron Binns col[ore]d of the second part. To wit, and have possession of the kitchen room also one half of the smoke house, one half the garden, access to the cistern for his and family use but not to allow any one else to use water without Howards consent also to cultivate all the ground except such as Howard sees proper to reserve; he Binns agreeing to repair the chimney of the Building he occupies so there will be no danger of fire injuring the primises also to repair the pailling and old fencing so as to keep out all kinds of stock and Binns agrees to watch the primises well so that no stock or person shall molest or distroy anything belonging to the primises giving Howard one half of all the produce raised by Binns on s[ai]d primises Howard agreeing to let Binns occupy the kitchen free of any charge except those specified in the foregoing article and Binns and mother or wife agree to work for Howard when ever called upon at a reasonable price.

       J. S. Howard
              his
Test   Aaron x Binns
    I Cain   mark

A Planter Views Black Freedom

"Correspondence," Records of the Bureaus for Refugees, Freedmen, and Abandoned Lands, Arkansas, Arkansas History Commission, Little Rock.

T. C. Flournoy was a white landowner in Arkansas County. His letter complaining to the Freedmen's Bureau illustrates how reluctant whites were to allow blacks even political or social freedom. His employees continued to be viewed as personal property, as Flournoy sought to control activities other than economic ones.

Cummins P.O.
Ark. Co. May 19, 1868
Genl. Smith

Sir

I had to leave Little Rock the next morning after seeing you and did not have time to make the writen statements you suggested. I take this opportunity to do so.

On Friday night the 9th May late at night my Freedmen and those of my neighbours were notified by a coloured messenger, that they must all assemble at the upper Jordan Plantation on the next day Saturday the 10th, to hear a speech from Maj. Hunt. And the messenger impressed upon them that all must be there, as something of importance was to take place. Upon this notice about half of my men employed in this Plantation (and I have 72 men) quit their work and went to the Jordan Place some ten miles distant. When they reached there, Capt. DeWolf the agent told them there was no meeting, and no speech to be made and they had done wrong to leave their work and that they must return to their home and their employment. And that they must not again leave their places of Employment upon any such notices. And when they did, they would be charged for the lost time. Capt. DeWolf's position and instruction to the Freedmen that assembled there had a good affect and they all returned to their Homes and work, seemingly much mortified at their folly, and say it should not occur again. I hope the Freedmen will adhere to this determination, as constant and attentive Labour is essential to make good crops of cotton. The crop prospects in the locality are splendid and a few more weeks constant work will finish them. And this the Freedmen seem determined in doing, if they are not disturbed or interrupted by such notices as that of Saturday the 10th. An order from you disapproving of such meetings and assemblys of the Freedmen upon any bodys notice will have a salutary effect, and add largely to the crop in this country.

Yours Respectfully
T. C. Flournoy.

Violence and the Freedmen

"Correspondence," Records of the Bureaus for Refugees, Freedmen, and Abandoned Lands, Arkansas, Arkansas History Commission, Little Rock.

The Bureau of Refugees, Freedmen, and Abandoned Lands was a government agency that started operations in Arkansas in 1865. Its primary role was to help blacks adjust to their new freedom. Often its officers had to protect blacks from the antagonism of whites and from efforts to restore some form of white social control. The following letters from bureau officers indicate the extent of the problems confronted.

Office BRF and AL
Lewisville, Fayette Co, Ark
August 23ᵈ 1868

Samuel M. Mills
1st Lieut 28th U.S. Infty.
Act. Ast. Adjt. Genl.

Lieut.

I have the honor to report for your consideration the state of affairs in this county.

During this month eight freedmen have been murdered by white men. Only one arrest has been made by the civil authorities. During the investigation of the case twenty-five men—friends of the party arrested—most of them armed, rode into town and filled the Court-house. They threatened that if the accused was committed to jail by the magistrate, that blood would be shed &c. &c. Their *evidence* cleared the accused.

On the night of the 21st a party of men went to a freedmans house, broke it open, searched it and took such things as they wanted. While the[y] were in the house the freedman came home. They shot at him several times when he shot one of the party & run. He came to my house on the night of the 22nd and told me the above narrated circumstances. I told him to go and stay in my smoke house for the present. In the morning I notified the magistrate and sheriff that he was there. They did not arrest him. On the night of the 22, about a dozen armed men surrounded my house and demanded the freedman. They searched the premises, my private apartments included, but could not find him, he escaped from the yard while they were there. Then left without otherwise molesting me *for the present.*

Mr. Hawkins who is building the school house here has been informed that it would be advisable for him to leave here immediately. There are a class of men who have arraid [*sic*] themselves against the law and swear that it shall not be executed. In orde[r] to protect the freedmen it will be necessary to have at least a company of U.S. Soldiers at this place.

I have been advised to leave the country until things get quiet. If I did so I anticipate that I would have to have a very long leave of absence.

Unless a detachment of soldiers are sent here I shall have to take leave or do as our *Circuit Judge* and others do in Columbia County—take to the woods at night.

> I am
> Very Respectfully
> Your Obdt. Servt.
> V. V. Smith.
> Agt. BRF & AL.

•　　•　　•

Bureau Refugees, Freedmen and Abandoned [Lands]
Office Superintendent Mississippi County
Osceola, Arkansas May 17, 1868

Brig. Genl C. H. Smith
Assistant Commissioner

General:

Again I have to record and report the malignant spirit that prevails in many sections of the state and the manner that it expressed itself last evening May 16th by burning the freedmen's church at this place. In the past month the Freedmen have been warned that the so called Ku Klucks would make the Union League a visit and kill the leaders P.C. The church was situated about one half mile from any building or residence also that distance from the traveled road and was so situated that the Freedmen's meetings could not disturb anyone. To show the building was intentionally fired, the fence near the house was removed. The church was owned and built by the Freedmen at a cost of four or five hundred dollars. They owned near one hundred at present in the same. Some two weeks since some party or parties broke windows, tables and committed other meanness in the building. It will be impossible to find and prove the guilt of any of the parties, yet they received encouragement from others who should be made to rebuild the Church. I would respectfully recommend that the town of Monroe or the county be required to rebuild the church within thirty days.

> I am Sir
> Very Respectfully
> Eli H. Mix
> Agent B.R.F. & A.L.

F. REPUBLICANS VERSUS DEMOCRATS DURING RECONSTRUCTION

The Republican Party that came to political power in Arkansas following the Civil War challenged the control over local politics that had been exercised by "The Family" through the antebellum era. In order to forge a coalition capable of maintaining power, the Republicans sought support from among blacks and the whites who had not been represented in the antebellum administrations. This support often required the handing out of governmental services or providing these various groups with such things as railroads, schools, and police protection. Services, however, cost money, thus opening the Republicans to charges of increasing taxes to levels that were too high. Given the general economic depression that encompassed the state after the war, the charge of exorbitant taxes was one readily accepted. The following documents illustrate the views Republicans and Democrats had of themselves and their opponents.

Conditions in Arkansas, March 1875

Charles Nordhoff, *The Cotton States in the Spring and Summer of 1875* (New York: D. Appleton & Co., 1876), 29–40.

In 1874, Charles Nordhoff, a Northern journalist and author, came to Arkansas as part of a trip across the South to report on local conditions. This document first illustrates the charges levied against the Republican Party that had come to power under Gov. Powell Clayton in June 1868. It is a catalog of Democratic accusations of fraud in government, a catalog that proved persuasive to most white voters. The document also indicates the growing tiredness in the North with Reconstruction and a willingness to accept a return of the Democratic Party to power as a means of ending the war once and for all.

The State of Arkansas celebrated on the 25th of March, 1875, a great deliverance. By proclamation of Governor Garland that day was kept as one of thanksgiving for the action of Congress, which, it is hoped and believed, restored the State to permanent and peaceful self-government. I arrived in Little Rock a few days before the holiday, and that day was singularly quiet. Banks and shops were mostly closed; many people went to church; there was turkey for dinner; and there were, among the older and substantial citizens, not a few heart-felt words of gratitude for quiet and peace, and the hope of prosperity. . . .

The truth is, it was time for strife to end. Nobody of either party who had anything, even his labor, to lose, could any longer afford it. Here are a few figures which prove it:

Arkansas has less than 650,000 people. It has about 120,000 voters.

These owed in 1868, when reconstruction began in this State, about $3,500,000, and had $319,000 in cash in their treasury. The debt was State debt. The counties owed little or nothing.

To-day, after seven years, the State owes at least $15,700,000 and most of the counties have debts of their own sufficient to make them bankrupt. And for this huge indebtedness, which amounts for State, counties, town, and school districts to probably $20,000,000 the people have nothing to show, except some miles of railroad, on which they must pay for their passage whenever they travel. There are no new public buildings; neither science or the arts have been advanced; the old State-house looks as dilapidated as when the reconstruction began, and has been changed in nothing except having its door-lintels mutilated that a Brooks cannon might be squeezed into the hall; the schools are almost all closed because the school fund was stolen; and Little Rock is unpaved, though the conquerors of 1868 issued nearly shinplasters enough to pave all the streets handsomely with the paper itself, and bonds enough besides to make dry crossings at the corners.

The State debt alone amounts to-day to more than $115 for every voter. State, county, township, and school debts, including scrip of all kinds, would probably bring the voters in debt $175 per head. And the whole of this prodigious burden has been laid upon an impoverished, and never very prosperous, people in seven years.

Arkansas was, in 1868, a tempting prize to speculators. It had a trivial debt, a handsome little sum in cash in the Treasury, hardly any railroads, and a people singularly innocent of political wiles. The young and enterprising men who then flocked in and seized on power, and who held it so many years, had had some experience in what we call "politics." "We showed them some new tricks," said one of them to me; "the damned fools didn't know a thing about organization. They just went around the state making stump-speeches, and thought that was politics. But that thing's played out."

The new *regime* framed a constitution admirably suited to their ends, of which I shall speak further on. And then they began the work of plunder with an act granting State aid bonds to railroads to the extent of 800 miles, at $15,000 per mile, or $10,000 for such roads as had also land-grants. Under this law 271 miles of road were built, of which the Fort Smith road is well built and well planned for 100 miles, and is to be completed. It has received $1,000,000 of bonds. The Memphis and Little Rock Company built 45 miles, and received $1,200,000 or $750,000 more than it should have got. The Ouachita Company built 28 miles, and got $600,000 or $180,000 more than it should have got. The Arkansas Central built 38 miles and got $1,350,000; under the law it was entitled to but $750,000. This was called Senator Dorsey's road. The Pine Bluff Company built 70 miles, and got $1,200,000, or $150,000 more than its share.

The whole issue of railroad aid bonds made by the State in less than four years amounts to $5,350,000. Many of the roads were not needed; all but the Fort Smith and the Memphis are unfinished, and will for some time remain so; $1,110,000 more bonds were issued than even the fragments of roads were entitled to; the roads were to pay the interest, but of course did not; and the State now owes the whole sum, and, when it can, must pay the interest as well as the principal. Citizens of Little Rock point out to a visitor the number of pleasant residences at the new or court end of the straggling town, which, they say, were built by the men who handled these bonds.

Next, in 1871, were issued $3,005,846 in levee bonds. The law authorizing this issue provided that no levees should be built except on the application of a majority of the property holders to be benefited, and then only in a specified way, and the land benefited was held by the payment of interest and principal of the bonds. Regular surveys were to be made, and competent engineers were to decide, after all, whether the levee should be built. In practice, one or two engineers and half a dozen contractors made a ring and built levees whenever they pleased; no formal petitions were required, no proper surveys made; logs and timber and even empty flour and beef barrels were crammed into the bank, and meantime the levee commissioner issued bonds whenever any body whom he knew asked for them, and actually kept no books to show to whom, for what work, or when they were issued. . . .

But these thefts are not nearly as amusing as the smaller ones. . . . In 1873, Faulkner County was formed out of fragments of surrounding counties. This making new counties was a custom of the reconstructors. They thus created new offices. The new Faulkner County had no debt. It had no public buildings, and has none yet, except an eight-by-ten court-house given it by a Methodist church. It contains 7000 people, and has a property valuation of about $900,000. Two young New Yorkers were appointed sheriff and county clerk by the governor. They collected the first year about $40,000 in taxes; and this being insufficient for their uses, they issued county scrip for $50,000 more. They collected the taxes in greenbacks, and turned them in in depreciated State scrip, some of which they bought at thirty-five cents on the dollar. They sold offices, released prisoners, engaged in fraudulent registration, and, finally, they departed with their plunder, and the State knows them no more. . . .

The reconstructors were wise in their generation. They not only robbed at wholesale and retail, but they took care to preserve their own supremacy. The constitution of 1868 gave the governor the appointment of almost all the local officers, even to the justices of the peace and registrars of elections. The governor, of course, selected his own adherents, and did not scruple to send them from Little Rock, sometimes a hundred miles away, into a strange county. So loosely was business conducted that when the new county of Howard was created, in 1873, an illiterate carpenter of Little Rock, being appointed county clerk, began his career by having county scrip printed before he even went down to take up his office, and issued the first of this scrip in Little Rock in payment for ambulance to take his family to Howard County. . . .

Under this monstrous system of centralization, as extreme as that of the later French empire, the ring had their adherents scattered all over the State. They absolutely controlled the elections; they ruled the people despotically. The governor was even careful to appoint, in many instances, local officers who did not live in the counties they were to rule, and who, of course, had no interest whatever in good government or in the decent administration of justice. . . .

The governor appointed the registrars of election, and they were actually manipulated to such an extent that the colored people were enticed away from their vocations for weeks before election-day, and gathered in crowds at barbecues and other camps.

Republicans Defend Themselves

Little Rock Daily Republican, September 18, 1874.

Republicans argued that Democratic charges of fraud and corruption were mere political propaganda. The following document comes from a Little Rock Republican newspaper during the gubernatorial campaign of 1874. It addresses many issues raised by the Democrats and defends the entire Republican program.

. . . We are impelled not only by a sense of duty, but in justice to the republican party to refute some charges made against us by our opponents. It is charged that the republican party is the author of high taxes in this state and that its administration is marked with more lavish and reckless expenditure of the public money than that of any which preceded it or followed it. To the end that the people may see how little truth there is in the charge, we have taken the trouble to ascertain the amount of taxes levied during the two years preceding the advent of the republican party to power. The tax for general revenue purposes, for the years 1866 and 1867, was as follows:

1866	$500,791.66
1867	278,089.80
Total	$778,881.46
1868	$341,979.37
1869	349,649.96
Total	$691,629.33

From the above statement, it will be seen that during the first two years the republican party were in charge of the state government it levied $87,252.13 less tax for general revenue purposes than the democratic administration that preceded it. When it is taken into consideration that, under the two years of republican rule alluded to, a deafmute institution and a blind asylum were built and the expense of supporting and maintaining the same paid out of the general revenue fund and that $160,000 of the same fund was used to subdue a Ku Klux rebellion, it may be doubted whether our opponents make anything by the comparison.

During the administration of Gov. Clayton state scrip never went below eighty cents [on the dollar] and at times was par. Under the administration of Elisha Baxter, the man who has won the admiration of the "white league," for the efficient manner in which he has conducted the finances of the state and the state government, state scrip never rose higher than sixty cents and has fallen as low as twenty-five cents. Where it stands today. These facts are only mentioned in passing that the public may judge for themselves which of the two administrations had the confidence of the people. Having compared two years of republican rule with two years of democratic rule, and finding the balance in our favor, let us make a comparison with that of Elisha Baxter. We have already seen that the general revenue tax for the years 1868–9 amounts in the aggregate to $691,629.33. Under the "economic administration" of Elisha Baxter the general revenue tax for the years 1873–4 is as follows:

1873	$1,024,987.93
1874	717,491.55
Total	$1,742,479.48

By deducting $691,629.33, levied for general revenue purposes, under the first two years of Governor Clayton's administration, from $1,742,479.48, the amount levied for the same purpose under the administration of Elisha Baxter, we find that *one million, fifty thousand, eight hundred and fifty dollars and fifteen cents* more tax was levied for general revenue purposes on "an oppressed and carpetbag ridden people," without a murmur by Elisha Baxter, than was in the same length of time under republican rule. . . .

"Knowledge and learning," so says the constitution of 1836, "generally differed through a community, *being essential to the preservation of a free government*, it shall be the duty of the general assembly to provide by law for the improvement of such lands as are or may hereafter be granted by the United States to this state for the use of schools and to apply any funds which may be raised from such lands, or from any other source, to the accomplishment of the object they are or may be intended." Now let us see how faithfully the democratic party observed this provision of the constitution. In the year 1827 congress granted Arkansas seventy-two sections of land, for the purpose of establishing a "seminary of learning." From the sale of these lands $18,432,000 was realized. The money has been squandered and no "seminary of learning" has been built. Having shown what became of a grant for educational purposes under democratic rule, let us see what a republican administration did with a grant of like character. Under an act giving to the different states a grant of land for the purpose of establishing "agricultural colleges," the state of Arkansas was entitled to 160,000 acres of land for which $135,000 was realized. With this money, and such donations as have been secured through the activity of the republican officials placed in charge thereof, a farm, costing $11,000, has been purchased, and a building, costing $130,000, has been erected thereon, and a endowment fund of $130,000 secured. At the time Elisha Baxter came into possession of the executive chair this institution was in a highly prosperous condition, with two hundred and thirty-two students in attendance. But we regret to say that under the administration of Elisha Baxter a change was made in the board of trustees, and from present appearances, it is soon likely to become an asylum where indigent survivors of the "lost cause" may be "pensioned off," and the youth of the country taught to hate the country that endowed the college. Having shown the difference between the two parties in relation to college, let us see the difference in relation to the "dissemination of knowledge," a thing the framers of the constitution of 1836 regarded as so "essential to the preservation of a free government." In a period of nearly thirty years, the democratic party erected, so Gov. Rector says in his message to the legislature of 1860, just twenty-six school-houses. In a period of four years, during all of which we had to combat a prejudice against free schools, the republican party erected eleven hundred and forty-six school-houses at a cost of $276,378. In addition to this, during the year 1869, it furnished 68,802 children with the benefit of a free common school education. In 1870, 107,908. In 1871, 109,309. In 1872, 93,633. Comparisons like these are odious but they are only so because the democratic party are opposed to free schools.

For the purpose of showing the utter fruitlessness of the democratic party, we desire to call the attention of the public to the fact that in the year 1841 the congress of the United States granted to the state of Arkansas 500,000 acres of land, the proceeds of which were to be applied to building "roads, railroads, bridges canals, and the improvement of water courses." . . . Instead of appropriating the money to some great work of improvement, as other states did, and to which a similar grant was made, it was first, in violation of the grant, distributed equally among the counties and second, by subsequent legislation, loaned to favorites and irresponsible persons. . . .

The republican party of Arkansas has much to be proud of. Organized, as it was, at the close of a wicked and uncalled for rebellion, ostracised as its members were, hated, maligned, and despised for its loyalty to the [national] government and prompt recognition of the rights of the colored men—its magnanimity has known no bounds. Under its reign, over six hundred miles of railroads were constructed. Under its advent into power, eleven hundred and forty-six school houses were constructed and one hundred thousand children annually received the benefits of a free school education, and life and property received a greater protection than during any period since the organization of the government. While it may not have been all that its friends would have desired, and while it may not have accomplished all that was expected, an era of prosperity, such as was never known before in the state, kept pace with its career of power. Its deeds of usefulness, and acts of fidelity to the best interests of the people, are no more to be compared to those of the democratic party than light is to darkness or loyalty to treason. It has committed no act to mantle the cheeks of its members with shame, and left a heritage to the people of Arkansas, which, if preserved, should embalm it in the memory of its loyal citizens.

FOR FURTHER READING

Of all the periods in Arkansas history, that from 1860 to 1874 has attracted the most students and writers. The earliest overview of the period was provided by David Y. Thomas in *Arkansas in War and Reconstruction, 1861–1874* (Little Rock: United Daughters of the Confederacy, 1926). His story has now largely been supplanted by Michael Dougan's *Confederate Arkansas* (Tuscaloosa: University of Alabama Press, 1976), especially with regard to the social, economic, and political life of the state during the war. The most recent overview of the war years is Thomas A. DeBlack, *With Fire and Sword: Arkansas, 1861–1874* (Fayetteville: University of Arkansas Press, 2003).

Several books provide insight into specific issues related to the Civil War. James M. Woods's *Rebellion and Realignment: Arkansas's Road to Secession* (Fayetteville: University of Arkansas Press, 19897) examines the course of the state to disunion and war. Focusing on changes engendered by the war is Carl H. Moneyhon's *The Impact of the Civil War and Reconstruction on Arkansas: Persistence in the Midst of Ruin* (Baton Rouge: Louisiana State University Press, 1994; repr., Fayetteville: University of Arkansas Press, 2002).

The military history of Arkansas in the Civil War was first written of in John Dimitry and John Harrell's *Confederate Military History* (Atlanta: Confederate Publishing Company, 1899), which devoted volume ten to

Arkansas affairs. A more recent overview of military operations in Arkansas is Mark K. Christ, ed., *Rugged and Sublime: The Civil War in Arkansas* (Fayetteville: University of Arkansas Press, 1994). An older but still useful study is *Military Operations in Missouri and Arkansas, 1861–1865* (Ann Arbor: Xerox University Microfilms, 1958), a two-volume study by Thomas A. Belser Jr. John Ferguson's *Arkansas and the Civil War* (Little Rock: Pioneer Press, 1957) offers original essays on various aspects of the war in the state as well as military reports from the *Official Records* (US War Department, *The War of the Rebellion: A Compilation of the Official Records of the Union and Confederate Armies,* 128 vols. [Washington, DC: G.P.O., 1880–1901]) on major campaigns in the state.

There has been much written on specific battles and on military units from the state. William A. Shea and Earl J. Hess, *Pea Ridge: Civil War Campaign in the West* (Chapel Hill: University of North Carolina Press, 1992); William L. Shea, *Fields of Blood: The Prairie Grove Campaign* (Chapel Hill: University of North Carolina Press, 2009); and Mark K. Christ, *Civil War Arkansas, 1863: The Battle for a State* (Norman: University of Oklahoma Press, 2010) offer superb modern views of the battlefield. Older studies that remain useful include *Steele's Retreat from Camden and the Battle of Jenkins Ferry* (Little Rock: Arkansas Civil War Centennial Commission, 1967) by Edwin Bearss; Cal Collier, *They'll Do to Tie It, 3rd Arkansas Infantry Regiment, C. S. A.* (Little Rock: J. D. Warren, 1959); and Wesley Thurman Leeper, *Rebels Valiant, Second Arkansas Mounted Rifles, Dismounted* (Little Rock: Pioneer Press, 1964). Battle as seen by a contemporary may be sampled in William Baxter's contemporary *Pea Ridge and Prairie Grove* (Cincinnati: Poe and Hitchcock, 1864).

Many Arkansans left memoirs of their experiences in the war. The nature of this bibliography prevents an exhaustive list, but *With the Light Guns in '61–65* (Little Rock: Central Printing Co., 1903), reminiscences of life in an Arkansas artillery battery by William Woodruff, whose father was the editor of the *Arkansas Gazette*, is typical and possesses the best literary merits of any of this genre.

It should be remembered that Arkansas provided more Union troops to the war than any other Confederate state except Tennessee. A contemporary view of Union sentiment during the war is A. W. Bishop's *Loyalty on the Frontier* (St. Louis, MO: R. P. Studley & Co., 1863).

Thomas S. Staples's *Reconstruction in Arkansas, 1862–1874* (New York:

Columbia University, 1927) is a study of Reconstruction in the interpretive school, based on the work of William A. Dunning of Columbia University. In general condemnatory of the efforts of the Republican Party at both the national and state levels, this study is countered by two fitting with the revisionist tradition: Martha Ann Ellenburg's *Reconstruction in Arkansas* (Ann Arbor, MI: Xerox University Microfilms, 1957) and George Thompson's *Arkansas and Reconstruction: The Influence of Geography, Economics, and Personality* (Port Washington, NY: Kennikat Press, 1976). A contemporary defense of the Reconstruction program is Powell Clayton's *The Aftermath of the Civil War in Arkansas* (New York: Neale Publishing Co., 1915). The best look at the conflict that ended the period of Reconstruction is *The Brooks-Baxter War* by John M. Harrell (St. Louis: Slawson Printing Co., 1893). These studies primarily focus on the politics of Reconstruction. A useful overview of the struggle of African Americans for freedom in this period may be found in Randy Finley, *From Slavery to Uncertain Freedom: The Freedmen's Bureau in Arkansas, 1865–1869* (Fayetteville: University of Arkansas Press, 1996).

CHAPTER V

Arkansas and the New South, 1875–1900

INTRODUCTION

The end of Reconstruction returned Arkansas to a normal relationship with the nation and ended fifteen years of turmoil that had been sparked by secession. Arkansans discovered that during those years the rest of America had changed and that their state's economy and society had to change also if they were to catch up. The United States had become more industrial, more urban, tied together by an extensive system of railroads. Arkansas was still agrarian—its cities little more than oversized towns—and lacked adequate transportation. The shift in the rest of the nation had brought problems. Laborers found themselves losing power and status, unable to deal with the large industries that employed them. The creation of a national market hurt many farmers, who were forced to compete not only with the produce of farmers throughout America but also with those of other nations. The traditional roles and occupations of women became less meaningful within the new society. The problems seemed minor, however, compared with the prosperity produced by the new system. Throughout the South, political and business leaders overlooked the difficulties as they rushed to share the wealth of the industrial system by creating a New South. Arkansans, like their counterparts elsewhere, did not hesitate in trying to enter the new era.

Those who argued for a New South wanted their section to imitate the economic life of the North. They had enough of agrarianism and the rural life, and they dreamed of a landscape covered with cities, factories, and thriving commerce. Whereas the planter and the politician had been the heroes of the antebellum years, the businessman and the developer became the leaders of the New South. These businessmen boosted the state throughout the nation, encouraging outside investment, construction of factories, immigration, and the development of natural resources. The railroads that had been given impetus during Reconstruction had their heyday during this period. Between 1880 and 1890 railroad mileage more than tripled, and almost every major town had its depot and steel ties with the rest of the state. The railroads, the lifeblood of the state's economy, became the most powerful political interest in the state during these years and developed almost without controls. Despite acquiring aid from the state in the form of financial help and tax breaks, the developers of the New South did not believe the government should attempt to regulate them. While Arkansas moved closer to industrialization and urbanization, the end of the nineteenth century would find the dream of the New South unfulfilled. Northerners, whom the boosters had sought as investors, had little interest in creating economic rivals to their own manufacturing firms. As a result, the money that came into the state usually went for the development of the state's resources, especially its timber and minerals, but not for the production of finished products. Industries tapped the wealth of the state, but the profits acquired from manufacturing remained outside.

For most Arkansans the New South period brought about change, often to their disadvantage. No one felt more pressure than the farmer. Mechanization, the opening of the local market to outside goods with the construction of the railroads, and competition for credit all undercut the farmer's economic position. More farm products meant lower prices, but the machinery necessary to farm and the credit used to prepare the next year's crops kept going up. At an economic loss, the shift of an industrial society also diminished the farmer's status as it increased the importance of the businessman. Used to thinking of themselves as the backbone of the nation, farmers in the 1880s and 1890s searched for explanations for their decline. Arkansas became the center of agrarian dissatisfaction and gave birth to organizations such as the Agricultural Wheel and the Brothers of Freedom. These groups encouraged cooperation among farmers and criticized the people that they believed were responsible for their plight, especially middlemen. Their protests finally led farmers into the Populist political movement in the 1890s. Despite their actions, the farmers found that the problems created by industrialization and urbanization were too difficult to be solved by the methods they chose. Into the twentieth century, agricultural depression would typify the condition of Arkansas's rural population.

Conditions for workers on the railroads and in the extractive industries that came to the state after 1875 placed these people in positions as bad as the farmers'. They did not share industrial prosperity but suffered through these years from low wages and terrible working conditions. The new industries operated for profits, not for the welfare of their workers; and the companies prospered, among other ways, by limiting the wages of their employees and restricting expenditures upon work facilities. When the individual laborer confronted a large mining concern, one that usually had its offices and owners out of state, the worker was unable to change the situation. In Arkansas, as in the rest of the nation, many workers thus tried to organize themselves into unions. The most effective of these was the Knights of Labor, which was effective in obtaining concessions from the Southwestern Railroad after a series of strikes in 1885. Many factors, however, prevented effective organization of the workforce. The availability of large numbers of nonunion workers who could be used to break strikes made many employed workers reluctant to join unions. The use of convict labor, especially in coal mining, also curtailed efforts at organization. In addition to the failure to organize, the industries that came to Arkansas generally did not require skilled labor and thus did not have to pay high wages, further hampering industrial workers in Arkansas from obtaining a portion of the New South's wealth.

Changing roles for women indicate the extensive nature of the modifications in society brought about in the New South. Especially in towns, more women entered the labor force as teachers, secretaries, clerks, and even professionals. The result was greater social freedom and an increase in demands by women for more control over their lives and a more expansive role in society. Excluded by tradition from many occupations, women demonstrated an increased agitation to be allowed entrance into whatever jobs they sought. Their efforts to obtain the vote indicated their desire to participate actively in political decision-making. Much of what the women sought would not be achieved in the nineteenth century, but the changes brought about in the New South would set in motion the demand for greater equality that would continue into the present day.

Of all the groups in Arkansas, none found the New South more disappointing than blacks. Through education and hard work, black Arkansans had prepared themselves for an equal place in society, but agricultural depression, industrial upheaval, and the development of ideas of scientific racism worked to frustrate them. In the 1890s, rather than accept black advances, whites began to reduce the place of blacks in the community. Fearing that a combination of blacks and farmers in protest movements might take over state government, Democrats obtained from the legislature in 1891 the first laws designed to prevent blacks from voting, and by 1893 an amendment to the constitution required the payment of a poll tax by all voters. More degrading in many respects was the move by whites in the 1890s to segregate blacks in public places such as railroad cars and public facilities. For blacks, the 1890s marked their relegation to second-class citizenship and a delay in their advancement to equality.

By 1900, the boosterism and the promise of development that characterized the years following Reconstruction had moved Arkansas along toward modernity. Many of the promises of the New South remained unfulfilled, yet the changes that had been accomplished altered the life of Arkansans.

A. THE NEW SOUTH SPIRIT INVADES ARKANSAS

Following Reconstruction, most Arkansans were ready to put the war behind them, to restore peace and prosperity. The best way to do that, many felt, was with economic expansion, and that would be achieved primarily by attracting the interest of outsiders who might invest in Arkansas. Boosterism emerged in the 1870s and 1880s, a movement to show to the nation that Arkansans were through with war and were now prepared to exploit their state's economic advantages.

Arkansas Life after Reconstruction

New York Times, May 31, 1874.

On May 31, 1874, the *New York Times* published a letter from Arkansas describing the state's people at the end of Reconstruction. It is useful in its description of conditions in the state, but it also provides insights into the way Arkansans viewed the potential of the state. This letter may be seen both as an accurate assessment of what existed and as a boaster's view of what might be as well.

Little Rock, May 25, 1874

Perhaps no other State in the Union has been more often written about than Arkansas. This is also true of its inhabitants. Yet little that is true is really known of the State, and no other people have been more misunderstood. It has for years been a favorite legend at the East that Arkansas was the home of every outlaw and renegade in the land, that the only law was Lynch law, and that the use of the pistol and knife was the daily custom and only recreation of all classes of its citizens. These stories are simply wild exaggerations. It is true that every one goes armed. Since the recent contest, pistols are to be seen worn in the belt by the judge and the minister of the Gospel, as well as by the planter living in remote and dangerous mountain districts. Such being the case it is but natural that shootings should be more frequent than they ought to be, but they occur chiefly in places of bad repute. People who mind their own business and do not visit gambling saloons and places of a like nature, are just as safe in Little Rock, Argenta, or Pine Bluff, as they would be in New York or Boston. . . .

The tone of society in the larger towns is not essentially different from that found in other portions of the country, but there is more freedom of action and speech allowed, and women are treated with far more deference and respect. Here in Little Rock, during the very worst stage of the recent (political) troubles, ladies on the streets were never interfered with, and it is a common incident to see a band of young roughs who would shoot at a man upon very slight provocation, respectfully get off the sidewalk and out of the way of a lady who may be passing. Houses and household establishments are generally on a smaller scale than in the West, the financial distresses occasioned by the war of the rebellion having substituted marked plainness for the somewhat gorgeous style of living which prevailed twelve or fifteen years ago. Among the natives of the State the size of a man's dwelling or his bank account does not materially affect his social standing. As an example may be cited the case of Mr. Chester Ashley, who lived in almost regal style, maintained a band of musicians organized from his slaves, housed his many horses in stalls of mahogany, and could ride all day without reaching the limit of his own plantation. Since the war his family have occupied a few rooms at the top of a humble house, without apparent or real change of social status. In Little Rock society is very sharply divided into two classes— the natives, and the Northern people who have settled here since the war. In other places, except perhaps in Pine Bluff, all classes mingle freely.

As a rule the planters live more simply than their fellows in the Southeastern States. Throughout the year they are dependent for their plantation supplies upon store-keepers and brokers, who make advances of provisions to them on their cotton crop. Consequently most of the planter's money comes to him in a lump at the selling season. The greater portion of the houses occupied by the smaller farmers and planters are of logs, the furniture being of plainest and most substantial material. These people fully understand the importance of education. Their children are sent regularly to school, many of the girls finishing at one of the Eastern academies. This is particularly the case among the people of the north-west. In that section it is not unusual for the traveler to hear issuing from a humble but comfortably-built log-house the tones of a well-played piano; or to find in some snug corner room a book-case, filled with a well-selected library. In the mountain districts, on the contrary, the mass of the people are poor and ignorant; many of them are unable to read; and, isolated as they are, they have to rely for political and other information upon a few unprincipled leaders. They are opinionated and independent almost to lawlessness. Among them is to be found the extreme type of border character represented in the "Arkansas Traveler" and other compositions of a like character.

The Cost of Living and Rate of Wages

In consequence of the contest for the Governorship which has just closed, the cost of living here in Little Rock is at present high beyond all comparison. Strangers are, particularly, required to pay three prices for everything. All the hotels are conducted on the European plan, and from twelve to fifteen dollars a week is demanded for a very ordinary room, without board. A simple, and not very palatable breakfast of eggs and ham (beefsteak is an unheard-of luxury) costs a dollar. For a dinner of hard beef, salt pork, potatoes, and corn-bread the modest price of $2 is demanded, and supper is charged for at the same rate as breakfast. These high prices, however, are as nothing compared to the demands for the "small things of life." A shave at the hands of a negro with a hand of iron costs thirty cents. Boot-blacks are insulted when offered less than a quarter, and the same amount is insisted upon for the washing of a shirt. People who like to drink pure water will do well to give Little Rock a wide berth. The water here is taken directly from the Arkansas River, and with it a disagreeably liberal allowance of mud. Other drinkables cost four times the price they do at New-York. Whisky is thirty cents, ale fifty, brandy seventy-five, and Rhine wine forty cents a glass. House-rents, too, are very high. A small house on an obscure street, costs five and six hundred dollars a year. In the country living is dear, but not anything like as high as at the capital. The salaries paid are in proportion to the rates of living. An ordinary clerk receives from one hundred to one hundred and fifty-dollars per month. Average book-keepers are paid $2,500 to $3,000 a year, and good men receive as high as $4,000. Good bricklayers demand from five to six dollars a day, carpenters from three and a half to five, blacksmiths from four to six, and common laborers in the cities and large villages, from one and a half to two dollars a day.

Characteristics of the People

The one great quality of the people of Arkansas which first impresses the traveler is their open-hearted generosity. They are hospitable to a fault. For a stranger, who is properly introduced, nothing is too good, and no trouble too great. Their courage, too, is unquestionable, as any one who saw them during the late disturbances would readily acknowledge. At the same time they are most apt to take offense without adequate cause. As an illustration of this may be mentioned an incident that occurred here a day or two since. A gentleman, who was a stranger in Little Rock, went to the desk of one of the hotels and asked if he could buy a postage-stamp. The clerk replied that he had none, whereupon a bystander took out his pocket-book and graciously handed the gentleman a number of stamps, telling him to help himself. The stranger took two of them, and, thanking the gentleman for his kindness, handed back the remainder of the stamps and six cents to pay for those he had taken. But the pennies had scarcely been placed in the hands of the other when he flung them on the floor, and exclaimed excitedly, "If you were not a d——d fool, Sir you would know that an Arkansian does not peddle postage stamps." No apologies would be accepted and the irate man walked out of the hotel muttering about his offended honor. The stories which have been circulated in the East to the effect that Northern people were badly treated by the natives is denied by some of the best-known gentlemen here. The men of the State cherish no hard feelings even against those who fought in the Union Army. On the other hand, the women of Little Rock pretend to look down on those who come from the Union States, and they refuse to visit Northern ladies.

The Needs of Arkansas

Nearly everything requiring mechanical construction is imported from other States. For wagons alone Arkansas pays annually a quarter of a million dollars, every cent of which could be kept in the State. There are not a dozen cart shops in the entire country, and the plow factories are far from being commensurate with the wants of the people.

Immigration is at present the one great need of Arkansas. The State is a large one, and so sparsely inhabited that even along the lines of the railroads tens of miles of country can be traversed without meeting a sign of human life. The population of the State does not exceed 600,000. The other great wants of the State are more schools, a better system of public instruction, a reformed Constitution, and honest office holders. Very many inducements are now being held out to immigrants and it is understood that still further efforts in the same direction are soon to be made by the State Government. Improved lands, of which 500,000 acres were given in 1841 to the State by the General Government, were selected with great care and comprised the best lands when unsold. A portion of these lands is still subject to entry. They can be bought from the State at $1.25 per acre annually, at six percent. Of the swamp of overflowed lands of the State there remain unsold about 1,000,000 acres, divided into two classes. The first class comprises those lying within six miles of a navigable stream, and are sold at seventy-five cents per acre. The second-class tracts sell at fifty cents an acre, and are situated at a greater distance than six miles from a navigable stream. These swamp lands are among the finest lumber districts in the world, but are not fit for habitation during certain portions of the year. With all these varied advantages of soil, climate, and cheap lands, there appears to be no reason why Arkansas, with a stable form of government, and a greater regard for human life among her citizens should not become the leading State in the South-west.

Address at the Opening of the Arkansas Building at the World's Columbian Exposition, Chicago, May 1, 1893

Mitchell Collection, UALR Center for Arkansas History and Culture, Little Rock.

James Mitchel was a prominent Democratic politician from Little Rock and editor of the *Arkansas Democrat*. At the Chicago World's Fair in 1893, he gave one of the addresses at the opening of the Arkansas Pavilion. Mitchel summed up the progress that boosters believed had been made by the state since Reconstruction. What had been accomplished was not enough, however, and he reflects the booster spirit in his appeal for even more aid from outsiders in pushing Arkansas forward.

We have assembled, ladies and gentlemen, to formally open to the public this building. It is especially fitting that we perform that task on this day, the anniversary of the admission of the State into the Federal Union.

Fifty-seven years ago to-day, (June 15, 1836) when Andrew Jackson was completing his second term, the Territory of Arkansas became the State of Arkansas. That is a considerable period in the life of a man, but in the history of a State or nation it is a very brief span. I do not propose to speak at length of Arkansas, her history, her great natural advantages, or her society and her people. In wealth and population and increase in her taxful values she has exhibited a wonderful progress in the last decade.

The census of 1890 discloses the fact that in the last decade she outstripped all the Southern States except Florida in her percentage of increase in population, while the percentage of increase in taxable values was exceeded only by Texas and Florida. The percentage of increase in population for the decade ending in 1890 was 40.37 percent, while the increase in taxable values was 102 percent. In her trade and commerce, her growth in manufacturing and mining, in the development of her agriculture, in her schools and colleges, and especially in the free common school system of the state, there has been a corresponding progress and advancement. . . .

It is not worthwhile to recount the struggles and difficulties we encountered in the erection of this building. They belong to the past. But it is a source of just pride and hearty congratulations to every citizen

---

of the State that we are here, with our sisters of the Union, in this great assemblage of the States and Nations of the world, the greatest spectacle of the kind since the birth of time. As citizens, we are proud of the progress and advancement made by the State in the past, and we look confidently and hopefully to the future. Nature has been bountiful and lavish in her gifts to us. With a sunny and delightful climate, where the extremes of heat and cold are unknown, and yet where we have all the advantages of well defined seasons, with a soil that yields graciously and bountifully to the labors of the husbandman; with nearly four thousand miles of navigable rivers; with a greater area of hardwood timber than is found in any State in the Union; with vast deposits of coal, iron, zinc, manganese, antimony, chalk, marble, onyx; with lime-stone, slate, granite and the celebrated novaculite of oilstone, the most valuable in the world; with a fruit belt that produces the finest apples in the world— apples that have taken the first prizes at the great fruit contests of the country, including the Wilder medal at the pomological contest in Boston; with far-famed and health giving mineral waters—including the Baden-Baden of America, the Hot Springs of Arkansas, with mountains, foot hills, valleys, plains and rich alluvial lands—a soil that produces in rich profusion everything that is grown in a temperate or semitropical climate—such a country is Arkansas, the "Crystal State." We are proud of it, proud of its history, its traditions, progress and advancement along the lines of improvement. We welcome the capitalist and the home-seeker, and invite them to go with us into partnership with the coming prosperity that is our certain heritage.

B. AGRICULTURE AND THE NEW SOUTH

The New South boosters wanted to make the South more like the North —to introduce industry and bring about urbanization. Agriculture, however, remained the major component of the state's economy throughout the nineteenth century, and there was little progress in that sector. For the former slaves, sharecropping and tenantry replaced their old place in the labor force, and the new system removed the efficiency and planning that were two of the few good things about the old plantation system. For the white small farmers, shortages of capital forced increasing numbers into a type of indebtedness in which merchants or bankers provided supplies or money in return for a lien or mortgage on the coming crop. The result of sharecropping, tenantry, and the lien system was continued emphasis upon the production almost solely of cotton, which destroyed the soil and diminished the productivity of the farmer.

A Farmer Looks at His Problems

Russellville Democrat, October 18, 1883.

The letter of J. T. Wharton to the *Russellville Democrat* provides testimony of the frustration of farmers in Arkansas in the 1880s. It captures the feelings of these people, the belief in their own value, and the constant questioning of how they had come to the point of poverty. Wharton's critique of the system would be at the heart of almost every farm movement of the era.

Illinois Township

October 15.—I notice your correspondent from Baker's Creek does not feel quite sure that the order of the Brotherhood of Freedom will result in any benefits to the farmers.

There appears to be an idea prevalent among the nonproducers and capitalists that the farmers will not hold together long enough to accomplish anything, and that there can be no unity of action among laboring people. Whether this is true, remains to be seen, and if true, the farmer may as well sell his lands for what they will bring and become the vassal of a rich man without further effort.

Our best farmers work hard year after year and after supporting their families in the most economical manner, they have nothing left at the end of the year wherewith to school their children or increase the fertility of their land and the laborer is scarcely able to keep the wolf from the door.

While this is the lot of the farmer, the merchant lives comfortably, if not in luxury; builds his brick houses and grows rich; railroads declare large dividends in largely watered stocks; wholesale and commission merchants grow into millionaires; bank and manufacturing companies make fabulous sums of money; lawyers wear fine clothes, and officers of the government live in elegance and ease.

This is pre-eminently an agricultural country and the farmer ought to be the most prosperous and independent man in the world; and he and the laborer begin to inquire: Why this condition of things? And these efforts at organization are healthy signs "that there is life in the old land yet." For destroy the whole race of merchants, bankers, lawyers, politicians, and tricksters and a single year will produce an average crop of new ones, but destroy the sturdy yeomanry of a country and you doom the country to decay. When once destroyed they have never yet been reproduced in any country.

I am not one of those who believe the world owes any man a living, not by any manner of means. The world owes a man just what he earns and no more. "By the sweat of thy face shalt thou eat bread." But when able, industrious people lack the necessaries and even comforts of life in a country like this, it is because there is no fair division of labor.

The United States government every three months makes a check by draft for $700,000 to Vanderbilt to pay interest on his bonds. $2,800,000 a year, and this is only part of his income.

I do not believe it would have been possible for Vanderbilt, Gould, Sage, Dillion, or any of the hundreds of millionaires of this country to have acquired this immense wealth if the farmers and laborers who produced all this had a fair showing in the fruits of their toil. The government literally legislated this wealth into the hands of these men by exempting them from taxation and granting them franchises and fat contracts, while the farmer and laborer is burdened with taxation to pay it all. Give the farmer a fair start at the beginning of the race and an equal chance in the course and he will come out all right in the end, but the capitalist has so long had the advantage that it becomes necessary that the farmer should have a little "Protection" to put him on equal footing.

J. T. Wharton

The Patrons of Husbandry and Politics

Crawford Bulletin, June 25, 1874.

One of the first farm organizations to appear in Arkansas was the Patrons of Husbandry, the Grange. It was not supposed to be a political organization. The following editorial from a Grange newspaper in Van Buren County shows, however, that members were not content to allow conditions to continue unchanged. This article provides clues as to how the Patrons of Husbandry viewed the farm situation, American life, and themselves.

The Power of the Patrons of Husbandry

So long as we have these opposing political parties in our country, the farmers organization can, if they will, be an important element in our body politic. Politics never can and never will purify themselves. We have seen this in the masterly efforts of the Republican party for the past two or three sessions of the National Congress, and their signal and sad failure to accomplish the good end proposed. Unless political parties are purified in some way, and compelled to put forward good men for official positions, the country is in imminent danger of losing its free government. The natural tendency of governments, is toward centralization of power. Political parties, as they have existed for many years past, in our nation, care but little for the spirit of free government, per se, but are chiefly concerned for their retention of power and place. These parties are led by corrupt men, and we can hope for no permanent reform in our public affairs until these leaders are deposed and good men substituted. One of the primary motives that prompted the organization of the granges was a purification of political parties. This is a noble and praiseworthy motive, and the accomplishment of this alone, would demand of the people of America unbounded thanks and never ceasing gratitude. To accomplish this great good, it was essentially necessary, the order of Patrons should be nonpolitical. As a foundation for this feature in the order the constitution provides that neither religion nor *politics* should even be discussed, and no farmer should be refused admission because of his opinions on these two subjects. But this provision was but the foundation. The superstructure to be erected upon it was to grow out of the teachings of the masters. We much fear the masters of the granges are sadly neglecting their duty in this regard, or do not fully understand the whole scope and meaning of being "nonpolitical." In our humble judgement, it was not meant merely, that political opinions should be no test of membership, and that political questions should not be discussed in the granges, but that it means further, that the organizations should keep aloof from political campaigns, and reserve to themselves the choice of candidates, put forward by the two political parties, with reference to the capacity and fitness of the man or men without regard to their political opinions or afilliations. Such being the case the political parties, earnestly desiring success, instead of resorting to chicanery and trickery in their nominations would vie with each other in putting out their best men for all the offices to be filled, so as to secure the support of the farmers of the country. The Patrons holding the balance of power could command the situation, and would be a power behind the throne greater than the throne itself. They would not only, in effect, dictate nominations, but would carry all elections. Then they could break down monopolies, eradicate corruption from official places, purify political parties, and arrest the dangerous tendency we now behold to centre all power in the central or Federal government. Then, indeed, would all power not only be "inherent in the people," but at each election they would make that power felt throughout the length and breadth of the land. With hearts uninfluenced by party passion, their minds would be untrammelled, their reason unclouded, and with an unerring certainty of judgement, they could select the best men and could easily apply the Jeffersonian rule, "Is he capable? Is he honest?" Then would we have the long-needed "civil service reform." This reform that civil service has utterly failed to secure to us, will come to us from the hands of the patrons of Husbandry. The bone and sinew of the nation would then have given us what the brain had failed to give us. Is not this a destiny to be courted? Is it not a power to be longed for? Will the farmers throw it away when it is in such easy grasp? Can they afford to let legislation run wild with their interests, as it has done for years past, squandering their treasure, and lavishly bestowing their public lands upon private railroad and other corporations? All this they throw away as soon as they enter the political arena. When they take a prominent part in political conventions, put forward candidates who are not as capable as those already in the field only for the purpose of opposing, they prostitute their high destiny and sink to the level of an oath-bound political conclave. Cannot the reflecting farmers of our county see the fatal mistake made in the nomination of Judge Sangster? Is he as capable as Gen. Thomason to perform the high and important duties devolving upon a member of a convention called to frame a fundamental law? He is fully as honest, but honesty is not the only requisite for the position. All should be equally honest; but an All-wise God has seen fit to give some of his creatures ten talents, and to others but two. It is no reflection upon Judge Sangster to vote against him because of his incompetency. For the position of county judge Sangster has shown himself fitted, but his own good sense should inform him that more information and capacity are needed in making a constitution.

Song of the Agricultural Wheel

Agrarian Reform Organizations, General Microfilm Collection, Arkansas History Commission, Little Rock.

In 1882, another farm protest movement emerged in Arkansas, this one known as the Wheel. Spawned by agricultural problems in Prairie County, the Wheel rapidly spread across the state. By 1884, leaders claimed almost seven thousand members. Songs were a part of protest then, as they would be in later movements—used at meetings to promote group spirit. The following song was one circulated among members in Independence County around 1884. It not only served as entertainment, but contained the Wheel's interpretation of problems in contemporary Arkansas.

There are ninety and nine that mortgaged a way
In want and hunger and cold
To the one merchant Every Day
and be happy with goods and Gold.
The ninety and nine in their homes so bar
The one in Merchandice so fair
They toil in their fields—the ninety & nine
for the fruit of our Mother Earth
They did and drive in rain and shine
to gain their treasures of Earth
And the Wealth of other Sturdy hands
Goes to the hands of one in Merchandice
It flows from the sweat of their brow
The cotton does bloom
The merchant says come farmer
in my books there is Room
and the ninety and nine their crops is short in the fall

And the one Merchant sayes
Come farmer I must have t'all
They stand firm and true
I must have it boys I've carried you through.

The Farmers' Alliance

Wylie B. W. Heartsill Papers, Special Collections, University of
Arkansas at Little Rock.

The last major farm movement in Arkansas in the nineteenth century was the Farmers' Alliance. The views of its members reflected
the thought of previous farm groups. The following document is
the Alliance Constitution, adopted at the state meeting in 1890.

Constitution and By-Laws of the Farmers' State Alliance of Arkansas. As
Amended at Dover, Ark., August 19, 1890

Declaration of Purposes.

Whereas. The general condition of our country imperatively demands
unity of action on the part of the laboring classes, reformation in economy,
and the dissemination of principles best calculated to encourage and foster
agricultural and mechanical pursuits, encouraging the toiling masses—
leading them in the road to prosperity, and providing a just and fair remuneration of labor, a just exchange for our commodities and the best means
of securing to the laboring classes, the greatest amount of good. We hold
to the principle that all monopolies are dangerous to the best interest of
our country, tending to enslave a free people and subvert and finally overthrow the great principles purchased to the fathers of American liberty.
We, therefore, adopt the following as our declaration of principles:

1st. To labor for the education of the agricultural classes in the science
of economical government, in a strictly non-partisan spirit, and to bring
about a more perfect union of said classes.

2nd. That we demand equal rights to all and special favors to none.

3rd. To endorse the motto: "In things essentially, unity; and in all
things charity."

4th. To develop a better state, mentally, morally, socially, and
financially.

5th. To constantly strive to secure entire harmony and good will to all mankind and brotherly love among ourselves.

6th. To suppress personal, local, sectional, and national prejudices; all unhealthful rivalry, and all selfish ambition.

7th. The brightest jewels which it garners are the tears of the widows and orphans, and its imperative commands are to visit the homes where lacerated hearts are bleeding; to assuage the sufferings of a brother or sister; bury the dead, care for the widows and educate the orphans; to exercise charity toward offenders; to construe words and deeds in their most favorable light, granting honesty of purpose and good intentions to others, and to protect the principles of the Farmers' State Alliance until death. Its laws are reason and equity, its cardinal doctrines inspire purity and thought and life, its intention is, "on earth, peace, and good-will to man."

C. LABOR IN THE NEW SOUTH

The industries that developed in Arkansas during the 1880s and 1890s were primarily extractive ones. Coal mining and the timber industry simply exploited the state's rich natural resources and then shipped its raw products elsewhere for processing. For the labor force this was unfortunate, since neither of the chief industries required skilled labor. Because the state's industrial concerns could draw upon a large pool of unskilled labor, the wages they paid tended to remain low. It was in an effort to better wages and working conditions that industrial laborers attempted to organize during this period, although their efforts were generally fruitless. The following documents indicate something about the condition of labor in Arkansas in the latter part of the nineteenth century.

Working on the Arkansas Railroads

"Investigation of Labor Troubles in Missouri, Arkansas, Kansas, Texas, and Illinois," House Reports, 49th Congress, 2d sess. (ser. 2502), 404–7.

This document is the testimony before a congressional committee investigating the strike against the Iron Mountain Railroad in 1884. James Yates, a member of the Knights of Labor, went out on strike and lost his job as a result. The strike was finally broken, with nothing accomplished by the union. Yates's testimony illustrates conditions among workers in Arkansas during this period, as well as their attitudes toward their situation and the companies for which they worked.

JAMES YATES sworn and examined.

By the Chairman:

Question. What grievance did you present to the Iron Mountain Company about the reduction of wages, if any?—Answer. Well, when I first commenced to work in the employment of the Iron Mountain Railroad I got $1.75 a day for ten hours. I was in the employ of the company at the time of this cut in October, 1884.

Q. How much did they cut you?—A. They cut me 10 cents on the day. Q. That was in October, 1884?—A. Yes, sir; we were working the nine-hour system and I was getting $1.65; I was getting $1.65 for ten hours and we were only working nine hours.

Q. Then your wages were $1.48½?—A. Yes, sir. I got notice in October that my wages were cut from what I had been getting. I did not know what to do, and I went to see Mr. Richardson, the master mechanic. He said he could not help that, which I did not suppose he could. I told Mr. Richardson the circumstances, that I would like to work there, that I had a family to support, and that I could not work for that wages and support them. Several of the boys quit that evening and said they could not stand it.

Q. Were your wages restored?—A. No, sir; they never have been.

Q. You still continued to work, did you?—A. I went in and talked to Mr. Richardson about my wages being cut, and that I could not make $10 a day, and that I thought I would quit. Mr. Richardson said that his advice would be to go on and work and that probably the thing would change. I told him if he could give me any definite word about it that I would be sure of I would work on. He said he could not do that; so I told him I had better take my time.

Q. What did you do?—A. I just voluntarily quit the business.

Q. When was that?—A. On the 11th day of October, 1884; the day I had this talk with Mr. Richardson.

Q. When did you quit?—A. On the 10th day of October, 1884. I quit that evening.

Q. Did you go to work again?—A. No, not then; I did come back January 19, 1885.

Q. At the same wages?—A. No sir; I did not commence at the same wages. I supposed I would get my former wages; some of those that had quit got it back, and I thought that I would.

Q. Had you no contract with the man who employed you as to what your wages would be?—A. I just went to work, and when the month was up I kept account of the hours and days that I worked in the month so as to see what my wages were, and when it was $1.65 a day for ten hours I went to the general foreman, Mr. Fuller, and told him my check was short. He looked at it and said it was not. I told him I was not getting $1.75. He considered it awhile and said, "Work on, I will right that for you." I worked on, and I counted up my hours again, and I got $1.70 a day for the next time I drew my check. I told him I was short a little more, and he said as I quit at the time, they had agreed to divide the spoils with me and let me have $1.70. I then called their attention to this notice of agreement of 1885, and called the attention of Mr. Richardson and the general foreman to the fact that it said that the rates were to be put back to the former price.

Q. What circular are you talking of, the Hoxie circular based on the Hayes agreement?—A. Yes, sir; I wanted it settled on that.

Q. Have you had your wages restored under that?—A. No, sir.

Q. Did you go out on the strike this last time?—A. Yes sir.

Q. What did you go out for?—A. I went out for one reason; I think I had grievance sufficient.

Q. Of your own?—A. Yes, sir.

Q. But you had gone out on a lone strike of your own in October, 1884, and came back?—A. I did not go out on a strike; I called for my time; I did not ask for my time.

Q. You mean you went out and left your money in the hands of the company?—A. Yes, sir.

Q. What good did that do you?—A. It was not due. I did not consider I had quit.

Q. You did not? Do you not think you have quit now?—A. Well, it would look that way now.

Q. Did you get your money from the company?—A. Yes, sir.

Q. Your private grievance then was that you did not get your wages restored as promised by the foreman of whom you spoke?—A. Yes, sir.

Q. But would you have gone out if you had not been ordered out by Martin Irons?—A. No, sir.

Q. Then really you went out because you were ordered out?—A. Partly.

Q. What other cause exists for your going out?—A. I did not get my pay according to promise, and the other was I was ordered out.

Q. There were two reasons?—A. There were the two.

Q. If you had received your former pay and Martin Irons had called you out would you have gone?—A. Yes, sir.

Q. Do you know why Martin Irons called you out?—A. I did not know then; I was not as well posted as I have been since.

Q. Then really when you were ordered out by those whom you regarded as the proper authorities you went out without inquiring into the cause?—A. Yes, sir.

Q. Did you seek re-employment by the company?—A. I did.

Q. Since the strike was ordered off?—A. Yes, sir.

Q. To whom did you apply?—A. To the master-mechanic.

Q. What did he say?—A. He said he had as many as he wanted; all that was necessary; and that he did not want any more.

Q. Did you ask Mr. Richardson how he thought prospects would be in the future?—A. He gave me to understand that it was no use sitting around expecting a job there, and I had better seek employment elsewhere else.

Q. Why?—A. I did not ask him why.

Q. Did he say that you had been engaged in these depredations committed on the property of the company?—A. No, sir; he did not.

Q. Did he say he would not give you employment because you were a Knight of Labor?—A. No, sir. He said at the time he was needing hands during the strike he sent for some of them to come back and they would not come back. He had to have men, and he had got men and he could not let them go now to take others. I did not expect him to discharge the man he gave my job to.

Q. You thought his view of the situation was correct?—A. I merely wanted to ask if my services were dispensed with.

Q. What do you understand by a strike?—A. There are two kinds of strikes; one a peaceable walk-out, where the men simply quit their work and permit other men to take their places without interference or molestation, and refraining from committing depredations on the property of the company.

Q. And also from interference with the transportation of freight. That is one kind of strike?—A. Yes, sir.

Q. Another kind of strike is one in which the strikers take possession of the property of the company, obstruct commerce and transportation of goods everywhere and interfere with employees who decline to go out on the strike, and also with any who are employed in the place of the old hands?—A. Yes, sir.

Q. Do you believe that either kind would remedy the grievances complained of by the men?—A. I do not believe in the kind of one you spoke of last.

Q. Do you believe in the first one?—A. I believe in none at all. That would be the best course.

Q. Tell me what your object would be in going out on one of those peaceable strikes. By going out on that kind of a strike, would you remedy grievance?—A. No, sir.

Q. What object would you intend to accomplish by going out on a peaceable strike?—A. I think that men who would present their grievances would get them quicker that way than any other way.

Q. Is it not better to present them before going out?—A. I supposed that had been done.

Q. If that is done and you go out on a peaceable strike your object is by action to force the company to redress your grievance, is it?—A. Well, I suppose it would lead them to do that if they pleased to.

Q. Would you not expect them to be compelled to it by your going out? If you did not think your going out would be effective, why go out?—A. The whole of our fellowmen would be benefited. Personally I am not much concerned in it. So far as I was individually concerned whether I got $1.75 a day or whether I never got it, I did not expect to be affected in any way by going out.

Q. Is there a surplus of railroad labor?—A. There is at the present day.

Q. Was there not at the time of the strike?—A. I so understand.

Q. You have been refused employment on the ground that the railroad company had plenty of labor, have you not?—A. Yes, sir.

Q. So long as there is a surplus of labor population in our country if you walk out peaceably, do not burn trestles, kill engines, or prevent men from taking your places, what possible good can result to you? If men take your places you will have to seek employment elsewhere and sell your homes. What benefit can you derive, therefore, from a peaceable walk-out?—A. I do not know about anybody but myself. I can not talk for anybody but myself. Of course all of us are liable to do wrong sometimes.

Q. If you walk out peaceably and quietly and there is another man ready to take your place, and he does take it, and you do not prevent him from taking it, and you do not interfere with the traffic of the country, and do not burn trestles and do not kill engines, what good can possibly accrue to you?—A. I cannot say.

Q. Is it any advantage to you?—A. I supposed it would be.

Q. (By Mr. Parker.) Have you a family?—A. Yes, sir.

Q. Are you at work now?—A. I am not.

Q. How much have you earned since the 6th of March?—A. I have earned but very little. I have had only one job and got $10 for that.

Q. Do you know of any employment you can get?—A. I have not yet tried until I saw if I could get any employment by the company.

Q. Why did you not try?—A. I did not deem it necessary.

Q. Have you had help from the Knights of Labor to support you?—A. Some, I have.

Q. When the strike was ordered off, did that help end?—A. Yes, sir.

Q. Then you have got to take care of yourself?—A. Yes, sir; I suppose so.

Q. Did you consider that in going into a strike like that you did your duty towards your family?—A. Well; yes, sir; I looked on it rather that way.

Q. Do you know that the wages paid to the men by the railroad company are paid by businessmen in paying charges upon freight?—A. Yes, sir.

Q. Do you think you have the right to throw the business of these men into confusion without any notice to them?—A. Well, I think I have.

Q. (By Mr. Buchanan.) What did you do when you were employed by the railroad company?—A. I was a machinist's helper.

Q. What were your duties?—A. I was in the running repair shop, and my duty was to do such work as I was ordered to do on the engine.

Q. Mechanical or simply laboring work?—A. Well, both of them, you may term it.

Q. Was it talked round among the men before that if they had a strike they would not allow the freight engines to run?—A. No, sir.

Q. Was anything of that kind said in your presence?—A. No, sir.

Q. Did you not understand that when the men struck they would not allow the company to use its property for transporting freight after they commenced the strike?—A. No, sir.

Q. Were you one of the seven appointed as guards?—A. I was left in reserve to do the passenger work.

Q. Tell me what you mean by that?—A. There were three or four men left there to do the running repair work on the passenger engines only.

Q. Why was that exception made?—A. Well, they did not want to conflict with the running of passenger trains, and wanted to keep up the repair work.

Q. Before the hour when the whistle blew on the 6th day of March, were you told you might remain there to attend to the passenger engines?—A. No, sir.

Q. Did you go out when the whistle blew?—A. Yes, sir.

Q. When did you go back to work?—A. Next morning.

Q. Who told you to go back?—A. My round-house foreman saw me, and George Gray told me I could go back.

Q. Did you go out on the strike?—A. No, sir.

Q. Did not somebody else give you leave to go back?—A. I do not know at whose orders we went. One man came from the executive board of the Knights of Labor.

Q. How do you know he had those orders?—A. He told me he had.

Q. On that you went back and remained there, how long?—A. That was on the Sunday morning I went back. I worked Sunday, Monday, and Tuesday until dinner. I went home, and my wife was sick, and I sent him word I could not come back until my wife got better, and I never went back at all.

A Hell in Arkansas

Arkansas Gazette (Little Rock), March 24, 1888.

A common practice during this period was the use of convict labor, particularly in coal mines in western Arkansas. In 1888, conditions had become bad enough that the state legislature sent a committee to investigate the Coal Hill camp. The legislature's report shows the view of laborers held by their contractors and the extremes to which the latter would go to ensure productivity. Such usage severely interfered with efforts to improve conditions among the free laborers in the industry.

The Light Thrown On the Coal Hill Convict Camp Through an Official Investigation—No Hearsay, But Blood-Curdling Facts.

Men Beaten to Death, Half Starved, Half Clothed, But Worked All the Same.

Facts Kept From Everybody, Lessees and Warden included Three Wards Who Killed Seven Men By Brutality Alone.

In order to obtain more definite knowledge of the way things are conducted at the Coal Hill convict camp the board of penitentiary commissioners left this city Thursday morning for the purpose of making as thorough as possible an investigation of affairs. . . .

The board first inspected the stockade and sent a representative down to inspect the mines. There are 140 men at the camp, 120 of these are employed in the mines, part of them working during the day and part during the night. The men sleep in a building ninety feet long, eighty feet wide and twelve feet high, in three tiers of bunks.

Black and White, Sick and Well and crippled all sleep along side of each other. At present five men with the measles are sleeping with the others, but three men who have broken legs and arms are provided with cots. The men sleep on beds made of shucks and straw, which have not been changed, so witnesses testified, but once in the last fifteen months and then not all of them; the beds are dirty and filthy, a sickening stench arises from them and many of them are covered with vermin. One blanket is the covering allowed each man and seems very meager, and the witnesses examined testified that in winter they suffered. The men, of course, sleep in the clothes which they wear when not at work in the mines. The clothes are cotton except a woolen shirt.

The board concluded to take some testimony bearing on the subject and in order to do so, decided to examine some of the convicts. . . . The men were not anxious to talk, in fact every man was AN UNWILLING WITNESS, and they would say: "Gentlemen, if I talk, when you go away, I will be beat to death; we can't tell anything about how we are treated." The members of the board assured the men that they would be protected and then after some hesitation they would talk. One man, who said his time was nearly out, positively refused to utter a word for fear of being hurt. The first convict who was called was asked how the men were treated by the wardens as regards whipping. The man replied that they were whipped all the way from ten to 150 licks at one time on the naked back, generally for failure to perform tasks. The heaviest and hardest whipping was done in J. B. Scott's time. Scott was warden from October 1 to January 1. He was drunk half the time and would whip the men unmercifully when drunk. One night he whipped about seventy-five men, hitting them on an average fifty licks with a leather strap, which had a piece of half sole leather on the end. The skin was broken on each man's back and the BLOOD RAN OUT ON THE FLOOR. . . .

FOOD

The men all testified that they were getting very good food and about enough now, but said that up to two weeks ago they had been almost starved ever since Spencer was Warden over a year ago. The present food consists of: bread, four biscuits or a piece of corn bread and a slice of salt pork and coffee for breakfast.

Bread, dried beans, or sour kraut, and a slice of salt pork for dinner.

Bread and molasses for supper; sometimes stewed dried apples or rice.

This is the bill of fare they have been having lately. The sick get the same thing as the others, but Mr. Kline has gotten some chickens and will give the sick chicken once in a while. The men get no fresh meat and no vegetables. This causes them to suffer much with flux, dysentery and diarrhea.

CLOTHING

The testimony showed that up to within the last month the clothing had been very scarce and some—quite a number [of men] had been compelled all winter to sleep in the same clothes in which they worked in the mines all day and which of course were wet and covered with coal dust. At present most every man has two suits. The mining suit is cotton, the other consists of pants and shirt, the former cotton, the latter wool. It was found that the men to about the number of thirty had worked all winter without shoes and this statement was corroborated by Mr. James Allister, who owns the mines, and leases them, and is the only man who has access to them. Two cases of shoes were received this week and each man is now well shod. The clothes should be washed once a month, but the men say it has not been done for months. Each man is given a small piece of soap once a week, with which to wash his body but none with which to wash his clothes, consequently they were all very dirty. A wash-room with sixteen tubs is provided for the men to wash in and change their clothes when they come out of the mine.

VISIBLE EVIDENCE

When some of the men who were coming off the "day shift" were washing in the washing room the party started in to look at the backs of some of the men who has been whipped by Gafford. They all left at the sight of the first man's back, except Dr. G. M. D. Cantreell and THE GAZETTE man and they examined the backs of the following white men who had been whipped from three to five weeks ago by Gafford. Sam Tobin, Will Keunerman, S. A. Carlisle, John Pearce, Jeff Davis, Coiman Stencil, all of who had been whipped for failure to get out their required amount of coal. Their backs were still raw and covered with sores from the size of a man's finger nail to the size of his hand. None of these men have been allowed to stop one day for this, but had been kept at work steadily. Mat Bailey's and other negroes' backs were examined and found in a horrible condition. Witnesses testified that in Scott's time he whipped a number of men so bad and their backs got so sore that even the convicts could not stand the smell from them when they were around. . . .

HOW THE MEN ARE WORKED IN THE MINES

The miners are leased by the Outia Coal company, which company employs the Arkansas Industrial company, lessees of the penitentiary, to mine the coal at so much per ton. The Ouita company has nothing to do with the convicts and receives the coal after it is loaded. The Arkansas Industrial company employs a warden to take full control of the convicts.

The men are worked in pairs or threes, two medium well men are put together, or one well man and two sick or crippled men. Two men are required to get out six carloads a day or three men to get out three carloads. Each carload weighs a little over 1400 pounds. The men are given two shots of powder with which to perform their daily task, and heretofore if one of these shots failed they have had to pick it out and almost always came out short on their task and at night got a lashing for doing so.

The convicts said they were promised pay if they would get more than their task, but men who have done it say they never got one cent for doing so, but if they failed to get their task next day after getting out additional lot they were whipped. If men strike bad luck, if they have much slate and slack to handle, a hard lot to make, or some accident befalls them by which they come up short, no matter how sick, there has been no plea of circumstances or anything else to save them from being whipped. If a well man and a sick man, a good man and a cripple, an expert and a new man are together and the task is short both have been whipped, but every man testified that such was not the case since Kline took charge. They say he is firm and requires the tasks done but don't whip for it. The vein is from two feet to three and a half feet thick, and of course when the coal is taken out the entry is small so that men work stooping over, kneeling or lying down, as, of course, they do in all other mines. There is water in most of the rooms of this mine and the men work in it all day or night as the case may be, but the temperature is good and it does not render them so very cold. The men complain now that of late there has been a lack of props to keep the roof from caving in, but the warden claims that a good supply is kept all the time by the superintendent of the Ouita mines, but it is also a fact that a great many of the accidents have been occasioned by falling slate. Some of the men, of course, as the convicts said, fail to take the necessary precautions and get hurt, and some men have not been able to do so on account of the officials not having taken the precaution of supplying posts. The air in the mines is not good at best, but men get along very well in it, but sometimes it is so foul that a lamp can hardly be kept burning, and this no doubt has a great deal to do with the sickness of the men. . . .

The investigating party returned to this city last night, glad that their work was over, but sickened at the results.

Miners' Strike

Wylie B. W. Heartsill Papers, Special Collections, University of Arkansas at Little Rock.

For workers in the state's new industries, the only recourse to labor conditions was to organize. The earliest activity in the state took place among coal miners in the western part of the state, where the Knights of Labor secured their earliest members. The following document reflects one effort by organized labor to rectify conditions in the mines. In this case the owners simply did not pay the workers.

MINERS AND MINE LABORERS, READ

WHEREAS, The Southwestern Coal Mining Company of Greenwood, Ark., under the control, supervision and general management of one J. P. Burton, one of the members of said firm, did, during the months of November and December, 1892, employ a large number of miners and mine laborers to work in and about said mines with the promise, expressed and implied, that said miners should receive full remuneration for their services; and

WHEREAS, Said miners and laborers did fulfill—well and faithfully—their part of the contract, causing said mines to produce large amounts of coal, and thereby making the business prosperous and productive of profits over and above expenses to the amount of $1,200 or $1,500; and

WHEREAS, On the twenty-third day of December, 1892, only two days before "pay-day" (which was fixed for the twenty-fifth day of said month), the said Southwestern Coal Mining Company failed, or pretended to fail and operations were suspended by the levying of attachments upon the mining plant of said company. That said property was placed in the hands of a receiver and operated by him from the thirtieth day of December, 1892, until the sixth day of February, 1893, at which time it was sold under and by virtue of an order of the Judge of the Circuit Court, subject, as advertised, to liens and mortgages in said advertisement set forth; and that at said sale one Will H. Burton, son of the said J. P. Burton, became the purchaser of said property at and for the sum of $30—a sum totally inadequate to pay the amount due miners and laborers for work done which amounts, as we are informed and believe, to about $1,700; and

WHEREAS, It appears from the complaint of P. H. Lequin (one of the partners in said company) vs. J. P. Burton and Will H. Burton that said failure was without cause, and said sale is, to say the least of it, open to grave suspicion of fraud; and believing from the allegations in said complaint, and such other information as we have been able to obtain corroborative of said allegations, that at the time said company pretended to fail the books of said company show that there should have been more than $2,000 in the hands of said J. P. Burton as General Manager—a sum amply sufficient to have fully paid every cent due the men for labor. We are also led to believe from the said allegations and corroborative circumstances and information that the failure of said company was not due to the failure of the mines to produce coal in profitable quantities, or the failure of said company to make sales of and receive the money therefore, but was solely due to a purpose on the part of said General Manager, by the adoption of such method, to cheat and defraud the men out of the money they had laboriously earned and to which they were justly entitled, and by robbing them of their means of sustenance, in midwinter, homeless, without supplies, and in debt, as many of them were, to reduce them to circumstances under which they would be powerless to resist his appropriation of their money to his own use, and being unable to get away, would be compelled to delve again in the mines for his profit. We believe the sale of said mine a fraudulent one, and that the purchase thereof by Will H. Burton and the restoration of J. P. Burton to the position of Manager means only that J. P. Burton still owns and controls said mines, and that the whole transaction is a sham and fraud. Therefore, be it

Resolved, That Greenwood Assembly, No. 239, Knights of Labor, wholly condemn said mine-owners for their action in the matters set forth; and while we exist only as a Mixed Assembly, we regard "An injury to one as the concern of all," and will faithfully stand by our mining brethren, demanding that no member of the Knights of Labor of the World shall again enter the mines of the Southwestern Coal Mining Company until payment or satisfactory settlement is made for the work done in November and December, 1892.

Resolved, That we request all Local Assemblies and other labor organizations in sympathy therewith to warn their membership against coming here to labor in said mines, and that they assist us in enforcing the "blackleg" penalty upon all who shall labor in said mines until matters are satisfactorily adjusted.

The above and foregoing is a true copy of resolutions, as presented by the committee to whom the matters and things contained therein were referred, adopted by unanimous vote of L.A. 239 at a regular meeting held on the fourth day of March, 1893, and I do hereby so certify. Witness my hand as Recording Secretary, and the seal of said Assembly, this sixth day of March, 1893.

W. B. W. Heartsill, Recording Secretary

D. WOMEN'S RIGHTS

For many women, the New South brought a change of roles. The traditional position of women in southern society had included a subordinate role before the law, political disfranchisement, and exclusion from economic, educational, and cultural opportunities. In Arkansas, as through the rest of the nation, women began to organize in an effort to change this situation. Their efforts varied from those of militant supporters of woman suffrage to those of much more moderate women who joined clubs designed to educate and improve their members and their communities. Both groups, however, were changing the long-held view of what women should do. Arkansas contained a strong contingent of advocates for women's rights. Several women's newspapers appeared in the state, educating women and the public about the aspirations of women.

Woman's Work

Woman's Chronicle (Little Rock), March 24, 1888.

One of the chief women's newspapers was the *Woman's Chronicle* of Little Rock, published by Catherine Campbell Cunningham. The *Chronicle* was a major proponent of changes in the status of women and of reforming society. The first document illustrates the view many women held of how they might better society.

No one is so well calculated to think for womankind as woman herself. In the province of administering to the wants of her sex, no one can be so well adapted as she. Her advancement is in no better way proven than by her progress in medicine and literature, to say nothing of the reform movements which she is steadily carrying on for the benefit of her sex.

The spirit which has worked the unpopular suffrage movement to its present advanced state is an indominitable one. And while these battles for reform are waging at a distance, in our own city the feminine spirit is a no less valiant one. The home work for women, by women, here in Little Rock during the past two years has been a noble one.

The Orphans' Home, so energetically and persistently worked up by Little Rock ladies, has borne fruit in the elegant home, bought and paid for, into which they are soon to move. The King's Daughters have shown in many ways the effect of their good works. And the Women's Exchange, so skillfully and successfully managed has given every evidence of the conscientious effort and financial ability of our Little Rock women. The reports of this work show the patronage and the benefits to congress to be something marvelous. So perfect is the satisfaction expressed in both sides—consumer as well as producer—that, as one is a necessity to the other, the scales balance perfectly, an object attainable only by the judgement and tact of womankind. It has placed the comforts of life within the reach of many a woman whose family cares prevent her from laboring outside the walls of home.

The Woman's Exchange is one of the noblest of the works of women in our society. But there is still room for another enterprise which women alone can work up with success. At a meeting of the Round Robin social club a few days ago, Prof. Ida Joe Bowles read a paper on the urgent need of a home for working women in Little Rock. It was an earnest appeal, and was listened to with rapt attention. May it bear good fruit in the near future.

The Old Ladies' Home is one of the well established institutions in our city, and the work of the women's auxiliary to the Y.M.C.A. bears ample testimony to the fact that the women of Little Rock are a strong element socially and morally, whether they ever care to be politically or not. The workers in the W.C.T.U. are the staunchest of the stout-hearted women and their work, well and widely known, looks to the near future to bring them an abundant and substantial harvest.

Woman Suffrage

Woman's Chronicle (Little Rock), December 6, 1888.

Although initially cool to suffrage for women, the *Chronicle* reflected the rapid change of view in many women in the 1880s. Within a year its editors had taken it into the suffrage movement. Through the 1890s, the suffrage movement made progress particularly among middle-class women in the state's towns and cities. Led by Clara A. McDiarmid of Little Rock, agitation continued until 1900, but with little success. It would not be till 1920 and ratification of the Nineteenth Amendment that women would be fully enfranchised in Arkansas.

Three years ago the advocates of equal rights to women were not only ridiculed and laughed at as visionary fanatics, but they were met with inumerable arguments based upon physical, economic, theological and political grounds.

It is wonderful to look around and mark the changes those three years have brought about. The ridicule has ceased, the laugh has died out to an echo, the fanatics have almost ceased to be called cranks. Arguments have been met with counter arguments that have shown this fallacy; facts have been brought forward to show the false base upon which anti-suffrage theories were built. Thousands of the best thinkers in the nation have been enlisted in the cause; tens of thousands of others have stepped up to the polls and emphasized their faith with their ballot. In fact nearly all arguments have ceased.

Now the anti-suffragists have about concentrated all their efforts upon the question, "Whether women themselves want to vote?" We are willing to admit that this is deserving of more consideration than anything else they have brought to bear upon the question, and believing this, we consider it the duty of everyone who believes in conceding equal rights, to turn their whole attention to this phase of the question and try to enlist the women, for we are convinced whenever any considerable portion of the sex demand the ballot, they will get it. Our experience is that whenever an unprejudiced, uninfluenced woman takes the matter under consideration, she sees at once its justice, and becomes one of its supporters. When she looks around her and sees the influence wielded by one class of foreigners who have the ballot, and the hopeless condition of other classes who have no vote, if she is a friend of her sex and a thoughtful woman, she at once sees the necessity.

Why, for instance, is it that women get less for the same work than men, if it is not that the political weight of the ballot is thrown into the scale of the men to destroy a fair balance. When we began to edit this paper nearly three years ago, it was almost impossible to meet here in the South a suffragist, now their name is legion.

E. CHANGING STATUS OF BLACKS

While blacks had never secured their full economic freedom in the post–Civil War years, they were not relegated to a position of complete subordination. In the 1890s, when it appeared that blacks might join with whites in the Populist Party, however, the politicians in power increasingly used demagoguery to prevent such a biracial coalition. They successfully destroyed the Populists by raising the cry of white supremacy and by asserting the inferiority of the black race. Their political tool unleashed such powerful forces in southern society, however, that racism could not be stopped with the defeat of Populism. Throughout the 1890s whites assaulted the rights of blacks, an assault that would end in segregation and total disfranchisement of the black community. The attack upon blacks did not go uncontested, though, with blacks providing their own best defense, yet their white opposition proved to be too strong to block. The following documents show the arguments used by whites in their efforts to segregate blacks on the railroads in Arkansas. They also show the efforts of blacks to retain equal access to these facilities.

Arkansas Separate Coach Law

Arkansas Gazette (Little Rock), January 30, 1891.

Black Arkansans were not truly integrated into white society after Reconstruction, but they were not legally segregated either. In fact, in 1873 the legislature passed a bill that required businesses to provide equal services to all races. In 1890, however, the Democratic Party made segregation of railroads a part of its political platform. State senator John N. Tillman, who would later go to Congress and would serve as president of the University of Arkansas, introduced a bill to accomplish that goal in 1891. The politically ambitious senator's comments explain the origins of the bill and some of the rationalizations for such a measure.

I introduced this bill (requiring railroads to provide separate and equal accomodations [sic] for whites and blacks) in response to a manifest demand on the part of the white people of this State looking to a more complete separation of the white and colored races. Arkansas has a large contingent of colored people and consequently is confronted with the same conditions that have caused other Southern states to adopt laws of this character. Mississippi, Louisiana, and other States of the South have set precedents that will at least justify a trial of the proposed law. This bill is modeled after the Mississippi statute which has been tested in the courts and pronounced constitutional. The bill provides that all railroad companies carrying passengers in this State shall provide separate but equal and sufficient accomodations for the white and colored races, separate coaches and separate waiting rooms. It makes the separation absolute and complete; even the clause permitting nurses to ride in the same coach with their charges was stricken out of the bill. There is, Mr. President, involved in this question issues of vital concern. We ought to discuss those issues calmly and carefully. A considerable number of our fellow citizens object to this kind of legislation. Their objection should be considered and weighed and if those objections are sound and reasonable they should influence us when we come to vote on this measure. I can see no material difference, Mr. President, in the aims and purposes of this bill than in the policy of separating the races in hotels, boarding houses and public schools. The colored people of this city have had several meetings and have adopted resolutions denouncing the measure. On the night of the 27th they met in considerable numbers in the hall at the other end of this building, and thundered phillipics [sic] against separate coaches. They say that if the bill is passed that the railroads will discriminate against them. I call attention to the language in the bill, which says that railroad companies must furnish equal, but separate and sufficient accomodations for both races. And if they violate any of the provisions of the act they are subject to heavy penalties. What more can they ask of the friends of the bill? Another objection that is urged by the colored people to this measure is that it does not compel railroads to provide first and second class fare on their lines, so that there may be given to the better class of negroes an opportunity to escape riding with inferior specimens of their own race. They insist upon a setting up of class distinctions which the white people will not attempt for themselves. They want to be delivered from members of their own race. They want us to draw the soap line. We propose to give them a coach and a waiting room all to themselves, equal in size and appointments to those used by the white people, and that ought to satisfy them. I think it unfortunate for both races that the colored people resist the passage of this bill. Their opposition will tend to contradict their oft repeated denial that they want social recognition from the white people. This is a step backward from solving what is known as the negro problem. The people of this State and the South as well have to deal with the negro problem. That problem first appeared in some arithmetic printed north of Mason and Dixon's line, but for that we would have never discovered the existence of such a problem. The way to solve this problem is for both races to strive to live together in peace and harmony. The white man should not oppose the negro and the negro should not become too agressive [sic] nor too bold to dispute the evident superiority of his white neighbor. The tendency of the times, and it should be encouraged, is to separate as much as possible the two races. It is the duty of both whites and blacks to allay race prejudice as much as possible. The negro ought to know by this time that the people of the South are his friends. They live among us and always will; they are here to stay and we want to live with them in peace. It would have been better for the South if our New England friends had never launched the ships that bore your ancestors to our shores. It would have been better if they had found slavery sufficiently profitable to have kept your fathers in the factories of the North instead of selling them to the Southern planters for a good round price. And it would have been much better for us if the Republican party had put a spelling book in your hand instead of a ballot when you first became freedman. Still those things were done and cannot now be helped, and we must make the best of the situation we can.

Sen. George W. Bell on the Separate Coach Bill

Arkansas Gazette (Little Rock), January 30, 1891.

George W. Bell, who represented Desha and Chicot Counties in the senate, was the first black senator in Arkansas since A. L. Stanford of Phillips County. Elected in 1890, he was one of twelve blacks sent to

Little Rock in that election. A graduate of Lincoln University in Pennsylvania and a schoolteacher, he proved an articulate spokesman against efforts to segregate blacks and whites. In the end, however, he failed to block the Tillman bill, which became a first step toward legal black segregation and virtual disfranchisement.

Mr. President—If the measure under consideration has for its object the regulation of passengers upon the basis of their deportment, I am, with a few exceptions in favor of it. But sir, after reading the bill with much care and deliberation, it appears to be pregnant with only one aim, and that is on the lines of color, which, in the light of reason, seems to me a most unfortunate affair. I am aware, Mr. President, of the fact that the press of the State, the great moulder of public sentiment, have been agitating the principles contained in this measure, to the detriment of the race with which I am identified. You have pictured to your minds only one side of the question, and have drawn your conclusions and deductions from a one-sided proposition. A just Judge will hear both sides of a case, and then render his decision in accordance with the facts presented. But to claim that certain citizens of our State are not comfortable, because their eyes happen to espy a man or a woman with African blood in his or her veins sitting at a distance from them within the same coach, seems to me, Mr. President, the height of inconsistency. The negroes have been riding upon and within the same coaches, in common with all other races, in this State for more than eighteen years. And during that entire period they have had no race wars, but, in the contrary, have behaved themselves quite as well, if not better, than some of the other races.

It is true that a few months ago, on the Altheminer branch of the Cotton Belt Road between this city and Pine Bluff, some trouble occurred between a few persons belonging to both races. This seems to have created in the minds of some the opinion that those negroes were rioting, and therefore, on that account, all the negroes in the State of Arkansas must be singled out and held responsible for the crimes committed by two or three drunken persons on a passenger train which ran through a country where the inhabitants thereof had never perhaps seen a steam car at any time before. As well might it be said that during last fall on the Valley Route two high toned white gentlemen created quite a sensation by fighting in a passenger coach in the midst of many high toned white ladies. No one would dare say, because these two men created this disturbance, "that all other white men, though peaceful and law-abiding, must be held responsible for the crimes of these two men." Nor of the negroes, that because a few are filthy and ignorant of the better ways of life, that it must necessarily follow, that all negroes are filthy and ignorant. It seems strange to me, and though there are five races of men known upon the face of the earth, many of which are represented in the United States, and in the State of Arkansas, as yet from among them all, the negro race has been singled out as the object of your scorn! That he should receive no better treatment than this, in his own native land, is a wonder to all lovers of justice. And yet the dirtiest peasants from Europe, the Nihilists, and cut throats of every government, can come here, though strangers to our Constitution and laws, and receive better protection before the law, and in their civil rights, than we, who have helped to make this country what it is. Turn your eyes where you may, in our Sunny South-land, you behold millions of broad and fertile acres, in a high state of cultivation, the trees from which were felled and the land cleared by my ancestors, and today, they are holding the supporting purpose of the South. The negro is your greatest wealth producer. He has taken an active part in all the great battles, for the protection of our country. His blood was the first offered upon the altar of his country to appease the wrath of the British Lion. His bones lie bleached upon many a battle field and his blood is mingled with that of the Caucasian race in the defense of his country, and is today flowing onward and upward through the fountain of liberty, crying for justice and equal rights before the law, and the protection of his life, property and the general pursuits of happiness! It is said that the founders of this government, having been oppressed in the country from which they came, sought this goodly land, upon which to build an asylum as a refuge for the oppressed and persecuted and unfortunate of every land. Actuated by the spirit of fairness and justice, the great and noble Jefferson, the father of Democracy, the author of the Declaration of Independence, an instrument sacred to the heart of every American (be he black or white, rich or poor), to write: "All men are created equal, that they are endowed by their Creator with certain inalienable rights, that among these are life, liberty, and the pursuit of happiness." To deny the negro these rights, guaranteed him by the Constitution of the United States, and the Constitution and laws of the State of Arkansas, you must first deny Jefferson's proposition, the author and finisher of your faith, that all men are created equal, and are therefore not endowed with certain inalienable rights, nor are they entitled to life, liberty and the pursuit of happiness. You will have to deny, that which is self-evident to every reasonable mind, that we are men. Science has demonstrated the fact that negroes are possessed with the same attributes in all respects in common with the human family of which he is a member. That he has not reached the highest stage of civilization is true. That the inhabitants of Africa, near the banks of the Nile, with negro blood coursing through every fibre of their bodies, were the first inventors, and from whom the historian tells us flows the stream of all knowledge, is also true. That when Grece [*sic*] and Rome lie steeped for centuries in the cesspools of illiteracy and barbarism, Africa, the home of our ancestors, could boast of a high state of civilization is also true. That the first inventors, though their inventions be crude, are the best inventors, is also true. . . . To reason, and conclude, that because a people have once lived in the lower state of degradation, or because their skins are different from ours, that they are not entitled to the same human and Christian rights that belong to other members of the human family is to destroy the very foundation stone upon which this mighty fabric rests so well planned by our ancestors, and so well built and protected by your and our fathers! Then, Mr. President, we hold that to single us out as objects worthy of scorn and derision, because our skins are black, is an injustice as odious, and as malignant and cruel as the grave! Are we yet slaves and therefore deemed unworthy to travel, on the public highways in common with freemen? We deny the assertion so often made by some of the friends of this bill, that the negroes seek social equality with the white people, when he rides in a coach for which he holds a ticket, in common with other passengers. I am frank to say, that no true negro desires social equality with the white race, to the extent of losing his race pride, that which God seems to have fixed unalterable as a characteristic mark into the heart and soul of all nations. We have our own churches separate and distinct from yours, our social entertainments and all our gatherings for pleasures. We have never sought to marry among you, though we have among us a peculiar people called mulattoes, the history of whom is a mystery to us, and an astonishment to the civilized and moral world. I regret, Mr. President, that this issue has been forced upon us. . . . I have witnessed with pride and patriotism the remarkable progress our grand old state has made since the days of reconstruction; I have sung her praises in Northern climes while others were striving to throw odium and dishonor upon her fair name and honorable citizens. I have boasted of the equal show that the negroes have in this State in the procuring and education, and the accumulation of wealth. How just and equitable her laws, and how liberal and well disposed her rulers. That in our State, race wars have never occurred. That even in the largest Republican districts throughout the State, the negroes are beginning to do their own thinking, and voting with their best friends, wherever sufficient encouragement is given them. This feeling of unrest and a desire to make peace with those interests [that] are in common with ours, seems to be permeating every Northern State wherein there are negroes. If this measure becomes a law, Mr. President, I venture the assertion that the hand of our fair State's progress will be turned back to the days of reconstruction when scheming politicians would take advantage of the times and engendered bitterness and violent controversies between the whites and blacks, which would excite mobs and massacres, and finally result in a war of races. We have always granted to you your boasted superiority, and your magnanimity in dealing with your humbler and weaker brother. You have given us schools and our children are learning and improving their conditions. They have a greater love for the State which gave them birth and a feeling of patriotism for their Sunny South-land that they never felt before. Then, Mr. President, we beseech this senate in the name of those, whose throbbing hearts are vibrating with the same love of country, with the same interest in his South-land to vote down these measures. . . . I thank God that the day is fast approaching, when reason and a proper regard for the rights and privileges of all our countrymen, North, East, West and South, will be recognized, and that all races, here in our fair and beautiful South-land, may feel and know that we have a common cause, a common humanity, and a common interest! And if we would triumph over wrong and place the emblems of peace upon triumphant justice, without distinction of race, color or previous condition, we must unite and cultivate that spirit of friendliness, which would make of us one people, in a truly solid South. [Bill passed 26 to 2.]

FOR FURTHER READING

The years following Reconstruction have attracted a considerable article literature but remain lacking in monographic treatments. Carl H.

Moneyhon's *Arkansas and the New South, 1874–1929* (Fayetteville: University of Arkansas Press, 1997) offers the only overview and is also useful for its bibliography. It may be supplemented with Waddie W. Moore's *Arkansas in the Gilded Age, 1874–1900* (Little Rock: Rose Publishing Co., 1976), a set of essays that had appeared in the *Arkansas Historical Quarterly* and that touch on many of the relevant issues of the postwar years.

As in earlier eras, politics has attracted more than its fair share of attention among scholars. Among the better of these studies are Garland E. Bayliss's *Public Affairs in Arkansas, 1874–1896* (Ann Arbor, MI: Xerox University Microfilms, 1972); Joe Seagraves's *Arkansas Politics, 1874–1918* (Ann Arbor, MI: Xerox University Microfilms, 1974); and Richard L. Niswonger's *Arkansas Democratic Politics, 1896–1920* (Fayetteville: University of Arkansas Press, 1990). Some attention to politics at the end of this period is provided by Gov. George Donaghey in *Building a State Capitol* (Little Rock: Parke-Harper Co., 1937). A view of one of the many third parties that arose in the state appears in *Socialism and the Southwestern Class Struggle, 1898–1918*, by James R. Green (Ann Arbor, MI: Xerox University Microfilms, 1972).

Judge Parker in Fort Smith has attracted almost as much attention as state politics. Among the works dealing with Parker are Fred H. Harington's *The Hanging Judge* (Caldwell, ID, 1951) and Glenn Shirley's *Law West of Fort Smith* (New York: H. Holt, 1957).

Works on the state's economy and society are sorely lacking. Typical of what is available are *Shortline Railroads of Arkansas*, by Clifton Hull (Norman: University of Oklahoma Press, 1969), and *The Quapaw Quarter: A Guide to Little Rock's 19th Century Neighborhoods* (Little Rock: Quapaw Association, 1976).

John William Graves's *Town and Country: Race Relations in an Urban-Rural Context, Arkansas, 1865–1905* (Fayetteville: University of Arkansas Press, 1990) broke new ground in its examination of race in the New South era.

PART III

Twentieth-Century Arkansas, 1900 to 1954

LeRoy T. Williams

CHAPTER VI

Arkansas in the Progressive Era

INTRODUCTION

Students of American history generally label the extensive socioeconomic and political reform activities spanning the years from roughly 1900 to 1920 as the Progressive Era. Beginning primarily on the local level in the Midwest, the movement quickly spread across the American landscape and into the legislative chambers of state capitals and, finally, of the national government.

In such varied places as Toledo, New York City, San Francisco, and Little Rock, the currents of progressivism were unleashed. A host of state governors, among them such personalities as Hiram Johnson in California, Woodrow Wilson in New Jersey, and Charles Brough in Arkansas, rallied the forces of reform against social inequities, political excesses, and monopolistic business practices. On the national level Theodore Roosevelt took up the cause; and his Republican successor, William Howard Taft, carried the reform still further. In 1912, Democrat Woodrow Wilson became not only the standard-bearer of his party but also the moral crusader of a "New Freedom" steeped in progressive rhetoric.

Primarily middle-class in its social and economic moorings, the progressive movement appealed to an assorted lot of political figures, religionists, and social gospelers (many of whom were rather recent converts to new interpretations of age-old scriptures), temperance leaguers, educators, writers, and businessmen. And while such diverse groups and individuals raised reform banners against a host of evils, one conviction, perhaps above all others, tugged simultaneously at their heartstrings. For the progressives, the almost uniquely American concepts of competition and opportunity were fast disappearing—if, in fact, they had not already—from the very fabric of society. Something, they argued, had to be done to return competitiveness and individual opportunity to society in the face of unbridled industrial growth and urbanization.

According to progressive thought, political corruption, abetted in many ways by the rapid urbanization of American life, had to be eliminated. So, too, did the giant corporations whose business activities stretched into every facet of the economic order, crushing the lifeblood of competitiveness, chance, and opportunity. If not eliminated, stated the progressives, such monopolistic concerns should be regulated closely by government. Here, the reformers advanced something of an ideological break with nineteenth-century laissez-faire economics. And when the progressives viewed the social order, they were appalled by urban squalor that seemed to spread like a cancer across the American landscape, the quality of education, and the industrial abuse of children. Moreover, a large segment of the society yet remained without political rights. To this end, the progressives championed the right of women to exercise the vote.

Sweeping though much of its rhetoric was, the progressive movement had some serious shortcomings. It did not extend to all groups and economic classes within American society, and, in fact, many progressives were comfortable in ignoring the larger humanitarian ideals regarding the issue of race. In large measure, the movement was but another in a series of reform efforts in which the rhetoric stood in marked contrast to the realities of the day. It can be argued, however, that despite certain limitations, the movement fostered a kind of ideological courage among those who remained outside the pale of progressive reform efforts.

In Arkansas, Jeff Davis, George Donaghey, and Charles Brough are representative of the progressive impulse. Davis, although fashioning himself as a commoner and veritable David against the Goliaths of big business and the city crowd, was a well-born attorney from Russellville. He was elected attorney general in 1898; from that office he went on to three unprecedented terms as governor, in 1900, 1902, and 1904.

Despite several lawsuits filed by Davis as attorney general against various business interests in Arkansas and despite his rather consistent fight against what he termed "unwise" spending by the legislature, his record as a reformer goes lacking. It was with the art of demagoguery that Davis succeeded with high marks. Whether the issue centered on Yankee business interests in the state or the city dwellers against the hill farmers or race relations, Davis knew best how to fan the flames of prejudice and distrust. In no small measure, however, the times, as much as Davis, were ripe for the exploitation of such issues.

In George Donaghey, Arkansas found a capable businessman whose principal interests lay in the construction of a new state capitol building (completed in 1915) and the improvement of the public schools. During Donaghey's administration, the State Board of Education was established, as were several agricultural schools and a teacher-training program.

Central to the development of educational programs during the progressive period was the belief that only through an informed and literate electorate could the state move toward national trends as well as economic development. Donaghey also called attention to Arkansas's notorious convict-lease system but failed to persuade lawmakers during his administration to pass legislation to end the practice. It appears that economic motives overshadowed any desire to eradicate this system that resembled closely the "peculiar institution" of another era. Shortly after Donaghey left office, the legislature technically ended the convict-lease system in the state.

A Mississippian by birth, Dr. Charles Hillman Brough served as governor of Arkansas from 1917 to 1921. In Brough, Arkansas's progressivism seems to have waxed strongest. It was during his administration that such progressive ideals as the eradication of illiteracy, the promotion of charitable concerns, the extension of medical care, woman suffrage, compulsory education, vocational schooling, and highway construction assumed greater meaning.

On the other hand, and despite such progressive inroads cited earlier, it was during Brough's second term as governor that the brutal Elaine Riot occurred in Phillips County. In October 1919, pitched battles raged for several days between landowners and black sharecroppers, resulting in the deaths of five whites and, officially, twenty-five blacks (other reports suggest that the number of blacks killed was considerably higher). The suspected causes of this outbreak of violence range from conspiracy on the part of blacks to kill whites in the area because of unfair farming arrangements to a new militancy among blacks that was spawned, in part, by America's credo during World War I to "make the world safe for democracy."

The violence in Phillips County was but one manifestation of the racial ills plaguing the nation during the Progressive Era. North and South, segregationists and "redeemers" fashioned a most repressive society, replete with political disfranchisement, Jim Crow laws, and mob violence. While the Elaine episode may have been the most brutal in terms of official and unofficial reports of deaths, more than two dozen race riots occurred across the United States in 1919. In all, the causes of such violence were many, and they acutely mark the failure of progressivism and the nation to extend the concepts of opportunity, freedom, and justice to all.

A. ARKANSAS AT CENTURY'S DAWN

During the late nineteenth and early twentieth centuries, American society plunged headlong into the modern era. Hand in hand, the forces of industrialization and urbanization ushered in a new day—of mechanical devices, greater wealth, leisure, human aspirations and expectations. The new age also called attention to some of society's more glaring ills. The selections in this section are illustrative of some of these forces and concerns as they were manifest in Arkansas at the dawn of the new century.

The "City of Roses"

Little Rock, *City of Roses* (Little Rock: Press of Arkansas, Democrat Company, 1901), 3–5.

The Progressive Era witnessed the first truly large-scale "City Beautiful" campaign in the nation's history. Green spaces of natural growth sprang up in countless cities to challenge impersonal stone structures. In the selection that follows, Little Rock—the "City of Roses"—is described at the turn of the twentieth century.

Nestled upon a spur of the Petit Jean Mountains at an elevation of about 300 feet above tidewater, the Arkansas River winding gracefully about it, offset by a majestic bluff against which the sunbeams play with vivid light and shadow effect, the "City of Roses," Capital and hub of the state, is no more beautiful than picturesque.

With a population approaching 50,000, covering an area of twelve square miles, sixty-two miles of improved streets, commerce aggregating more than $20,000,000, 1,500 business houses, twenty-seven newspapers and periodicals, twelve banks, railroads running in seven different directions and river transportation, Little Rock is no small pebble in spite of its name. A cotton market that is reported daily on the bulletins of New York and New Orleans exchanges, showing total receipts of $9,086,263 in 1901, gives Little Rock rank among the first in this industry. . . . Little Rock is the largest producer of oil from cotton in the world, there being five cotton seed oil mills turning out all kinds of cotton seed products. . . .

. . . During the year 1901, there were upwards of 2,000 real estate sales, the consideration being $215,921 in excess of the previous year. Authorities state that a larger percent of the laboring classes own homes in Little Rock than in any other city of corresponding size. . . . The City has a thorough and efficient paid fire department and the streets are lighted by [an] electric light plant. There are four gas and light companies operating here and two telephone systems. The electric street car system is the most perfect of any operating in the South. . . . The graded free school system is one of the best in the United States. . . . the white and colored pupils are taught in separate buildings, but of equal convenience and attractiveness.

. . . In the rapid commercial growth of the city, the equal development of religious, benevolent and educational institutions has shown the moral worth of our citizenship. The social features are unsurpassed for refinement, culture and liberality. True southern hospitality characterizes the home and individual. Notwithstanding the darts and shafts that have been hurled, the men and women of Arkansas maintain a chivalry and dignity worthy of the "South of long ago."

. . . The artistic and profuse display in garden and yard of every variety of flower known to the temperate zone which justly gives the title "City of Roses," bespeaks an eye and heart for the true and beautiful where the Southern girl, too often forced into business circles, is still the same sweet woman, whose ideal is under the marriage bell. . . . Arkansas is not a bloody waste as our neighbors saw us thirty-five years ago, but a great, progressive, resourceful state, greatly undeveloped.

The Public School System of Arkansas

George B. Cook, "The Public School System of Arkansas,"
in *The Book of Arkansas* (Little Rock, 1914), 130–31.

In the following selection, George B. Cook, superintendent of public instruction, reports on the advancement of education in Arkansas between 1900 and 1913.

"Intelligence and virtue being the safeguards of liberty, and the bulwark of a free and good government, the state shall maintain a general suitable and efficient system of free schools, whereby all persons in the state, between the ages of six and twenty-one years, may receive gratuitous instruction."—Constitution of Arkansas.

The present public school system of Arkansas, based upon the above provision of the state Constitution, has had almost its entire growth within the past four decades, or since 1875.

With the beginning of the twentieth century, there has become manifest in this state a wonderful awakening and increase of interest in . . . the public schools on the part of the entire citizenship of Arkansas. Even a casual review of the statistics . . . will show a substantial development during the past fourteen years which is unprecedented. During this period the school population has increased twenty-seven percent and the average daily attendance . . . has increased forty-two percent, the average length of the annual school term has increased two and one-half months and is now almost six and one-half months for the entire state, as against less than four months in 1900. . . . In 1900 approximately one and one-third million dollars were expended in public school education, whereas as for 1913 this sum had become more than four and one-quarter million dollars. . . .

During the past several years, the awakened interest of the state for popular education of all its youth has been clearly reflected by legislative enactment, raising the standards and broadening the scope of public schools. . . . In 1909, the legislature passed an act to establish four agricultural schools and . . . a Compulsory School Attendance Act. The legislature of 1911, however, will be recorded in history for its constructive and progressive education legislation. During this session, which followed a statewide campaign conducted by the Arkansas Education Commission, the State Board of Education was established, [as were] state aid for high schools, consolidation of weak schools, transportation of pupils and a law standardizing all institutions of higher learning in the state. . . .

During the past decade, the advancement of higher education in the state has kept pace with the common school progress. The State University at Fayetteville has been constantly increased and improved in all its departments. . . . The State Normal for negroes at Pine Bluff, received generous support from the state. . . . Closely related to the general educational institutions . . . are the School for the Blind, and Deaf-Mute Institute at Little Rock. Among the private and denominational schools for negroes, institutions doing valuable work for the colored race, may be named Arkansas Baptist College, Philander Smith . . . and Shorter College.

Probably the most significant and reassuring factor in education in Arkansas is the spirit of cordial cooperation. . . . Persons of all religious and political beliefs may be assured of welcome and place both in the public schools and . . . private or denominational schools.

Jeff Davis Describes the Workings of the County Farm

L. S. Dunaway, *Jeff Davis: Governor and U.S. Senator, His Life and Speeches* (Little Rock, 1913), 46–49.

The "county farm," in Arkansas and several other southern states, was an exploitative institution for exacting human labor. It posed a particular problem for progressives. In the selection that follows, Arkansas's one-term attorney general and three-term governor, Jeff Davis, recounts in his own inimical style, during a campaign speech before the residents of Center Point in Howard County, a question raised by black attorney Scipio A. Jones regarding the county farm.

Scipio A. Jones, a Nigger lawyer in Little Rock, an insignificant personage, submitted to me and to my office [as attorney general] a very important question, and that was this: "How much shall county convicts confined upon the county farm to work out their fine and costs be allowed upon their fine and costs for each day that they labor?" I do not know what your practice is, but with us it is this way. A man is tried for carrying a pistol here. He is fined fifty dollars. The Sheriff's and Clerks's costs are about ten dollars. The Prosecuting Attorney's is ten dollars more. This makes seventy dollars. If he can not pay it he has to go to the county farm and work it out.

Up to the time of rendering this opinion, the practice had prevailed all down the Mississippi River and in Pope County on the Arkansas

River, to allow him fifty cents a day. If he was sick and did not work, he was charged fifty cents for his board; if it was a rainy day and he could not work, he was charged fifty cents per day for his board; if it was Sunday and he could not work, he was charged fifty cents a day for his board. So, gentlemen, an unfortunate man was absolutely working *into* the county farm instead of working *out*.

I instructed Scipio A. Jones, a Nigger lawyer, that, in my judgment, every convict that was confined upon the county farm to work out his fine and costs should be allowed under the law seventy-five cents per day for the time he was confined, whether he labored or not. That revolutionized the county farm in Arkansas. Men were turned *out* of the farm. They had been kept overtime.

Bone Dry: An Assault upon "Demon Rum"

Public and Private Acts and Joint and Concurrent Resolutions and Memorials of the 41st General Assembly of the State of Arkansas (Little Rock: Democrat Printing and Lithographic Co., 1917), 41–49.

The Progressive Era witnessed the culmination of several decades of agitation by temperance leaguers and others to prohibit the sale and manufacture of alcoholic beverages in American society. And while many today consider prohibition to have been less than wise, numerous progressives believed it vital to the foundation of American family life. Following the lead of the US Congress in passage of the Webb-Kenyon Bill in 1913, prohibiting the transportation of liquor into any area where it was outlawed, and in advance of national prohibition, the Arkansas legislature enacted the "Bone Dry Law" in 1917. The following are excerpts from that act.

ACT 13.
Approved January 24, 1917
An ACT to prohibit the shipment of intoxicating liquors into this State, and to prevent shipments of the same from one point or locality in this State to any other point or locality within this State; prohibiting the storage or possession of said liquors; forbidding the solicitation or taking of orders for the liquors defined in this Act; prohibiting the storage

of liquors in lockers, or other places in any social club or fraternal organization for use therein, or carrying liquor thereto or keeping the same therein; prohibiting the keeping or maintaining of unlawful drinking places as defined by the Act, which drinking places are made nuisances; and providing for the forfeiting of the charter of any incorporation, club or association violating the law against keeping or maintaining said drinking places, regulating procedure and fixing punishment and penalties; and for other purposes, as detailed in the Act.

Be It Enacted by the General Assembly of the State of Arkansas: Section 1. That it shall be unlawful for any railroad company, express company, or other common carrier, or any officer, agent or employee of any of them, or any other person, to ship or to transport into, or to deliver in this State in any manner or by any means whatsoever, any alcoholic, vinous, malt, spirituous, or fermented liquors or any compound or preparation thereof commonly called tonic, bitters or medicated liquors from any other State, Territory or District of the United States, or place now contiguous thereto, subject to the jurisdiction of the United States, or from any foreign country, to any person, firm or corporation within this State, when the said liquors, or any of them, are intended by any person interested therein, to be received, possessed or sold, or in any manner used except as provided in Section Seventeen (17). . . .

Section 5. That it shall be unlawful for any person, firm or corporation to store, keep, possess, or have in possession, or permit another to store, keep, possess or have in possession, any liquors and beverages . . . in or at fruit stand, restaurant, store, drug store (except alcohol in a drug store as permitted by law, or wine for sacramental purposes as may be permitted by law [Section 17 exempted wine for sacramental purposes and alcohol for strictly medicinal or mechanical purposes. Records of such transactions, however, were to be filed with the clerk of the circuit court within ten days of delivery]) . . . or in any club or club room of any social or fraternal organization or of any other organization or association of persons, or in any livery stable, dining room, wagon yard, or in any public building of the State, county or municipality, or district . . . bowling alley or pool[room] . . . this shall not prevent any officer from storing or having such liquors in a public building for a safe keeping when seized in the enforcement of the law.

Needed Reforms: A Call to Action

Charles H. Brough, "Needed Reforms in Charities and
Correction in Arkansas," in *Proceedings of the Third Annual
Meeting of the Arkansas State Conference of Charities and
Correction* (Fort Smith, 1914), 18–23.

Prior to his inauguration as governor in 1917, Arkansas's leading
progressive politician, Charles Hillman Brough, served on the fac-
ulty at the University of Arkansas. It was here, as a university pro-
fessor of considerable mark, that he delivered a call for extensive
social reforms. In the selection that follows, the scholarly Brough
makes use of history, reason, and even poetry as he pleads the cause
of reform before the third annual meeting of the Arkansas State
Conference of Charities and Correction.

The sacredness of human life and the value of constructive philan-
thropy are no longer mere principles. They are rules of action and have
found expression in intelligent legislation and voluntary efforts to reduce
human suffering and disease. Much practical good has already been
accomplished in Arkansas, a State that is rapidly meriting the stately
eulogy of [Roscoe] Conkling upon [Ulysses S.] Grant, "Great in the arduous greatness of things done." The establishment of a reform school and
a tuberculosis sanatorium, the relatively liberal support given our charitable institutions by the General Assembly, the abolition of the nefarious
convict lease system, the creation of a State Penitentiary Board and a
State Medical Board, with power to collect and register vital statistics—
these and other notable reforms accomplished in Arkansas within the
last decade are worthy of commendation. But much more remains to be
accomplished. . . .

Paramount to every other reform in this field is the enactment of a
law providing for the health, safety and welfare of our children by forbidding their employment in certain occupations and under certain specified ages; by regulating the hours and conditions of employment and
the conditions under which employment conditions may be issued. . . .
Not relief, but prevention is the slogan of modern social work; not pal-
liatives, but fundamental social reforms, are demanded today. . . .

The second reform which I would suggest is the passage of a series of
laws for the protection and preservation of the health and morality of

female delinquents. . . . Imprisonment of women and girls in the penitentiary or in county jails is not consonant with the most progressive methods of modern criminal administration. Another needed reform in Arkansas is the abolition of the lease system as applied to our county almshouses, by which the poor of each county are placed on the tender mercies of the lowest bidder. Our secretary [of the Conference of Charities and Correction], Hon. M. A. Auerbach . . . calls attention to the deplorable conditions of poorhouse administration throughout the South, where oftentimes to grow old is a disgrace and to be poor is a crime.

Legislative authority for the creation of juvenile courts in cities of the first class would seem to be a desirable innovation in the administration of justice in Arkansas. . . . As a handmaid of the juvenile court system, and absolutely necessary to make it a success, the next General Assembly should pass a law requiring the establishment of parks, public playgrounds and recreation places in every city of the first and second class in the State. . . . Finally, everything possible should be done for the betterment and encouragement of our rural population, which constitutes eighty-six percent of the total population of Arkansas. Oftentimes our country people are a sad faced race of people, making misery their worship and paying their orisons in groans. . . . We should tie our country boys and girls to the farm and country life by the tie of attractiveness. . . . "Ill fares the land to hastening ills a prey, Where wealth accumulates and men decay; Princes and lords may flourish or may fade—A breath can make them, as a breath has made; But a bold peasantry, their country's pride, When once destroyed can never be supplied."

Motion Pictures and Sex Education

Murray A. Auerbach, "The Drama and Moving Picture in Sex Education," in *Proceedings of the Third Annual Meeting of the Arkansas State Conference of Charities and Correction* (Fort Smith, 1914), 63–69.

It was during the Progressive Era that the "new leisure" came to American life. In fact, the era became known for its leisure class. In the home, gas and kerosene replaced coal, creating valuable time to engage in other activities. As an abundance of "new" and poor immigrant women took jobs as servants in countless homes, more and more women were free to pursue leisurely activities. New feature pages in magazines and newspapers, romance novels, poetry, the theater, and social columns all echoed the good life. Spectator sports, the new architecture, the green space crave, and, finally, the movies were symbols and manifestations of the new leisure. Perhaps few other industries have been as controversial as that of motion pictures. In 1900, movies were novelty items. By the time the United States entered World War I, motion pictures were common in cities and towns, large and small. In the selection that follows, Murray A. Auerbach, secretary of the Conference of Charities and Correction, sees a valuable use of the motion picture in sex education.

The moving picture is, after all, only another method of presenting a story. Like the theater, too, the moving picture has been abused, and censure became common. Mob psychology is a most peculiar phenomenon, and when a few leaders rise in protest over the picture playhouses, the cry is immediately taken up by the multitude, and moving picture places are ranked with places of ill repute. There may be some reason for this condemnation so far as certain places are concerned. But why include all? It is as reasonable to condemn all churches because occasionally one hears of a minister who falls from grace. The moving pictures have become a power for good. . . . So [do they] exert an influence in sex education. Very recently there appeared the widely heralded "Traffic in Souls," which was shown to thousands of people in most of the larger cities. Unfortunately, this film was prohibited in certain places, among these cities being Chicago. . . . The "Traffic in Souls," however, proved to be a story with a powerful sermon. Aside from the action and interest in the story itself, it showed the manner in which girls are procured by the white slavers and their treatment after they fall into the hands of these parasites.

Have these pictures so bad an influence on girls? Do they tend to demoralize our growing children? Those who have seen such pictures as the "Traffic in Souls" may well wonder how a young, unsophisticated girl could escape the clutches of the many procurers unless she were acquainted with their methods. How many an innocent girl, indeed, has gone to her ruin because she innocently accepted the attention of some dapper young man, or because she put her trust in some woman whom she met in a business way, and who pretended to be a friend, while in reality she was a hireling of the white slaves? An hour spent with these pictures serves to fortify the girl against the machinations of the procurers. Does the girl get as strong a lesson or as vivid a picture in the home or in the school? How many parents and teachers talk these things over with their children? The subject is tabooed; it is too delicate. Until false modesty is thrown to the seas, the theater and the moving picture must play their part, and they play an important part, despite the adverse criticisms leveled at them. . . .

. . . Instead of concentrating on the pictures, consider the low ceilings, the inadequate ventilation, the narrow aisles, the paucity of exits, the general danger to the health of the audience and the fire hazard [in the moving picture houses].

B. POLITICAL TRENDS

Politics in the largely Democratic New South during the Progressive Era did not include participation by black citizens except in those instances when black votes could be used by one white political faction against another. The Republican Party—the so-called party of Lincoln—also drifted steadily to the right during the period and accorded blacks little in terms of active participation. And while women secured their long-awaited right to participate fully in the political process and new measures for more direct involvement of the citizenry dotted statute books across the land, progressive political rhetoric had some serious flaws. The documents in this section are indicative of the conflicting forces of progressive politics. They reflect, on the one hand, efforts to broaden the political participatory base and, on the other, an exclusive view based upon race.

The Initiative and Referendum

Public and Private Acts and Joint and Concurrent Resolutions and Memorials of the General Assembly of the State of Arkansas (Little Rock: Democratic Printing and Lithographic Co., 1909), 1238–40.

Among the inclusive measures of progressive politics, the initiative and referendum garner high marks. In 1909, Arkansas amended its constitution to reflect greater political participation by the citizenry.

Senate Joint Resolution No. 1.
Approved February 19, 1909

Senate Joint Resolution submitting to the qualified voters of the State of Arkansas an amendment to the Constitution thereof, providing for the Initiative and Referendum:

Be it Resolved by the Senate and House of Representatives of the State of Arkansas, a majority of both Houses agreeing thereto:

That the following is hereby proposed as an amendment to the Constitution of the State of Arkansas, and the same being submitted to the electors of the State of approval or rejection at the next general election. . . .

Section 1. The legislative powers of this State shall be vested in a General Assembly, which shall consist of the Senate and House of Representatives, but the people of each municipality, each county and of the State, reserve to themselves power to propose laws and amendments to the Constitution and to enact or reject the same at the polls as independent of the legislative assembly, and also reserve power at their own option to approve or reject at the polls any act of the legislative assembly. The first power reserved by the people is the Initiative, and not more than 8 percent of the legal voters shall be required to propose any measure by such petition. . . . Initiative petitions shall be filed with the Secretary of State not less than four months before the election at which they are to voted upon.

The second power is a Referendum, and it may be ordered (except as to laws necessary for the immediate preservation of the public peace, health or safety) either by the petition signed by 5 percent of the legal voters or by the legislative assembly as other bills are enacted. Referendum petitions shall be filed with the Secretary of State not more than ninety days after final adjournment of the session of the legislative assembly which passed the bill on which the referendum is demanded. The veto power of the Governor shall not extend to measures referred to the people. . . . Any measure referred to the people shall take effect and become a law when it is approved by a majority of the votes cast thereon and not otherwise. The style of all bills shall be, "Be it Enacted by the People of the State of Arkansas."

The Commission Form of Government

Acts of the General Assembly of the State of Arkansas (Little Rock: Democrat Printing and Lithographic Co., 1913), 1–40.

The Progressive Era witnessed the coming of new forms of government for the management of cities. Among these, the commission plan provided for a division of city functions into various departments, each headed by a commissioner. In 1913, Fort Smith took the lead in adopting the commission plan of government. The following are excerpts from Legislative Act Number 13, providing for the commission plan.

Act No. 13
Approved February 5, 1913; Amended and Approved January 18, 1917.

Be it Enacted by the General Assembly of the State of Arkansas.

Section 1. That any city of the first class having a population of over 18,000 and less than 40,000 according to the United States census in pursuance of this act, may become organized as a city under the provisions of this act by proceeding as hereinafter provided.

Section 2. Upon petition of electors residing within the corporate limits of the city, equal in number to twenty-five per centum of the votes cast in such city for all candidates for governor at the preceding election, filed with the mayor thereof, the mayor shall by proclamation submit the question of organization of a city under this act at a special election to be held at a time specified therein and within thirty days after said petition is filed. The said proclamation together with a copy of this act shall be published at length in two daily newspapers, if two are published in the city in which the election is to be held, and in one daily newspaper, if only one is published in said city, once a week for two weeks. . . . If said Plan is not adopted by a majority of the voters voting on that issue at the special election called, the question of adopting said Plan shall not be resubmitted to the voters of said city for adoption within two years thereafter, and then the question to adopt shall be resubmitted upon the presentation of a petition . . . equal in number to twenty-five per centum of the votes cast for all candidates for mayor at the last preceding city election. . . .

Section 4. [as amended and approved January 18, 1917] There shall be elected at the first municipal election held after the adoption . . . of this act, a mayor and two commissioners, who, together, shall be known and designated as the Board of Commissioners. The mayor shall be elected for a term of four years, and of the commissioners, one . . . for a term of four years, and one for . . . two years, the term to be determined by lot; but thereafter, all commissioners shall be elected for terms of four years, one of the commissioners to be elected biennially. . . .

Section 9. The Board of Commissioners shall have, possess and exercise all executive, legislative and judicial powers and duties now had, possessed and exercised by the mayor, city council, board of public affairs, and all other officers and offices in cities of the first class. The executive and administrative powers, authority and duties in such persons shall be distributed among the three departments, as follows: The mayor (a) Department of Public Affairs. Commissioner No. 1: (b) Department of Accounts and Finance . . . Health and Public Safety. Commissioner No. 2: (c) Department of Streets and Public Improvement . . . Parks and Public Safety. Before [engaging] in their duties . . . each Commissioner shall take an oath [and post a bond of] $5,000.00 to the city, conditional upon the faithful performance . . . and accounting for all moneys or property of the city coming into their hands.

Suffragettes and the Political Equality League

Ida Husted Harper, ed., *The History of Woman Suffrage* (New York: Fowler and Wells, 1920), 6:16–26.

The struggle by women to gain the vote came to an end with the declared ratification of the Nineteenth Amendment to the US Constitution on August 26, 1920. In the selection that follows, some of the early efforts of Arkansans to secure the vote for women are recounted.

There was little general suffrage activity in Arkansas before 1911; perhaps the only specific work after 1900 was an occasional article written by Mrs. Chester Jennings of Little Rock and published in various papers in the state. She was called "the keeper of the light." Arkansas was not affiliated with the National American Association prior to 1913, there was only correspondence between individual suffragists and national officers.

In January, 1911, the Political Equality League was organized in Little

Rock. This organization came about indirectly as a result of an article written by Mrs. D. D. Terry of [Little Rock] and published on the front page of the *Arkansas Gazette,* the largest paper in the state. It was in answer to a scathing criticism of women by another paper for attending the trial of a child victim and was a demand that the suffrage should be given to women.

. . . Under the auspices of the [Political Equality] League the first National Suffrage May Day was observed in Little Rock with speeches from the steps of the Old State House. Seventy-five letters were sent out to prominent men in the state, asking them to make five-minute speeches and after ten days Dr. L. P. Gibson, the well-known physician, was the first to accept. . . . The intensely interested crowd stood two hours and a half earnestly listening to these leading citizens asking the right of suffrage for Arkansas women.

In October, 1915, the first annual meeting [of the Political Equality League] took place in Little Rock, eleven counties being represented. . . . [T]he principal business of this convention was to lay plans for the legislative work early in the following year. In October, 1916, the second annual convention was held in Pine Bluff, its principal work being to devise ways and means of raising money for continuing the organization of the state. . . . Mrs. Carrie Chapman Catt, President of the National American Suffrage Association, had come to Little Rock in April and spoken most acceptably to a large audience. . . .

The first state-wide Primary election in which women had the right to vote was held in May, 1918, between 40,000 and 50,000 voted and all [news]papers commented on the intelligence of the new electors. . . . The legislature met January 13, 1919, after thousands of women had voted at the Primary election. Not one member had been asked to present a resolution proposing a constitutional amendment for woman suffrage. In fact the women were following closely the advice of the National Association and were ardently hoping to avoid a state campaign. They were reckoning from past experiences but times had changed. Twenty-five men came ready to propose a full suffrage amendment; Representative Riggs . . . was the first man on the floor after the House was organized and his bill got first place on the calendar. It passed the Senate January 30 by 27 to one, and the House February 3 by 73 to three. In November [1919], it went to the voters and was defeated. It received the largest favorable vote of any of the amendments submitted but not a majority of the largest number cast at the election, as required by the Constitution. The women had felt certain that this would be impossible. In August, 1920, full suffrage was conferred by the federal amendment.

Race as a Political Factor

L. S. Dunaway, *Jeff Davis* (Little Rock, 1913), 50–60.

In this selection, Jeff Davis, candidate for reelection as Arkansas governor in 1904, exploits the racial issue in a speech that castigates one of his opponents.

Ladies and gentlemen, I now come to a question in Judge [Carroll D.] Wood's life, in his official career that is unequaled, that has no parallel in Arkansas politics. He served as circuit judge from 1887 for six years. Ashley and Drew, two large Democratic, two large white counties, were in the judicial district. At each term of the court, while he served as judge, he appointed three men as jury commissioners to select the petit and grand juries for the next term. Whom do you think he selected as jury commissioners to do this work? He selected two white men and one Negro at every term of the court. Did you ever hear of such a thing in Arkansas before? Would the circuit judge of your district do such a thing? My fellow citizens, the statute of this state does not require that the jury commissioners be even selected from opposite political parties, and no one would presume that a white man born and raised in the South would select a Negro as jury commissioner to select a jury for the county, to pass upon the rights of white people in the civil and criminal courts of the county. But Judge Wood did this; he does not deny it.

. . . My fellow citizens, if he would do this to secure the Negro vote for circuit judge, what would he do to be elected Governor of Arkansas? . . . My fellow citizens, the Negro question is the biggest question now confronting the American people. Teddy Roosevelt is trying to force it upon us, trying to force Negro equality in the South. Roosevelt only wanted to eat with Negroes; Judge Wood appointed them as jury commissioners and on the juries of the county. . . . Do you know what the qualifications of jury commissioners are? The statute says that they shall be men of sound judgement, reasonable information and approved integrity. We do not have any Negroes like that in my county. . . . Ah, my fellow citizens, imagine a judge appointing [a Negro] as . . . jury commissioner; but in justification of this, [Judge Wood] says that I appointed two Negroes as Justices of the Peace since I have been in office in Chicot County. I want to say to you that I never in my life KNOWINGLY appointed a negro to any office. I find upon examination in my office, that my private secretary in my absence signed a commission for a Negro in Chicot County as Justice of the Peace who had been elected but had failed to be sworn in, and the sheriff and clerk of that county asked that a commission be issued to him inasmuch as he had been elected. This was done without my knowledge; of course I am responsible for the action of my private secretary, but I say to you ladies and gentlemen that when I went into office as Governor I announced this rule and have never knowingly violated it; that no man could be appointed to office under my administration unless he was a white man, a Democrat and a Jeff Davis man; these have been the qualifications and requirements for appointments in my administration.

Scipio Africanus Jones on Republicanism

Scipio A. Jones, "Speech before the Black Republican League of Arkansas," *Arkansas Gazette (Little Rock),* October 24, 1916.

In the following selection, Scipio A. Jones, a black attorney from Little Rock, a social activist, and a Republican, decries the state of politics in Arkansas and across the nation during the Progressive Era.

It is needless for me to say that I am a Republican. From the day that I received at the hands of the Republicans of Pulaski County a nomination for state representative until this good day, my influence, my time, my money, whatever political ability I possess has been at the disposal of the party of my fathers, the party of the immortal Lincoln and the illustrious Grant. And I recall with feelings of fond recollection when the Republican Party of Arkansas was untainted by the monster "lily-white-ism." In those days we had Republicans in county offices, in those days county conventions were not held in boarding houses and hotels, where men of my color were not permitted. But you all know what is the condition in the Republican Party in our State at this time. County conventions such as was held in the Marion Hotel this spring are now a farce; lily whites are trying to drive us from the party councils; they say to us you can not enter into the inner circle, but here is our candidate for governor, here is our county ticket, [now] you Negroes, despite what we have said to you and done to you, vote for the men we, THE LILY WHITES, put up for office. My friends, the line has been drawn by these lily whites. What side are you on? Inch by inch your right to participate in the deliberations of your party has been taken from you until now you are denied a single representative to the Republican National Convention. Heretofore you have had from three to four delegates and [a] number of alternates to the National Convention. What a contrast with the delegation sent from this state last June? Arkansas is the only Southern state that did not have a Negro delegate to the last Republican Convention. The Negroes of this State hold more than sixty thousand poll tax receipts. Will they be used in the interest of political equality or will they be cast so as to encourage lily white-ism, political discrimination, and advance the interests of those who even in the Republican Party would deny us a man's chance? But the lily whites cry out if it were not for the Negroes the Republican Party in Arkansas would grow. I say let's give the lily whites an opportunity to prove it this year by scratching their candidates for office. There are ten Negro Republicans to every white Republican holding poll tax receipts in Arkansas. And yet, no Negro delegates to the National Convention, practically without representation on the State Central and Executive Committees. But the lily whites claim they are after the Negro leaders of Pulaski County, because they are not loyal Republicans! If that be true, why did they not send some Negro from some other county as a delegate? Are we disloyal? No, my friends, the Negro in Arkansas nor in any other place has not been disloyal to the Republican Party. I challenge any lily whites or their defenders to show where any race or set of men anywhere in the history of our State or Nation have been more loyal in their support or steadfast in their devotion than has the Negro been to the Republican Party. But whenever a Negro contends for his political rights he is disloyal and must be destroyed. Fellow citizen, no race has ever succeeded without a leader. The contemptible lily whites and their paid black allies are asking you to assist them in destroying what few leaders you have. Will you do so? God forbid that the black men of my race whose bravery shines as a beacon light from the patriotic field of Bunker Hill to the blood stained prairie of Carrizal shall ever be found crucifying on a cross of racial treachery the true, tried leaders of their race.

These lily whites are the same gentlemen who declared it would not be good policy for the Republican State Convention to declare itself in opposition to the Grand Father Clause. When your right to vote was at stake and you and I were working day and night to defeat this damnable grandfather clause, where was this distinguished crowd then? But now, since you and your leaders have led you out of the wilderness of disfranchisement they come to you and say crucify your leaders and give us your vote! Will you do so? No, no, a thousand times NO.

If you favor holding conventions in hotel parlors and denying Negroes the right to go to Republican National Conventions, then vote for those who advocate such things. But if you are opposed to lily white-ism in Arkansas, if you value your manhood, if you believe in opportunity for unborn sons and justice and honor to unborn daughters, vote against these lily white oppressors of true Republicanism and show your resentment of them and their methods by scratching the names of every one of their candidates. Choose you this night who you will serve! Be men, cast your vote for right, for political freedom to all men regardless of color.

At the recent convention of Negro Republicans held in this city, I was in favor of Bishop J. M. Connor's suggestion that we fight the lily whites by placing a Negro candidate for Governor in the field against [Wallace] Townsend, the candidate of our opponents. But since the convention thought best not to nominate a candidate for Governor but recommended that we scratch the so-called Republican State Ticket, let's follow out their wishes and abide by the counsel of Bishop Connor, Dr. Morris, Col. Havis and our other leaders. I appeal to you men, who fought side by side with me as your chosen captain and with your assistance, I marshalled our black host against Amendment 11, the grandfather clause, and administered unto it a crushing defeat, to now help me deal the death blow to lily white-ism in Arkansas Republican politics. Register your protest against the lily white and his method of scratching those who have scorned you. Listen my friends, in the first Congressional District, the Negroes hold a majority of all the poll tax receipts, and still we were denied a delegate to the National Convention.

. . . Every qualified Negro elector in Arkansas should go to the polls early on November 7 [1916] and cast his vote for electors pledged to the support of Charles Evans Hughes and Charles Warren Fairbanks. Our National Republican Party could have chosen no greater nominees than these men. The great and lasting service rendered their nation by these great citizens of our republic is in earnest what may be expected of them if by the suffrage of our citizenship they shall be called to the high offices of President and Vice President.

. . . In conclusion, permit me to say to you that the eyes of millions now look down upon you, wondering whether as men you will resent insult and injury and discrimination, or whether as craven cowards you will yield to the beck of your persecutors and lick salt from the hand of them that seek to slay you. God grant that as you go to the polls on November 7, your minds will be enveloped in such heroic thoughts as stood well your illustrious sires at Bunker Hill, New Orleans, Milligan's Bend, Port Hudson and Fort Wagner to the end that you may deal a death blow to the lily whites of Arkansas and their candidates, and win a glorious victory for Negro manhood, Negro honor, Negro representation and true Republicanism.

C. THE COMING OF WORLD WARFARE

During the waning years of progressivism, the United States found itself drawn into world conflict. World War I also witnessed the coming of a Communist-revolutionary form of government—Bolshevism—to Russia. This latter development, as viewed by the democracies of the West, set in motion a wave of hysteria commonly known as the Red Scare. In city after city across the United States, a veritable crusade began: to ferret out "Bolsheviks" and those deemed less than 100 percent patriotic to the nation's flag in the war against German tyranny. On more than one occasion during the period, ultrapatriotic fervor triumphed over basic human rights. The selections herein are illustrative of Arkansas's response to World War I and its reaction to what was perceived as the Bolshevist threat.

Military Preparedness and Patriotism

Arkansas Gazette (Little Rock), May 23, 1917.

Authorized by Gov. George Donaghey and composed of prominent citizens, the Arkansas State Council of Defense symbolized Arkansas's patriotism during the war years.

The Arkansas State Council of Defense met [on May 22, 1917] and organized in the office of H. L. Remmel. . . . General Lloyd England, commanding the Arkansas National Guard, is chairman. . . .

. . . The President of the United States, the Department of War and the Governor of Arkansas have asked that registration day be made a national holiday, which may be converted into a magnificent demonstration of the unity and patriotism of our country. President Wilson, in issuing the proclamation announcing the date of registration, used these words: "It is in no sense a conscription of the unwilling; it is rather selection for a nation which has volunteered in mass. It is no more a choosing of those who shall serve an equally necessary and devoted purpose in the industries that lie behind the battle line."

Speaking before the National Defense Conference, recently, the Secretary of War said: "All prejudice will be gone, if, when the day comes, flags are floating from public and private buildings and bands are parading the streets, and the people of the cities and countryside are accompanying their sons and brothers and husbands of suitable age to the registration place in the feeling that here in America is the alter [altar] of free institutions, and that every man who is putting his name down is making an acceptable sacrifice."

The Arkansas State Council of Defense urges all patriotic citizens and organizations in Arkansas to make arrangements at once to hold, in all cities, towns and voting precincts of the state, on June 5, public meetings where patriotic programs will be given. Meetings may be held in churches, schoolhouses, or other convenient places. . . . The program may consist of band music, singing of national airs, flag raising, reading of the Declaration of Independence, reading of the president's proclamation announcing the date of registration. . . . There are thousands of people in Arkansas who are perfectly able to buy a bond for $50 or $100 or more, who do not realize the necessity of helping to float [the war effort] loan. The banks of the state have risen to the occasion and will offer opportunity for buying bonds by means of small payments.

It is suggested also that there be at each registration place a committee of ladies to serve lunch to the enrolling officers, and to see that each man enrolls, has some evidence of the fact that will be apparent to the passers-by. A small piece of red, white and blue ribbon, or the blue enrollment card, might be pinned on each man.

. . . The people of Arkansas, as yet far removed from the scene of conflict, pursuing peacefully the daily routine of their lives, wishing only to be unmolested in the conduct of their affairs, and not having at hand the sources of information possessed by the United States government, do not realize the magnitude of the crisis confronting the nation. We are not at war with Germany because of the sinking of a few ships and the destruction of a few American lives. If that were the cause, we would have declared war immediately after the sinking of the *Lusitania.*

We entered the war because the president and the Congress of the United States, whom we have chosen to direct our government and to conserve our national interests, having at their command means of securing information not accessible to the private citizen, became absolutely certain that the question in this war is to settle . . . whether the world—including America—is to be free, or is to [become] slave to Germany; that a German victory over England and France would be followed, as certainly as the night follows day, by an immediate attack on America.

Arkansas Responds to the Red Scare

General Acts and Constitutional Amendments Proposed and Joint and Concurrent Resolutions and Memorials of the 42nd General Assembly of the State of Arkansas (Little Rock: Democrat Printing and Lithographic Co., 1919), 388–89.

The document that follows describes Arkansas's legislation to deter the introduction and spread of "Bolshevist" doctrines in the state.

ACT 512.
Approved March 28, 1919

AN ACT to Define and Punish Anarchy and to Prevent the Introduction and spread of Bolshevism and Kindred Doctrines, in the State of Arkansas.

Be It Enacted by the General Assembly of the State of Arkansas:
Be It Enacted by the People of the State of Arkansas:
Section 1. That hereafter it shall be unlawful for any person or persons, to write, indict, dictate, speak, utter, publish, or declare or be interested in writing, indicting, dictating, speaking, uttering, publishing or

declaring any word, sentence, speech or article of whatsoever nature or kind, with the intent to encourage, advise, aid, assist or abet in the infliction of any personal injury upon any person or the taking of human life, or destruction or injury to either public or private property, without due process of law, or in any manner to disseminate knowledge or propaganda which tends to destroy or overthrow the present form of government of either the State of Arkansas, or the United States of America, by any violence or unlawful means whatsoever or whoever shall employ any such means aforesaid, which are calculated to cause such results aforesaid, shall be guilty of a misdemeanor, and upon conviction, shall be punished by a fine of not less than ten dollars ($10), nor more than one thousand dollars ($1,000), and may be imprisoned in the county jail, not exceeding six months, or both, at the discretion of the court.

Section 2. That hereafter it shall be unlawful for any person or persons, to wear, use, exhibit, display or have in possession any symbol, token, device or flag, the meaning, object, purpose or intent of which is to encourage, aid, assist or abet with such intent or incite with such intent to, or which is calculated to encourage, aid, assist, abet or incite any person in, the infliction of personal injury upon another person or the taking of human life, or the destruction of either public or private property, without due process of law, or to destroy or overthrow or which tends to destroy or overthrow the present form of government of either the State of Arkansas or the United States of America. [The same penalty applied to Section 2 as Section 1.]

FOR FURTHER READING

For Arkansas in the Progressive Era, the following works should be consulted: Carl H. Moneyhon, *Arkansas and the New South, 1874–1929* (Fayetteville: University of Arkansas Press, 1997); Calvin R. Ledbetter Jr., *Carpenter from Conway, George Washington Donaghey as Governor of Arkansas, 1090–1913* (Fayetteville: University of Arkansas Press, 1993); George Donaghey, *Building a State Capitol* (Little Rock: Parke and Harper Publishing Co., 1937); Foy Lisenby, *Charles Hillman Brough: A Biography* (Fayetteville: University of Arkansas Press, 1996); James R. Green, *Socialism and the Southwestern Class Struggle, 1898–1918* (Ann Arbor, MI: University Microfilms International, 1972); Richard L.

Niswonger, *Arkansas Democratic Politics* (Ann Arbor, MI: University Microfilms International, 1973); and Joe Seagraves, *Arkansans Politics, 1874–1918* (Ann Harbor, MI: University Microfilms International, 1975). The books by Green, Niswonger, and Seagraves examine political and social currents of the period. For an account of the woman suffrage movement in Arkansas and across the nation, see Ida Husted Harper, ed., *The History of Woman Suffrage* (New York: Fowler and Wells, 1920). *Long Is the Way and Hard: One Hundred Years of the NAACP* (Fayetteville: University of Arkansas Press, 2009), edited by Kervern Verney and Lee Sartain, provides an overview of that organization's challenge to the racism and violence of the period.

CHAPTER VII

Between the Wars, 1920–1940

INTRODUCTION

The progressive impulse in Arkansas and across the nation did not die suddenly with the conclusion of World War I. Certain reform trends—improving the quality of education, road construction, and public services and addressing the plight of the nation's farmers, for example—continued into the 1920s. There was, however, a new spirit of economic development afoot as the nation enjoyed new and expanded trade markets around the world. Perhaps President Calvin Coolidge expressed the mood best when he boldly stated, "The business of America is business."

Arkansas witnessed significant economic growth during the early 1920s. The value of the state's factory output in 1920, for example, stood at $200 million, an all-time high. In 1922, the value of Arkansas's mineral products was estimated at $60 million, while the value of all crops and livestock produced was $300 million during that same year. Perhaps of all the areas of growth, the state's mineral production was most impressive during the period from 1900 to 1925. In the former year, the total value of all minerals produced was only $2,390,788. By 1925, this figure had risen to $87,185,532. The increased use of bauxite both during and after World War I was a tremendous impetus to this growth, and Arkansas had a virtual monopoly of bauxite production, as the vast reserves of this chief ingredient in the making of aluminum seem to rest solely within the state's borders.

With economic growth and development, many concerned Arkansans sensed the need to bolster the state's reputation throughout the nation. To accomplish this, the Arkansas Advancement Association took up the challenge and launched what can best be described as a crusade to tell the world about "Ar-kan-*saw*." For many boosters of the state's image, the older title, "The Bear State," was no longer appropriate; in 1923, the legislature adopted a resolution officially dubbing Arkansas "The Wonder State." In all, it seemed as though the good times would never end.

But they did. In October 1929, the American economic bubble burst, as the stock market crash ushered in a decade of hard times. The subsequent Great Depression of the 1930s constituted an economic and intellectual crisis of the greatest magnitude. In Arkansas, where cotton was still king and 80 percent of the 1,854,482 people lived in rural areas, the depression was acute. Cotton prices plummeted, and, with prices low, farmers could not meet mortgages, causing displacement to run rampant.

Even before the Great Depression set in, a large portion of the state's farmers had taken a financial and spiritual drubbing at the hands of Mother Nature. In 1927, the rain-swollen Mississippi overflowed its banks into the Arkansas River, destroying thousands of acres of farmland and drowning countless livestock. And then during the summer of 1930 came the great drought that parched land, crops, and men. Such was the uncertain nature of farming. So, after these disasters, many Arkansas wondered just what else could there be in the way of hardships? The Depression answered this question.

In 1933, J. Marion Futrell took the reins of state government. Despairing of incurring further state debts in any attempt to ease the economic crisis, Futrell cut back the operating cost of running the state by instituting a most painful austerity program that included a reduction in state services, employees, and salaries.

On the national level, Arkansans, solidly within the democratic tradition, gave their support in 1932 to Franklin Delano Roosevelt as the thirty-second president of the United States. Many residents had been particularly impressed by Roosevelt when during the campaign he stated, "I pledge you, I pledge myself, to a new deal for the American people. Let us all . . . constitute ourselves prophets of a new order of competence and courage. This is more than a political campaign; it is a call to arms." After assuming office in 1933, Roosevelt immediately set about to restore American confidence and the economy.

The historical debate over the effectiveness, the direction, and purpose of the New Deal yet rages. Perhaps its true significance lies in the efforts exerted by a host of alphabetic agencies and programs based largely upon the concept of systematic government planning for the economy. For New Dealers, laissez-faire economics would not cure the ills of the American economic system. In short, the natural workings of the economy needed a helping hand.

A helping hand came to many Arkansas farmers as they complied with the Agricultural Adjustment Administration's program of plowing under already planted crops as a stimulus to increased prices. In the face of breadlines, crops were destroyed; so, too, would there be the slaughter of millions of pigs across the nation. Terrible though this logic was, it worked. With increased shortages, farmers received higher prices. Thus, farmers who owned their land witnessed some economic relief, but sharecroppers who leased or rented theirs found little or no recourse. The plight of this group of farmers found expression near Tyronza in eastern Arkansas in July 1934, when H. L. Mitchell, a former sharecropper, along with several other whites and blacks formed the Southern Tenants Farmers' Union. The reception given this union by local landowners and law officers, particularly after the union staged a strike among cotton pickers in 1935, was largely hostile.

The 1930s were, of course, dominated by the Great Depression, but other events were also of significance to Arkansans. In 1936, Arkansans celebrated the state's one hundredth birthday. Times were still hard, but for many the jubilant celebration held out the promise of a brighter day. On the international horizon, however, things were growing dim as Adolph Hitler fanned the flames of ultra-German nationalism and as Japan announced a new order in Asia in which Japan alone would rule.

A. ECONOMIC DEVELOPMENT AND BOOSTERISM

In the aftermath of World War I, the United States turned inward and vowed to remain outside the realm of Old World politics and foreign conflicts. The nation, however, given its continued industrial growth and development and the concomitant reality of an ever-shrinking globe, would be hard pressed to remain true to such isolationist sentiment. In the meantime, Americans turned their attention to internal development and prosperity. The selections in this section reflect Arkansas's efforts to foster both internal economic progress and the state's image.

Mines, Manufacturers, and Agriculture

Jim G. Ferguson, *Arkansas Handbook: Mines, Manufacturers and Agriculture* (Little Rock, 1923), 33–48.

This selection utilizes statistics to illustrate Arkansas's economic growth and development. It is interesting to note that at this time Arkansas ranked fourth among the states in petroleum; the state has dropped considerably in the rankings since then.

In 1920 Arkansas had 656 saw mills each reporting an annual production of 50,000 or more board feet. Mills of smaller output were not included. . . . The aggregate quantity of lumber cut by all mills reporting was 1,148,158 thousand board feet.

Value of factory output reaches $200,000,000 in one year. Being abundantly supplied with raw materials and possessing vast stores of cheap fuel, including oil, natural gas, coal, lignite and wood, and with exceptional water power possibilities, Arkansas is becoming an important manufacturing state. In 1919 there were 3,123 manufacturing establishments in the state, employing 58,202 persons, utilizing 274,469 primary horse power, and capital to the amount of $138,818,000. There was expended in wages $47,186,000 and for materials $102,813,000. The value of the products of these industries was $200,313,000. One-half of these industries were timber-working plants and their output was valued at $84,008,000; cottonseed oil mills were second in importance with an output of $25,304,000. More than thirty other industries are included in the list.

FACTORY PRODUCTION, 1919

PRODUCT	VALUE
Lumber and Timber	$84,008,309
Cottonseed Oil and Cake	25,304,034
Railroad Car Construction	11,030,409
Rice Cleaning and Polishing	8,995,856
Flour and Grist Milling	8,645,569
Planning Mill Products	7,064,791
Zinc Smeltering and Refining	4,423,398
Printing, Newspapers, etc.	3,405,163

Cooperage Products	3,367,254
Furniture	3,199,537
Bread and Baking Products	2,596,333
Confectionary and Ice Cream	2,592,993
Food Preparations	2,548,792
Canning and Preserving	2,420,922
Ice, Manufactured	2,132,331
Printing, Book and Job	2,014,930
Carriage and Wagon Material	1,807,497
Mineral and Carbonated Water	1,669,822
Foundry and Machine Shops	1,652,456
Coffee Roasting	1,542,441
Wood Turned and Carved	1,427,048
Printing and Publishing	1,247,078
Slaughtering and Packing	1,218,191

MINERAL PRODUCTION IN ARKANSAS
STATE ESTIMATES, 1922

Petroleum	$31,739,270
Coal	10,000,000
Clay	3,000,000
Bauxite	2,500,000
Natural Gas	1,000,000
Sand	1,500,000
Stone, Marble, and Granite	1,750,000
Manganese, Zinc, and Lead	250,000
Mineral Waters	150,000
Diamonds	125,000

Arkansas is one of the most important states. Its most valuable product is petroleum, which was discovered in the southern part of the state, adjacent to the producing Louisiana oil field, in 1921. The annual production the first year placed Arkansas fourth among the states in oil production and, with this new field much extended, she has since outranked Pennsylvania, the pioneer oil state, in total production. . . . From Arkansas the world obtains 70 percent of its supply of bauxite, the ore of aluminum. The output is 500,000 tons annually. . . . The total value of all mineral products in 1922 is estimated at $60,000,000.

AGRICULTURE

	VALUE
Cotton (lint)	$117,457,000
Corn	38,951,000
Cotton Seed	17,986,000
Swine Slaughtered	2,400,000
Dairy Products	33,574,861
Cattle Sold	1,578,890
Oats	3,612,000
Garden Vegetables	12,500,000
Rice	6,283,000
Eggs and Poultry	22,972,302
Peaches	2,040,000
Mules and Horses Sold	1,768,000
Wheat	1,185,000
Swine Sold	2,366,700
Sweet Potatoes	3,346,000
Irish Potatoes	3,094,000
Timothy, Clover, etc.	9,942,000
Sorghum and Sugar Cane Syrup	2,061,500
Apples	2,448,000
Strawberries	1,923,000
Cantaloupes	425,600

The total value of all crops and livestock grown on Arkansas farms in 1922 was nearly $300,000,000 according to the report of the State-Federal Crop Reporting Service.

Paving the Wilderness

Charles Hillman Brough, "Paving the Wilderness—An American Commonwealth out of the Mud," in the Charles H. Brough Papers, Arkansas History Commission, Little Rock.

As president of the United States Good Roads Association, Charles Brough, governor of Arkansas from 1917 to 1921, took special pride in the state's progress in the development of an efficient highway system. Below, Brough describes efforts, literally, to pave a wilderness.

A few leaders in their respective communities, whose names are worthy of mention for their courage and tenacity, realizing the hopelessness of the situation as long as inadequate transportation facilities existed, banded together for the purpose of discussing ways and means of paving . . . bottom lands and taking southeastern Arkansas out of the mud. Among these leaders were Senators John L. Carter of Chicot County, Robert L. Collins of Drew County and George F. Brown of Desha County. . . . These empire builders were faced with a tremendous problem. Aside from the physical difficulties presented in a road project of the size contemplated and the natural obstructions of the surrounding country, a bland wall of opposition faced them—the Constitution of 1874 of Arkansas forbids the issuance of either state or county bonds for internal improvements. . . .

However, these sturdy modern road builders recognizing the truth of the celebrated dictum of [Edward] Gibbon, the great historian that "the progress of any civilization is measured by the character and improvement of its roads," availed themselves of legal creation of judicial decisions known as the district improvement unit, which was authorized under the decision of our Supreme Court, to issue bonds on the taxable real property within the district for the improvement of these lands. In 1917, they secured the passage of Act 265 by the progressive Forty-First General Assembly . . . authorizing the creation of the Arkansas-Louisiana Highway Improvement District, under the terms of which bonds aggregating $3,100,000 were authorized for the construction of a hard-surfaced road 156 miles long and 18 feet wide, with a modern concrete base of 5 inches and an asphaltic top of 2 inches. . . .

. . . The entire project will probably be completed by January 1, 1920. . . . It is difficult to realize the magnitude of this highway without appreciating the wilderness of the country. The greater part of the road is being cut through virgin timber, a wide pathway tearing apart the . . . jungle, which a scant 15 years ago lay under 10 to 15 feet of water at springtime.

. . . Today our progressive citizens, riding over the Arkansas-Louisiana and other hard-surfaced roads, which have . . . paved a wilderness, can exclaim with one acclaim: "Hence forth O Arkansas, We look up to thee, not down at other states, arise, arise, be not proud, be humble and be wise, and bow thy head to the Great Supreme one who on high, hath willed that as a state, Arkansas shall never die."

Arkansas Boosterism

The Arkansas Advancement Association, pamphlet (1921), UALR Center for Arkansas History and Culture, Little Rock.

Whether for a sense of well-being, the attraction of newcomers, or commerce, American communities have sought to project a favorable and positive image. The Arkansas Advancement Association outlined an extensive campaign to promote the state during the 1920s.

Organized for the purpose of correlating the agencies which endeavor to convey to the outsider the great word about Arkansas thereby establishing a central body which has but one purpose—to preach the gospel of Arkansas, the Arkansas Advancement Association is getting down to real business. This association represents the ideals which have made you an incessant fighter for the proper recognition of your state. It is not a new idea, just a new determination and a sensible way of handling the proposition by uniting the strong men of the state for a common purpose. Every commercial organization, civic and patriotic body will be asked to take a prominent part in this work. . . .

[The] program of [the] Arkansas Advancement Association [is] to place a button, "I am Proud of Arkansas," on every Arkansan going out of the state. . . . To prepare a card containing on one side twenty or more reasons why Arkansas is the greatest state. . . . To place on every visitor and traveling salesman possible, a button, "I Have Been to Arkansas and I Like It," and give them plenty of information to back up the assertion.

To awaken the counties of Arkansas to a realization of their resources through visits to them by talented journalists who will immediately recognize that to which the citizen has become so accustomed that it no longer charms him, and will prepare the story for home, as well as foreign consumption.

To dismiss the School for Scandal, and by co-operation with the press of Arkansas, omit the sordid and the harmful from the news columns, giving preference to constructive articles which will show the world we are prosperous, contented people, instead of a house divided against itself. . . .

To prepare a series of catechisms which will be taught in the public schools, and read by all people of the state. . . . To conduct letter writing campaigns . . . telling of developments in Arkansas. It should be an easy matter to get 1,000 letters written for each county of the state, once each week. This would be 75,000 letters arriving in as many homes, where they would be read by an average of four members of a family—300,000 a week. This 300,000 would convey a portion of the letter to several times as many people, and Arkansas would be on the tongues of over 1,000,000 new people every week. . . . To induce leading novelists and magazine writers to come to Arkansas. . . . To have an Arkansas Day in New York during the winter. The very audacity of such a thing is sure to open the columns of the New York papers to our publicity agents.

. . . To keep after the fruit and vegetable shippers until they label their packages . . . inviting the purchaser to ask for Arkansas fruit, the possessor of the greatest of all hidden charms—a flavor equalled by none.

To combat outside agencies which seek to discountenance Arkansas enterprises, by meeting their propaganda at its source. . . . To influence the popular song writers to occasionally insert the word Arkansas in their effusions.

. . . To prepare an automobile map of Arkansas. . . . [T]he automobile is every day extending its field of usefulness. . . . The modern tourist travels by automobile. He is a good booster for the places which appeal to him. . . .

To induce motion picture concerns to get on the ground . . . so that Arkansas will be shown in thousands of moving picture theaters in the news of the day. . . . To maintain a staff that will devote 24 hours a day to seeking new and varied ways of putting Arkansas before the world in a garb so attractive that it is indeed a hard-hearted person who does not fall a victim to the attractions of this charming young miss.

B. MOTHER NATURE AND HUMAN SOCIETY

Many were the currents of the 1920s. These were, of course, the Roaring Twenties, years of the speakeasy, installment buying, and unprecedented business growth and expansion. In human relations, the period harbored expressions of a deep-seated distrust, suspicion, and hatred for the culturally different and foreign. The decade also witnessed an outpouring of artistic and literary achievements of considerable import. Simultaneously, the South, particularly, experienced the ravages of drought and then flood waters that brought the human order to its knees in awesome wonder at the majestic powers of nature. It was, indeed, a most action-filled period of American life.

The Great Flood of 1927

Frederick Simpich, "The Great Mississippi Flood of 1927," *National Geographic Magazine* 3 (1927): 243–89.

Frederick Simpich, a journalist for the *National Geographic Magazine*, described the ravages of the Mississippi River flood of 1927. In the article, Simpich evokes images of great floods from mythical, historical, and biblical sources to convey the magnitude of this one.

Since time began, the fact that water runs downhill has warped the fate of men and nations. In Babylonia, kingdoms fell with floods and the famines that followed. Some say a Hebrew prophet could foretell the Seven Lean Years because he knew the habits of the Nile. The Mongols, cutting the Tigris levees, conquered Baghdad. In China, more men drown than die in battle. One Yellow River flood claimed more than a million who drowned or starved. . . . Along our cruel Colorado and marauding Mississippi, man has long matched his wits against the powers of Nature.

When white men founded New Orleans, 200 years ago, they had to throw up dirt banks to bar the river from their rude camp. From that day to this, with men, mules, machines, and money, the towns and planters along the river, aided in more recent years by the Government, have fought a losing fight against the floods. It is a stupendous struggle. Its battle front is flung from the Ohio to the Gulf. In heat, mud, and miasma, slaving men and sweating animals, toiling through the years, have thrown up 2,500 miles of huge, fort-like levees. Higher and higher they build them, hoping always that some day, somehow they may achieve perfect flood control.

. . . Today the most destructive flood in all the annals of this rapacious river [the Mississippi] is rolling from Cairo to the sea.

Parts of seven states are under water. Nearly 800,000 people have been driven from their homes or rescued from housetops, trees, levees, and railway embankments.

To save New Orleans, levees are blown up. Tons and tons of dynamite are used, throwing masses of mud and driftwood high into the air repicturing in a way the shell-torn fields of France in war times.

In the flood's wide path from Arkansas to Louisiana, unknown thousands of farm animals have been drowned, marooned on mounds and levees, or here and there rescued by cruising boats. . . .

To human victims of the flood more than 50,000,000 grains of quinine have been given and more than half a million people inoculated against disease.

Final property loss may be nearly a billion dollars. The whole nation, at first amazed and appalled, quickly and magnificently rallies with millions in money, with trainloads of clothing and food to comfort hungry helpless victims of the worst American flood of all time. . . .

From Cairo, from Little Rock, from Memphis, far down through the lowlands to where Evangeline searched for her lover, the waters wreak their wrath. Levees tumble and farms are flooded. Swollen, crowded bodies of mules, hogs, horses, and cows glut the bayous. Buzzards come, and on the levees wolves prey on the deer, tired from swimming.

Far and wide, rescue steamers churn the yellow tide, hauling bargeloads of silent, stupefied people, coaxed from their perilous retreats. Overhead roar the scout planes. As soaring, keen-eyed hawks scour a field for hiding quail, so these planes seek out groups marooned on levees or housetops; then whiz back to report, that rescue boats may be sent.

On levees, ridges, ancient Indian Mounds, wet, miserable man huddles with his domestic animals. Crawling up from the flood come foxes, rabbits, quail, deer, wild turkey, to climb freely over man's piled-up furniture, bedding, and bundles, unmindful now of him and his dogs. Only the snake is denied refuge. Animals shrink from it; man kills it. Probably it was so in the first flood.

A clumsy, creaking, weather-beaten old side-wheeler was one rescue boat I saw creep in. . . . Forward, on the deck, after the boat had docked, a small group of old women began singing hymns. And, heedless of the hymn-singers, a gum-chewing, giggling maid of the marshes, skylarking with the sunburned crew, boldly declared, "Noah oughta stuck around; he'd a seen a real flood!"

"The most immediate danger," said the skipper of one rescue boat, "was from the crevasses, rather than from the more slow-moving flood behind the levees. One levee break, for example, was at Pendleton, above Arkansas City. When it came couriers raced the lowlands, warning those who had no telephones. At Noon the streets of Arkansas City were dry and dusty. By 2 o'clock mules were drowning in the main streets of that town faster than they could be unhitched from wagons. Before dark the homes and stores stood six feet deep in water."

. . . How to fight fever, smallpox, and all the dread disease that follows a vast, receding flood is the biggest of all tasks that now face the Red Cross and Public Health Service. . . . Fifty thousand dead animals must be burned or buried in flooded sections of Arkansas and Mississippi alone.

The Arkansas Federation of Women's Clubs

The Arkansas Federation of Women's Clubs Report, n.d., Arkansas History Commission, Little Rock.

Efforts to improve the health and social conditions of Arkansans during the 1920s are reported by the Arkansas Federation of Women's Clubs, which offered helping hands to those in need.

Not exactly "from the center all around to the sea" but from Little Rock east to Lee County; west to Sebastian, to Washington on the north and south to the Louisiana line, the working members of the Department of Public Welfare have been pushing their plans for making the Wonder State a better place in which to live. The chairman . . . and chairmen [of the Arkansas Federation of Women's Clubs have] found the inspiration to work in all lines of welfare. . . .

Through the enthusiasm of Mrs. Vaughn W. Root . . . Occupational Therapy has been placed in practically all the State institutions where it is indicated. . . . Mrs. Florence McRaven is watching with zeal the problems of industry that affect the lives of women . . . and considering the need of new laws to govern industrial affairs. . . .

The legal and social status of the disadvantaged children is the phase of life that has commanded the energies of Mrs. Katherine Gibson, whose committee deal with . . . juvenile and adult offenders against the law, probation and parole, the prevention of crime . . . to bring about better conditions in Arkansas. The Division of Child Welfare, presided over by Mrs. C. E. Daggett of Marianna whose committee on dependent children and hospitalization, the orphan child, pre-natal care and allied problems has found warm response in the hearts of the women and their efforts to prove to them the need of real work along this line.

Here we want to give credit to the Parent Teachers Association and their pre-school committee for the splendid work done for the children of pre-school age and if we can now find an organization interested in doing maternal and infancy.

Mrs. Anne M. Blakeney as Chairman of the Division of Health has been at work, interesting her committees on public health nursing, mental hygiene, tuberculosis, social hygiene, occupational therapy, narcotics, cancer and vital statistics. As Chairman of Health for the State Parent Teachers Association, she has received enthusiastic response from these groups.

By the efforts of these combined groups there has been established an official standard of child health in Arkansas which requires that every blue-ribbon child shall have normal vision or properly fitted glasses, normal hearing, sound throats without adenoids or infected tonsils, good teeth and gums, correct posture; shall be properly nourished, being neither 20 percent overweight nor 10 percent underweight; shall be immunized against typhoid, diphtheria and smallpox, and shall be able to show that his birth is of record.

Trachoma clinics have been reported from counties widely distributed over the state. In some of these counties few cases have been found, but in a few localities many active cases have been discovered and placed under the supervision of the medical officer of the government trachoma hospital at Russellville.

Practically all over the state there has been nutrition work in the schools, taking the form of milk given in the mid-morning or hot lunches at noon. Local home economics teachers and the university extension workers have cooperated splendidly and good results have been noted in all schools where the nutritional program has been tried.

That the effect of poor teeth on health has been widely taught is shown by the fact that dental corrections are eagerly sought by the children in every section of the state. A number of schools are reporting 100 percent dental corrections, and from one official source in a report of 2,640 physical corrections made 1,740 were dental corrections.

Immunization against smallpox and diphtheria has been administered wholesale. The state has a law requiring vaccination against small pox as a prerequisite for entrance into school, the first state in the Union to take this forward step. A large percentage of the population of southern and eastern Arkansas was vaccinated against typhoid and smallpox in combating outbreaks following the floods of 1927. There were reported at that time 152,000 complete immunizations against typhoid, and 5,084 administered since, and 37,000 smallpox immunizations in the emergency and 8,850 since that time. Recent diphtheria immunizations amount to 3,912.

In 1927, 220 pre-natal, infant and pre-school conferences were held and the work has begun well in this year, there having been held 48 of the same type conferences in the first three months of 1928, at which parents were instructed in child care, and shown the necessity for corrections.

This year-round program culminated in a "May Day—Child Health Day" celebration and plans have been carried out in more than 25 counties of the state. Celebrations were held in the form of picnics, pageants, plays and parades, in which every form of health habit or practice was featured. Dairies made floats and exhibits showing the value of milk in maintaining health; grocers displayed the foods requisite for balanced meals; health organizations visualized the fundamentals of good health, pure water, sewage disposal, screening houses, mosquite control and other phases of health promotion. . . .

Your Chairman for Public Welfare would respectfully recommend that more serious consideration be given by the club women to the study of mental hygiene and that an additional committee, which would be coordinated with the legal health authorities of the State, be appointed to study the prevention of blindness.

A Knight of the Long Trail: The Travels of a Circuit Rider

John C. Glenn, *Reverend Drury Harrington Colquette: The Worker and His Work, An Appreciation*, pamphlet (October 1927), UALR Center for Arkansas History and Culture, Little Rock.

In a fashion similar to that of his counterpart who rode the dusty trails of America dispensing justice, the religious circuit rider carried with him words of redemption and salvation. In this selection, Rev. John C. Glenn, of the Little Rock and North Arkansas Conferences of the Methodist Episcopal Church, South, recounts the work of one such circuit rider.

We can never fully appreciate the final summing-up of any life until the "lights and shadows" of childhood and youth are known. . . . Heredity puts its stamp upon people; there is no doubt in the world about that. What a man's parents were, and what his environment was until his majority, stamp themselves indelibly on the life and character of the man. Lincoln was one who rose above his environment and is admiringly called a "self-made" man. Reverend Drury Harrington Colquette is, in the accepted sense of that term, a "self-made" man. . . .

The childhood and boyhood life of . . . Colquette was not unlike that of other boys of his station in life. A native of Tennessee, having been born just outside of the corporate limits of Trenton, young Colquette came to Arkansas with his parents in December, 1878, when he was a lad of ten winters. He passed through the public schools of his native state and Arkansas. He attended a normal school in Mississippi. After spending five years in the school-room, he entered Hendrix College at Conway. . . . He began his ministry before he was out of his teens. In 1887, at a church near Walnut Ridge, [Colquette] was licensed to preach.

. . . Now we come to the heart of the life, labors and achievements of the subject. . . . The "rule and guide for our faith and practice"—the Holy Bible—was seldom found in many of the "out-of-the-way" places that Drury Harrington Colquette visited. . . . To this thoughtful and faithful minister, this work constituted a great field. He willingly accepted the challenge, and for many years he carried Bibles, Testaments, good books and tracts on his monthly rounds. As a pastor he placed Bibles in the homes of more people than any other minister in the Methodist Church in Arkansas. . . . [According to] Mr. Colquette . . . the great purpose of the Bible is declared in the words: "These are written that ye might believe that Jesus is the Christ the Son of God; and that believing ye might have life through His name." [The Bible] is the Magna Charta of the poor and the oppressed, the mother of popular education, and just as easily the most powerful educative force that has ever entered humanity.

. . . We direct [our] attention to [Colquette's] 1921 annual report. It reveals remarkable progress and wonderful service, with a grand total distribution of [Bibles] of 16,062 volumes. He made twenty trips to penal institutions, conducted services in other institutions, and traveled nearly 5,000 miles. He seems to have achieved unusual success in 1923, according to the office files and the annual report. He traveled 8,000 miles on foot, in buggy, automobile, horseback, and on freight and passenger trains, and in a few instances in Pullman cars. He worked in 53 towns and cities, visited forty prisons, hospitals and pauper houses, conducting services and giving out Bibles and Testaments. . . .

. . . In 1925 [Colquette] visited 1,259 "shut-ins" of state penal institutions alone, distributed approximately 40,000 volumes, traveled nearly 7,000 miles and held 202 special services. He had the privilege of preaching to scores of others and held services for ten condemned men during the year. No less than forty accepted Jesus.

During the [1927 Mississippi] flood when an area larger than that of Massachusetts, Connecticut, Rhode Island and Deleware [*sic*] combined, was under water in the three states of Mississippi, Louisiana and Arkansas, Reverend Colquette lost no time in the canvass of the flood district. He did not stop with the rains. . . . He says: "In all of my eleven years' experience as one of the exclusive state agents of the American Bible Society I have not known of a greater hunger for God's word than I found among the distressed and frightened people of almost every age and color who were driven from their homes by the flood." In Dermott Mr. Colquette distributed Gospels to refugees living in forty-three box cars. In some instances he reached the flood sufferers only by motor boat. . . .

. . . Mr. Colquette's balance sheet is not closed. There may be other and greater chapters to be added before the final summing-up of accounts. . . . But I submit my questions to the judgement of those who may chance to read this. . . . Is such a life worth while? Does it deserve a place among the records of human documents? Does it not carry a message more precious than gold? His life means, first of all, the inexhaustible resources of God's grace; second, the imperial majesty of the human will when surcharged with a presiding purpose; lastly, the certain triumph of a dedicated life.

The Authors' and Composers' Society of Arkansas

The Arkansas Writer, July–August 1921, UALR Center for
Arkansas History and Culture, Little Rock.

Founded originally in 1914, the Authors' and Composers' Society,
through its official organ, *The Arkansas Writer,* dedicated itself to
the preservation and promotion of Arkansas's cultural life. Literary
figures, artists, actors, and musicians (an active membership by 1921
of 122 from across the state) were determined to show that the state
could hold its own in the world of culture. The following selection
describes the state of arts and letters in Arkansas to the early 1920s.

The time-worn idea that Arkansas is a state without ideals, a state
without traditions, a state without literary attainment, has long since
been refuted, and Arkansas has secured recognition among the ranking
producers of the country. It is generally conceded that Arkansas has won
"first place" in pioneer literature, through John Gould Fletcher; in classical poetry through J. Brookes More; in school classics through Mrs.
Walter H. Pemberton; in pure, princely poesy and song through Fay
Hempstead; in historical novel through Mrs. Bernie Babcock; in religious
song through Will M. Ramsey; in composition through Prof. Emile
Trebing, . . . Mrs. De E. Bradshaw, Miss Lillian Hughes, . . . Mrs. C. E.
Whitney. There are other Arkansas writers of story, song, drama and
verse, whose literary and musical articles take high rank. Among these
are Clio Harper, C. T. Davis, T. Elmore Lucey, Mrs. Ruby Livingston
and Mrs. Robert Forster. Their productions are eagerly accepted by the
Eastern publishers, and they have experienced the supreme test of leading
publishers clamoring for more. . . . Other states of the South and West
are "lining up" with Arkansas; others have long ago taken first rank and
are now known as the "Old Liners," but, after careful, just and conservative weighing of works, we find that Arkansas is altogether able to "hold
her own" with even the most ancient of code, and loudest of acclaim.

And while not altogether satisfied with ourselves and results; yet the
total average-up is quite compensating and cause of comfort. Each of
you should feel a real, a personal pride in [the Authors' and Composers'
Society]. 'Tis said that everything takes on new life every seven years, so
the "Pioneer Age" of this society has passed into the "Progressive," a
surety of plan and purpose; a steady and steadfast development, and some

degree of success. . . . We know where we stand, we know what we are doing, we know what we intend to do.

The Anti-evolution Law: A Challenge to the New Science

Acts, Concurrent Resolutions, Memorials and Proposed Constitutional Amendments of the 47th General Assembly, State of Arkansas (January 14–March 14, 1929), Little Rock, 1929.

Perhaps few other issues so stirred US society and threatened traditional values during the 1920s as did the scientific theory of evolution. Following the 1925 John T. Scopes trial in Dayton, Tennessee, in which Scopes was found guilty of violating that state's anti-evolution laws, Arkansans, through the initiative and referendum process, voted in their own anti-evolution law.

INITIATED ACT NO. 1.

AN ACT to Prohibit in Any University, Normal, Public School, College, or Other Educational Institution in the State of Arkansas That is Supported in Whole or in Part, From Public Funds, the Teaching that Man Descended or Ascended from a Lower Order of Animals and Providing a Penalty For Violation Thereof.

Be It Enacted by the People of the State of Arkansas:

Section 1. That it shall be unlawful for any teacher or other instructor in any University, College, Normal, Public School, or other institution of the State, which is supported in whole or in part from public funds derived by State and local taxation to teach the theory or doctrine that mankind ascended or descended from a lower order of animals and also it shall be unlawful for any teacher, textbook commission, or other authority exercising the power to select textbooks for above mentioned educational institutions to adopt or use in any such institution a textbook that teaches the doctrine or theory that mankind descended or ascended from a lower order of animals.

Section 2. Be it further enacted that any teacher or other instructor or textbook commissioner who is found guilty of violation of this Act by teaching the theory or doctrine mentioned in Section 1 hereof, or by using, or adopting any such textbooks in any such educational institution shall be guilty of a misdemeanor and upon conviction shall be fined not exceeding five hundred dollars ($500.00); and upon conviction shall vacate the position thus held in any educational institutions of the character above mentioned or any commission of which he may be a member.

Section 3. This Act shall be in full force and effect from and after its adoption by vote of the people of the State of Arkansas.

Section 4. That all laws and parts of laws in conflict herewith be, and the same are, hereby repealed.

Filed in the office of the Secretary of State on the 6th day of June, 1928. Voted on at the General Election October 6th, 1928. For, 108,991; against, 63,406.

The Ku Klux Klan Speaks

"Roman Catholics United, Protestants Divided," *The Torch: A Magazine of Enlightenment* 3 (April 1931): 12.

Founded anew in 1915 by William B. Simmons of Atlanta, Georgia, the Knights of the Ku Klux Klan, for whatever reason, got a late start in Arkansas. According to Charles C. Alexander, in *The Invisible Empire in the Southwest: The Ku Klux Klan in Texas, Louisiana, Oklahoma, and Arkansas, 1920–1930*, the Klan did not appear in Arkansas, at least in a demonstrable fashion, until late 1921. Once established, however, this anti-black, anti-Semitic, anti-Catholic, and anti-immigrant, self-appointed defender of moral purity and 100 percent Americanism "committed its share of physical attacks on sinners." For example, the Klan moved through the oil fields of El Dorado, flogging and driving out those elements deemed by it to be undesirable. In 1924, the Klan supported Lee Cazort for governor of Arkansas on a platform that smacked clearly of the Klan's brand of law and order. In the document that follows, the women of the Little Rock Klan rally the forces of Protestantism against a united Roman Catholic front during the opening years of the twentieth century's third decade.

It is true that we are going through a period of financial depression. It is a fact that many are out of employment. Those who are employed are working at greatly reduced wages. Without question money is not as easy to obtain as it was in the recent past.

These conditions are as true among Roman Catholics as they are among Protestants. And yet we find that a majority of the Protestant organizations have lost some of their supporters because they claim to be unable to pay their dues. Therefore, their potential strength and force is reduced to that extent.

If we turn our attention, however, to the activities of the Roman Catholic Church, we find that it is promoting a major program for the furtherance of its cause and is making substantial strides, gaining ground and becoming more and more potential. It is spending large sums of money for advertising by radio, moving pictures, colored editorials and long articles of propaganda accentuating the virtues of its faith and practice. We are, therefore, constrained to believe that the Roman Catholic membership is more willing to serve and sacrifice than are the Protestants.

All the Priests of the . . . Catholic Church are of one accord. All its well organized official family is of one accord. All its membership is of one accord. On the other hand, the Protestant Ministry, officials, and membership are divided as to what is the best method of maintaining Protestant supremacy in America, and what is the best method of supporting our free public schools and sponsoring a thorough-going American program.

Too many preachers and teachers of the Gospel faith are prone to find a cause for division that will prevent their presenting a solid front on the matters to which we have referred. Some go so far as to oppose the Ku Klux Klan without being able to assign a valid reason for their objections.

If all the Protestant ministers, officials and communicants could have a unity of mind, purpose and action, there would be no division, but there would shortly develop established sentiment that would induce all Protestants to move toward one end—the supremacy of Protestantism, free public schools, obedience to law and higher ideals of Americanism. Let there be no minor questions raised that would cause or have a tendency to cause a division of thought or action to destroy the potentiality of a combined force which, in its application, would keep America safe at all times and free from Roman Catholic influence and control.

The women of the Ku Klux Klan have set forth their views on the subjects mentioned above. They invite every Protestant and non-Catholic to embrace these principles and begin at once giving a helping hand to the Women of the Klan in bringing about a victory for all. Let us put a ban on holidays and vacations until the close of this campaign.

Arkansas's Centennial Celebration

Arkansas Democrat (Little Rock), June 10, 1936.

In 1936, Arkansas celebrated one hundred years of statehood. In the midst of unparalleled economic dislocation and hardship, Arkansans, at least for the moment, had their emotional spirits renewed by a visit from President and Mrs. Franklin Delano Roosevelt. As chairman of the Arkansas Centennial Commission, Harvey C. Couch entertained the Roosevelts at his Couchwood estate on Lake Catherine in Hot Springs. Even the dinner menu at Couchwood did its part to both publicize Arkansas and bolster residents' morale: it included, among other things, "Arkansas Fried Chicken, South Arkansas Parsley Potatoes, Blytheville String Beans, Malvern Rolls, Rockport coffee, centennial tea, Ozark salad, Lake Catherine cookies, Couchwood Candy and Hot Springs' mineral water." The following is an excerpt from a report in the *Arkansas Democrat* on Roosevelt's visit to Hot Springs in 1936.

A mass of humanity packed into the city for the presidential visit, highspotting the Arkansas Centennial celebration, and every conveyance, from automobiles, trucks, farm wagons and pack animals, appeared to have been pressed into use to bring the spectators in.

One farmer, on muleback, told bystanders he had ridden 30 miles out of the mountains "to see the president."

The special train brought the White House party into Hot Springs early in the morning and shortly afterwards, Mrs. Roosevelt left it to drive through the crowded streets, waving to the cheering throng, to breakfast with 500 Arkansas women at the Arlington hotel. Later President Roosevelt appeared amid shouts from the crowd massed at the station and held back by police and state rangers and entered a black seven-passenger automobile for a drive around the city. Riding with him were Gov. J. M. Futrell, Senator Joe T. Robinson, Mayor Leo P. McLaughlin and Centennial Chairman Harvey Couch.

. . . Preceded by the Hot Springs High School band, the presidential car moved slowly along the crowded streets to the Army and Navy hospital, where [the president] greeted patients and chatted. . . . After a drive over the mountain roads of the government reservation, the president headed for the Arlington hotel, where Mrs. Roosevelt was just finishing the women's breakfast in her honor there.

... The Roosevelts then went to the Hot Springs bathhouses for an inspection tour and the president left his car for the first time to enter one of the establishments and chat with the operators. While there, also, he greeted six small children receiving the thermal baths for infantile paralysis as beneficiaries of the Roosevelt Birthday Ball Fund. After the inspection, the party drove over West Mountain and then, waving final adieus to the Hot Springs gathering, headed for Couchwood, home of Harvey Couch on Lake Catherine. The official cars drove slowly over the winding mountain roads leading down to the artificial lake, and crossing the narrow bridge leading out to the island on which the Couch place is located in the heart of the Ouachita mountains. Arriving shortly before noon, the party rested at the Couch lodge before luncheon. The press corps accompanying the president meanwhile ate at barbecue pits at the side of the lake.

Four women who fainted in the crush to see the president during his stop at Arlington hotel were given emergency treatment there. With the completion of luncheon at Couchwood, the party headed for Rockport and the religious services scheduled at the old church there.

C. THE ONSLAUGHT OF HARD TIMES

While the decade of the 1920s had not been free of periods of economic stagnation and even dislocation, none of these could compare to the hard times of the Great Depression:

> Once underway the spiral of the depression swept out in an ever-widening curve. Millions of investors lost their savings; thousands were forced into bankruptcy; over 5,000 banks closed their doors in the first three years of the depression. Debts mounted, purchases declined, factories cut down production, workers were dismissed, wages and salaries slashed. Real estate sagged in value and tax collections dropped alarmingly, forcing governments to cut essential services. Construction work, except for government operations, practically ceased. . . . The depression struck a devastating blow at the farmer, already hard hit, and when he was unable to meet his obligations, his mortgage was foreclosed, sometimes on land that had been held in his family for generations. . . . Grown men worked for 5 cents an hour in sawmills. Negroes learned the cruel truth of the saying that they were the "last to be hired first to be fired."

(Samuel E. Morison, Henry Steele Commanger, and William E. Leuchtenburg, *The Growth of the American Republic* [1969], 2:471–72.)

Such were the hardships of the Great Depression, the impact of which on Arkansas can be felt from the documents in this section.

Demands for Food

Arkansas Gazette (Little Rock), January 4, 1931.

The acute nature of the Great Depression drove men and women to do the heretofore unthinkable. For example, a riotous situation was narrowly averted in England, Arkansas, as farmers demanded food for their families.

A deplorable economic situation reached a climax here today when 300 farmers, mostly white men and half of them reported to have been armed, swarmed into England and threatened to loot the stores unless they were provided with food.

The mob was quiet and orderly, but the spokesman seemed determined. England merchants held a conference and provided food for all who demanded it. The march began this morning when families who have been receiving aid from the Red Cross reported at the various precincts, and were told that the Red Cross blanks [vouchers] were exhausted. Lacking these blanks, no food could be distributed.

People came from all directions to England, in cars, on horseback, in buggies, and on foot, and when they arrived, they found their neighbors assembled on the streets, milling about uncertain what to do next. It is believed that many feared they would get no more help from the Red Cross. Citizens of the town had flocked on the streets, which soon were filled. For the most part the crowd [remained] orderly.

. . . It is estimated that the families of the 300 men represented a total of 1500 persons supplied with food by England merchants, whose business had been poor, because the farmers have no money. Red Cross headquarters at St. Louis [Missouri] was called by telephone and advised of the situation. The merchants were told that a supply of blanks would be sent here, but that distribution of food could not be authorized except through regular Red Cross channels, and on food blanks.

While the excitement was high pitch, George E. Morris, attorney, tried to pacify the farmers, who were, however, in no mood for a speech. Mr. Morris told them that the people of England understood and appreciated the predicament of the farmers, most of whom . . . were prosperous and hard-working citizens, and would work with them to feed their starving families. He was interrupted continually by cries of "we want food!" "Our children are crying for food and we're going to get it!" "We're not beggars!" Men shouted from the crowd. "We will work for any amount if we can get it. We're not going to let our families starve!"

. . . By nightfall, all had received rations and returned home, but this food will last only three or four days, and by the end of that time, they will be hungry again.

. . . England merchants will urge the Red Cross to pay for the food distributed today, but there is no assurance this will be done.

The Arrogance of Authority: A Citizen's Complaint

Paul G. Branch to Gov. Marion Futrell, August 16, 1934, "Welfare Folder," Futrell Papers, Arkansas History Commission, Little Rock.

In this selection, Paul G. Branch, a resident of Elm Springs, Arkansas, and a recipient of relief aid, complains of treatment received at the hands of a relief official.

Aug. 16, 34
Elm Springs, Ark.

Honorable Gov. Futtrell [*sic*]

Dear Sirs. I am writing you in regards to Mr. [John] Rhea at Fayetteville, Ark. supposed to be the head of the Drouth [*sic*] Relief there for Washington Co., Ark. I was investigated about the 30th day of July last and put on the relief roll as one in need of food & feed also received $5.00 order itemized for groceries to be purchased at Elm Springs for 2 weeks supply. I got them July 31 and have eaten same and fed the 100 lb sack of feed to the chickens and 2 horses am completely out of said 2 weeks supply and no other source of getting more. I went to Fayetteville yesterday Aug. 15 and wanted to get more food and was absolutely flatly refused under any circumstances. . . . I left for home hungry and my wife and child hungry[.] I had walked most of the 21 miles to get there and had no dinner at all and had to walk over half way back home on hungry guts.

Now then this Mr. Rhea acts like a hardboiled penitentiary warden or something worse. I was shown to his office and he absolutely refused to talk sensible to me[;] he asked what I wanted. I told him relief food and then he started balling [*sic*] me out something shameful and told me to go write my funny jokes in the newspapers and turned his back on me and refused any further conversation. I was angry enough to cut his head off but I left for home without any disturbance to my hungry 4 yr. old girl and my wife.

Now then if Mr. Rhea acts like that to many more hungry people someone is very liable to do him serious harm besides making us go hungry back to our children who were expecting something to eat when daddy got home.

Experiment in Economic Recovery: The Dyess Colony

Arkansas Gazette (Little Rock), January 8, 1938.

The severity of the Great Depression prompted bold, new measures by the federal government in an attempt to hasten economic recovery. More than tangible results, many federally sponsored programs simply brought renewed hope to thousands of Americans beset by economic disaster. One such project was the Dyess Colony in Jackson County. Established in the spring of 1934, the colony offered a second chance to many Arkansas farmers during the Depression era. In the selection that follows, we are given a measure of its success and accomplishments.

This oldest and most spectacular New Deal experiment in the rehabilitation of distressed farmers—in which the government has gambled $2,500,000 on the pluck, industry and determination of rural Americans to make their own way—presents today a character remarkably different from that in evidence here May 22, 1934, when Dyess Colony was inaugurated.

On the physical side, progress at Dyess Colony has been startling. Of the original 15,400 acres of cypress and oak studded bottoms and near-swamps, colonists have hewed, hacked and chopped 9,000 acres of cleared land—and obtained more than 12,000,000 feet of lumber.

Homes for 500 families have been built in addition to 60 miles of gravel roads and 90 miles of drainage canals. A city has been created, including a 35-bed hospital, post office (with rural free delivery), four schools, bank, barber shop, "general store," service station, garage, feed mill, gin, canning plant, motion picture theater, poultry plant, library, shoe shop, machine shop, furniture factory and woodwork shops, printing shop—and, of course, a WPA (Works Project Administration) office. Two churches are scheduled for construction next. Then will come power lines, and other refinements.

On the invisible side, the principal progress has been in the matter of morale. This comes out in conversation with the colonists. Take Harve Smith, ruddy, 45 year-old self-described "cotton farmer," for instance. Harve was the first colonist to move onto the colony tract, back in October, 1934. He has a family of nine. "What do you think of this place now?" he was asked. "It's the best proposition a poor man ever had." "In what respects?" "Well, there's nothing against a man here. A man does need more acreage, but still I've got feed enough to do two mules and my other stock this winter. Here, they've given a man a chance when it looked like no one else would."

"Think you'll have any trouble buying your place?" (Colonists get deeds to their farms and homes, must pay about $150 a year, plus about $45 a year in taxes, for 30 years). "Nope I'll buy it all right." "What do you think of the cooperative idea for operation of the community center?" (That's the "town.") "Swell idea." "What do you like best about the place?" "Well, I've got a home and some good land—best in the world—and an opportunity to buy them (directors of the colony) they'll back us, but we wouldn't have a chance without this place. Let me tell you, the sentiment of the farmers is looking up."

"Anything you don't like about it?" "Well, yes, but it can't be helped. The only thing hurtin' now is the 'PWA' [Public Works Administration] that is putting us on jobs and keeping us off our farms. We ought to be plowing. Of course, they can't give us a living when we're broke; we've got to earn it. But why not give me a $25 mortgage on my cow and let me go on my farm and make it back?"

The Southern Tenant Farmers' Union Decries Lawlessness

H. L. Mitchell to Denver L. Dudley, January 20, 1936, Futtrell
Papers, Arkansas History Commission, Little Rock.

In it's effort to gain greater economic well-being for the sharecropper and the landed poor, the Southern Tenant Farmers' Union was
an unwelcomed development in many parts of Arkansas and other
southern states. In this selection, H. L. Mitchell, the union's executive secretary, implores the prosecuting attorney of Jonesboro to
enforce the law.

January 20, 1936
Mr. Denver L. Dudley
Prosecuting Attorney
Jonesboro, Arkansas.

Dear Sir:

At the suggestion of Hon. J. Marion Futrell, Governor of the state
of Arkansas, I am writing to you in regard to whole sale violations of the
laws of the state and the nation in your district. I am sure that you are
fully aware of the disgraceful actions of local peace officers of Poinsette,
Mississippi, and Crittenden Counties last Spring when they aided and
encouraged the formation of bands of outlaws known as "night-riders."
As an official who is sworn to uphold the constitutional guarantees and
the rights of American citizens, you at that time took no action whatever
for the protection of members of the Southern Tenant Farmers' Union,
an organization of legal and lawful purpose chartered under the laws of
the state of Arkansas.

At this time we wish to bring to your attention a matter that
demands immediate action on your part, or an admission that the entire
forces of law and order in Crittenden County have utterly disappeared.

On the night of January 16th a lawful meeting of the Southern
Tenant Farmers' Union was raided by officers of the law; J. D. Peachers,
and Deputy Sheriff Hood. The meeting was broken up, and two of our
members were shot by these men as they were returning home. Local
officers have done nothin only arrested Union men who were innocent
of any wrongdoing.

On Friday, January 17th, a meeting on the outskirts of the town of

Earle was raided by a band of outlaws composed of plantation owners or their retainers whose names are as follows: "Boss" Dulaney, L. L. Barham, A. L. Lancaster, Otis Belford, Jerome Hood, Charlie Hood, Frank Hill and Ernest Richards. There were other men in the mob who took no part in the breaking up of the meeting, but who sanctioned it by their presence. These outlaws forcibly removed Rev. Howard Kester, who was speaking in behalf of the Union, from the church. On the inside Otis Bedford let the clubbing of innocent men, women and children, both white and Negro. Rev. Kester and H. I. Goldberger, an attorney from Memphis, were then escorted out of the town and threatened with lynching by members of the mob. These thugs also threatened to repeat the Elaine massacre, making it this time both white and black workers who would be slaughtered.

On a previous occasion, J. D. Peachers, City Marshal of Earle, Arkansas, stated in the presence of witnesses that he intended to break up the union with Winchester rifles if necessary.

We are prepared to prove the above statements in any court of justice in which the plantation owners in Northeastern Arkansas have no control. The situation which we have just described to you demands immediate action.

Yours very sincerely,
H. L. MITCHELL
Executive Secretary.

HLM:es
Copy to Gov. J. Marion Futrell

D. STATE INDEBTEDNESS

During the Great Depression, the term *default* echoed resoundingly throughout the US financial community. Arkansas, too, found itself unable to meet certain agreed upon financial obligations, particularly its bonded indebtedness. The two selections that follow offer some insight into the concerns of bondholders and the problems of the state's indebtedness.

Default: A Bondholder's Plea

Roff P. Hastey to Gov. Marion Futrell, July 4, 1933, "Bond Folder,"
Futrell Papers, Arkansas History Commission, Little Rock.

Few were spared the ravages of the Great Depression. In time, the
ordinary citizen and the business community, as well as state and
local governments, came to know the real meaning of economic
hardship. In this letter, a Chicago holder of Arkansas bonds pleads
to the governor to honor the state's debt.

July 4th 1933
1131 East 45th St.
Ch. Ill.
The Governor State of Arkansas

Dear Mr. Governor—

It seems incredibable [*sic*] that your office permits such conditions
as exist and I am taking [*sic*] this opportunity to put this matter before
you.

Here in the face of returning prosperity your state is refusing to pay
interest long past due of Road Bonds and School districts and absolutely
ignoring the public that ivested [*sic*] their funds in your State Bonds feeling that if there was a source of security surely it was in a state and school
obligation and now we find you repudiating such trust and faith as was
entrusted to you.

I have several thousand of road bonds that were deposited over ten
months ago and interest that was due to that time and I have no returns
on same and nothing has been done to pay same. If you want to refi-
nance, why not borrow money from the Federal Gov and pay off your
obligations. I understand the money to pay interest on Road Bonds was
collected and can see no reason why it was not used to pay interest and
bonds falling due. I can't understand you permitting your state to get
into such bad repute, I am sure nobody in the futire [*sic*] shall consider
buying Arkansas Bonds.

I also have school bonds in your state that are not paying their inter-
est and I feel you should see that this is done. The following are the
School Districts I have in mind. Union Special School District, Pulaski
County . . . Kelso Special School District, Desha County, Fairview

Special School District Lonoke County, Halley Special School District Desha County.

I shall appreciate hearing from you and hope it is not the intention of your state to repudiate your debts like the French. Why not set an example to others and pay up your obligations in full.

Yours Truly.

Support for the Highway Bond Refunding Bill

C. J. Farin to Gov. Marion Futrell, February 1, 1934, Futrell Papers, Arkansas History Commission, Little Rock.

In an effort to meet the state's financial obligations on bonds for highway construction and improvement, the General Assembly passed a bond-refunding bill. In no small measure, Gov. Marion Futrell played an important role in the passage of this legislation. In the letter that follows, the governor's efforts are applauded.

Feb. 1st, 1934
Hon. J. M. Futrell
Governor
Little Rock, Ark.

Dear Governor:

First, I want you to pardon my boldness in writing you, but your stand on the Refunding Bill, just passed by the legislature, was one of the best pieces of work done in many years, and I feel like you are directly responsible for it, and you certainly are to be commended for your gallant stand, I read every word that was printed in the papers, that you said, in regards to the Refunding Bill, and the pleas you made were certainly inspired by the Lord, and I feel like your old state has been granted a new leases [sic] of life.

I did not support you in the last race, but you have won me completely, and I travel over the state, especially in the south part quite a bit, and you have not only won me, you have won friends by the thousands, it would do your heart good to hear the many nice things said about you since your stand to pass a satisfactory refunding bill, I own the filling station and store at the junction of 167 and 48 in Dallas County, and when the Mill is not running I go over there and that being on a main highway, I have a good chanch [*sic*] to hear what folks from other sections of the state have to say, and it[']s all in your favor, surely you would be surprised to know how many friends you have won, and my best wishes go to you in your good efforts. Anytime I can be of any assistance to you, I want you to feel at liberty to call on me, day or night, you'll find me ready.

Again wishing you
God speed, I am
yours very truly.
C. J. Farin

Mr. J. A. DuVall, the Voucher Clerk, in the Highway Dept. is one of your strongest supporters, and it was he, who first started winning me to your cause.

FOR FURTHER READING

Works related to Arkansas history during the period 1920–1940 include Ben Johnson, *Arkansas in Modern America* (Fayetteville: University of Arkansas Press, 2000); Anthony J. Badger, *New Deal/New South* (Fayetteville: University of Arkansas Press, 2007); Jeannie Whayne and Willard B. Gatewood, *The Arkansas Delta: Land of Paradox* (Fayetteville: University of Arkansas Press, 1993); Charles C. Alexander Jr., *Invisible Empire in the Southwest: The Ku Klux Klan in Texas, Louisiana, Oklahoma, and Arkansas, 1920–1930* (Ann Arbor, MI: University Microfilms International, 1977); Pete Daniel, *Deep'n as They Come: The 1927 Mississippi Flood* (New York: Oxford University Press, 1977); Donald Grubbs, *The Cry from Cotton* (Chapel Hill: University of North Carolina Press, 1971); Donald Holley, *Uncle Sam's Farmers: New Deal Farmers in the Lower Mississippi Valley* (Urbana: University of Illinois Press, 1975); H. L. Mitchell, *Mean Things Happening in This Land* (Montclair, NJ: Allanheld and Osmun, 1979); David E. Rison *Arkansas during the Great Depression* (Ann Arbor, MI: University Microfilms International, 1982); and Donald W. Whisenhunt, ed., *The Depression in the Southwest* (New York: Kennikat Press, 1980).

CHAPTER VIII

Arkansas during War and Peace, 1941–1954

INTRODUCTION

Perhaps no other event in the history of the United States so shocked and horrified the American people as did the Japanese attack on Pearl Harbor, December 7, 1941. Almost without exception, Americans cast aside their isolationist leanings and projected a unified front in the face of military aggression.

Arkansans responded along with their countrymen, as more than two hundred thousand residents of the state served in the various branches of the armed forces. And for those on the home front, the ravages of war could be felt in shortages of food stuffs and the rationing of gasoline. Victory gardens dotted the countryside and the green areas of urban places as Arkansans and the nation dug in for a fight. Gov. Homer Adkins probably expressed the sentiment of most when he affectionately called a group of 135 US Navy and Marine Corps enlistees "Avengers of Pearl Harbor." Adkins continued: "You typify the American way of life—a part of the right-thinking people of the world embarked upon a great crusade to rid this earth of gangster governments and make it a livable place again."

One of the realities of war is that it very often brings economic growth and development, particularly to the victors and those outside the pale of actual combat. For the floundering US economy, World War II brought recovery. So, too, did it bring economic lifeblood to Arkansas. Defense plants and installations marked the landscape from Jacksonville to El Dorado. Bauxite became even more important, and its production grew by leaps and bounds to satisfy the nation's aircraft industry. The net effect of this growth was the employment of more Arkansans and a lessening of the Depression-inspired hardships of the past decade.

Arkansas also became the home of thousands of Japanese, as the nation's leaders came to believe that the entire West Coast of the United States might be in danger of attack from the Japanese and their saboteurs. And so the government removed more than 110,000 Japanese, two-thirds of whom were American citizens, to detention centers (also known as concentration camps) within various parts of the interior. Arkansas's facilities were located at Rohwer in Desha County and at Jerome in Chicot County. It was one of those times when widespread fear and suspicion ruled the day.

Arkansas experienced some currents of social change during the decade of the 1940s. These came in the form of a US Supreme Court decision regarding Jim Crow rail travel and agitation by the Arkansas Negro Democratic Association to gain the vote in state primaries. Before the decade came to a close, inroads had been made in breaking down Jim Crow barriers in the state's institutions of higher education: Silas Hunt and Jackie L. Shropshire were admitted to the previously all-white University of Arkansas Law School, and Edith Erby was admitted to the Arkansas School of Medicine in Little Rock.

Significantly, and despite a net loss in population, Arkansas entered a phase of greater urbanization during the fifth decade of the twentieth century. According to census figures, slightly more than one-half of the state's population of 1,949,387 resided on farms in 1940. By 1950, only 35 percent of the state's 1,909,511 residents made their homes on farms.

In some other areas of life, conditions stagnated. The quality of education and educational facilities, for example, remained well below trends on the national level. And while the state had indeed made gains in improving its highways during earlier years, much remained to be done.

Perhaps the most significant political event in the state was the hotly contested US Senate race in 1944. Four candidates challenged Sen. Hattie W. Caraway, the first woman elected to the US Senate, for her seat. Out of the pack emerged J. William Fulbright, who, until his defeat three decades later, was probably Arkansas's most respected and influential senator. In national and international affairs, as well as in efforts toward world peace, Senator Fulbright set high standards.

On September 2, 1945, Arkansas's Gen. Douglas A. MacArthur,

supreme commander of Allied forces in the Pacific, accepted the surrender of Japan on board the USS *Missouri,* and World War II came to a close. The war years represent a major watershed in the course of US political, economic, and social life. Moreover, they mark the beginning of a new era in international affairs. No longer could the nation withdraw unto itself and let the world go on without active US participation. So determined were some that the nation keep its hand on the pulse of the world that the prospects for conflict, both domestic and foreign, loomed ever large. Between 1945 and 1954, the American nation was forced to make a painful yet necessary decision. In fact, ever since the bombs of Japan slammed into Pearl Harbor, few doubted that the United States could remain outside the affairs of global politics. And so almost two centuries of largely isolationist thought came to an end, and the nation embarked upon a more active role within the world community of nations.

The postwar years also witnessed new currents of social and political change. Under his catchword title of a "Fair Deal," President Harry S. Truman called for a series of reforms that included higher wages for workers, the eradication of slum housing, extension of social security benefits, and federal aid to education and health programs. According to the more conservative elements in the nation, such efforts marked a new and dangerous height in federal encroachment. Moreover, Truman's call for antidiscrimination measures in employment, desegregation of the armed forces, and a general civil rights bill thoroughly outraged many others. In fact, the civil rights plank in the Democratic Party's 1947 platform drove many conservative southerners into a new political faction known as the Dixiecrats. These "secessionists" from the Democratic fold had one basic motto: "The South Says Never!"

Arkansas also responded to the new social thrusts of the Truman administration. Gov. Ben T. Laney became a leading force in the state's Dixiecrat or States' Rights Democratic Party during the 1940s. According to Laney, "the foundation of democracy is found in the right of the . . . people to govern themselves," and "if that right [was] ever surrendered by the people, or usurped by any government (state or federal), the individual [would] lose both his unfettered opportunities and his freedom to pursue happiness in his own way."

Deeply rooted in the American experience, the states' rights philosophy represented a formidable force against the more inclusive concept of government extension to promote the collective good. And given the inequities of life within the society at large, it was, perhaps, inevitable that new conflicts as well as champions of broader social principles would arise.

In 1949, Arkansas voters elected Sidney Sanders McMath governor. Having garnered statewide recognition as a leader of the GI revolt against the corrupt political practices of Mayor Leo P. McLaughlin in Hot Springs, McMath proved to be a counterforce within the generally conservative framework of Arkansas politics. In fact, he has been termed a leading force in the southern reform tradition. It is also significant to note that with McMath came a small number of blacks to serve on the local political scene during the late 1940s and early 1950s, most notably as city councilmen. Among these were Fred Martin of Hot Springs' Second Ward and Reverend L. R. Williams of Malvern's Fourth Ward. Black Arkansans also gained limited visibility on state-appointed boards and commissions. Moreover, Governor McMath repeatedly called for adherence to the Fourteenth Amendment's provision regarding equality under the law and sponsored antilynching legislation to this end. He also opposed the poll tax that so effectively discriminated against the poor and disadvantaged in their right to vote. Such reform zeal, however, was not shared by the state legislature. And except for McMath's highway construction and revitalization program, his social efforts went unrewarded by the state's lawmakers. But despite legislative rebukes, the McMath years may still be called futuristic. They were real indications of things to come.

Texas-born Francis Cherry defeated McMath when the latter attempted to gain a third term as governor in 1952. Here, the reformer McMath himself fell victim to charges of corruption in his administration's practice of placing state purchase orders with select business interests. Moreover, Cherry's use of the radio "talkathon" to exploit this and other charges, as well as opposition to McMath by the Arkansas Power and Light Company, proved politically disastrous for the reformer from Hot Springs.

When Francis Cherry took the reins of state government in 1953, Arkansas stood at the door of an uncertain future. Politically, the issue of states' rights had yet to run its course. Moreover, the impact of the rather recent participation of black Arkansans in the democratic political process was still to be felt. On the social level, few could know that a series of tests would try the collective will of the state. Economically, while post–World War II growth had brought improvement to the quality of life, Arkansas yet needed industry to balance its economy. Uncertain though the future was, Arkansas had little real choice but to pass through its door.

A. THE OUTBREAK OF A SECOND WORLD WAR

Pearl Harbor catapulted the American people into collective support for US intervention in World War II. In Arkansas, residents rallied to the cause and prepared once again to meet the enemy. This section of documents ranges from state efforts at military preparedness to an exchange between a native Arkansan and a Japanese resident of the Jerome Relocation Center.

The Arkansas State Guard

Arkansas Gazette (Little Rock), December 8, 1941.

In a fashion similar to the state's response during World War I, Arkansas mobilized a state guard to show its preparedness for military conflict.

Governor [Homer] Adkins, who hurried to the Capital from his Hot Springs County farm last night, said that: "Immediate steps" will be taken to organize an Arkansas State Guard. No special session of the legislature is contemplated.

Japan's action [the bombing of Pearl Harbor] "unifies all America." A volunteer force of 500 men, divided into two battalions, is planned for the State Guard, Mr. Adkins said. Ex-Army officers who have received training in the past few years and men recently discharged from service will be its officers.

. . . Approximately $50,000 will be needed to provide uniforms and tents for 500 men. . . . Regarding developments in the Pacific, the governor, a world war veteran, said [that] . . . the time has arrived for every person in America to make any necessary sacrifice to win this war. We should be very grateful for the foresight of the President in having the Navy ready for this emergency.

. . . Arkansas ranks high among the states in Navy personnel. Our men in both the Army and Navy have always acquitted themselves in a creditable manner.

. . . Senator Hattie W. Caraway of Jonesboro planned to return to Washington immediately, Senator Lloyd Spencer of Hope, a seaman in the world war, expects to board a Washington-bound plane at Memphis this morning. Congressman W. F. Norrell of Monticello was reported to have left Washington for his home Saturday night. It was expected that he would return immediately.

The Rev. Jeff Smith, Director of the Lighthouse for the Blind, telegraphed President Roosevelt last night that the blind people in Arkansas stand 100 percent behind him during this emergency. "Although, [said Smith], we do not have eyes we are ready to do our part."

Arkansas's Defense Industries

Arkansas Gazette (Little Rock), June 3, 1942.

Arkansas, not unlike countless other communities across the nation, profited from the expansion of wartime industries. The state had defense plants or installations at or near Little Rock with Camp Robinson, Jacksonville, and Marche. Others included the Pine Bluff Arsenal, the Helena Air School, Camp Chaffee at Fort Smith, and centers for communication and transportation at El Dorado, Hope, Texarkana, Jonesboro, Hot Springs, and Malvern. The defense industry of Texarkana is described below.

When the United States plunged into its gigantic defense-war program—the biggest job in human history—towns in peaceful agricultural regions became arsenals for the production of increasing quantities of arms and munitions for the battle fronts of the United Nations.

Texarkana, the home of the Lone Star Ordnance Depot, is one of these cities. In the Texarkana [*Gazette*] . . . no production figures are given, nor the dimension of the plants. But on one of them, $50,000,000 was spent in 18 months and both are still growing.

. . . Texarkana [is] advantageously placed as a potential industrial city. It is on the main lines of four trunk line railroads and four United States highways, and it has an airport on the improvement and enlargement of which $429,000 has been spent recently. It is on the Arkansas-Texas state line and just a little below Oklahoma and above Louisiana.

As Texarkana shoulders her share of the work of the present her eyes are on the future. In the older industrial centers of the country, plants long in the production of consumer goods were changed over to the war effort, and the [people of Texarkana are] looking forward to the day when great plants built for the battle can be converted to making the goods the world will need when peace comes again.

One Arkansan's View of the Japanese

Arkansas Gazette (Little Rock), November 26, 1942.

Arkansas had two relocation centers—concentration camps—for the resettlement of a sizable number of more than 110,000 Japanese (many of whom were American citizens) removed from the West Coast of the United States during the war years. These were located at Rohwer in Desha County and Jerome in Chicot County. The presence of increased numbers of Japanese in the state, and the war against Japan, prompted one Arkansan, Lynn Hall of Hazen, to address the issue of the Japanese and racial superiority in a letter to the *Gazette*.

To the Editor of the *Gazette*:

If there are people in Arkansas who have felt a bit superior and looked with suspicion on the "Americans with Japanese faces," it seems to me that the letters in this column from these American-born Japanese should prove, even to the most skeptical, that America is a nation composed of many nationalities. Every American should be proud of every other American regardless of race or color. If any of us are feeling a bit superior merely because our skin happens to be white, maybe we should remember that while our race has produced many great and good people, it has produced some demons, including Adolph Hitler. I imagine that every race has its proportion of the mentally deficient and also of the normally intelligent and of geniuses. So where is there any real inequality?

We Americans disdain Germany's claim to "German Kultur" and the superiority of Aryan people, also the claims of imperial Japan that they are divinely destined to rule the world.

We Southerners do feel, perhaps pretty strongly, that races should not mix too freely socially but I don't think that ever should mean a feeling of superiority. Every race should be proud to keep its own distinctiveness, proud to be as God made it and proud to be able to do its own part to prove it equal to any.

If some feel peeved because our government seems to be furnishing these evacuees with some luxuries which some of us native Arkansans never have been able to afford, hadn't we rather that the government make the mistake of being too generous rather than the opposite?

I am sure every sensible white American regrets that one of our race took a shot at a Japanese-American soldier [in Dermott, Arkansas].

I am a native of Arkansas, white race, Anglo-Saxon descent. I always claim that my ancestors came over on the Mayflower but would hate to try to prove it. I hope I never kick a person on account of his color. I want to be accepted—not tolerated—and I'm sure you feel the same. Unless you treat me shabbily, I accept you as a friend and truly believe that all men are created equal. I believe that just about expresses the typical American sentiment.

Hazen, Ark.   Lynn Hall

"Americans with Japanese Faces": A Letter to Mr. Lynn Hall

Eddie Shimano, "A Letter to Mr. Lynn Hall, Hazen, Ark.,"
The Communiqué, December 1, 1942, Japanese Relocation Center Files, UALR Center for Arkansas History and Culture, Little Rock.

In this selection, Eddie Shimano, resident Japanese-American editor of the Jerome Relocation Center *Communiqué,* responds to Lynn Hall.

Dear Mr. Lynn Hall:

I have just finished reading your letter of Nov. 29 [1942] to the editor of the Arkansas *Gazette* and I am filled with conflicting emotions, predominant of which is the feeling of gratitude for having some native Arkansan understand the meaning of Americanism as it applies to us. We are American citizens accidentally born to parents whose place of birth, in turn, was accidentally in a country now engaged in a war with our nation, the United States.

I gather from your references to "Americans with Japanese faces" that you have read the book in which this phrase is used as a chapter heading. We are glad to inform you, Mr. Hall, and all the Arkansans, that a great majority of Japanese Americans (and please note that I do not believe in hyphenating Americans) are as American as the one referred to in this book . . . and many are better Americans, if not more, than some of their white brother-citizens.

The regrettable shooting in Dermott of a Japanese American soldier shocked me, not because the soldier shot at was of Japanese descent, but because the act of shooting an American soldier wearing the uniform of the United States seems to me to be an act of treason!

This is not what we have been brought up to believe—that the measure of an American soldier is by the color of his face, or that the measure of any American, citizen or soldier, is by the differences in pigmentation. The great majority of us regret that we are not allowed as full a participation in the war effort as this soldier is engaged in.

When we were removed from our homes on the Pacific Coast, many of us accepted the evacuation in the belief that this would be our contribution to a total war effort—to eliminate a molehill squabble which in time might have grown to mountainous proportions and thereby disrupted a unified war effort on the Coast. This we did in good grace, sacrificing all but our lives (which many of us are yet willing to do).

We are dumbfounded at the accusations made by people ignorant of these relocation centers that "our government seems to be furnishing these evacuees with some luxuries which some of us native Arkansans never have been able to afford." The only luxury we boast is our claim to Americanism, and our fervent desire to live up to it.

This must be a rare luxury indeed for some people on the outside of these centers who claim Americanism but dare not pay the price of Americanism which are tolerance, fair play, democratic thinking, and the belief that "all men are created equal."

And so, Mr. Hall, I wish to extend my hand to you as one American citizen to another—in friendship, in fellow citizenship, and in a firm belief that each of us, in our own way, will win not only the war for democracy but also the peace. The future of America will be dismal indeed if we substitute the "Horst Wessel" song of racial-superiority for the glorious refrain of "the land of the free."

Sincerely yours,
Eddie Shimano
Editor, *Communiqué*

B. AGRICULTURAL AND INDUSTRIAL DEVELOPMENTS

In prosecuting the war effort, the federal government regulated, often with a stern hand, the domestic production of goods and services. The selections herein describe the state of agriculture during World War II and the link between economic development, education, and Arkansas's population loss during the 1940s.

The State of Agriculture

Ross Mauncy, "The State of Agriculture," *Arkansas Extension Service Review* (December 1942).

In this selection, Ross Mauncy, farm extension economist at the University of Arkansas, assesses the state of agriculture during the war years.

Three basic conditions, which color the outlook for the next year, must be recognized, these are: First, the war, the increasing certainty of its continuance through 1943, and its increasing demands for larger volumes of agricultural products; second, the possibility of war conditions in 1944 and 1945; and third, the nation's most completely controlled economy ever experienced. Uncle Sam will practically, if not actually, tell farmers what to produce and the price they will receive for their products.

Agricultural economists list seven important factors in the farm situation which lead them to conclude that 1943 will not be as favorable as the current year. These are: (1) Total agricultural production is likely to be lower than the 1942 record crop, largely because of shortage of labor and machinery, (2) Demand for agricultural products will exceed supplies, as the result of increased industrial production, higher wages, and increased purchases for armed forces and lease-lend shipments, (3) Relationship between farm prices and production cost will be less favorable next year because of expected rising costs of production, (4) Gross farm income in 1943 likely will be higher, but net income probably will be lower due to higher taxes and labor costs, (5) Farm labor shortage is expected to become more troublesome as the war progresses, (6) Farm machinery shortage will become more acute in 1943, since manufacturers will be allowed to make only 20 percent of their 1940 output, [and] (7)

Transportation facilities will be taxed to the limit, although it is hoped that sufficient trucks and railroad cars will be available to move agricultural products without losses by discontinuance of shipping such bulky products as watermelons long distance.

Economic Development and Education: The Link

Report of the Arkansas Commission on Higher Education, to the Governor and the General Assembly (January 1951), 14–20, UALR Center for Arkansas History and Culture, Little Rock.

This document offers poignant insight into the connection between Arkansas's industrial development and education.

In past years Arkansas has not compared favorable with its neighbors in the number of years of formal education possessed by its people. The Census figures for 1940 disclose that 8.7 percent of the persons twenty-five years of age and over had completed four years of high school. Among the states in that section of the country only Mississippi had a lower percentage of high school graduates. The percentage for the United States as a whole was 14.1. The 1940 Census data also show that the percentage of persons twenty-five and over who had completed one to three years of college was lower in Arkansas than in any other South-central state. Similarly, Arkansas was the lowest of the South-central states in the percentage of persons in that age group who had completed four or more years of college.

. . . In 1939–40 [Arkansas] ranked 46th among the forty-eight states in the number of residents of the state per 10,000 population who were enrolled in institutions of higher education. By 1949–50 the number of Arkansas students in higher institutions in relation to the population was very much larger than it had been ten years earlier but, because large gains had also been made in other states, Arkansas continued to rank 46th among the states.

The most important single reason for this situation is to be found in the relatively low level of income of the people of the state. Obviously, this means for one thing that, in general, the share of the cost of this education that the students themselves can bear is relatively low; it also means that the monies available for state support of education are relatively limited.

However, conditions in Arkansas have, in recent years, been changing rapidly. There is a new spirit abroad in the state—a recognition of the fact that Arkansas is rich in human and material resources awaiting development. There is strongly in evidence a determination to do those things that will contribute to the physical, moral and aesthetic well-being of the people of the state.

Economically, notable progress is being made. The trend toward crop diversification is strengthening the agricultural economy. Poultry and livestock production are assuming a place of growing importance. The rich mineral resources of the state—bauxite, barite, cement, clay products, coal, natural gas, petroleum—are being developed. Arkansas' forest, among the finest in the nation, will, under good management and with continued growth of wood using and processing industries, play a part of increasing importance in the economy of the state. There has been and will doubtless continue to be significant growth in such fields as manufacturing, construction, wholesale and retail trade, transportation, and the service occupations. As the wealth of the state increases through the development of its material resources it will be possible to make more and better provisions for education. Development of the state's human resources through better education will provide more effective workers and citizens and will thus contribute in turn to the more effective utilization of the material resources.

Arkansas's Population Loss

Arkansas Gazette (Little Rock), October 25, 1955.

The causes of Arkansas's dwindling population during the 1940s are explored in this newspaper article.

A Census Bureau report shows continued loss of population by Arkansas. . . . Sadly enough, among the seven states of the nation which lost people during that period [1940–1950], Arkansas lost more than any of the others on a percentage basis. If there is any consolation in having neighbors suffering the way we do, both Mississippi and Oklahoma lost population during this time.

While Arkansas, Mississippi, Oklahoma, Alabama, West Virginia, Vermont, and Maine were losing people, the nation as a whole was gaining some ten and half million. The trend is westward, with California, Nevada, and Arizona showing substantial increases. Texas, which is both Southern and Western in numerous respects, is one of the high gainers again.

What does a continued loss of people mean? Why is Arkansas losing instead of gaining when the national trend is upward? What can we do to turn the Arkansas trend up instead of watching it move steadily downward? These are questions on which there will be a variety of answers in almost any discussion held on the matter. They are questions which need intelligent answers. The continuing loss is a drain upon energies and brains which our communities—and the state as a whole must have if Arkansas is to capitalize upon the opportunities our natural resources and geographical location offer.

There are many good reasons to cause us to believe that Arkansas' loss of people started back in the 1920s—is caused primarily by the tremendous agricultural and industrial revolution which our nation experienced, and which is still in process. Various communities in Arkansas during these years have shown substantial gains in population. For the most part they are the ones that have progressed industrially. It is encouraging that many Arkansas communities are today striving to diversify their economies through industrial expansion. And at the same time more attention is being given to diversify farming, soil and water conservation, mechanization on the farms, and kindred measures. Arkansas is making many gains in many fields. Surely there must be ways by which we can make our wonderful state more attractive to our own people—especially our young people—so that they remain here and help Arkansas grow.

C. BLACK CITIZENS AND THE QUEST FOR GREATER EQUALITY

If there was a "New Negro," as author Alan Locke describes during the period of the First World War, there was also during the late 1930s and 1940s a new determination on the part of blacks to gain greater equality and become "just Americans" within the body politic of the society. The leadership of the Arkansas Negro Democratic Association, the National Association for the Advancement of Colored People (NAACP), and, later, the black-owned *Arkansas State Press* newspaper all signaled a new direction and determination among black Arkansans. The following selections are indicative not only of the new climate afoot regarding the place of blacks within society but also of the inequities that yet remained.

A Blow against Jim Crow

Cases Argued and Decided in the Supreme Court of the United States (Rochester, NY: Lawyers Co-operative Publishing Company, 1941), 1208–12; *Arkansas Gazette (Little Rock),* April 29, 1941, and November 20, 1941.

In 1896, the US Supreme Court decided the case of *Plessy v. Ferguson.* The court held, against the lone protest of Justice John Marshall Harlan, that Louisiana's Jim Crow law requiring separate but equal railway coaches for blacks and whites was constitutional. While the *Plessy* decision would not face a full frontal assault in the courts until the *Brown v. the Board of Education of Topeka* decision of 1954, the Supreme Court did undercut *Plessy* substantially in 1937. In that year, Arthur W. Mitchell, a black Democratic member of the US House of Representatives from Illinois, was forcibly ejected from a Pullman railcar in Arkansas while traveling from Chicago to Hot Springs. After appealing unsuccessfully for relief to the Interstate Commerce Commission and the Federal District Court for Northern Illinois, Mitchell took his case to the US Supreme Court. The following are excerpts from the Supreme Court decision in *Mitchell v. United States,* decided April 1941, a test case of the Interstate Commerce Act of 1887; they are followed by newspaper commentary.

Mr. Chief Justice [Charles Evans] Hughes delivered the opinion of the court: Appellant, Arthur W. Mitchell, filed a complaint with the Interstate Commerce Commission alleging an unjust discrimination in the furnishing of accommodations to colored passengers on the line of the Chicago, Rock Island & Pacific Railway Company from Chicago to Hot Springs, Arkansas, in violation of the Interstate Commerce Act. The Commission dismissed the complaint . . . and appellant brought this suit to set aside the Commission's order. Upon a hearing before three judges, the District Court found the facts as stated in the Commission's findings, and held that the latter were supported by substantial evidence and that the Commission's order was supported by its findings. The court then ruled that it was without jurisdiction, and dismissal of the complaint was stated upon that ground. The case comes here on direct appeal.

. . . We have repeatedly said that it is apparent from the legislative history of the [Interstate Commerce] Act that not only was the evil of discrimination the principle thing aimed at, but that there is no basis for the contention that Congress intended to exempt any discriminatory action or practice of interstate commerce which it had authority to reach. . . . Paragraph 1 of [the Interstate Commerce] Act says explicitly that it shall be unlawful for any common carrier subject to the Act "to subject any particular person . . . to any undue or unreasonable prejudice or disadvantage in any respect whatsoever." From the inception of its administration the Interstate Commerce Commission has recognized the applicability of this provision to discrimination against colored passengers because of their race and the duty of carriers to provide equality of treatment with respect to transportation facilities; that is, that colored persons who buy first-class tickets must be furnished with accommodations equal in comforts and convenience to those afforded to first-class white passengers. . . .

We find no sound reason for the failure to apply this principle by holding the discrimination from which the appellant suffered to be unlawful and by forbidding it in the future.

That there was but a single instance was not a justification of the treatment of the appellant. Moreover, the Commission thought it plain that "the incident was mentioned as representative of an alleged practice that was expected to continue." And the Commission found that the ejection of appellant from the Pullman car and the requirement that he should continue his journey in a second-class car was " in accordance with custom," that is, as we understand it, according to the custom which obtained in similar circumstances.

Nor does the change in the carrier's practice avail. That did not alter the discrimination to which appellant had been subjected, and as to the future the change was not adequate. It appears that since July, 1937, the carrier has put in service a coach for colored passengers which is of equal quality with that used by second-class white passengers. But, as the Government well observes, the question does not end with travel on second-class tickets. It does not appear that colored passengers who have bought first-class tickets for transportation by the carrier are given accommodations which are substantially equal to those afforded to white passengers. The Government puts the matter succinctly: "When a drawing room is available, the carrier practice of allowing colored passengers to use one at Pullman seat rates avoids inequality as between the accommodations specifically assigned to the passenger. But when none is available, as on the trip which occasioned this litigation, the discrimination and inequality of accommodation become self-evident. It is no answer to say that the colored passengers, if sufficiently diligent and forehanded, can make their reservations so far in advance as to be assured of first-class accommodations. So long as white passengers can secure first-class reservations on the day of travel and the colored passengers cannot, the latter are subjected to inequality and discrimination because of their race."

. . . It is the individual, we said, who is entitled to the equal protection of the laws,—not merely a group of individuals, or a body of persons according to their numbers. . . . And the Interstate Commerce Act expressly extends its prohibitions to the subjecting of "any particular person" to unreasonable discriminations.

. . . On the facts here presented . . . the discrimination was palpably unjust and forbidden by the [Interstate Commerce] Act. The decree of the District Court is reversed and the cause is remanded with directions to set aside the order of the Commission and to remand the case to the Commission for further proceedings in conformity with this opinion.

Reversed.

•   •   •

Although this case originated from an incident taking place in Arkansas, the Attorney Generals of nine other states joined with Arkansas' Counsel in a common brief. These states were Alabama, Florida, Georgia, Kentucky, Louisiana, Mississippi, Texas, Tennessee, and Virginia. The Supreme Court, however, finding that segregation was not involved, had no occasion to consider the questions discussed in this brief. . . . No dissenting opinion was filed (by the U.S. Supreme Court Justices). On November 19, 1941, the Interstate Commerce Commission ordered the Chicago, Rock Island and Pacific Railway to provide Negroes traveling in Arkansas and paying first-class fares on through journeys from Chicago to Hot Springs with accommodations "substantially equal" to those provided for white passengers. This must be done by December 24 [1941]. Of course the order will affect all other railways selling first-class tickets through states having "Jim Crow" laws.

Black Arkansans Seek the Vote

Arkansas Gazette (Little Rock), July 29, 1942.

In this selection, black citizens challenge the prevailing state Democratic Party rules barring their participation in the primary election process.

Election officials in Arkansas' Democratic Preferential Primary adhered to party rules and turned away Negro Democrats who attempted to vote in the primary election held on July 28, 1942. This seems to have been the practice followed throughout the state except at Camden where a number of Negroes were allowed to cast ballots. The Negroes who requested the right to participate in the primary were members of the Arkansas Negro Democratic Association. The denial of their request may result in a legal test before the Federal Court. At any rate a report on the developments of election day is to be sent to a special counsel for the N.A.A.C.P. (National Association for the Advancement of Colored People) in New York City. The intentions of the Negro Democrats to seek suffrage in the primary had been indicated as far back as May, 1941, after the U.S. Supreme Court held unanimously in a Louisiana case that state primaries and nominating conventions are subject to Federal regulations. The officers of the [Arkansas Negro Democratic Association] stated that had the Negroes been admitted to the primary, they would have voted only the contests for U.S. Senator and Congress.

The effort of the Negroes to vote aroused interest not only in Arkansas but throughout the South. The State Chairman of the Democratic Executive Committee for the state of Mississippi coupled it with the campaign for the proposed abolition of the Poll Tax and warned further that Federal appropriations for schools might be made contingent upon a surrender of state control to Federal authorities. Speaking the day before the state primary in Arkansas, the Mississippi man said, "our sister state of Arkansas is going to have an awful serious time tomorrow forgetting these two things."

Economic Justice:
A Report on the Little Rock Black Community

"Employment," Industrial Relations and Education, Report of
Survey Community Relations Project, Greater Little Rock,
Arkansas, vol. 2 (The Greater Little Rock Community Council,
September–December 1946), UALR Center for Arkansas History
and Culture, Little Rock.

In 1946, the National Urban League and the Community Chest
and Council of Greater Little Rock conducted a study of the city's
black community. The following is an excerpt from the study's economic findings.

A study of the employment patterns of Greater Little Rock show[s]
that the Negro worker is not a part of the main stream of employment but
instead is relegated to the service and unskilled categories unless employed
to give direct service exclusively to the colored population. Of course, there
are some exceptions to this but not many. The governmental agencies fall
in line with this pattern with the exception of the post offices where a large
percentage of the carriers are colored. The City of Little Rock follows it,
having failed to even give equal status to the Negro policemen, while the
City of North Little Rock simply does not employ any Negroes. This is
also true of the Little Rock offices of Veterans Administrations, the State
Employment Service and the State Unemployment Compensation Office,
none of which employ colored workers although giving service to a large
number.

The jobs which Negroes have are usually among the lowest paid.
Wages in the community have increased during the last five years as evi-
denced by the average pay offered to domestics through the Urban
League. Such increases, however, have failed to bring the pay to a livable
level. Among the A.F. of L. [American Federation of Labor] craft unions
the bricklayers set a good example for the community to follow. Its members meet together and work together without friction. Most of the other
locals, where white members outnumber Negro members, do not follow
this example. Instead they either bar colored workers or place them in
auxiliary locals.

The existing inadequacies briefly described in this report are not new. Individuals who know the community have long been cognizant of them. . . . Therefore it is recommended:

1. That the Subcommittee on Education and Industry continue to function in an effort to put into effect as many of the recommendations as it finds acceptable, and that this committee be strengthened through the addition of the Principal of the Dunbar School and a representative from the American Federation of Labor and the Congress of Industrial Organizations.

2. That this committee work to widen the opportunities for employment of qualified colored workers in the semi-skilled, skilled and clerical categories. One technique that could be used is to have a small committee, representing both races, to discuss employment opportunities with the management of new plants opening in the Greater Little Rock area, making a special effort to sell management the idea of giving equality of opportunity for employment to qualified colored applicants. Two companies that this subcommittee should begin to work with at once are Westinghouse Electric Company, which plans to employ 800 people in its new plant, and Leylind Manufacturing Company, which plans to employ 250 by June 1, 1947.

3. That the labor unions be requested to arrange educational programs for their locals designed to give equality of opportunity for employment and membership to qualified colored applicants, especially in those locals where conditions indicate such programs are definitely needed.

4. That the Chamber of Commerce of both cities be urged to arrange similar programs for their members. This is of vital importance since these bodies usually wield a great deal of influence on new companies' personnel policies regarding the employment of minority groups.

D. THE POLITICS OF REFORM AND REACTION

A new political zeal came to Arkansas with the conclusion of World War II. A number of returning war veterans, centered primarily in Hot Springs, Garland County, launched political careers in response to allegations of old guard politics and corruption. The following documents offer some insight into the politics of reform and reaction.

The GI Revolt

Arkansas Gazette (Little Rock), July 5, 1946.

Named for its leaders' status as veterans of the Second World War, the "GI Revolt" rallied the forces of a new era of political accountability.

In the heat of Arkansas' first postwar Independence Day, Garland County's slate of GI candidates launched their campaigns . . . with a full-scale assault on the political machine of Hot Springs' Mayor Leo P. McLaughlin.

If the enthusiasm of the 800 who crowded the air-cooled auditorium of Londale's Colony House is any gauge, McLaughlin's regime faces a far more serious threat than the mayor has publically admitted. The speeches of Sidney S. McMath, candidate for prosecuting attorney, and Q. Byrum Hurst, GI aspirant for county judge, were interrupted frequently by applause, and several citizens in the auditorium's amen corner responded to the candidates with vocal encouragement.

"That's Leo for you," one shouted as Mr. McMath compared McLaughlin with Hitler and Mussolini. . . .

. . . Charging that his opponent, Prosecuting Attorney Curtis Ridgeway, had failed to protect the civil rights of the people, Mr. McMath asked why there had been no prosecutions arising out of the 1942 Garland county vote frauds reported by the Grand Jury. The basic right of the people to vote and have their votes counted for a candidate of their choice was endangered by that failure, [McMath] charged. . . .

. . . The returning soldier is zealous of his heritage as an American citizen, perhaps because he has recently fought for it. When he returns to his own community from the war and finds his own people deprived of their right to vote, when he discovers that their lives and liberties are not secure, when it is threatened that if he exercises the right of citizenship and runs for public office without the consent of the political boss, he will be scarred for life and ruined, what is his reaction? How does he feel?

He feels that the principles of human decency which he fought to the gates of hell to retrieve, have been corrupted and thrown in his face by those whose fortunes were made and whose lives were made secure by reason of his sacrifices and his loss of blood. He feels that the war is not over, that there is another battle to be fought, another beachhead to be taken. He feels that before he can take off his pack and stack his arms, before he can rest secure in the heritage for which he had fought, he must join with the other red-blooded men and women of our community in an assault upon the island of dictatorship in Garland County, an island of dictatorship which has become more entrenched during the war, and which has waxed fat from the profits of war.

One View of Arkansas Politics at Midcentury

Mrs. Willard Steele to Francis Cherry, September 10, 1952, Francis Cherry Papers, Arkansas History Commission, Little Rock.

In this letter, we are given a sense of the explosive political currents in Arkansas and the nation prior to the general election of November 1952.

September 10th
Judge Francis Cherry
Jonesboro, Ark.

Dear Judge Cherry—

There was great rejoicing among many people outside of Arkansas when you defeated the [Harry] Truman approved Sid McMath—I was one who was very happy over your election—

I have reasons to feel very close to Arkansas—It was my father's boyhood state—and his parents are buried at Viney Grove—His father fought in the Confederate Army and my father spent many weeks in a Yankee prison—I have many many friends in Arkansas and I wrote to them on your behalf—I even have several friends in Jonesboro—as a young girl I traveled with the Will R. Stucks and knew Walter very well—Charlie Claunch who now lives here is a real friend of ours and lawyer. I could go on and on—as I have visited in so many places in Arkansas—and love the state—

So I felt that with your election—Arkansas would have what the country needs, a change—and an escape from Trumanism—the New Deal—and the effect that the Mess in Washington is having upon the whole country—

I read with real disappointment and regret in the paper this morning—that you will support the New Deal—Socialistic platform and candidates—and that Arkansas will not have the change that was expected.

As I [am a] Southern Democrat—and I have no candidate—no ticket—I must choose between the New Deal and the Republicans and every time I will take Americanism with [Dwight] Eisenhower and [Richard] Nixon—to Socialism with [Adlai] Stevenson and [John] Sparkman (who has openly betrayed the South). My hats off to Texas—now they are doing the patriotic thing—they are putting the good of the country first and party second—we can all STAY Democrats and vote for a Republican—We do not change our party at all—we simply choose the best man and platform for the country—and the time has come when all Americans should put principle ahead of the label.

. . . Thank goodness we have some patriots in Texas and a few Southern states and I am awfully sorry that Arkansas seems to follow the label and support the man Mr. Truman selected and controls—If you think Mr. Stevenson can clean up the Mess in Washington you have another guess coming—the men who made the Mess nominated him—do you think he will clean them out—

Thank goodness [Joseph] McCarthy won—he has the courage to fight the Communists—even if he gets smeared . . .

I hope as the campaign goes on you will change your mind as so many of our Southern leaders are doing—I hate to be so disappointed in you and Arkansas.

Yours very truly
Mrs. Willard Steele

The Revenue Stabilization Act

Acts of Arkansas of the 55th General Assembly (January–March 1945), 721–53.

As a method for financing state government, the Revenue Stabilization Act has had far-reaching implications for the Arkansas community. The following are excerpts from that act.

AN ACT to Provide a Method of Financing All of the Necessary Functions of the State Government Without the Levying or Collecting of Any New Taxes; To Reallocate All State Revenues On a Basis Which Will Provide an Equitable Apportionment of Funds for the Cost of Maintaining Public Services; To Provide Definite Funds for the Speedy Retirement of the State Debt; To Stabilize the Funds of the State Treasury for Current and Further Needs of the State Government; To Provide a Means for the Reduction of Taxes.

Be It Enacted by the General Assembly of the State of Arkansas:

Section 1. It is the purpose of this act to provide for the prompt payment of the bonded debt of the state and the financing of all the functions of the State Government by reallocating revenue, and by creating current and general surplus funds by means of which the Government may be stabilized, without the necessity of levying any additional taxes; and to provide a means for the reduction of taxes. This act shall be referred to as the "REVENUE STABILIZATION LAW" of Arkansas.

Section 2. As to the special taxes, permits, licenses, fees and other exactions contributing to the "special revenues," and "trust funds," or "non-revenue receipts," as hereafter defined, it is not the purposes of this act to change the levy of such taxes, as now provided by law, either as to the amount or rate thereof, or as to the purpose or purposes for which such special revenues are levied; and as to all taxes contributing to "general revenues," as hereafter defined, it is not the purpose of this act to change the amount or rate of such taxes but all such taxes for "general revenues" of the state are hereby levied for the purposes hereafter provided in this act; and all such revenues collected after the effective date of this act and deposited in the State Treasury on or after June 1, 1945 (date beginning of the "revenue year," as hereafter defined), shall be distributed in the manner and for the purposes provided in this act; provided that all such revenues collected after the effective date of this act and deposited in the State Treasury prior to June 1, 1945, shall be distributed in the manner and for the purposes provided by the prior acts levying or allocating such taxes or revenues, provided further, that any unencumbered balance in any fund in the State Treasury at the close of the fiscal year on June 30, 1945, shall be used only for the purposes for which the fund was collected, and as hereafter provided.

Section 3. Revenues required by law to be deposited in the State Treasury, and such grants as are received from the Federal Government, shall be classified in one or more of the following groups:

(a) General Revenues.

(b) Special Revenues.

(c) Trust Funds.

(d) Federal Grants.

(e) Non-revenue Receipts.

•   •   •

Section 9. There is hereby created in the State Treasury a fund to be known as the State Apportionment Fund.

As relates to the State Apportionment Fund, a "revenue year" is hereby established which shall begin June 1 and end May 31 of the following year, and "general revenues" and "special revenues" deposited in the State Treasury on and after June 1, 1945, shall be credited to the State Apportionment Fund; provided that in establishing such "revenue year," it is not intended to affect the "fiscal year" or "bond year" used for other purposes.

Section 10. Revenues deposited in the State Apportionment Fund during any calendar month shall be designated as "gross revenues" for the respective month.

All departments, officers, boards, commissions, agencies or institutions of the state depositing any money in the State Treasury during any calendar month, which under the terms of this act is required to be credited to the State Apportionment Fund, shall at the end of the month file a report thereof with the State Treasurer, and the State Treasurer, after comparing such reports with his official receipts issued at the time of deposit, shall prepare a statement showing the "gross revenues" deposited in the State Apportionment Fund during the respective calendar month.

From such "gross revenues" for each month, the State Treasurer shall deduct the amounts paid in refund of taxes erroneously collected, as provided for by law, and the amounts represented by uncollected checks, and shall keep a record thereof for accounting purposes. The remaining revenues in the State Apportionment Fund shall be designated "gross revenues available for distribution."

Section 11. It is declared to be the policy of the State Government that every department, office, board, commission, institution, agency or activity supported from the State Treasury shall contribute in part to the following general expenses of the state:

(1) For the services of the Legislative, Executive and Judicial Branches of the State Government.

(2) For the support of the Revenue Department, and any other collecting agency of the state which is supported from the General Revenue Fund.

(3) For the state's part of paying salaries and expenses of county assessors and clerks.

(4) For the upkeep and maintenance of the State Capitol Building.

(5) For expenses of budget control and auditing.

•   •   •

Any unencumbered balances on June 30, 1945, . . . which are merged with the General Revenue Fund, shall be transferred to the General Revenue Fund, but used only for the support of the departments for which the funds were originally provided by law until such funds are exhausted, and thereafter such departments shall be supported out of any other monies in the General Revenue Fund. . . .

•   •   •

Section 52. Provisions of this act, with reference to the allocations of funds, are declared to be in compliance with Sub-Section A of Section 3 of Amendment No. 22 to the Constitution of the State of Arkansas.

Section 53. The revenues allocated from the State Apportionment Fund during any "revenue year" are for the purpose of providing funds for the operation of state agencies during the "fiscal year," and no revenues allocated during any revenue year may be used for the payment of vouchers or warrants issued against the appropriations for the previous fiscal year; and no disbursing agent of the state shall be permitted to issue vouchers during any fiscal year, unless there has been allocated to the fund for the support of his agency sufficient monies during the revenue year for the payment of said vouchers, together with all previous vouchers issued by him during such fiscal year, or unless there is sufficient unencumbered balance carried over from previous years to pay such vouchers.

Section 54. It is not the intention of this act to abolish any fund carried on the Treasurer's books, and heretofore provided for by law, unless such fund is merged with or transferred to another fund mentioned in this act to be used for the same purposes as originally provided for, and the identity of any fund so merged or transferred shall be maintained so far as the revenues to the credit of such fund are concerned until such balances are used, as provided for in this act.

Section 55. The State Comptroller, State Auditor and State Treasurer are directed to set up the necessary records which will reflect at all times the condition of the revenues, accounts and funds, as herein provided. The State Comptroller and State Auditor, with the approval of the Attorney General, shall prescribe the form of vouchers to be used by all state agencies and the warrant to be used by the State Auditor in payment of all vouchers, and the State Comptroller and State Treasurer, with the approval of the Attorney General, shall prescribe the form of all receipts to be issued for the deposit of all monies in the State Treasury, as provided for in this act.

All vouchers for the payment of obligations which are incurred, or which become due, prior to the close of any fiscal year on June 30, must be presented to the State Comptroller's Office not later than August 15 following the close of the fiscal year, and the Auditor of State shall issue his warrant in payment of such voucher not later than August 31 following the close of the fiscal year, unless such warrant had previously been issued and cancelled or lost, and the issuance of a new warrant becomes necessary.

•　　•　　•

Section 59. It has been found and is hereby declared by the General Assembly of the State of Arkansas that: (1) existing laws providing for the distribution of state revenues are such that a moderate diminution of certain of the revenues would have the effect of curtailing the activities of certain necessary agencies of the State Government; (2) that under the provisions of this act all revenues of the state are allocated in such manner that during any given year sufficient funds will be received to perform all necessary functions of the State Government; (3) because of the fact that future revenues only are affected by the provisions of this act, and it is necessary to collect and handle a great many of our taxes before depositing the same in the State Treasury, thereby making it necessary to clear the records on such taxes in order for the provisions of this act relating to the allocation of funds to commence on June 1, 1945; and (4) that only the provisions of this act will correct a situation which otherwise may deprive the citizens of this state from receiving the benefits for which the operation of State Government contemplates. Therefore, an emergency is hereby declared to exist, and this act being necessary for the preservation of the public peace, health and safety shall take effect and be in full force from and after its passage. [Approved March 23, 1945.]

E. A NEW DAY DAWNING

Standing at the threshold of yet another new era in its history, Arkansas faced a series of important challenges. Economically, its long-touted aim of sustained industrial development had not been realized. Politically, the forces of demagoguery stood ready to overtake reason and common sense. On the social scene, much remained to be accomplished. Dim though the times were, Arkansans could still believe that a new day was dawning, in the quest for greater economic prosperity and upon the future of education in the state.

The Arkansas Plan

"'Selfish' Arkansas Power," *Fortune* (October 1952), reprint by Time, Inc., C. Hamilton Moses File, Arkansas History Commission, Little Rock.

This excerpt from *Fortune* magazine outlines a course of industrial development for the state as expounded by C. Hamilton Moses.

At the dedication of the Bull Shoals Dam in Arkansas last summer, Harry Truman introduced a theme for the Democrats to plug in Dixie. Set to music this one might have been titled, "Especially for You-All"; its burden was how much the government has done for the South in spite of those old special interests. This fine dam, Mr. Truman said, was an example "of how people have to fight to overcome not only the forces of nature, but also the forces of reaction and selfishness." The private companies, he charged, had opposed this dam, and while this accusation was not entirely justified, what made it interesting was that for once Mr. Truman was specific. He pointed directly at the Arkansas Power & Light Co., C. Hamilton Moses, President.

. . . Now, as one of the few "selfish interests" ever thus positively identified, A.P.&L. provides a rare opportunity for analyzing the Democratic charges against business and determining what substance they have. No cursory examination will do. A caricature, either benign or malign, can too easily be drawn. It can, for example, be said that A.P.&L. is a monopoly and a Wall Street monopoly at that. It can be charged, as Harry Truman did, that A.P.&L. carted an expensive model dam all over the state trying to prove that multipurpose dams like Bull Shoals are a contradiction in terms—which they are, although not necessarily an irreconcilable contradiction. It can be said that A.P.&L. has opposed the "wheeling" of federal power to farm customers over its transmission lines, and the right of the Rural Electrification Administration to lend farmers money to build generating and transmission facilities. Finally, to round out the picture of big business sitting toadlike on a backward state, it can be alleged that A.P.&L. meddles in politics to an unseemly degree. There are elements of truth in all these charges.

Those more favorably disposed to capitalism, on the other hand, can point to A.P.&L.'s accomplishments not only in providing power but also in advancing the well-being of Arkansas. They can show that the company has multiplied its generating capacity more than three times since 1946 and is the biggest taxpayer in the state; that next year [1953] it will install two and a half times as much power as it had in toto at the end of World War II; that Arkansas, which ranked fourth from the bottom in rural electrification in 1946, is now close to the top. They can point to electric rates that compare favorably with the national average, and in some cases are the lowest in the land. And they can truthfully say that Moses and A.P.&L. led the effort to pole the state of Arkansas out of the economic backwaters and into the mainstream of U.S. progress. But this would not be a complete portrait of A.P.&L. either.

. . . Arkansas has a lot of catching up to do. As Moses puts it, "we wore ourselves out whipping the North and then quit." Ranking twenty-sixth among the states in area and thirtieth in population, the "Wonder State" today ranks next to last in per capita income ($950). Only Mississippi [is] lower. During the 1940's, moreover, Arkansas [lost 2 percent of its population].

To Hamilton Moses this emigration seemed intolerable, unwarranted, and unavoidable. For Arkansas is relatively rich in resources. It is the third largest producer of cotton and sixth producer of lumber in the nation. It has virtually all the deposits of bauxite in the U.S. and sizable reserves of other minerals. It has a temperate climate and a large potential force of intelligent labor. What Arkansas lacks is industry. According to the last business census (1947), Arkansas contributed less than four-tenths of 1 percent of the value added by manufacture in the U.S.

Realizing that A.P.&L. could grow only as Arkansas grew, Moses decided early in World War II that a major bootstrap operation was in order. To lure industry he took the lead in setting up the Arkansas Economic Council, a private research-and-development agency, and got the state to create a similar body. Together with newspapers and other public agencies (A.P.&L. intentionally stayed in the background), these groups pushed Arkansas' industrialization and progress. When local money was needed to build a factory to attract industry from outside the state A.P.&L. usually ponied up one-twentieth of the cost.

The backbone of the plan, however, was the "Build Your Home Town" program. Forums were arranged all over the state and the citizens of hundreds of communities drew up blueprints for self-improvement. A.P.&L. contributed leadership, advice, and financial assistance, awarded prizes to communities making the most progress. Last year it launched a similar project in more than 300 farm communities, hopes soon to have 1000 rural communities competing for prizes. For fostering and promoting the "Arkansas Plan," Moses received considerable personal recognition.

Ham Moses, however, does not devote his time or his company's money to civic affairs for recognition or even because he is offended by the growing tendency to look to Washington for economic succor and subsidies. And if there is one firm Moses does not want to attract to Arkansas it is the federal government. He can never forget that just across the Mississippi to the east lies the domain of the Tennessee Valley Authority.

... A.P.&L. may fit Harry Truman's definition of a "selfish interest." If it does the country could use more of them.

The Little Rock Council on Education: The Winds of Change

"The Little Rock Council on Education Report," George Iggers Papers, UALR Center for Arkansas History and Culture, Little Rock.

In 1952, the newly formed, biracial Little Rock Council on Education reported on the quality of education for blacks and whites in the city. The following is an excerpt from the council's report.

What are the reasons for the much poorer results achieved by the segregated Negro high school as against the white one? Why does the slight difference between white and Negro performance at the beginning of the second year of school become a tremendous gap at the twelfth. It is clear that the segregated school system does not offer an equal quality of education. But why? The factors involved are doubtlessly many, the poorer facilities playing a definite role. But there is strong reason to believe that a decisive part is played by certain intangibles which cannot be overcome merely by equal appropriations and which make any real equality under segregation impossible. The crux of the matter is that the Negro children, members of a minority group which has in the past been generally excluded from the fullness of American life and its heritage, are not admitted to the cultural advantages of the privileged majority. The segregated school system perpetuates this semi-isolation of the Southern Negroes and makes it difficult for the Negro child to absorb that part of education which the white child learns not necessarily through formal instruction but acquires more indirectly from fellow students and teachers. . . . The Negro teacher, himself a product of the segregated school system of the semi-isolated minority, generally cannot be as effective a school teacher as his white counterpart unless he is permitted to participate in the full advantages of the education of the privileged majority. The school achievement tests point this out too clearly. Equalization of school facilities, an extremely expensive proposition, can remove some of the physical obstacles of better instruction, but cannot succeed in providing education of the same quality. Only by the integration of Negro pupils and teachers in the white school system can intangibles which prevent any real qualitative equality be overcome.

. . . The separate educational facilities for Negroes in this city are not equal to those for whites. . . . The material basis of education could, of course, be equalized but at a staggering cost to the taxpayer. . . . The only practical, realistic, and ethical answer is integration.

Segregation in public facilities is bound to pass. With the increasing social and political awakening of the Negroes in the South, increasing pressure is being brought upon this system and is finding increasing sympathy among the enlightened white citizens. Recent developments in the South have opened most graduate and undergraduate facilities to Negroes. The attack on segregation in secondary and elementary schools is in the making, with a number of cases pending before the courts of Arkansas. Arkansas has been very fortunate in having seen most of the progress in this direction during the past few years made through mediation rather than through court action. During the past few years, the University of Arkansas opened its doors, several colleges are considering a plan to admit Negro students to their campuses for graduate extension courses, an increasing number of professional societies has admitted Negroes, the Little Rock Public Library was opened, no segregation was practiced at the opening of the first Little Rock community center, all major department stores have removed drinking fountain segregation signs, the Rock Island RR has abolished segregation on its trains. . . . All this seems to indicate the increasing understanding of Arkansas for peaceful and gradual solution of the problems of segregation outside the courts.

Full integration may come in two ways, either suddenly through court action or gradually through planned integration and the fullest utilization of the human and physical resources of the school system. . . . Sudden integration through court action would have as its consequence increased social tension for a period of time, resentment on the part of pupils and teachers, the casting of unprepared students into the integrated situation, and . . . [the inability of] many Negro pupils and teachers to play a full role under integration and introduce them into the common school system step by step as they become ready. Such a plan would also condition white public opinion to a situation which in the long run would result in greater social harmony and a better trained citizenry.

FOR FURTHER READING

For the post–World War II period in Arkansas history, students should see Ben E. Johnson III (Fayetteville: University of Arkansas Press, 2000); C. Calvin Smith, *War and Wartime Changes: The Transformation of Arkansas, 1940–1945* (Fayetteville: University of Arkansas Press, 1986); Harry S. Ashmore, *An Epitaph for Dixie* (New York: Norton Publishing Co., 1958); and Daisy Bates, *The Long Shadow of Little Rock: A Memoir* (New York: David McKay Co., 1962). For an informative account of Arkansas political issues during the late 1940s and early 1950s, see James Lester, *A Man for Arkansas: Sid McMath and the Southern Reform Tradition* (Little Rock: Rose Publishing Co., 1976); and Sidney S. McMath, *Promises Kept: A Memoir* (Fayetteville: University of Arkansas Press, 2002).

PART IV

Modern Arkansas, 1955–

C. Fred Williams

CHAPTER IX

Modern Arkansas

INTRODUCTION

Modern Arkansas saw a revival of the spirit that characterized its development prior to the Civil War. Originally an ambitious, economically expansive state, Arkansas spent almost a century trying to overcome the devastating influence of the Civil War and Reconstruction. In the Modern Era, business and political leaders made a major commitment to industrial development. That, and a surge in population caused in part by a national demographic shift to southern and western states, restored much of the state's antebellum vitality.

In the hundred years prior to 1960, Arkansas grew accustomed to heavy indebtedness and limited revenues in the state treasury. Much of that changed in the Modern Era. For the first time since the Civil War, Arkansas consistently showed a surplus in state revenues, its products were marketed around the world, and commerce on the Arkansas River boomed as in the steamboat era.

Politically, the new era saw the revival of the Republican Party. Devastated in southern states by association with the Civil War and Reconstruction, Republicans challenged Democrats in much the same way that their predecessors, the Whigs, did in antebellum days. Although still limited in statewide elections, the party selectively applied its influence and made the political process more competitive.

Much of the success of the revived Republican Party was due to the personal fortune of Winthrop Rockefeller. A transplanted New York businessman, Rockefeller first entered the political arena as director of the Arkansas Industrial Development Commission in Orval Faubus's first administration. Faubus won the gubernatorial election in 1954 on a mildly progressive platform but turned increasingly conservative after his involvement with the Little Rock School Crisis, 1957–1959. Disenchanted with Faubus's new direction, Rockefeller resigned his position in the administration and began an all-out effort to rebuild the state's Republican Party. His success led to a confrontation with Faubus in 1964, when he challenged his former boss in the race for governor. Although soundly defeated, Rockefeller was considered a viable alternative by a growing bloc of moderate to liberal voters who became increasingly unhappy with Faubus's segregationist policies and ties to men of wealth in the state. When Faubus did not seek a seventh term in 1966, Rockefeller again entered the race and defeated former state senator Jim Johnson, an outspoken segregationist and nominee of the Democratic Party. A significant factor in Rockefeller's victory was the support given him by moderate Democrats.

Even though his tenure was short lived—he was defeated in 1970 while seeking a third term—Rockefeller was successful in pressuring the Democratic Party into liberalizing its practices. Dale Bumpers, winner of the 1970 gubernatorial election, did so by reclaiming many Democratic voters who had bolted the party in Faubus's later years. Bumper's successors, David Pryor and Bill Clinton, continued the Democratic tradition by utilizing essentially the same campaign appeal as the former. While Democrats maintained a large majority of registered voters, the three decades following World War II demonstrated that the party could not take voters for granted. Arkansans have traditionally shown a tendency to act independently and often ignore official party recommendations. Perhaps the biggest surprise in the state's Modern Era came in the 1980 gubernatorial election, when Republican candidate Frank White defied all opinion polls and defeated Democratic incumbent Bill Clinton.

Change was not limited to politics. For two decades following World War II, Arkansas experienced a slow but steady decline in its population. Thousands of the state's native born sought opportunities elsewhere, and new immigrants were slow to be attracted to the "Land of Opportunity." In the mid-1960s, however, these trends began to change. Not only did the economic climate improve, but also changing lifestyles—with an emphasis on a simpler, less hurried pace—led many newcomers to discover Arkansas. They were attracted to the state's natural beauty, its relatively unpolluted environment, and its open spaces. The dramatic rise in energy costs in the mid-1970s also stimulated immigration into the "Sunbelt" from northern and eastern states.

Ironically, this influx of people returned the state to its more traditional settlement pattern. Through much of the nineteenth century, counties in the mountainous regions had a larger population than the delta counties. However, in the first half of the twentieth century, the lowlands became the more heavily populated region. But the new migration after 1960 was in large measure a shift back to the Ozarks and Ouachitas. These shifting patterns created problems, not only at the state level, in congressional redistricting for example, but in local communities as well. In scenes reminiscent of early statehood days, newcomers vied with old timers for political and social control. Some analysts interpreted these creative tensions at the local level as strategic and suggested that the state was undergoing a fundamental change in its political and social attitudes. Other observers argued that the variety of interests represented in the state preserved a balance of opinion and that Arkansas would continue to be an independent state, although admittedly southern in culture.

A. POLITICS

Arkansas politics in the Modern Era shifted from traditional patterns. To be sure, an overwhelming majority of the state's officeholders were members of the Democratic Party. However, there was an increasing tendency by the electorate to vote independently—for the man, as pollsters say—with less dependence on official party endorsement. The office of the governor underwent significant modification. Traditionally limited by constitutional constraints, governors in the three decades following World War II reorganized the executive branch, to increased administrative salaries, and used increased federal aid to the state as a means for strengthening the office. But political changes were not limited to the executive branch. Reapportionment of the General Assembly, as mandated by the "one person, one vote" ruling of the US Supreme Court, had a major impact on that body by shifting power to the more urban areas of the state.

Official Results of 1968 General Election

Arkansas Gazette (Little Rock), November 19, 1968.

This document reflects the independent temperament of Arkansas voters. In the 1968 general election, Arkansans gave majorities to George Wallace (American Party) for president, Winthrop Rockefeller (Republican) for governor, and William Fulbright (Democratic) for US senator. This apparent contradiction in voter attitudes can best be interpreted by recognizing that each candidate represented anti-establishment views and was outside the mainstream of traditional party politics.

Governor Rockefeller won re-election by 29,969 votes . . . the official tabulations by Secretary of State Kelly Bryant showed Monday.

Mr. Rockefeller won a second term with 52.4 percent of the vote against Democrat Marion H. Crank.

Senator J. William Fulbright won with 59.1 percent and a lead of 106,110 votes over Republican Charles T. Bernard of Earle.

The total vote in the governor's race—a record—was 615,595. The vote cast in the presidential race was 619,119. . . .

Here were the final results as tabulated Monday:

President

George Wallace	239,364
Richard Nixon	191,659
Hubert Humphrey	188,096

United States Senate

William Fulbright	344,678
Charles Bernard	238,568

Governor

Winthrop Rockefeller	322,782
Marion Crank	292,813

A Ranking of State Governors in the Twentieth Century

Cal Ledbetter Jr. and C. Fred Williams, "Arkansas Governors in the Twentieth Century: A Ranking and Analysis," *Arkansas Political Science Journal* 3 (1982): 41.

The following evaluation of the state's governors in the twentieth century was made by a group of historians, political scientists, and journalists. The poll reflected the traditional weakness of the governor's office. In the judgment of those surveyed, none of the state's chief executives could be rated as "great" in the performance of official duties. The survey excluded those governors holding office in the last ten years.

GOVERNOR	# RESPONDENTS	RANKING	CATEGORY	TOTAL POINTS
Charles H. Brough	31	4.16	Good	129
George W. Donaghey	29	4.10	Good	119
Winthrop Rockefeller	35	3.97	Good	139
Sid McMath	35	3.86	Good	135
Carl E. Bailey	31	3.74	Good	116
Thomas C. McRae	27	3.56	Good	96
Ben T. Laney	33	3.33	Average	110
John E. Martineau	24	3.21	Average	77
Jeff Davis	27	3.15	Average	85
Orval Faubus	34	3.12	Average	106
George W. Hays	24	2.88	Average	69
Francis Cherry	35	2.83	Average	99
Homer M. Adkins	30	2.80	Average	84
J. M. Futrell	29	2.76	Average	80
Harvey Parnell	29	2.59	Average	75
Tom T. Terral	24	2.04	Below Average	49

53 Questionnaires Mailed
35 Responses by Survey
6 Responses by Letter
Ranking Scale: 5.0–4.5 = Great; 4.4–3.5 = Good; 3.4–2.5 = Average; 2.4–1.5 = Below Average; 1.4–0 = Poor

Rockefeller's Plans to Reorganize Agencies and Functions

Max Milam, "Organization Chart of the Executive Branch, State of Arkansas," *Arkansas Gazette (Little Rock)*, September 5, 1971.

The executive reorganization plan put forth by Winthrop Rockefeller and enacted with minor modifications during the administration of Dale Bumpers was the first major restructuring of state government since the Constitution of 1874. Although the plan was revised somewhat, it nevertheless represented a significant realignment of responsibilities and provided the governor with more administrative control over the executive branch.

A proposal that would extensively reorganize state agencies and their functions into 13 major departments was revealed Tuesday by Governor Rockefeller.

The proposal would create seven new departments and place more than 100 state agencies and their functions under the new departments, the existing departments, and the constitutional officers.

Most state agencies would be affected and the proposal would appear to increase the power of the governor, who would appoint all department heads. The governor would be allowed to "establish, combine, abolish or otherwise reorganize" any division with the departments.

The new departments would be the Departments of Higher Education, Natural Resources, Commerce, Local Affairs, Human Services, Public Safety and Planning and Development.

The Highway Department, the Game and Fish Commission, and Department of Corrections apparently would not be affected. The proposal said the Game and Fish Commission would "co-operate" with the Department of Natural Resources and the Highway Department with the Department of Commerce.

Some of the major changes proposed were to remove some functions from the offices of the Secretary of State and the Treasurer and give the duties to the Department of Administration and to merge the Department of Welfare into the new Department of Human Services. Some changes would alter existing titles without substantially changing the functions of the office.

Three types of transfers were suggested. Type 1 would transfer managerial functions to a department and the existing organization would

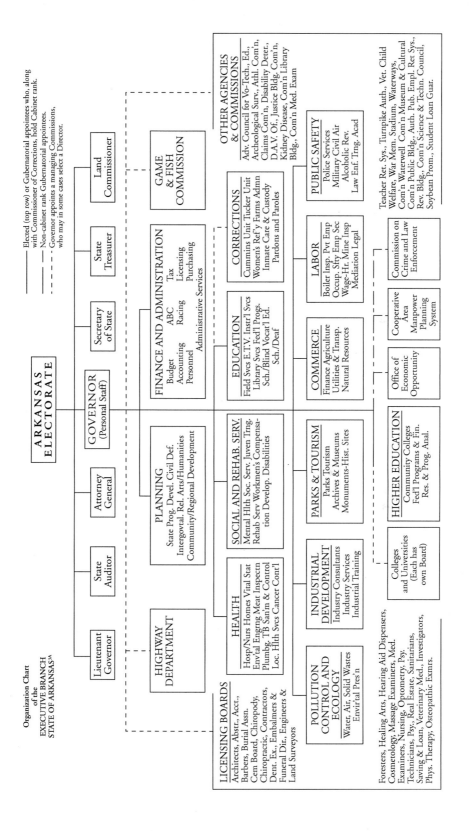

Organization Chart
of the
EXECUTIVE BRANCH
STATE OF ARKANSAS^{SM}

retain its substantive power and authority; type 2 would transfer all power and authority to the head of an existing or newly created department but would retain the organization as part of the new department, and type 3 would abolish an agency. Most transfers would be type 2 changes.

Assembly Reapportionment Illustrates Population Shift

Arkansas Gazette (Little Rock), August 22, 1965.

This newspaper report of reapportionment in the General Assembly described the first reorganization to be done following the US Supreme Court's *Baker v. Carr* ruling in 1962. The realignment reflected increasing political strength for the cities and a declining influence for rural Arkansans as a result of post–World War II population shifts.

The new reapportionment of the Arkansas General Assembly illustrated a trend that has been in progress since before the turn of the century—the movement of the center of population eastward and southward.

Its reshuffling of representational strength also means that 12 of the present members of the House of Representatives will lose their seats because they have been thrown into districts with other incumbents against whom they must run.

Did the reapportionment do what it really was supposed to do—give perfectly equal representation on the one man–one vote basis. The answer to this question is: It's perhaps closer to ideal than the old system, but inequities are scattered through the new system. The Board of Apportionment hopes that the flaws in the new are not so great as to cause the courts to reject the plan.

Between 1900 and 1960, 37 Arkansas counties showed a net loss of population, while 38 showed a gain. With few exceptions all of those showing losses were in the western part of the state—the majority in the mountains of the northwest. . . .

People Were Moving Eastward in 1900

If an imaginary line had been drawn from Blytheville to Texarkana in 1900 (Blytheville then being a muddy crossroads), most of the state's population lived to the left (west) of it.

But even then the movement was eastward. A telling illustration of the final effect is a comparison of the Congressional Districts of Arkansas as they existed in 1901 and in 1950. In both years Arkansas had seven districts.

In 1900, First District in the east had a population of only 180,790. In 1950, the same district had grown to 425,861—an increase of 245,071 in half a century.

Meanwhile, the Northwest Arkansas Third Congressional District had 177,492 population in 1900, and had increased by only 508 to 178,000 in 1950. Most of the growth was in one county—Washington.

So long as each county had at least one state representative the full impact of the population change was not readily apparent. The 1874 Constitution provided at least one representative per county, with the remaining 25 divided up among the more populous counties.

Counties Will Share Representatives

The one man–one vote rule of the United States Supreme Court on reapportionment has changed that. It made it necessary for smaller counties to share representatives, and most of the sharing is being done in the northwest and western hill counties.

In the days of its early settlement why did more people go to the hill counties than to the delta and flat counties and why the change back in later years?

The early settlers—those not connected with the large plantations, were attracted to the hills because of good drainage, little danger of flooding, absence of malaria and other lowland diseases and a good water supply.

With the levee districts in the delta came flood control; then came increased farming and improved drainage, which lessened malarial breeding areas. There was more money in the farms of the delta than the marginal farms of the rocky northwest. There was also better transportation.

The population began to shift—downhill.

B. SOCIETY

In many respects Arkansas society in the Modern Era was a reflection of national norms and trends. For example, women and minorities became increasingly vocal in expressing positions unique to their interests. Both groups organized and applied political and economic pressure to achieve desired results. Assisting the underprivileged also became a matter of concern for the post–World War II generation. Lacking major urban areas and inner-city ghetto-living conditions, attention in Arkansas centered on the state prison system: a series of sensational exposés in the 1960s identified deplorable conditions. Such conditions gained national exposure and became a source of major embarrassment for the state. But even in the midst of these disturbing and unsettling events, Arkansans were able to offset the trauma by a newfound pride in the arts and in the improving fortunes of the football team at the University of Arkansas, Fayetteville. Few things have had a more unifying effect on Arkansans or been the object of more boastful conversation than Razorback football. However, even with the publicity given to athletics, attendance at fine and performing arts events more than doubled that at all college sporting activities in the state in every year after the mid-1960s. Changing migration patterns and a revived interest in local culture contributed to a growing cultural awareness in the state.

Van Dalsem's Formula for Handling "Nosey" Women

Arkansas Gazette (Little Rock), August 28, 1963, March 28, 1966, and July 28, 1966.

This series of newspaper accounts includes a speech made before a civic club in Little Rock by Paul Van Dalsem, state representative from Perry County and a long-term, old-guard politician. His jesting comment on the role of women in his home county became the major rallying point for unifying women voters in the state and to a great extent marked the modern beginning of the Arkansas women's movement. The results of their activities are reflected in related newspaper reports. Herb Rule III, who defeated Van Dalsem, was a Little Rock lawyer making his first race for the General Assembly.

Representative Paul Van Dalsem of Perry County told the Little Rock Optimist Club yesterday what he thought was the matter with the women who lobby in the legislature and what he thought should be done.

"They're frustrated," he said.

"We don't have any of these university women in Perry County but

I'll tell you what we do up there when one of our women starts poking around in something she doesn't know anything about, we get her an extra milk cow," Van Dalsem said. "If that doesn't work, we give her a little more garden to tend. And then if that's not enough, we get her pregnant and keep her barefoot."

Van Dalsem said the women lobbyists were getting out of hand.

"I've seen as many as 30 of them on the floor of the House at one time," he said.

The women, whom he did not identify beyond "university women," frustrate the Pulaski County legislators, he said. He said they did not bother him.

Van Dalsem was at odds with several women's organizations over a voter registration bill during the 1963 legislative session. The women lobbied against some provisions of the bill that he favored, particularly an amendment that would have allowed any member of a voter's family to register for him and another amendment incorporating a literacy test. No bill was passed.

Various women also opposed Van Dalsem on the attempted ouster of Winthrop Rockefeller as chairman of the Arkansas Industrial Development Commission (which Van Dalsem favored).

The Optimists met at the Albert Pike Hotel.

•   •   •

DO NOT FALL FOR VAN DALSEM'S LINE
GROUPS WARN PULASKI COUNTY WOMEN

PERRYVILLE—Two women's political groups in Perry County have warned women voters in Pulaski County not to fall for the blandishments of Representative Paul Van Dalsem, who is expected to file for a position in the new combined House district of Pulaski and Perry Counties.

The Perry County Federation of Republican Women and the Perry County Women in Politics have approved a resolution addressed to the women voters in Pulaski County outlining what they consider the shortcomings of the veteran Perry County legislator.

The Perry County Women in Politics group was organized in 1963 shortly after Van Dalsem made his now-famous remark about how women in his County are kept out of politics. . . .

The resolution said that other legislators in Arkansas should be given a chance to take care of state affairs without "the big showman from Perry County," the resolution said.

"Without the Van Dalsem tactics and tantrums perhaps the necessity for costly special legislative sessions in the future could be curtailed," they said.

The resolution charged that Van Dalsem had prospered during his years in the legislature. It is easy to see, it said, how persons could be taken in by Van Dalsem's "gift of gab."

"We hope and pray that the voters in Pulaski County will not succumb to Mr. Van Dalsem's promises that he will do for Pulaski County what he has for Perry County—which is virtually nothing," the resolution stated.

•　　•　　•

VAN DALSEM LOSES, TO POLITICAL NOVICE; OTHER RACES CLOSE

As the returns from Tuesday's Democratic Party primary trickled in at a painfully slow rate Wednesday night, veteran Perry County Representative Paul Van Dalsem was trailing Herbert Rule of Little Rock with only 35 percent of the vote reported.

POSITION 13
Paul Van Dalsem   11,535
Herbert Rule   21,300

Rule–Van Dalsem Race Was in Spotlight

The Rule–Van Dalsem race generated a lot of interest, and it provided the sharpest contrast in the District's 22 races. Van Dalsem, 59, is a Perryville farmer, landowner and businessman who had been a power in the legislature for 26 years. Rule, 28, a lawyer, was making his first political race.

Prison Conditions in Arkansas

Senate Committee on the Judiciary, *Juvenile Delinquency: Hearings before the Subcommittee to Investigate Juvenile Delinquency of the*

Committee of the Judiciary, 91st Cong., 1st sess., 1970, Senate Resolution 48, Part 20, 4836–40, 4921–22, 5244, 5247, 5251, 5253, 5255–59, 4841–43, 4845–47, 4852–53, 4858–59, 4865.

Joint statements made by Thomas Murton, former director of the state's prison system, and Robert Sarver, the newly appointed (November 1968) director, before a US Senate subcommittee and an edited version of an official investigation by the state police reveal some of the conditions, both real and perceived, in the state prison system in the 1960s.

Statement of Thomas O. Murton, Former Superintendent of Arkansas State Penitentiary.

MR. MURTON. Mr. Chairman, my testimony today describes my one year as superintendent of the Arkansas State Penitentiary. . . .

The Arkansas penitentiary system remained an isolated remnant of an ancient philosophy of retribution, exploitation, corruption, sadism, and brutality. The sordid history of this penitentiary is indelibly recorded on the bodies of those citizens who had the misfortune to be committed to penal servitude in this barbaric system.

In this prison there are no guards; that is, there are no "free world" guards. The Arkansas system consists of state-owned and inmate operated prison farms. Inmate labor had been exploited as a business for the profit of the State and selected individuals.

While slavery was officially abolished in the South over a century ago, landholders quickly looked to the prisons for a cheap source of labor. The continuance of the master–slave relationship between the free man and the convict has been reflected in the prison language.

The inmate speaks of the "free world," "free people," and the "free line" thus indicating his self-concept for what our society has made him—a penal slave. . . .

The peculiar philosophy of imprisonment led inevitably to decadence, exploitation, corruption, barbarism, and ultimately to torture. Physical cruelty was used not only to extract information, but to secure greater production, on the theory that a man can be more easily driven than led. Through fear, stark terror, and intimidation, the prison evolved as a closed system which was self-perpetuating. . . .

At Tucker, there were four free world, that is freemen, in charge of the institution to guard 300 inmates operating on 5,000 acres, and there were in addition to that 49 inmates who carried guns. They carried 12 gauge shotguns, rifles, pistols. These are all issued from the armory every morning and they are supposed to turn them in at night. . . .

In Arkansas, the detention of juveniles has been officially outside the jurisdiction of the prison system. However, in the absence of a viable juvenile court code, many juveniles aged 14 to 18 are committed to prison. In fact, boys 14, 15, 16 and 17 years old comprised the majority of the population at Tucker. . . .

On the Arkansas prison farms, a group of armed inmates, some of whom are vicious, violent, and emotionally deranged felons, have life and death power over the other inmates. These inmate guards have been backed up by a number of "freeworld" staff who have been contaminated by the system so that they are often as brutal, callous, and amoral as many of the prisoners. Inmates were beaten without provocation by the trusties in charge of operating the prison or by the staff of the institution.

Inmates had to pay for better jobs, better food, or living conditions. And they were exploited and abused in every possible way. One of the more sadistic devices that was used to torture inmates was the "Tucker telephone," a device that was used to run electrical current through two wires attached to genital parts of the body.

CHAIRMAN DODD. How does that work?

MR. MURTON. Well, this is in Arkansas in the rural areas, this is the normal telephone system. It is battery powered and you crank it and it sends a charge across the line. But they converted it to be used in this manner. The inmate would be taken to the infirmary, stripped naked, tied down on the operating table and one wire would be run to his big toe and the other to his penis and then either a warden or an inmate would sit down and ring him up as they say. This would send an electrical charge through his body.

CHAIRMAN DODD. How many volts passed through?

MR. MURTON. Six volts. . . .

•   •   •

CHAIRMAN DODD. I suppose that was that whip, was it, that was being used?

MR. MURTON. Yes, it was . . . about 5 feet long.

The inmate, if I may explain how it is administered, is laid spread-eagled on the floor, bare naked, at least his pants are off, and an inmate sits on each arm and each leg to hold him down because the body convulses and lifts off the ground, and they lay the hide on from the floor over the top and down this way.

CHAIRMAN DODD. Well, how often were they administered . . . ?

MR. MURTON. Well, during the fall of 1967 when I was at Tucker they took 104 Negroes out of the barracks one night at Cummins and laid them on the floor, sequentially, and beat them.

CHAIRMAN DODD. Well now, was this provided or allowed rather as a matter of law?

MR. MURTON. The Arkansas statutes have delegated to the prison board the authority to administer disciplinary set rules. This was rather loosely done in 1966. As a result of a petition to the Federal court, the Federal court ordered Arkansas officials to set a limit on the number of strikes that could be made. They ordered that it not be more than 10 administered in any one day, and the prison warden was ordered by the Federal court to implement that. They never did.

CHAIRMAN DODD. What I want to make clear is whether or not it is still the practice there?

MR. MURTON. No, it is not.

CHAIRMAN DODD. All right. Go ahead.

MR. MURTON. One of the main problems is the public does not care about the men it sends to prison. It does not care whether or not prisoners are beaten, exploited, or subjected to inhuman conditions. The public does not want prison reform because it actually does not want to know what goes on in prisons and thus the inmate is at the mercy of his guard.

I am convinced that what we uncovered on the Cummins Prison Farm were traces of inmates murdered by the trusties or the staff.

It is almost self-evident that when men in prison have to fear for their lives, when they are beaten, brutalized, degraded, and humiliated, there can be no question of rehabilitation. If anything, these men come out more violent, more hostile, and more prepared to vent their vengeance upon society that has subjected them to the barbaric prison conditions. . . .

●　　●　　●

MR. MURTON. Conditions under which female prisoners were incarcerated in Arkansas were also atrocious. There were impossibly restrictive rules, poor food, unhealthy and unsafe facilities, and abuse. As recently as two weeks prior to my appointment at Cummins, one of the male wardens beat a female inmate with the hide. One of the former superintendents had a buzzer installed near his bed to summon his favorite inmate from the women's reformatory to perform unnatural sex acts with him.

Female prisoners were transported to and from the prison in a closed van with male prisoners. Consequently, they were raped. . . .

Work for the female inmates consisted of clipping grass with fingernails (for the Negro prisoners) and sewing clothes by the white prisoners. The inmates were forced to sew clothing for relatives of the staff as well as the prisoners.

By clipping I mean the inmates sat down on the ground and clipped the grass this way and the inmates can show you gnarled hands and no fingernails. It is pretty bad.

The Negro prisoners were segregated in even worse facilities than the whites. They ate only the scraps from the table after the whites finished eating. They were also forced to wash personal laundry for the matrons on the scrub board although there was a modern prison laundry available. These were the conditions in Arkansas.

Following is a summary of what we're able to accomplish at Tucker in only a few months: Abolition of corporal punishment, brutality, torture, exploitation, special privileges, and intimidation; we eliminated the American money, brozene (prison money), money lending, gambling, inmate control over the mail, radio, telephone, records, and the institution.

We improved the physical facilities by constructing a new slaughter house, new infirmary, new staff houses, painted the barracks, upgraded the livestock herds, improved the crop population, and issued clothing.

An adequate diet was provided. We established a viable religious program, instituted education classes (from which 45 eventually received the high school equivalency certificate), created a library, conducted vocational training classes, provided medical service, established parole and counseling services at the institution, and integrated condemned prisoners into all aspects of the prison programs and activities.

And, perhaps most significantly, through adequate classification procedures we were able to make it unnecessary for the majority of the prisoners to work under the gun. Consequently, there were fewer inmates carrying guns. During the last five months I was at Tucker, we had only one escape.

Then I went to Cummins and started doing the same things there.

The State asked me for reform and I was making broadscale improvements in Arkansas.

But when I tried to overhaul the degenerate system at its very roots, the state failed to back me up. They did not want that much reform.

Mr. Chairman. I dug up bodies I believe were murdered. This was done with the full knowledge and support of the administration, yet when the publicity surrounding these uncoveries became a political liability, a new investigation was ordered to cover it up. This new investigation was really a whitewash of the system and served no constructive purpose.

After a year, I was forced to leave the Arkansas prison system and the conditions have essentially reverted to their previous levels. In the midst of the 20th century, Arkansas tenaciously preserves the status quo in penological philosophy which has proven unsuccessful and undesirable in nearly all other jurisdictions not for years or decades, but for centuries. Arkansas still has corporal punishment, no segregation by ages and offense, brutality, no classification, no industry, no vocational training, limited educational training, and inmate guards.

The old headknockers are in charge. The exploitation is being perpetrated throughout. I get letters weekly from inmates telling me how it really is.

•　　•　　•

Statement of Robert Sarver, Commissioner, Arkansas Department of Corrections
[Mr. Sarver's prepared statement follows:]

Mr. Chairman, I appreciate very much the opportunity of presenting testimony before this committee on behalf of Governor Winthrop Rockefeller and the citizens of the State of Arkansas. . . .

As a consequence of testimony presented here last Tuesday, by a former employee [Mr. Murton] of the Arkansas Prison System, an entirely distorted picture has been presented to this committee. To say that the testimony was replete with untruths, half-truths, innuendos, and unwarranted conclusions would be an understatement and serve no useful purpose for this committee. Suffice it to say, that prison reform in Arkansas began before his employment and continues today in spite of his termination. . . .

Act 50 of the First Extraordinary Session of the 1968 Arkansas General Assembly established the Department of Corrections. It prescribes, among other things, that the Department shall ". . . provide for the custody, treatment, rehabilitation and restoration of adult offenders as useful, law-abiding citizens within the community." This is our legislative mandate. It is the reason for our existence. Underlying the very foundation of our system is the elementary and irrefutable belief that our prescribed purpose cannot be achieved by coddling, brute force or humiliating punishment.

Corporal punishment has been abolished, in every form in Arkansas. It is not going to return. In spite of overt allegations and implications to the contrary, the people of Arkansas are making headway in the development of our correctional program. Our staff is dedicated to a philosophy of rehabilitation. . . .

An entirely distorted picture of the situation in Arkansas has been presented to this committee.

I think that if any person will take the time to go look at a prison—just take the time to go look at it—practically any person can point out the problems, the deficiencies, the things that are lacking. There would be no difficulty whatever. I think that most inmates of most correctional institutions can pretty quickly articulate some kind of opinion as to what ought to be done to straighten out the situation. I know that, practically daily, most correctional administrators receive letters or telephone calls suggesting various types of reform or various types of programs that would be helpful, and usually they are educational or vocational and technical training, more psychiatrists, better staffs, more staff.

CHAIRMAN DODD. You are not finding fault with that?

MR. SARVER. Oh, no, not at all. I am just simply saying that everybody seems to know the answers and everybody seems to recognize the problem, but thus far nobody does anything about it.

I do not think that there is a panacea for the problem. I think, if we are looking for one answer, we are not going to find it, certainly I do not think that any person can be placed in a correctional institution in this country, typed and separated and put into any kind of a training program along with hundreds of other people and be expected to respond like everybody else responds.

I think probably, however, the most misunderstood portion of our whole system of criminal justice is the institution, because people simply do not want to take the time to look at it. It is not a fun and games place; it is not a happy, pleasant place. . . .

It is pretty difficult to convince a taxpayer that money which could be used to build new highways, to build new high schools and colleges and increase teachers' salaries ought to be paid to the prisons. I think we can admit that the prisons in this country are woefully inadequate, and I do not think that anybody takes issue with that.

When I read of an expose of homosexualities, bribings, escapes, political corruption in prisons, I think most knowledgeable correction administrators think "So, what else is new?"

CHAIRMAN DODD. Think—what?

MR. SARVER. "So, what else is new?" This has been going on long before I got here, and, I am sure, Senator, long before you came.

CHAIRMAN DODD. . . . I am concerned about what else you just said, that people in the field of correction, when they see these whips and these knives and clubs, and hear about the brutalizing incidents and about the dreadful problem of homosexuality, and all of these other abuses, that they simply say, "So, what else is new?"

MR. SARVER. We have been living with it for years, Senator. People have been operating prisons with inadequate financial structures, totally inadequate and incompetent staffs, no money, and I do not know what else we expect from them, to make an expose as if this has never been known before. I think it is unwarranted.

CHAIRMAN DODD. I thought you wanted to rebut the testimony of Mr. Murton.

MR. SARVER. Senator, I see nothing to be gained by taking item by item the things the witness testified to and attempting to refute them. I do not think that is what we need. I am sure that is not what the Governor had in mind. I know that the Governor and the Arkansas Legislature and the General Assembly have invited each member of the committee to come to Arkansas and see our prison system just as it is.

CHAIRMAN DODD. Could we come at an unexpected hour?

MR. SARVER. By all means, anytime, Senator, and have dinner with us.

CHAIRMAN DODD. And make an inspection of it.

MR. SARVER. Just anytime at all, Senator.

CHAIRMAN DODD. Is it true that this whip was used down there?

MR. SARVER. I have not any idea, sir. At this point in time we are not attempting to defend what happened years ago. The point is that it has been implied that this is continuing in Arkansas to this day, that the headknockers are there and the brutality continues, and that is simply not true.

CHAIRMAN DODD. We are just concerned. You know, you called him [Murton] a liar.

MR. SARVER. That is right, I mean, if that is what it boils down to.

CHAIRMAN DODD. But what did he lie about?

MR. SARVER. He lied in implying that brutality is now existing in Arkansas, that "the headknockers are back," and that is a quote.

CHAIRMAN DODD. Yes.

MR. SARVER. That is not true, Senator. There is no brutality going on there.

•   •   •

Case Report, Criminal Investigations Division [Arkansas State Prison]
Arkansas State Police
File Number: 9160166–66.
Investigators: H. H. Atkinson, Investigator, Criminal Investigations Division, Little Rock, Ark.; James M. Beach, Investigator, Criminal Investigations Division, Pine Bluff, Ark.; Billy Skipper, Investigator, Criminal Investigations Division, Little Rock, Ark.
Subjects: 1. Robbery (41–3601); 2. Larceny (Over $35.00) (46–130) (43–2156) (41–3917); 3. Maiming (41–2502) (41–2504) (41–2507); 4. Extortion (12–1738); 5. Liquors into Prison (41–3109); 6. Excessive Punishment (46–158); 7. Personal use of provisions (46–129); 8. Gifts to Officers or Personnel (46–167); 9. Housing and Treatment (46–108); Investigation by board.
County: Jefferson.
Time and Place: As indicated in facts section of report.
Name and type of establishment: Tucker State Prison Farm, Tucker, Arkansas.
Loss: As indicated in facts section of report.
Victims: State of Arkansas. Others as indicated in facts section of report.
Facts: On 8–19–66, at about 11:30 A.M. this investigator was instructed to proceed to Tucker State Prison Farm by Major W. C. Struebing,

Commanding Criminal Investigations Division. Further instructions were to report to the Superintendent, Mr. O. E. Bishop, and to assist him in the investigation of an incident involving intoxication among a group of inmates or in any other matter as requested.

At about 1:30 P.M. 8–19–66, this investigator reported to Mr. Bishop at the Administration Building, Tucker Farm, and was advised that several inmates, on the previous night had left the Prison and gone into town to purchase whiskey and beer. When they returned to the prison, they were arrested by Wardens Fletcher, Mays, and Wilson and a quantity of whiskey and beer was confiscated from them. Also, a number of inmates had become intoxicated during the afternoon and early evening from intoxicants obtained in an earlier visit to an off premise liquor store in Tucker, Arkansas. Mr. Bishop requested this investigator to take charge of the investigation at hand, and, in addition, to assume full charge of the Prison Farm in an effort to correct the security situation until such a time as another person was obtained to assume the responsibility of the office of Assistant Superintendent. This request was cleared by Mr. Herman E. Lindsey, Director, Arkansas State Police, and Major W. C. Struebing, Commanding Criminal Investigations Division. All personnel employed at Tucker Prison were advised of this move by Mr. Bishop and concurred that security was in "poor" condition.

Investigator Note: All persons interviewed in the course of this investigation were advised of their rights under the Fifth Amendment to remain silent and to have legal counsel present. Subject waived all rights prior to interview.

On 8–19–66, at about 4:45 P.M., this investigator discontinued the interviews [of the incident involving intoxication of inmates] and proceeded to the Inmates kitchen to inspect the Inmates as they were eating. Upon inspecting the kitchen, this investigator observed that the entire was filthy. The floors, tables, walls, and kitchen appliances appeared to have been wiped off rather hurriedly but were not sanitary. Flies were very thick and there was no screen on the door leading to the wash rack and vegetable room. The food and meat were piled on the cook tables completely exposed to the flies and nothing was done to protect it. Tin cans with the tops cut out were used as cups. The pitchers and trays were badly bent and damaged. All cooking utensils were in a state of disrepair or damaged beyond repair.

Food had been prepared and was observed to be a very thin, watered down serving of rice. One large spoonful per Inmate. The bread was a tasteless cornbread. One medium slice per Inmate. Upon being questioned, the kitchen personnel stated that meat was served to the Inmates once a month, on visiting Sunday, and it was served in small portions at that time. . . . Kitchen personnel stated that the Inmates received one egg per year on Christmas morning and were never given milk to drink. One kitchen helper suggested that the food supply records be examined, as the majority of the meat was being sold by the kitchen rider (Trusty Supervisor) or carried out the "back door" by the Wardens.

At about 5:30 P.M., 8–19–66, this investigator inspected the Inmates on the long line (field workers) as they were brought to the kitchen to be fed. The entire group appeared to be forty to sixty pounds under their normal weight. Their clothing (whites) were filthy, torn up, and in bad states of repair. Their shoes were in terrible disrepair and seemed to be several sizes too large for each of them. They were worn out, had no strings, and had holes along the soles and across the tops. Upon being questioned, the Inmates stated that they had no shoes and either were required to wear the rubber boots or go barefooted. In addition, the Inmates stated that they had never been issued underwear, and socks were issued only twice a year. Two pair of socks were in each issue. This investigator issued orders to forward requisitions to the proper authority at Cummins Prison to correct this situation.

At about 6:45 P.M., 8–19–66, this investigator proceeded to the Inmates barracks and conducted an inspection. The mattresses were filthy and rotten and appeared to be badly discolored. The cotton was spilling out of the majority of the mattresses from worn and torn spots. The sheets were dirty and appeared to have been used for two or three weeks without change. Over half of the beds did not have any pillows on them, and the beds that had pillows were dirty and discolored. The showers were pouring water from leaks. The commodes were stopped up or would not flush. The urinals were stopped up and in general disrepair. The entire barracks area smelled from filth. The floors were filthy.

On 8–20–66, at about 7:30 A.M., this investigator interviewed Inmate Clifford Cash, Laundry Rider (Supervisor), who stated that he was aware that many jobs were sold to Inmates for the laundry by Inmates Jim Reaves, Yard Man, and Winston Talley, Floor Walker. Inmate Cash stated that the jobs sold for as "much as the traffic will bear," at times as low as thirty dollars and others times as high as one thousand dollars. He continued that almost anything could be had at Tucker Farm if you could get the money. He stated that much of the whiskey was bought by Warden Wilson and brought in to the Inmates for a price. Cash stated that he had seen Inmates buy a bottle of whiskey through Warden Wilson by buying him a bottle at the same time. Cash stated that "pills" could be had for a price and that he believed the "pills" were brought over from Cummins Prison Hospital. Inmate Cash was cooperating with this investigator until Assistant Superintendent Bruton came into the office, and Cash seemed to "freeze up." He would not discuss anything pertaining to the operation of the Prison Farm and seemed to either avoid answers or speak in riddles. This investigator excused Inmate Cash from the interview, and when we were both outside, he said to me, "What are you trying to do? Get me killed?" Interview was terminated at this time.

On 8–21–66, at about 8:30 A.M., this investigator received information from Inmate Informer F1–17 that the "Tucker Telephone" had been hidden in the residence of former Assistant Superintendent [Jim] Bruton. This investigator had been told of "long distance calls" and the "Tucker Telephone" by several Inmates since arrival at Tucker Prison Farm. . . .

F1–17 stated that an Inmate Doctor (Doc Morgan) had used this device extensively at the order of Mr. Bruton and the other Wardens. Mr. Fletcher was mentioned as having ordered and observed a great number of these torture periods. F1–17 stated that while he had never been subjected to the "Tucker Telephone," he could and did furnish a list of Inmates who had been "rung up" at the order of Mr. Bruton.

F1–17 stated that while he was afraid, he would testify to everything that he had said in the event this case comes to trial. This interview was terminated with the understanding that this investigator could return for further information.

On 8–21–66, during the afternoon visiting hours in the death cells, Inmate Jim Reaves called this investigator to the bars and asked if he was to be punished for activities that were authorized by Mr. Bruton. He continued that he was acting as Mr. Bruton's representative in job selling and loaning money to the other Inmates. He stated that in order to conduct this business, it had been necessary to carry a large amount of "green." (Prison term for paper money. Reaves had $507.00 in paper money at the time of his arrest which was confiscated by Superintendent Bishop.) Reaves stated that this was with the "full knowledge" of the "man" (Mr. Bruton).

On 8–21–66, during the evening hours, this investigator conducted an extensive search of the Assistant Superintendent's house, including all closets and storage areas. In the upstairs, south bathroom, this investigator found the "Tucker Telephone" in a hat box on the top shelf of a linen closet. This instrument was photographed in its resting place and also in a more detailed manner on the bathroom floor. (See exhibit Nos. 41–45). This search was conducted on the basis of state property and the "invited guest" rule of search and seizure. Following the photographing of the instrument, it was returned to its original hiding place.

On 8–22–66, at about 8:00 A.M., this investigator interviewed Inmate informer F1–1, who stated that he had observed Mr. Bruton commit many brutal beatings upon inmates in the past two years. F1–1 stated that no hearings were ever conducted prior to whippings in accord with the Prison regulations. F1–1 stated that Mr. Bruton would hit inmates for anything he suspected they might have done and with anything he could get his hands on. . . . F1–1 stated that he had known of some of the job selling deals of Jim Reaves and Mr. Bruton, and he mentioned the John Tolliver and Jimmy Roman case in particular. He stated that anyone could get anything on Tucker Farm if he had the right amount of money.

The following paragraphs are a synopsis of statements from Inmates of Tucker Prison Farm by State Police Investigators on the night of 8–26–66.

LL–1 stated that in June of 1963, a long line rider and he got into a fight, and he was hit on the foot with a hoe. He stated that Mr. Fletcher brought him to the hospital where he stayed for three days. He stated that Mr. Bruton came to the hospital where he was and asked him what happened, and when he told him, Mr. Bruton had Bill Morgan, Inmate Doctor, wire him up on the telephone. . . . He states that Morgan cranked the telephone five or six times. He stated that he was put on a table in the Prison hospital and belted down with one strap across his chest and one across his legs.

LL–2 states that he came to Tucker in March of 1965 and was assigned to the long line. He stated that the long line was cleaning ditches and two of the long line riders were beating the Inmates with rubber hoses and blackjacks. He continues that one day at lunchtime, the two riders called Walter Perry to the end of the line and made him stand there while they shot at his feet and near his head. The riders were named as Butch Harper and Douglas Burke. He stated that during strawberry season last year, he was beaten four or five times by riders and his ear began to bleed one night in the building. He stated that his hearing had been affected from these beatings. He stated that the yardman or floorwalker charged from $1.00 to $5.00 to give the Inmates a good bed. He stated that the food in the mess hall was very bad, consisting mostly of greens that had bugs in them, but if an Inmate would pay the kitchen rider, he could have better food. He concluded, stating that on visiting Sunday, when some of the family would bring food or clothing to Inmates, the Trustys would take it for themselves as soon as the family left. LL–2 stated that he would testify in court to any of the happenings.

LL–94 stated that in July of 1965, he had about $20.00 on the books when the long line rider (Dale Johnson) . . . approached him and told him for $30.00, he would let him make it [get a new job]; if not, he would beat his head with a "blackjack." He stated that he was told to pay Inmate Bill Morgan and what he [lacked of] the $30.00, Morgan would loan to him, and he could pay Morgan when he got his next money. He stated that the loan would be $2.00 for each $1.00 loaned. He stated that he refused and was beaten by the rider. He stated that on the next visit, his father paid Morgan $150.00, for which he stayed in the building for two weeks, then went to work in the laundry. He stated that after a new yard man came, he was ranked, and Mr. Fletcher approached him and asked for money to get him a better job. He stated that he refused, and after that, he could do nothing right and was abused and beaten repeatedly.

LL–15 stated that he was whipped by the long line rider for not picking enough cotton, and has had money taken away from him. He stated that he had done without food.

LL–17 stated he has used hoes and shovels with rough tree limbs for handles that cut his hands. He stated that he was whipped, with his pants down, by Mr. Fletcher until he bled. He stated he has been whipped by the line riders with "blackjacks," trace chains, axe handles, hoe handles, and rubber hoses for things that they did not like.

LL–18 stated he was whipped with a rubber hose and the "hide" for not picking enough cotton. He stated that he was whipped by the line rider (Douglas Burke), on Mr. Bruton's orders and in front of Mr. Bruton.

LL–23 stated that he paid the Prison Doctor (Bill Morgan) $20.00 to be turned into a trusty. He stated that he has seen Inmates brutally beaten and tortured by Inmates Richard Davis, Ray Varner, and Tony DeShazo, all line riders. He stated that he has seen needles run under Inmates fingers . . . and has seen Inmates set on coke bottles, and if they fell off, they would get whipped.

LL–2 stated that he has been whipped many times for not doing enough and being fast in his work. He stated that he was whipped by line riders, Douglas Burke, Nelson Henderson, Sam Bean, and Richard Wilson. He stated he had seen Mr. Bruton kick and rupture an Inmate.

LL–27 stated that the long line rider tried to force him to do unnatural sexual acts.

LL–29 stated that he was whipped with the "hide" by Mr. Wilson and was put in the hospital. He stated that he was kicked out of the hospital for not paying any money to stay, by the Inmate Doctor (Bill Morgan).

LL–32 stated that he was whipped several times with the "hide" by Mr. Bruton and Mr. Fletcher for not picking enough cotton. He stated that the whippings were administered with his pants off.

Hog Frenzy Spreads over State

Arkansas Gazette (Little Rock), December 4, 1969.

> Few things reflected Arkansas society more clearly in the Modern Era than Razorback football at the University of Arkansas. It was the one institution that drew together young and old, rich and poor from all sections of the state.

Although the 1964 team had won a national championship, the 1969 game with Texas recounted below illustrated the stature of the football program at the university. Even the president of the United States traveled to Fayetteville to watch "the game of the century."

Sixth-graders at Walnut Ridge have sent a big letter to the Razorbacks and a club of elderly women at El Dorado has postponed a meeting scheduled for Saturday so they can watch the GAME.

All over Arkansas it was the same as frenzy increased over the University of Arkansas–University of Texas game for the Southwest Conference championship, a national title in football's centennial year and a chance to play Notre Dame in the Cotton Bowl.

Football fever spread all the way to Washington, D.C., where a demonstration developed at a House Ways and Means Committee meeting.

Girls from the office of Representative Wilbur D. Mills (Dem., Ark.) the Committee chairman carried "Beat Texas" signs. A counterdemonstration developed when Texans from the office of Representative George Bush (Rep., Tex.) paraded with "Hook 'em Horns" signs.

"They're ape down here. I tell you," said a Warren resident Wednesday. There are signs all over town, practically everbody is wearing "Beat Texas" buttons and business is expected to grind to a halt while the game is on television, he said.

Lieutenant Governor Maurice (Footsie) Britt made a speech at the Warren High School auditorium Wednesday morning. After he finished, School Superintendent James M. Hughes said he had never allowed a pep rally to be held at the auditorium but that this was a special occasion.

With that, he invited the high school cheerleaders onto the stage to "call the Hogs" with Britt, a former U of A end.

"With all the stomping, and whooping and yelling, I thought the whole building was going to come down," a spectator said.

At Dumas, Rev. Mason Bondurant, pastor of the First Baptist Church, went out about noon Wednesday to put a new sign on the bulletin board in the church yard. It said:

"God is neutral. We are human, Beat Texas!"

This in a good-natured way was getting back at Texas Coach Darrell Royal, who in commenting on a Baptist Church sign in Fayetteville urging "beat Texas," said he thought God was neutral in such matters.

A large "Go, Hogs, Go. Beat Texas" sign has been placed on a tall tower at Matthews on U.S. Highway 65 near Dumas and it can be seen for miles in the flat Delta country. John Puryear put up a sign in his hardware store at Dumas urging "Go, Hogs, win the presidential citation."

President Nixon, who will be at the game, will present a plaque to the winner.

Up the highway at Pine Bluff, buttons and bumper stickers were all over town and marquees on restaurants around town advertised the

Razorbacks instead of roast beef. Some were predicting the score—Razorbacks 24, Texas 17.

Lots of traffic headed to Fayetteville passes through the little Johnson County town of Altus, where a group of young people got together and made a large "Razorback, Go Hogs" sign and a mutilated steer, which they erected on the highway Tuesday. Someone stole the big Razorback. The young folks made another Wednesday.

The Walnut Ridge students sent an oversized 4 by 6-foot letter bearing more than 200 signatures to their football heroes at Fayetteville wishing them luck in the big clash.

Dr. Lawrence Edwards, a Crossett physician, who takes a planeload of friends to every Razorback game, has the front window of his home decorated with a Razorback and a picture of the Cotton Bowl tied with a red ribbon.

At El Dorado, residents wearing buttons and driving cars with Razorback signs are listening to a radio station on which the announcers are interspersing music with "Beat Texas." The Arkansas Pioneers chapter called off their Saturday meeting so the ladies could watch the game.

The Holiday Inn at Harrison, a stopping place for many East Arkansans on their way to Fayetteville, is full and has been reserved for months.

In fact, there was no hotel or motel space available within 50 miles of Fayetteville. A Methodist Church in Fayetteville put up 300 beds in its recreation hall and all were rented quickly.

A Fayetteville radio announcer and one at Austin, Tex., have exchanged dares.

Ed Brandon of KTAP at Austin told Ken Rank of KFAY at Fayetteville that if Texas lost he would push Rank around the University of Arkansas in a red and white wheelbarrow. If Texas wins, Rank will go to Austin and push him around the Texas campus in an orange and white wheelbarrow.

A Little Rock bank has given away 10,000 "Beat Texas" lapel buttons in less than two days and has ordered another 5,000. A Little Rock radio station has distributed 15,000 bumper stickers and 4,000 posters.

On radio stations, a favorite song this week is "Short, Squashed Texan," which was recorded in 1965 after the Razorbacks beat Texas 27–24 in 1965 when the Longhorns were ranked no. 1 in the nation.

A "Beat Texas" sticker even adorned the forehead of a Longhorn steer at the Little Rock Zoo for a short time before it fell off.

Arts in Arkansas

New York Times, February 2, 1977.

Traditionally, Arkansas has been perceived as lacking distinctiveness in the arts. However, for a variety of reasons, interest in cultural activities increased rapidly in the 1960s. The following article appeared in the *New York Times* and was written by Roy Reed, a native Arkansan. In it he examined some reasons for this interest and cited examples of creative work in music and literature.

Ten years ago [1967], Arkansas did not have a symphony orchestra worthy of the name. Now it has five. Whether all are worthy of the name is debatable, but at least two are attracting highly competent musicians and one has begun to play occasionally outside the state.

Two years ago, the state had no serious indigenous theater. Little Rock now has a repertory group that is causing a rare excitement in the community, and some of the state's universities report a growing interest in the theater among their students.

A state that once regarded a corn shuck doll as a work of art now has a number of serious painters and artistic craftsmen. Half a dozen nationally known novelists call Arkansas home. Every hamlet seems to have at least one poet, and in the alluring remoteness of the Ozark Mountains the poets are almost as numerous as razorback hogs.

As with many cultural movements, the artistic budding in Arkansas is touched with mystery. No one is certain of the reason for it. Some credit a more relaxed political atmosphere after the easing of racial tensions. Some point to the greater affluence since industrialization. Some attribute it to a chance spark that ignited a blaze. Some simply say the state was ready.

There is a certain evenness in the artistic development here. The state has no Faulkners or Weltys, but the creative ferment is bubbling in every corner. Now and then, in the telling of it, a person will shiver, as if electrified by its essence.

The most widely discussed growth is in music. A group that liked to play classical music formed an amateur orchestra in Little Rock in 1966. Five years later, the orchestra was taken over by Dr. Francis MacBeth of Ouachita Baptist University. Dr. MacBeth is a ranking composer of band music and, by all accounts, a persuasive musical leader. During his two-year tenure, Little Rock got the idea that it could afford a first-rate symphony orchestra.

Then came a happy accident. Arkansas, like most of the older Southern states, had long had a balance of talents problem. It exports more than it imports. One of its exports a few years ago was Mignon Dunn, the Metropolitan Opera mezzo, who had grown up on a plantation in the delta of eastern Arkansas.

Some years ago, in Dusseldorf, she met and later married an Austrian opera coach and symphony conductor named Kurt Klippstaetter. She lured him as far as Memphis, where he worked as musical director of the city's opera theater. Then in 1974, with Miss Dunn's encouragement, Little Rock lured him on across the Mississippi River to conduct the Arkansas Symphony Orchestra.

Mr. Klippstaetter began hiring strong professional string players to go with the orchestra's dedicated amateurs. The professionals, who earn $10,000 to $12,500 a year, divide their time between the orchestra and teaching music in the state's public schools.

The orchestra and Miss Dunn performed at the Kennedy Center in Washington last spring. Paul Hume, music critic of the *Washington Post*, called the group "a truly fine orchestra under a first-rate conductor."

The orchestra and its chamber group become more popular each season. Concerts draw upward of 2,000 people a night. This season, the main orchestra will play four concerts in Little Rock, each repeated once, and seven in Arkansas towns. About 500 people hold season tickets. That gives the orchestra a $57,000 head start toward its $400,000 budget. . . .

Mr. Klippstaetter is pleased by the amount of government support for the arts in Arkansas. In less than five years, Arkansas has gone from somewhere near the bottom to 13th in the United States in per capita state government spending on the arts. A new state agency called the Office of Arkansas State Arts and Humanities—headed by Sandra Perry, the author of *Charles Ives and the American Mind*—reports that just under $2 million was spent on the arts in the state last year. Of that, $283,000 came from state government and $509,000 from the Federal Government. The rest was from ticket and membership fees and other private sources. . . .

In addition, the state has its first serious opera group, the Arkansas Opera Theater. It uses Arkansans for most roles and imports lead singers like Robert Schmorr of the Metropolitan Opera and Chester Ludgin of the New York City Opera. Mr. Schmorr sang the part of the Duke in *Rigoletto* in 1975. Mr. Ludgin sang Olin Blitch in *Susannah* the year before.

The new Arkansas Repertory Theater is causing even more excitement than the musical organizations in some circles. . . . [It] came about through another happy accident. Years ago, the late Gov. Winthrop Rockefeller and his wife, Jeanette, began pouring millions of dollars of their own money and countless hours into promotion of the arts in Arkansas. They spearheaded the building of an arts center here that included an excellent amateur theatrical company. The company produced *Marat/Sade* one year and took it on tour. Cliff Baker, a serious young drama student at the University of Missouri, saw the production when it played there. He was so impressed that he came to Little Rock and got a job at the arts center. One thing led to another and last year he formed the repertory company. Everyone who mentioned his name here one recent week used the word "genius" to describe him.

In the old barefoot days of scorn and backwardness, when people thought of poetry in Arkansas they probably hummed "The Arkansas Traveler" or chuckled over the hill country verse that went like this:

Every time I go to town
People keep kicking my dog around
I don't care if he is a hound,
They got to quit kicking my dog around.

Actually, Arkansas has a tradition of excellence in poetry, but the tradition has never been much known beyond the state. The late John Gould Fletcher won the Pulitzer Prize for poetry he wrote here before World War II.

Arkansas poets have now become so numerous and popular that they are giving public readings all over the state and people are willingly paying to hear them. Poets lecture on their art in the schools. Two have started a literary magazine here called *Black and White*.

Probably the best known of the state's current poets is Miller Williams, who teaches at the University of Arkansas at Fayetteville. He won the coveted Prix de Rome for poetry last year. One of his friends and fellow teachers, James Whitehead, who also writes novels, is considered a major sonnet writer.

Among the other Arkansas poets who are known nationally are Besmilr Brigham, Jack Butler, John S. Morris and Sue Abbott Boyd. Mr. Whitehead says the most exciting young Arkansas poet he knows is Frank Stanford, who has already published several volumes and is not yet 30 years old.

The novel was a neglected art in Arkansas until after World War II. Francis Irby Gwaltney earned a reputation as a novelist during the 1950's. Then a young Korean War veteran named Charles Portis, tiring of newspaper reporting and unable to bear the tea and tailors of London, came back to the hills and wrote a small comic masterpiece called *Norwood*. It attracted just enough attention among publishers to insure the sale of his second novel, *True Grit*.

The latter earned him fame and enough fortune to support him in indignant seclusion. He is said to be writing another novel in a back room of an out-of-the-way motel, emerging after dark sometimes to visit a favorite honky-tonk and swap war stories with old Marine Corps buddies.

Since *True Grit*, a number of Arkansas novelists have enjoyed a measure of success—Mr. Whitehead (*Joiner*), Bill Harrison (*Rollerball*), Donald Harrington (*The Architecture of the Arkansas Ozarks*). The most recently published novel from the state, *The Court-Martial of George Armstrong Custer* by Douglas C. Jones, reportedly is hovering just under the best-seller list.

Migration Patterns by Age, 1950–1970

Arkansas Industrial Research and Extension Center, *Migration Patterns by Age, 1950–1970* (Little Rock, 1978).

Population analysis of the state's migration patterns between 1950 and 1970 and a projection of the state's growth through 1990, based on two different assumptions, demonstrated that the state was able to check its outward migration in the 1960s and experience a population increase greater than the national average. Between 1970 and 1980 the state's population grew 18.8 percent. Where the growth occurred was equally important to political and economic developments in the state.

As to the state's counties, only 19 of the 75 experienced growth between 1940 and 1950, even though Arkansas' population loss was relatively small (40,000) for this intercensal period. These growth counties were for the most part the State's more heavily populated ones. By the time of the 1960 Census, the number of counties with increases during the 1950's had fallen to a low of six: Crittenden, Jefferson, Pulaski, Saline, Sebastian and Washington. A substantial change in the trend of county population movement accompanied the growth of the State's population during the 1960's. The 1970 Census shows that 46, or almost two-thirds (61.3 percent), of Arkansas' counties experienced increases in their numbers since 1960.

Projected Population Change

Projected 1980, 1985 and 1990 Series A and Series B county populations are contained in Tables 2 and 3. The Series A and Series B numbers should be regarded as a projected population range, reflecting an interval within which it is assumed that the actual population will fall. Practically all of the numerical disparity between the two series is attributable to the difference in the birth assumptions underlying each. Actual births are not expected to rise above the birth level of the Series A projections or to fall below that projected for Series B. However, the current level of actual State births is on a trend line approximating the birth level assumed in the Series A projections.

The State's 1980 population is expected to reflect a growth rate ranging between 14.4 percent (Series B) and 16.6 percent (Series A) above the 1970 Census count. Absolute growth is projected to range from 277,000 to 320,000 or from 2.0 to 2.3 times that of the 1960's. The data also indicate that the number of growth counties is expected to exceed the 46 of the 1960's. Population increases are projected for 64 or 65 (approximately 86.0 percent) of the State's 75 counties. However, growth rates of less than 5.0 percent are projected for from 10 (Series A) to 15 (Series B) of these counties.

Population growth is projected to continue between 1980 and 1990; the State increase is expected to range between 12.0 percent (Series B) and 18.9 percent (Series A) above corresponding 1980 levels.

PROJECTED SERIES A, POPULATION OF ARKANSAS COUNTIES, 1980, 1985, AND 1990

GEOGRAPHIC AREA	CENSUS 1970	ESTIMATE 1975	PROJECTED 1980	PROJECTED 1985	PROJECTED 1990	CHANGE, 1970–1980 NUMBER	CHANGE, 1970–1980 PERCENT	CHANGE, 1980–1990 NUMBER	CHANGE, 1980–1990 PERCENT
ARKANSAS	1,923,295	2,086,000[a]	2,242,807	2,439,922	2,666,762	319,512	16.6	423,955	18.9
Arkansas	23,347	23,596	23,724	24,101	24,479	377	1.6	755	3.2
Ashley	24,976	25,197	25,478	26,021	26,636	502	2.0	1,158	4.5
Baxter	15,319	21,904	27,898	35,636	45,508	12,579	82.1	17,610	63.1
Benton	50,476	58,597	66,811	77,349	90,133	16,335	32.4	23,322	34.9
Boone	19,073	22,795	25,776	29,161	33,675	6,703	35.1	7,899	30.6
Bradley	12,778	12,597	12,392	12,290	12,190	–386	–3.0	–202	–1.6
Calhoun	5,573	5,709	5,947	6,336	6,825	374	6.7	878	14.8
Carroll	12,301	14,099	15,308	16,778	18,402	3,007	24.4	3,094	20.2
Chicot	18,164	17,708	17,407	17,281	17,200	–757	–4.2	–207	–1.2
Clark	21,537	21,996	22,770	23,762	24,970	1,233	5.7	2,200	9.7
Clay	18,771	20,001	20,579	21,454	22,270	1,808	9.6	1,691	8.2
Cleburne	10,349	14,305	17,564	21,698	26,709	7,215	69.7	9,145	52.1
Cleveland	6,605	5,797	6,956	7,213	7,511	351	5.3	555	8.0
Columbia	25,952	25,895	26,533	27,344	28,144	581	2.2	1,611	6.1
Conway	16,805	17,798	18,590	19,695	20,963	1,785	10.6	2,373	12.8
Craighead	52,068	57,895	62,541	68,121	74,152	10,473	20.1	11,611	18.6
Crawford	25,677	29,901	33,481	38,181	43,830	7,804	30.4	10,349	30.9

[a]The population estimate for Sebastian County for July 1, 1975, does not include 24,178 Vietnamese refugees temporarily housed at Ft. Chaffee.

Source: Census data from US Bureau of the Census. Estimates and projections prepared by the Industrial Research and Extension Center, University of Arkansas, Little Rock, February 1978.

PROJECTED SERIES A, POPULATION OF ARKANSAS COUNTIES, 1980, 1985, AND 1990 (continued)

GEOGRAPHIC AREA	CENSUS 1970	ESTIMATE 1975	PROJECTED 1980	PROJECTED 1985	PROJECTED 1990	CHANGE, 1970–1980 NUMBER	CHANGE, 1970–1980 PERCENT	CHANGE, 1980–1990 NUMBER	CHANGE, 1980–1990 PERCENT
Crittenden	48,106	50,499	52,681	55,752	59,146	4,575	9.5	6,465	12.3
Cross	19,783	20,503	20,961	21,700	22,534	1,178	6.0	1,573	7.5
Dallas	10,022	10,196	10,487	10,889	11,288	465	4.6	801	7.6
Desha	18,761	17,699	16,938	16,329	15,747	−1,823	−9.7	−1,191	−7.0
Drew	15,157	15,700	16,305	17,113	18,042	1,148	7.6	1,737	10.7
Faulkner	31,572	37,498	44,433	53,281	64,509	12,861	40.7	20,076	45.2
Franklin	11,301	12,801	13,866	15,285	16,941	2,565	22.7	3,075	22.2
Fulton	7,699	8,896	9,954	11,327	12,947	2,255	29.3	2,993	30.1
Garland	54,131	61,698	68,369	76,546	85,702	14,238	26.3	17,333	25.4
Grant	9,711	11,998	14,002	16,607	19,816	4,291	44.2	5,814	41.5
Greene	24,765	28,302	30,355	32,869	35,566	5,590	22.6	5,211	17.2
Hempstead	19,308	20,197	20,946	22,076	23,465	1,638	8.5	2,519	12.0
Hot Spring	21,963	24,503	26,126	28,054	30,062	4,163	19.0	3,936	15.1
Howard	11,412	13,094	14,223	15,670	17,376	2,811	24.6	3,153	22.2
Independence	22,723	24,301	25,534	27,175	29,036	2,811	12.4	3,502	13.7
Izard	7,381	9,596	11,208	13,153	15,457	3,827	51.8	4,249	37.9
Jackson	20,452	20,997	21,162	21,517	21,834	710	3.5	672	3.2
Jefferson	85,329	83,706	92,224	95,318	97,644	6,895	8.1	5,420	5.9
Johnson	13,630	15,299	16,625	18,291	20,159	2,995	22.0	3,534	21.3
Lafayette	10,018	9,401	9,286	9,319	9,394	−732	−7.3	108	1.2

PROJECTED SERIES A, POPULATION OF ARKANSAS COUNTIES, 1980, 1985, AND 1990 (continued)

GEOGRAPHIC AREA	CENSUS 1970	ESTIMATE 1975	1980	PROJECTED 1985	PROJECTED 1990	CHANGE, 1970–1980 NUMBER	CHANGE, 1970–1980 PERCENT	CHANGE, 1980–1990 NUMBER	CHANGE, 1980–1990 PERCENT
Lawrence	16,320	18,401	19,422	20,588	21,703	3,102	19.0	2,281	11.7
Lee	18,884	17,602	16,858	16,225	15,607	-2,026	-10.7	-1,251	-7.4
Lincoln	12,913	13,194	13,550	14,165	14,847	637	4.9	1,297	9.6
Little River	11,194	11,805	12,506	13,469	14,629	1,312	11.7	2,123	17.0
Logan	16,789	18,298	19,133	20,368	21,895	2,344	14.0	2,762	14.4
Lonoke	26,249	31,203	35,035	40,099	46,278	8,786	33.5	11,243	32.1
Madison	9,453	10,104	10,533	11,185	11,946	1,080	11.4	1,413	13.4
Marion	7,000	9,395	11,472	14,126	17,413	4,472	63.9	5,941	51.8
Miller	33,385	33,897	34,624	35,765	37,102	1,239	3.7	2,478	7.2
Mississippi	62,060	64,094	64,592	65,843	67,017	2,532	4.1	2,425	3.8
Monroe	15,657	14,799	14,370	14,068	13,785	-1,287	-8.2	-585	-4.1
Montgomery	5,821	6,498	6,915	7,423	7,976	1,094	18.8	1,061	15.3
Nevada	10,111	10,399	10,621	11,003	11,446	510	5.0	825	7.8
Newton	5,844	6,698	7,217	7,917	8,759	1,373	23.5	1,542	21.4
Ouachita	30,896	29,539	29,455	29,443	29,328	-1,441	-4.7	-127	-0.4
Perry	5,634	6,799	7,602	8,623	9,833	1,968	34.9	2,231	29.3
Phillips	40,046	38,604	37,615	37,006	36,445	-2,431	-6.1	-1,170	-3.1
Pike	8,711	9,498	10,087	10,829	11,676	1,376	15.8	1,589	15.8
Poinsett	26,822	27,599	27,820	28,410	28,981	998	3.7	1,161	4.2
Polk	13,297	14,700	15,647	16,816	18,154	2,350	17.7	2,507	16.0

PROJECTED SERIES A, POPULATION OF ARKANSAS COUNTIES, 1980, 1985, AND 1990 (continued)

GEOGRAPHIC AREA	CENSUS 1970	ESTIMATE 1975	PROJECTED 1980	1985	1990	CHANGE, 1970–1980 NUMBER	PERCENT	CHANGE, 1980–1990 NUMBER	PERCENT
Pope	28,607	33,598	38,761	45,341	53,277	10,154	35.5	14,516	37.5
Prairie	10,249	10,599	10,865	11,320	11,841	616	6.0	976	9.0
Pulaski	287,189	316,602	344,175	378,423	415,215	56,986	19.8	71,040	20.6
Randolph	12,645	16,002	18,343	21,216	24,528	5,698	45.1	6,185	33.7
St. Francis	30,799	31,201	31,488	32,107	32,728	689	2.2	1,240	3.9
Saline	36,107	42,701	49,347	58,246	69,394	13,240	36.7	20,047	40.6
Scott	8,207	9,099	9,758	10,652	11,739	1,551	18.9	1,981	20.3
Searcy	7,731	8,198	8,572	9,124	9,748	841	10.9	1,176	13.7
Sebastian	79,237	84,801[a]	90,423	97,838	106,121	11,186	14.1	15,698	17.4
Sevier	11,272	12,400	13,238	14,399	15,809	1,966	17.4	2,571	19.4
Sharp	8,233	10,703	12,824	15,447	18,625	4,591	55.8	5,801	—
Stone	6,838	7,994	8,868	10,026	11,374	2,030	29.7	2,506	28.3
Union	45,428	44,605	44,955	45,758	46,584	–473	–1.0	1,629	3.6
Van Buren	8,275	9,900	11,126	12,659	14,444	2,851	34.5	3,318	29.8
Washington	77,370	87,901	100,437	115,848	133,745	23,067	29.8	33,308	33.2
White	39,253	45,398	50,201	56,182	63,081	10,948	27.9	12,880	25.7
Woodruff	11,566	11,095	10,745	10,478	10,205	–821	–7.1	–540	–5.0
Yell	14,208	16,403	18,167	20,465	23,222	3,959	27.9	5,055	27.8

PROJECTED SERIES B, POPULATION OF ARKANSAS COUNTIES, 1980, 1985, AND 1990

GEOGRAPHIC AREA	CENSUS 1970	ESTIMATE 1975	PROJECTED 1980	PROJECTED 1985	PROJECTED 1990	CHANGE, 1970–1980 NUMBER	CHANGE, 1970–1980 PERCENT	CHANGE, 1980–1990 NUMBER	CHANGE, 1980–1990 PERCENT
ARKANSAS	1,923,295	2,086,000[a]	2,200,717	2,328,846	2,465,885	277,422	14.4	265,168	12.0
Arkansas	23,347	23,596	23,286	23,018	22,667	−61	−0.3	−619	−2.7
Ashley	24,976	25,197	24,984	24,779	24,513	8	0.0	−471	−1.9
Baxter	15,319	21,904	27,541	34,510	43,112	12,222	79.8	15,571	56.5
Benton	50,476	58,597	65,579	73,794	83,146	15,103	29.9	17,567	26.8
Boone	19,073	22,795	25,360	28,298	31,459	6,287	33.0	6,099	24.0
Bradley	12,778	12,597	12,169	11,744	11,287	−609	−4.8	−882	−7.2
Calhoun	5,573	5,709	5,811	5,959	6,134	238	4.3	323	5.6
Carroll	12,301	14,099	15,064	16,127	17,203	2,763	22.5	2,139	11.2
Chicot	18,164	17,708	17,068	16,464	15,807	−1,096	−6.0	−1,261	−7.4
Clark	21,537	21,996	22,260	22,528	22,819	723	3.4	539	2.5
Clay	18,771	20,001	20,195	20,438	20,512	1,424	7.6	317	1.6
Cleburne	10,349	14,305	17,333	21,006	25,306	6,984	67.5	7,973	46.0
Cleveland	6,605	6,797	6,820	6,857	6,893	215	3.3	73	1.1
Columbia	25,952	25,895	25,994	26,000	25,870	42	0.2	−124	−0.5
Conway	16,805	17,798	18,249	18,793	19,342	1,444	8.6	1,093	6.0
Craighead	52,068	57,895	61,248	64,782	68,206	9,180	17.6	6,958	11.4

[a]The population estimate for Sebastian Country for July 1, 1975, does not include 24,178 Vietnamese refugees temporarily housed at Ft. Chaffee.

Sources: Census data from US Bureau of the Census. Estimates and projections prepared by the Industrial Research and Extension Center, University of Arkansas, Little Rock, February 1978.

PROJECTED SERIES A, POPULATION OF ARKANSAS COUNTIES, 1980, 1985, AND 1990 (continued)

GEOGRAPHIC AREA	CENSUS 1970	ESTIMATE 1975	PROJECTED 1980	PROJECTED 1985	PROJECTED 1990	CHANGE, 1970–1980 NUMBER	CHANGE, 1970–1980 PERCENT	CHANGE, 1980–1990 NUMBER	CHANGE, 1980–1990 PERCENT
Crawford	25,677	29,901	32,891	36,490	40,553	7,214	28.1	7,662	23.3
Crittenden	48,106	50,499	51,517	52,772	53,991	3,411	7.1	2,474	4.8
Cross	19,783	20,503	20,235	20,612	20,660	752	3.8	125	0.6
Dallas	10,022	10,196	10,280	10,366	10,404	258	2.6	124	1.2
Desha	18,761	17,699	16,605	15,556	14,523	-2,156	-11.5	-2,082	-12.5
Drew	15,157	15,700	15,953	16,241	16,525	796	5.3	572	3.6
Faulkner	31,572	37,498	43,439	50,417	58,575	11,867	37.6	15,136	34.8
Franklin	11,301	12,801	13,638	14,659	15,781	2,337	20.7	2,143	15.7
Fulton	7,699	8,896	9,793	10,863	12,034	2,094	27.2	2,241	22.9
Garland	54,131	61,698	67,261	73,533	80,115	13,130	24.3	12,854	19.1
Grant	9,711	11,998	13,750	15,842	18,283	4,039	41.6	4,533	33.0
Greene	24,765	28,302	29,829	31,473	33,058	5,064	20.4	3,229	10.8
Hempstead	19,308	20,197	20,554	21,040	21,600	1,246	6.5	1,046	5.1
Hot Spring	21,963	24,503	25,667	26,852	27,922	3,704	16.9	2,255	8.8
Howard	11,412	13,094	13,976	15,006	16,171	2,564	22.5	2,195	15.7
Independence	22,723	24,301	25,089	25,993	26,902	2,366	10.4	1,813	7.2
Izard	7,381	9,596	11,048	12,681	14,519	3,667	49.7	3,471	31.4
Jackson	20,452	20,997	20,754	20,505	20,149	302	1.5	-605	-2.9
Jefferson	85,329	83,706	91,105	93,212	94,529	5,776	6.8	3,424	3.8
Johnson	13,630	15,299	16,341	17,530	18,777	2,711	19.9	2,436	14.9

PROJECTED SERIES A, POPULATION OF ARKANSAS COUNTIES, 1980, 1985, AND 1990 (continued)

GEOGRAPHIC AREA	CENSUS 1970	ESTIMATE 1975	1980	PROJECTED 1985	1990	CHANGE, 1970–1980 NUMBER	PERCENT	CHANGE, 1980–1990 NUMBER	PERCENT
Lafayette	10,018	9,401	9,102	8,863	8,626	-916	-9.1	-476	-5.2
Lawrence	16,320	18,401	19,110	19,799	20,343	2,790	17.1	1,233	6.5
Lee	18,884	17,602	16,522	15,419	14,277	-2,362	-12.5	-2,245	-13.6
Lincoln	12,913	13,194	13,269	13,435	13,589	356	2.8	320	2.4
Little River	11,194	11,805	12,254	12,789	13,376	1,060	9.5	1,122	9.2
Logan	16,789	18,298	18,806	19,460	20,198	2,017	12.0	1,392	7.4
Lonoke	26,249	31,203	34,412	38,335	42,906	8,163	31.1	8,494	24.7
Madison	9,453	10,104	10,352	10,699	11,073	899	9.5	721	7.0
Marion	7,000	9,395	11,321	13,662	16,451	4,321	61.7	5,130	45.3
Miller	33,385	33,897	33,969	34,085	34,150	584	1.7	181	0.5
Mississippi	62,060	64,094	63,250	62,517	61,468	1,190	1.9	-1,782	-2.8
Monroe	15,657	14,799	14,084	13,386	12,684	-1,573	-10.0	-1,400	-9.9
Montgomery	5,821	6,498	6,803	7,114	7,408	982	16.9	605	8.9
Nevada	10,111	10,399	10,425	10,495	10,549	314	3.1	124	1.2
Newton	5,844	6,698	7,081	7,540	8,070	1,237	21.2	989	14.0
Ouachita	30,896	29,539	28,889	28,090	27,116	-2,007	-6.5	-1,773	-6.1
Perry	5,634	6,799	7,475	8,256	9,133	1,841	32.7	1,658	22.2
Phillips	40,046	38,604	36,843	35,158	33,442	-3,203	-8.0	-3,401	-9.2
Pike	8,711	9,498	9,932	10,404	10,897	1,221	14.0	965	9.7
Poinsett	26,822	27,599	27,255	26,997	26,606	433	1.6	-649	-2.4

PROJECTED SERIES A, POPULATION OF ARKANSAS COUNTIES, 1980, 1985, AND 1990 (continued)

GEOGRAPHIC AREA	CENSUS 1970	ESTIMATE 1975	PROJECTED 1980	PROJECTED 1985	PROJECTED 1990	CHANGE, 1970–1980 NUMBER	PERCENT	CHANGE, 1980–1990 NUMBER	PERCENT
Polk	13,297	14,700	15,413	16,167	16,933	2,116	15.9	1,520	9.9
Pope	28,607	33,598	38,058	43,161	48,967	9,451	33.0	10,909	28.7
Prairie	10,249	10,599	10,652	10,755	10,855	403	3.9	203	1.9
Pulaski	287,189	316,602	337,137	359,929	382,243	49,948	17.4	45,106	13.4
Randolph	12,645	16,002	18,089	20,525	23,172	5,444	43.1	5,083	28.1
St. Francis	30,799	31,201	30,814	30,455	29,986	15	0.0	-828	-2.7
Saline	36,107	42,701	48,376	55,289	63,365	12,269	34.0	14,980	31.0
Scott	8,207	9,099	9,596	10,193	10,873	1,389	16.9	1,277	13.3
Searcy	7,731	8,198	8,414	8,696	8,983	683	8.8	569	6.8
Sebastian	79,237	84,801[a]	88,684	93,271	97,945	9,447	11.9	9,261	10.4
Sevier	11,272	12,400	13,005	13,742	14,574	1,733	15.4	1,569	12.1
Sharp	8,233	10,703	12,661	14,954	17,609	4,428	53.8	4,948	39.1
Stone	6,838	7,994	8,704	9,545	10,464	1,866	27.3	1,760	20.2
Union	45,428	44,605	44,101	43,625	42,979	-1,327	-2.9	-1,122	-2.5
Van Buren	8,275	9,900	10,961	12,194	13,561	2,686	32.5	2,600	23.7
Washington	77,370	87,901	98,236	109,918	122,525	20,866	27.0	24,289	24.7
White	39,253	45,398	49,282	53,627	58,200	10,029	25.5	8,918	18.1
Woodruff	11,566	11,095	10,536	9,980	9,401	-1,030	-8.9	-1,135	-10.8
Yell	14,208	16,403	17,858	19,591	21,541	3,650	25.7	3,683	20.6

C. ECONOMICS

Arkansas's traditionally agrarian-based economy yielded significant gains to other sources of economic activity after the mid-1950s. The Arkansas Plan in the immediate post–World War II years opened the way for diversified economic development in the state. Even the disruptive influence of the Little Rock school crisis did not permanently interrupt the increased volume of industrial investment. To many Arkansans the new symbol for industrial expansion in the 1970s became the Arkansas River Navigation and Comprehensive Development Project. Commonly known as the McClellan-Kerr Project, it was completed in 1970 by the US Army Corps of Engineers. The project made year-round navigation possible on the river and provided an outlet for Arkansas products to international markets. Of course, agriculture continued to play a major role in the economy, but it too changed. Changing lifestyles and dietary habits allowed new crops of rice and soybeans to replace cotton, the traditional leader in agricultural production. Another factor in the state's economic development in the Modern Era was the low profile of organized labor. Arkansas voters repeatedly rejected efforts to require company-wide union membership in favor of right-to-work options. Because Arkansas was a labor exporter, business and political leaders sought to increase technical training opportunities for individuals in an effort to attract industry and check workers' out migration.

Little Rock Industry and the School Crisis

Gary Fullerton, "New Factories a Thing of the Past in Little Rock," *Nashville Tennessean*, May 31, 1959.

Although the 1957 Little Rock school crisis focused attention on integrated education, the incident had a major secondary impact on the state's economic development. The following chart taken from a Nashville, Tennessee, newspaper compares industrial development in Little Rock prior to the school crisis and afterward.

YEAR	# OF NEW PLANTS	VALUE	# OF NEW JOBS	# OF EXPAN- SIONS	VALUE	# OF JOBS
1950	7	$835,000	143	6	$2,110,000	—
1951	7	945,000	255	3	475,000	—
1952	6	295,000	163	9	2,150,000	—
1953	2	100,000	30	7	820,000	—
1954	3	1,350,000	150	1	500,000	—
1955	5	1,393,000	565	8	1,250,000	192
1956	2	325,000	70	8	1,350,000	213
1957	8	3,092,000	1.002	3	913,985	70
1958	None	—	—	1	325,000	50
1959**	None	—	—	1	268,000	—

**Through May

Arkansas River Navigation and Comprehensive Development Project Report

House Committee on Public Works, *Arkansas River Navigation and Comprehensive Development Project*, 90th Cong., 2d sess., 1968, 1–14.

Developing the nation's inland waterways was a goal for many business and political leaders since the nineteenth century. The McClellan-Kerr Arkansas River project discussed below was one of the first and largest projects of its kind on an interior river. The testimony presented by business leaders and Army Corps of Engineers officials before a US Senate subcommittee revealed not only an ambitious prediction for the economic value of the project, but also a brief explanation of its actual conditions.

TUESDAY, APRIL 30, 1968
House of Representatives,
Committee on Public Works,
Washington, D.C.

The committee met at 10 a.m., in Room 2167, Rayburn Building, Hon. Ed Edmondson, acting chairman, presiding.

Mr. EDMONDSON. The Committee on Public Works will be in order.

Before I present the general who is going to lead this presentation, I would like to turn the microphone over to my colleague from Fort Smith, who shares the interest that I have in the forward progress of this project.

Congressman Hammerschmidt.

Mr. HAMMERSCHMIDT. Thank you, Mr. Chairman.

I would like to take just a moment, of course, to welcome the members we have here, constituency from Arkansas, the Third District, and all other districts.

I would also like to take the opportunity to pay tribute and to thank the members of this committee who have seen fit to follow through on authorizations for this largest civil works project that has ever been done by the Corps of Engineers. We thank them for their foresight. . . .

Mr. EDMONSON. Thank you very much, Paul. . . .

Statement of Charles D. Maynard

Mr. Chairman, I am Charles D. Maynard. I appear here today as chairman of the 15-man Arkansas, Kansas, and Oklahoma Tri-State Committee. This Committee consists of five representatives from each of the aforementioned states, appointed by the respective Governors to represent him, his state and the common interests of the three states in matters pertaining to the development of the water resources of the Arkansas River Basin. The statement which I will make today represents the unified viewpoint of these three great states in the development of the Arkansas River and its tributaries in our area.

In private life I am Manager of Industrial Development for the Arkansas Louisiana Gas Company and its subsidiaries, which operates throughout the three states traversed by this great river, and I live in Little Rock, Arkansas. . . .

. . . I am pleased to tell this Committee that the people of the Arkansas Valley are going to use this navigable waterway as it is completed. At our principal cities—Pine Bluff, Little Rock, Fort Smith, Muskogee and Tulsa—port facilities are financed and construction is underway on the various features needed to make them operable. In addition to these, many other applications for other cities such as Clarksville,

Arkansas, and private port facilities, loading and/or unloading docks or facilities are being processed by the 2 Engineer Districts involved.

Plant Development to complement the navigational aspects is accelerating rapidly in this area. Already plants involving expenditures in excess of $300 million have been announced along the river course. Included in these are such as:

Arkansas Power and Light Company announced plans for a $140 million nuclear generating plant to be located on the Dardanelle Reservoir near Russellville, Arkansas. . . .

Little Rock is spending $4.3 million for port development; Muskogee, $2.5 million. Similar developments are also going on at Fort Smith and Pine Bluff. . . .

The Maumelle Ordnance Works on the Arkansas River near Little Rock has been purchased for $1 million by private developers who have announced it will become the site of a $20 million industrial and residential complex which they call Maumelle New City. . . .

"Early birds" already on or near the river because of the promise of navigation include: . . . Arkansas Craft Corporation's $10 million plus paper mill at Morrilton, Arkansas . . . [at] Pine Bluff, Central Transformer Corporation, $1.5 million expansion . . . and docks or port facilities at Pine Bluff, Little Rock, Clarksville, Fort Smith and Muskogee.

Just recently Dow Chemical announced a $10 million aluminum extrusion plant near Russellville, and Chicago Iron and Bridge Company this month announced a plant using some 100 people at Conway.

Additionally, our area is being investigated, studied and eyed for plant expansions and additional locations by many firms—some large, some small. To a great extent they are attracted to this area by the promise of economic advantage along this developing area of commerce. They recognize that this development makes possible the release and utilization of many of the great resources that have been dormant in our area. . . .

We are talking about thousands of jobs and millions of dollars in investment made possible by the wisdom and leadership of Congress. What you have done makes possible the shining horizon we see in the Arkansas Valley. We know that for each 100 new jobs created at a new plant, an additional 65 non-industrial jobs come into being. These will be created in retail trade, in transportation, in construction, in service facilities and in other industries. These 165 new jobs will produce about

100 new households and place about 300 more people in our communities. As a consequence, the school population will increase about 90 students. Each 100 new jobs increase the annual personal income of a community about $700,000, which means added retail sales of some $300,000 and a rise in bank deposits of approximately $230,000. Three or four retail stores plus other service establishments will come into being to accommodate these people.

Starting this fall, navigation will be a reality to Pine Bluff, Little Rock and the Central Arkansas Valley, and the first of our 3 navigation targets will be a reality. . . .

Near Little Rock this fall we plan a celebration to mark the achievement of our first goal. We have to have President Johnson present upon this auspicious occasion. The Post Office Department has authorized the issuance of a special commemorative stamp to mark the day and the nation's achievement.

●   ●   ●

STATEMENT OF GEN. HARRY WOODBURY, U.S. ARMY CORPS OF ENGINEERS: ACCOMPANIED BY COL. CHARLES L. STEEL, DISTRICT ENGINEER, LITTLE ROCK, ARK.

This project is the program for the comprehensive development of a major segment of the Arkansas River. This is a truly multiple-purpose project which will produce benefits of low-cost transportation, flood damage prevention, low-cost electric power, dependable water supply, recreation, fish and wildlife enhancement, and water quality improvement. This project has already produced tremendous benefits by its control of floods on the Arkansas and Mississippi Rivers. Several of its hydro-electric powerplants have been and are pumping electrical energy into the electrical distribution network for consumption throughout the Southwestern United States.

By the end of 1970 we will have realized one of its principal purposes, the extension of barge navigation from the great Mississippi River across the state of Arkansas and into Oklahoma to a point near Tulsa. A more immediate milestone—completion of navigation as far as Little Rock— is expected this year. Public and private ports are being developed and many commercial enterprises have already located along the waterway. Additional industries have announced plans for future plants to take advantage of low-cost water transportation on the Arkansas. Another milestone—water carriers have been licensed by the ICC to operate on the new waterway. And farsighted interests in the valley are already looking to the further extension of low-cost water transportation west into Oklahoma, and north. . . .

Next, Col. Charles L. Steel, the district engineer, Little Rock. He is responsible for construction and operation of that portion of the project in the State of Arkansas. He is the man whose feet you kept in the fire to insure that water transportation was available in Little Rock this year. He joined the district in December 1967 from Germany where he commanded the 39th Engineer Group and was engaged in providing facilities for redeploying U.S forces within NATO. . . .

Col. Steel will open the presentation. . . .

Col. Steel.

COLONEL STEEL. Thank you General Woodbury. . . .

I will start off the presentation with some general comments; then we will discuss the major structures on the Arkansas in the State of Arkansas, stressing the location and dams and the bridges.

I will then cover the dredging that will be required on the entire river and will conclude my presentation with a few comments about the people who will use this river.

This project is one of the largest projects that has ever been attempted by the Army Corps of Engineers with respect to navigation. It starts on the Mississippi River, goes 10 miles up the White River, and then across another 10 miles of the Arkansas Post Canal. There it flows into the Arkansas River and continues up 450 miles to the Port of Catoosa, with the last 50 miles being on the Verdigris River, which it joins at Muskogee.

During this 450-mile trek, the 17 locks and dams along the way raise the water 420 feet in the 17 steps, with the steps being between 14 feet and 54 feet, the highest one being at Dardanelle.

This project, when it is completed, will cost about $1.2 billion. Through fiscal year 1967, we had already appropriated $768 million, which left about $430 million to be spent.

In this fiscal year we have appropriated $155 million, and it is anticipated that next year we will have $136 million.

. . . [The first] lock and dam, No. 1, is at the junction of the White River on the downstream side, in the Arkansas Post Canal on the upstream side. Each of the locks in the entire stretch of river are the same size. They are 110 feet wide and two football fields in length, 600 feet. They will accommodate the normal barge, which is used throughout the rest of the inland waterways of America.

This structure is unique in that it is controlled by the level of the Mississippi River. The Mississippi River will vary as much as 60 feet in this region and when the water is at its highest, the whole structure will be inundated to include the first floor of the control building . . . at the lock.

In these conditions, the barges will have to traverse the weir, over on the side, and continue to go upstream.

All of our locks and dams use both horns and visual signals to tell the barge operators to start and stop. But to insure that they know that they are supposed to use the weir, instead of the red and the green, we have developed a purple light, so if they see a purple light, they go over the weir instead of through the lock.

Everyone Talks about Other Things but Agriculture Is Still the King

Arkansas Gazette (Little Rock), January 21, 1968; US Department of Agriculture, *1980 Agriculture Statistics for Arkansas* (Little Rock: USDA, 1981), 5, 7–8.

Although traditionally considered a rural state (as recently as 1970, 50 percent of the population lived in communities of less than 2,500 people), in the post–World War II years, Arkansas leaders made a determined effort to increase the industrial base and saw significant gains in this area. However, as the following document illustrates, agriculture continued to hold its lead in the state's economy.

The changing patterns of modern economy have tended to relegate agriculture to the back burner when the chef devotes most of his attention to the fancy concoctions related to industrial and professional development. This situation is particularly true in Arkansas, which once derived most of its basic income from farm production but which has concentrated on the task of attracting factories to its cities and towns.

Admittedly, the farm has become less important as a creator of jobs and a contributor to total employment. The number of farm workers in the state has declined steadily for several years and, primarily for this reason, a tendency has developed to "write off" agriculture as a significant factor.

Nothing could be further from the truth. Despite the fact that the manpower needs of agriculture have declined in recent years, the value of farm productions has increased and a fresh viewpoint is needed. Farming should not be regarded as a declining segment of the economy, simply because the manpower needs are not as great as they were when walking cultivators were used to plow cotton. Instead, the technological progress that has been achieved in farming should be seen as a change that has released workers for industrial and professional jobs.

The important fact is that agriculture still is the "meat and potatoes" of the Arkansas economy and will continue to play this role so long as the world needs food and fiber. The soups, salads and desserts of industrial and professional developments are essential but the main course still comes from the farm.

Arkansas agriculture contributed almost $1 billion last year [1967] to the Arkansas economy—if only the value of raw material is considered. When the added value of manufacturing and processing is brought into the balance sheet, it becomes apparent that the economy of the state still is geared to the farm. . . .

Arkansas agriculture will continue to adjust to changing conditions and the manpower requirements may decline still further. The real need, however, is that people should understand that a reduction in the number of farm workers is simply an indication of the increasing efficiency of those who remain with the land. The total value of farm commodities produced in the state can be expected to increase as goods become more important and as farmers make better use of their land resources.

No one should make the mistake of ignoring the value of agriculture to the economy of Arkansas. It will remain the meat and potatoes of business in the state, even though we succeed in rounding out the menu.

REALIZED GROSS INCOME AND NET INCOME
OF FARM OPERATORS FROM FARMING

YEAR	REALIZED GROSS FARM INCOME*	FARM PROD-UCTION EXPENSES	REALIZED NET FARM INCOME	NET CHANGE IN FARM INVENT-ORIES	TOTAL NET FARM INCOME
			Million dollars		
1960	743.3	502.7	240.6	4.4	244.9
1961	855.4	556.5	299.0	5.2	304.1
1962	853.6	602.2	251.4	13.1	264.5
1963	919.1	660.7	258.4	.3	258.7
1964	983.3	706.6	276.7	21.0	297.7
1965	1,001.5	757.5	244.0	−7.2	236.8
1966	1,151.5	801.6	349.9	8.0	357.9
1967	1,101.9	859.1	242.8	13.5	256.2
1968	1,170.5	905.2	265.3	13.1	278.4
1969	1,266.8	986.6	280.2	−11.4	268.8
1970	1,378.5	1,064.8	313.7	15.3	329.0
1971	1,403.9	1,112.1	291.8	15.4	307.2
1972	1,550.4	1,195.7	354.6	38.0	392.6
1973	2,285.4	1,521.1	764.4	49.7	814.0
1974	2,307.8	1,721.1	586.7	269.0	855.7
1975	2,316.2	1,654.0	662.2	99.5	761.7
1976	2,556.0	1,850.8	705.2	−170.9	534.3
1977	2,657.1	2,077.0	580.1	−12.5	567.6
1978	3,184.2	2,235.6	948.6	−67.6	881.0
1979	3,455.4	2,596.6	858.8	191.3	1,050.1

Details may not add to totals because of rounding.

*Includes cash receipts from farm marketings, government payments, value of home consumption, and gross rental value of farm dwellings.

FARM REAL ESTATE: AVERAGE VALUE PER ACRE, ARKANSAS AND SURROUNDING STATES, AND 48-STATE TOTAL, FEBRUARY 1, 1977–1981

STATE	FEB. 1977	FEB. 1978	FEB. 1979	FEB. 1980	FEB. 1981*
			Dollars		
Arkansas	521	619	769	922	1,061
Louisiana	581	822	1,002	1,293	1,526
Mississippi	404	568	682	826	1,049
Missouri	526	636	726	878	939
Oklahoma	365	451	513	605	666
Tennessee	545	735	863	957	1,024
Texas	286	336	384	445	490
48 states	450	533	628	720	790

*Preliminary, November data have been discontinued.

DISTRIBUTION OF CASH RECEIPTS FROM
ARKANSAS FARM PRODUCTS

YEAR	COTTON (LINT & SEED)	CATTLE AND CALVES	BROIL-ERS#	SOY-BEANS	RICE	DAIRY PROD-UCTS	HOGS	EGGS	TUR-KEYS	OTHER
					Percent					
1960	33.4	9.3	13.4	16.3	8.4	4.8	2.3	3.8	1.5	6.8
1961	34.9	9.5	12.2	16.2	9.1	4.4	2.1	4.9	1.4	5.3
1962	32.1	9.2	14.6	14.6	11.1	4.3	1.9	5.8	1.3	5.1
1963	34.0	8.2	14.4	13.5	10.9	3.9	1.6	6.7	1.4	5.4
1964	28.4	7.4	14.1	21.3	8.9	3.3	1.4	7.5	1.6	6.1
1965	27.2	9.3	15.7	17.0	10.3	3.2	1.5	7.9	2.1	5.8
1966	11.3	9.2	17.8	27.5	11.1	3.4	1.7	9.0	2.7	6.3
1967	8.7	10.2	16.6	25.1	12.4	3.8	1.6	9.7	3.4	8.5
1968	14.0	11.2	17.6	20.4	12.2	3.7	1.6	10.3	2.8	6.2
1969	13.9	11.0	19.8	19.9	12.4	3.5	1.7	10.0	2.4	5.4
1970	11.3	13.1	16.6	26.9	9.8	3.2	1.5	8.8	2.8	6.0
1971	15.6	12.5	18.2	22.1	9.6	3.3	1.4	8.5	2.9	5.9
1972	15.4	14.0	18.9	19.7	9.9	3.2	1.5	8.4	2.6	6.4
1973	10.1	11.4	20.3	23.8	15.3	2.4	1.5	8.3	2.4	4.5
1974	6.0	5.8	17.6	34.1	16.8	2.7	1.2	8.7	1.8	5.3
1975	13.1	9.7	21.3	20.2	15.0	2.7	1.7	8.5	2.1	5.7
1976	11.0	8.0	19.4	52.2	13.5	2.9	1.9	8.5	2.9	6.7
1977	11.3	12.5	20.9	19.6	15.2	2.9	1.7	7.3	3.0	5.6
1978*	7.0	12.7	20.3	26.5	15.1	2.6	2.0	5.9	3.6	4.3
1979*	6.1	13.2	20.9	25.5	14.8	2.7	2.5	6.6	2.9	4.8

Source: Farm Income Branch of Economic Research Service.
#Starting in 1974, percent is for all chickens.
*Revised data.

1980 AGRICULTURAL STATISTICS FOR ARKANSAS
ARKANSAS'S RANK AMONG STATES:
VALUE AND PRODUCTION OF CROPS AND LIVESTOCK, 1980

COMMODITY	UNIT	PRODUCTION RANK	PRODUCTION THOUS. UNITS	VALUE OF PRODUCTION RANK	VALUE OF PRODUCTION THOUS. DOLLARS
CROPS					
Corn for grain	Bu.	40	1,036	40	3,678
Cotton	Lb. Bale	6	444	6	164,316
Cottonseed	Ton	5	181	4	23,349
Oats	Bu.	24	2,079	23	3,846
Rice	Lb. Cwt.	1	52,615	2	*
Sorghum grain	Bu.	10	5,887	10	16,955
Soybeans, for beans	Bu.	8	69,600	7	560,280
Sweetpotatoes	Cwt.	13	36	13	360
Wheat, all	Bu.	19	31,160	19	118,408
HAY & SEEDS					
Hay, all	Ton	29	1,221	32	57,387
Lepedeza seed	Lb.	4	465	3	293
Tall fescue seed	Lb.	4	3,380	5	625
FRUITS & NUTS					
Apples. commercial	Lb.	35	5,000	35	415
Grapes	Ton	8	6.6	9	1,122
Peaches	Lb.	10	27,000	11	3,645
Pecans, all	Lb.	11	900	11	742
TRUCK CROPS					
Strawberries	Lb.	13	2,600	13	793
Tomatoes	Cwt.	13	241	9	7,897
Watermelons	Cwt.	15	80	15	362
LIVESTOCK & POULTRY					
Cattle & calves#	Head	17	2,300	20	376,222
Milk	Lb.	34	745,000	34	100,575
Hogs & Pigs	Head	20	720	20	86,546
Commercial broilers	No.	1	634,877	1	657,733
Eggs	No.	4	4,153,000	3	209,727
Farm chickens	No.	3	27,450	3	13,720
Turkeys, raised	No.	4	14,500	4	106,416
Honey	Lb.	34	1,472	38	824
Beeswax	Lb.	38	28	38	51

#Number on farms, January 1, 1981.
*Not available for 1980.

Arkansas Freedom to Work Law

State of Arkansas, *Constitution of Arkansas,* Amendment No. 34;
Associated Industries of Arkansas, Inc., "Answers to your
Questions About Arkansas' Freedom to Work Law," Pamphlet
Collection, Little Rock Public Library, Little Rock; and J. Bill
Becker, "Remarks by J. Bill Becker, President Arkansas State
AFL-CIO before [the] Little Rock Chamber of Commerce,
March 4, 1976," Pamphlet Collection, Little Rock Public Library,
Little Rock.

Few issues in the Modern Era were more controversial, or emotional, than Arkansas's right to work law. Business leaders, working
to stimulate economic growth, cited the law as a major asset in
recruiting new industry and thus more jobs. Many labor leaders,
however, argued that the law stifled economic development by
keeping workers in a subservient position and limiting their purchasing power. The following documents illustrate the nature of
the law and pro and con arguments about it.

CONSTITUTION OF ARKANSAS
Amendment No. 34

Be it Enacted by the People of the State of Arkansas: That the following
shall be an amendment to the Constitution:

"Section 1. No person shall be denied employment because of membership in or affiliation with or resignation from a labor union, or because
of refusal to join or affiliate with a labor union; nor shall any corporation
or individual or association of any kind enter into any contract, written or
oral, to exclude from employment members of a labor union or persons
who refuse to join a labor union, or because of resignation from a labor
union; nor shall any person against his will be compelled to pay dues to
any labor organization as a prerequisite to or condition of employment."

"Section 2. The General Assembly shall have the power to enforce
this article by appropriate legislation."

Proposed by Initiated Petition. Voted upon at General Election
November 7, 1944. For 105,300; against 87,654.

•　　•　　•

Act 101

AN ACT FOR THE ENFORCEMENT OF THE PROVISIONS OF AMENDMENT NO. 34
TO THE CONSTITUTION, AND FOR OTHER PURPOSES.
BE IT ENACTED BY THE GENERAL ASSEMBLY OF THE STATE OF ARKANSAS:

SECTION 1. Freedom of organized labor to bargain collectively, and freedom of organized labor to bargain individually, is declared to be public policy of the State under Amendment No. 34 to the Constitution.

SECTION 2. No person shall be denied employment because of membership in, or affiliation with, a labor union; nor shall any person be denied employment because of failure or refusal to join or affiliate with a labor union; nor shall any person, unless he shall voluntarily consent in writing to do so, be compelled to pay dues, or any other monetary consideration to any labor organization as a prerequisite to, or condition of, or continuance of, employment.

SECTION 3. No person, group of persons, firm, corporation, association, or labor organization shall enter into any contract to exclude from employment, (1) persons who are members of, or affiliated with, a labor union; (2) persons who are not members of, or who fail or refuse to join, or affiliate with, a labor union; and (3) persons who, having joined a labor union, have resigned their membership therein or have been discharged, expelled, or excluded therefrom.

SECTION 4. Any person, group of persons, firm, corporation, association, labor organization, or the representative, or representatives thereof, either for himself or themselves, or others, who sign, approves, or enters into a contract contrary to the provisions of this Act shall be guilty of a misdemeanor; and, upon conviction thereof shall be fined in a sum not less than $100.00 nor more than $5,000.00 and each day such unlawful contract is given effect, or in any manner complied with, shall be deemed a separate offense and shall be punishable as such as herein provided.

The power and duty to enforce this Act is hereby conferred upon, and vested in, the Circuit Court of the county in which any person, group of persons, firm, corporation, unincorporated association, labor organization, representatives thereof, who violate this Act, or any part thereof, resides or has a place of business, or may be found and served with process.

SECTION 5. This act shall not apply to existing contracts, but shall apply to any renewals or extensions thereof.

SECTION 6. The provisions of this Act are severable, and the invalidity of one shall not affect the validity of the others.

SECTION 7. Labor controversies, the disruption of industrial and agricultural labor by labor disputes, the effort to force laborers to join, or to refrain from joining, labor organizations, are a menace to the peace, quietude, safety and prosperity of the people of the State; an emergency is therefore declared, and this Act shall take effect from and after its passage.

Signed by Governor Ben Laney, February 19, 1947
APPROVED: February 19, 1947

•   •   •

Answers to Your Questions About Arkansas' Freedom to Work Law

1. Does the Arkansas Freedom to Work Law abolish labor unions?

   No. The law does not abolish the right of employees to join a union.

2. Does the law protect the right of an employee to join a union?

   Yes. (See Section 1 of the law.)

3. Does this law also protect employees who do not wish to join a labor union?

   Yes. (See Section 1.)

4. May an employer compel his employees to stay out of a labor union under the terms of the Right to Work Law?

   No. (See Sections 1 and 3.)

5. Does the law permit an employer to force his employees to join a union?

   No. (See Sections 1 and 3.)

6. Does the law protect an employee in his right to join a union of his choice?

   Yes. (See Section 1.)

7. Does this law prohibit the firing of a union member because he is expelled from the union?

   Yes. (See Section 3.)

8. Was the Arkansas Freedom to Work Law passed to benefit the employer?

No. The law was passed to protect and benefit the individual employee. Both employers and labor unions are subject to fines and other penalties for violations of this law. (See Section 4.)

9. What is meant by Freedom to Work?

Freedom to Work means that an employee may join or not join a union, as the employee sees fit. It means that an employee cannot be forced to join a union—or any other private organization—in order to get a job or hold a job.

10. What does Federal law say about State Freedom to Work laws, such as the Arkansas law?

Enactment of State Freedom to Work laws, such as the Arkansas Freedom to Work Law is authorized by Section 14b of the Taft-Hartley Act which is as follows:

"Sec. 14 (b) Nothing in this Act shall be construed as authorizing the execution of application of agreements requiring membership in a labor organization as a condition of employment in any State or Territory in which such execution or application is prohibited by State or Territorial law."

11. Does the law deny employees their right to strike?

No. The Arkansas Freedom to Work Law does not relate in any way to the right to strike. Employees are free to strike for better wages, hours, working conditions, or for any other legitimate objective.

12. Are paid vacations and other fringe benefits affected by the law?

No. The Freedom to Work Law does not interfere with a labor union's right to bargain for paid vacations or any other benefits.

13. Has the United States Supreme Court ever ruled on the constitutionality of the State Freedom to Work laws?

Yes. In the Nebraska, North Carolina and Arizona cases, the United States Supreme Court ruled that State Freedom to Work laws are constitutional. References: Lincoln Union v. Northwestern I & M Co., Jan. 3, 1949. AFL v. American Sash & Door Co., Jan. 3, 1949.

14. Do State Freedom to Work laws reduce union membership?

    No. Union membership has increased in every one of the states that have Freedom to Work laws, according to figures compiled by Dr. Leo Wolman, Professor of Economics at Columbia University.

15. Do Freedom to Work laws reduce wages?

    No. U.S. Department of Labor figures show that wages have increased in all Freedom to Work states.

16. Do Freedom to Work laws guarantee a man a job?

    No. Freedom to Work creates no new rights. It serves to protect the individual's fundamental right to work without having to join a union against his will.

17. Was the Arkansas Freedom to Work Law enacted in accordance with the wishes of the People of Arkansas?

    Yes. Amendment 34 to the Constitution of Arkansas was adopted by a large majority of the voters of Arkansas at the General Election of 1944. Act 101 received approval of the General Assembly in 1947.

●   ●   ●

A View From Organized Labor on Arkansas' Right to Work Law
Remarks by J. Bill Becker, President, Arkansas State AFL-CIO
Before Little Rock Chamber of Commerce
March 4, 1976

Working people all over the great state of Arkansas are celebrating the Bicentennial Year in a way which shows the vitality of our democratic system, raising an important issue for voters to decide.

We are circulating a petition to place on the fall ballot an amendment—or modification—to Amendment 34 in our State's Constitution, the "Rights of Labor" provision. It sounds, and is, a bit complicated.

What we seek, however, is a basic redress of a grievance that has plagued us for over thirty years.

Let me put the problem in context. Suppose the Government of Arkansas had adopted a law placing a free rider on the street where you live. He sends his kids to your schools. He uses the same sewer and water system as the rest of the neighbors. He gets the same fire and police protection. But instead of helping pay for these things through taxes, the government required you and the rest of the neighbors to come up with his share.

Do you think that free rider would be popular, or would you resent him?

Well, the State of Arkansas has such a law. It affects those working men and women who belong to trade unions, and they, too, resent it. It's a compulsory open shop requirement. Here's how it works.

Before a trade union can represent a group of working men and women, it must be certified as the bargaining agent. The same Taft-Hartley Act that sets up the procedures requires the local union to represent everybody in the bargaining unit, members and non-members alike.

You negotiate a wage increase, the non-member gets it.

You negotiate better pensions, better insurance, better vacation provisions. The non-member gets those, too.

You're even supposed to give his grievance the same consideration you do the grievances of the member who attends every meeting and helps organize the Labor Day picnic.

Okay so the non-member is a chiseler. He's a free rider. He is not liked or respected by his fellow workers.

The appeal is to the worst of man.

Let's look at it from his standpoint.

You're in the line. You're going to get the same merry-go-round ride as everybody else. You can ride free or pay for the ticket. It's up to you. Which way are you going to go?

I know that everybody here would pay. I can tell by your faces that you're all pure of heart and motivated chiefly by compassion. But can you believe that there are people in the world so self-centered, so eager to take care of No. 1, that they say, if you can get it for free . . . take? Why not?

Management knows who they are. It can spot them. It can work to keep a trade union weak . . . by hiring the probable free riders every chance it has. It can encourage others to be free riders . . . chiselers if you will, by its own system of rewards.

When the compulsory open shop was adopted a generation ago, the people of Arkansas were promised great returns. Keep the unions weak, the promoters said, and we'll all be the stronger for it. It just hasn't worked out that way.

Today, the enlightened employers know better.

Major Arkansas employers not only stand ready to put union security clauses into their contracts, they have actually signed contracts with "If and When" provisions which will go into effect just as soon as Arkansas' voters adopt an enabling "Rights of Labor" provision for our Constitution.

These clauses are in contracts already signed by representatives of major corporations and Arkansas local unions. They provide for union security clauses which will go into effect "IF" they are approved by a majority of eligible employees and "WHEN" such provisions are legal in Arkansas.

Outstanding retailers like J. Weingarten, Kroger and Safeway, many Arkansas garment makers, major manufacturers like Reynolds Metals, Brown Shoe and Teletype, major service organizations, including Southwestern Bell, are among firms which have agreed to "If and When" agreements in current contracts.

Enlightened employers simply do not want this state or any other to get in the way of free collective bargaining. Here labor and management can be on common ground.

Farsighted employers are just as disturbed as the rest of us over revelations of wrong doing between some giant corporations and governments. They are just as concerned as the rest of us over the way Gulf Oil, Lockheed, Northrop and others have used corporate resources illegally and unethically to get governments to do their bidding.

Enlightened corporate executives do not want the State of Arkansas to use the power of government to keep trade unions weak. That has to be a healthy attitude on their parts.

Nobody, including those of us in the labor movement, is pushing for the opportunity to impose union security provisions on working people without their voting for them. But relaxing the compulsory open shop requirements in Arkansas' Constitution will be a sign that a new day is dawning. The existence of "If and When" agreements suggests that management and labor may be able to turn their backs on hateful yesterdays and find more ways to cooperate in the search for brighter tomorrows.

Merchants, farmers, professional people and, above all, housewives, have just as much a stake in the proposed new "Rights of Labor" provision as do the unions and management. Getting rid of the compulsory open shop straightjacket is one of the things we must do to bring per capita earnings in Arkansas up to the national average.

When the present compulsory open shop provisions went into affect in 1947, Arkansas wages were 57 cents an hour below the national average. Today they are $1.18 below.

We cannot have a broadly-based prosperity while Arkansas ranks 48th in the nation in income per resident. We cannot secure an enduring prosperity with high bank buildings and low wages. It can only come by putting purchasing power in the hands of people.

Thus giving working people and management the right to work out union security matters voluntarily without government interference is not only morally right, it is right economically as well.

It is morally wrong to require trade unions to bargain for all eligible employees in a work unit and then to require the workers who join the union to carry the freight for those who don't.

It is morally wrong for a state government to deny working people the right to make their own union security decisions by majority vote.

While I see glimpses of a new Arkansas, I am not so naive as to think there will not be spirited opposition. The John Birch Society, for one, will hardly be able to resist getting into the fight. Neither will the so-called "National Right-to-Work Committee," a front group financed in part by reactionary employers whose primary purpose is to make unions ineffective.

Still I think this is the right issue on which to take a stand, and our Bicentennial Year is the right year in which to take it. Accordingly I hope all who believe in fair play will join with us in this campaign. Our goal is to give Arkansas' working people the same voting rights working people enjoy in 31 other states. Our goal is also to give due support to the processes of free collective bargaining without an oppressive government standing in the way.

You will notice that right up to now I have carefully avoided using the phrase "Right-to-Work" in connection with this presentation. The phrase is an advertising gimmick which must have been dreamed up by some Madison Avenue huckster.

The compulsory open shop provision gives the worker the *right-to-work-for-less,* here and in every other state where the provision is in effect.

It gives the anti-labor management the *right-to-work-over* the union certified as the bargaining agent.

It gives the something for nothing person the *right-to-work-out* the rationalizations that will enable him to ride on the backs of his fellow workers.

I have no doubt that in due time we will be seeing television commercials asking us all to side with the poor fellow who would be denied the right-to-work by the evil labor bosses . . . commercials paid for by forces eager to see to it that the poor fellow enriches others by working for just as much . . . and no more . . . than is needed to keep body and soul together.

That's a right he can always enjoy in one of the many places where the benefits of the trade union movement do not flow.

The hard facts of life are that few industries can afford to pay their employees much more than their competition pays. The bald facts are that without the right to bargain collectively, those who work for wages have little power to bargain at all.

The compulsory open shop movement was and remains an attempt to stake out low wage sections of the country in the hope that industry would rush in to exploit the situation. It doesn't happen. Further, Dr. Charles N. Kimball, President of the Midwest Research Institute of Kansas City, told the Arkansas State Chamber of Commerce a few years ago, any industries attracted by such shoddy bait are "hardly worth having." We need firms that are attracted by the good things we have to offer; not the bad.

Thus, while we in the labor movement have a problem, it's your problem, too.

We can poke along with our great pockets of poverty and our rising crime related, in part, to lack of decent jobs, or we can move ahead.

Adopting the proposed "Rights of Labor" provision is not the whole answer to the problem, but it is a big step in the right direction.

Join with us. We believe the course on which we have embarked is the road to progress for all Arkansas citizens.

In Summary

Passage of this measure will remove a government obstacle to free collective bargaining. It will give management and labor the right to agree to union security provisions in contracts if two conditions are met:

1. A majority of all eligible employees in the bargaining unit must

indicate their desire for a union security clause by a secret ballot election, and

2. The employer approves.

D. EDUCATION

Education had a tremendous impact on Arkansas in the post–World War II era. Although the state ranked near the top among the states in the percentage of its budget committed to education, in the area of per capita expenditures for students and teachers' salaries the state consistently rated near the bottom of the fifty states. Two major influences on public education in the Modern Era were court-ordered desegregation and the consolidation of rural school districts. The following documents illustrate those actions.

The Little Rock School Crisis

Aaron v. Cooper, 163 F. Supp. 13 (E.D. Ark, 1958).

This document represented the view of district judge Harry T. Lemley regarding the Little Rock school crisis following the US Supreme Court decision ordering school desegregation in the *Brown v. Topeka* decision in 1954. The judge provided a historical background to the crisis, outlined the issues before the Little Rock Board of Education, and, finally, issued an order to delay integration at Central High School until 1961.

IN THE DISTRICT COURT OF THE UNITED STATES
FOR THE EASTERN DISTRICT OF ARKANSAS
WESTERN DIVISION

JOHN AARON, ET AL,   } Plaintiffs
    vs.

WILLIAM G. COOPER, ET AL,
Members of the Board of Directors   Civil Action No. 3112
of the Little Rock, Arkansas
Independent School District, and   } Defendants
VIRGIL T. BLOSSOM,
Superintendent of Schools

Memorandum Opinion

This cause is now before the Court upon the petition of the defendants, members of the School Board of Little Rock, Arkansas, and the Superintendent of Schools, for an order permitting them to suspend until January, 1961, the operation of the plan of gradual racial integration in the Little Rock public schools, which plan was adopted by the Board in 1955, and was approved by the Court in 1956, the Court of Appeals affirming. *Aaron* v. *Cooper*, DC, Ark., 143F. Supp. 855, aff'd., 8 Cir., 243 F2d 361. This petition has been tried to the Court and the Court having considered the pleadings, briefs and evidence, and being well and fully advised, doth file this memorandum opinion, incorporating herein its findings of fact and conclusions of law.

In order that the issues tendered by the Board's petition may be intelligently understood, a brief history of this litigation is desirable:

Prior to the decisions of the Supreme Court of the United States in the Brown cases (*Brown* v. *Board of Education,* 347 U.S. 483, and 349 U.S. 294) the public school system in Little Rock, like all other public school systems in the State of Arkansas, was operated on a racially segregated basis. A few days after the first Brown decision was rendered the Board announced that it was commencing studies looking toward the establishment of an integrated school system; and in 1955, a few days prior to the rendition of the second Brown decision, the Board announced a plan of gradual integration extending over a period of years, the plan to go into operation with respect to the high school grades at the commencement of the 1957–58 school year.

Thereafter, the plaintiffs in this case, who are Negro Children of school age residing within the Little Rock School District, commenced a class action against the members of the Board and the Superintendent of Schools attacking the plan. The case was tried by Judge John E. Miller of Fort Smith, who was sitting in the Eastern District of Arkansas under a special assignment. As indicated, the plan was approved, and the Court dismissed the prayer of the complaint for declaratory and injunctive relief, and retained jurisdiction of the case for the purpose of entering such other and further order as might be necessary to obtain the plan's effectuation.

At the time the plan was adopted, the Board recognized that the vast majority of the people of Little Rock was opposed to integration, but it was felt by the Board that the plan would be acceptable as the best one obtainable under the circumstances, and that it would be workable if put into operation in September, 1957. As time went on, however, opposition to integration increased in intensity not only in Little Rock but throughout the State as a whole, as is shown by the fact that in the general election in November, 1956, the people of the State by substantial majorities adopted: (a) Amendment No. 44 to the Arkansas Constitution of 1874, which amendment directs the Arkansas Legislature to take appropriate action and pass laws opposing "in every Constitutional manner" the decisions of the Supreme Court in the Brown cases; (b) A resolution of interposition, which among other things, called upon the people of the United States and the governments of all of the separate states to join the people of Arkansas in securing the adoption of an amendment to the Constitution of the United States, which would provide that the powers of the federal government should not be construed to extend to the regulation of the public schools of any state, or to include a prohibition to any state to provide for the maintenance of racially separate but substantially equal public schools within such state; (c) A pupil assignment law dealing with the assignment of individual pupils to individual public schools.

And the 61st General Assembly, which met in January, 1957, passed four statutes, one of which established a State Sovereignty Commission; another of which relieved school children of compulsory attendance in racially mixed public schools; the third of which required certain persons and organizations engaged in certain activities including those affecting integration, to register with and make periodic reports to the State Sovereignty Commission; and the fourth of which authorized local school boards to expend district funds in employing counsel to assist them in the solution of problems arising out of integration.

In August, 1957, Mrs. Clyde Thomason, a white person, filed a suit against the Board and the Superintendent in the Chancery Court of Pulaski County, the purpose of which suit was to enjoin them from putting the plan into operation; that suit was based, in part at least, upon the legislation heretofore mentioned. A hearing was held before the Chancellor, and on August 29, 1957 a temporary restraining order was issued. At that time Judge Ronald N. Davies of Fargo, North Dakota, was sitting in the Eastern District of Arkansas under special assignment, and on August 30, upon the application of the Board in this cause, he enjoined further proceedings by the plaintiff in the state court litigation. His decision was appealed, and he was affirmed. *Thomason v. Cooper,* supra.

The 1957–1958 school year was due to commence on September 3,

1957, and the Board had arranged to enroll nine Negro students in the formerly all-white Central High School pursuant to the plan. On the night of September 2, however, the Governor of the State of Arkansas announced that in the interest of preserving the public peace and tranquility he had called out units of the Arkansas National Guard and had directed that the white schools be placed "off limits" to Negro students, and that the Negro schools be placed "off limits" to white students. The Board, learning of the Governor's action, requested the nine Negro students not to attempt to enter the school the following day, and on the morning of September 3 the Board applied to Judge Davies for instructions. As a result of that application Judge Davies entered an order on the same day directing the Board to put its plan of integration into operation "forthwith."

On September 4 the Negro students attempted to enter the school but were turned away by the national guardsmen. The next day the Board filed a petition for a temporary suspension of the operation of the plan, which petition upon a hearing by Judge Davies was denied.

On September 9, 1957, Judge Davies entered an order inviting the Government to come into the case as amicus curiae and to commence injunction proceedings against the Governor and his subordinates "to prevent the existing interferences with and obstructions to the carrying out of the orders heretofore entered by this Court in this case." Thereupon the Government intervened, and after a hearing held on September 20, a preliminary injunction was entered restraining the Governor, the Adjutant General of the State of Arkansas, and the Unit Commander of the guardsmen on duty from "(a) obstructing or preventing by means of the Arkansas National Guard, or otherwise, Negro students eligible under said plan of school integration to attend the Little Rock Central High School, from attending said school or (b) from threatening or coercing said students not to attend said school or (c) from obstructing or interfering in any way with the carrying out and effectuation of this Court's orders of August 28, 1956 and September 3, 1957, in this case, or (d) from otherwise obstructing or interfering with the constitutional right of said Negro children to attend said school." See *Aaron* v. *Cooper,* DC, Ark., 156 F. Supp. 220.

The Governor obeyed the order entering the temporary injunction just mentioned, while at the same time prosecuting an appeal therefrom and withdrew the national guardsmen. Judge Davies' decision in question was affirmed by the Court of Appeals on April 28 of the current year. *Faubus et al.* v. *United States et al.*, 8 Cir.,__F2d__. On Monday, September 23, the Negro students entered Central High School under the protection of the police department of the City of Little Rock and of certain members of the Arkansas State Police. A large and demonstrating crowd, however, had gathered around Central High School, which crowd officers on duty could hardly control, and they advised the Superintendent to remove the Negro children from the school which was done.

A short time later the Negro students were readmitted to the school under the protection of combat troops of the regular United States Army which the President sent into Little Rock for that purpose, and eight of these students remained enrolled for the balance of the school year which closed on May 28, 1958. During the entire school year the grounds and interior of Central High School were patrolled first by regular army troops and later by federalized national guardsmen.

The petition for a stay with which we are concerned was originally filed by the Board on February 20, 1958; that pleading, reduced to essentials, alleged that federalized national guardsmen were on duty at the school and were preventing interference with the attendance of the Negro students, that a small group of students with the encouragement of certain adults had created almost daily incidents making it difficult for pupils to learn and teachers to teach, that there existed unrest among students, parents and teachers, which likewise made it difficult for the school district to maintain a satisfactory educational program, and that educational standards were being impaired. The prayer of the original petition was that "the plan of integration heretofore ordered by this Court be realistically reconsidered in the light of existing conditions and that in the interest of all pupils the beginning date of integration be postponed until such time as the concept of 'all deliberate speed' can be clearly defined and effective legal procedures can be obtained which will enable the District to integrate without impairment of the quality of education it is capable of providing under normal conditions." On February 25, 1958, the plaintiffs filed a motion to dismiss the petition on the ground that it stated no claim upon which relief could be granted, and the further ground that it stated no claim for relief from a judgement or order cognizable under Rule 60(b) of the Federal Rules of Civil Procedure.

Although this case had never been on our docket, due to the fact that at the time there was no other judge regularly commissioned in the Eastern District of Arkansas, and in view of the public interest involved in the Board's petition, the Honorable Archibald K. Gardner, Chief Judge of the Court of Appeals for this Circuit, on April 18, 1958, designated us to hear and determine the issues presented by the petition, "and to do such work as may be necessary and incidental to acting upon said petition." This special assignment was made to run from April 21, 1958, to September 1, 1958, both dates inclusive.

On April 28, 1958, we held a preliminary proceeding in this matter, in the course of which we read a prepared statement, which, among other things, directed that the original petition be amended so as to disclose whether the Board desired time to reconsider the plan, or whether it simply wanted a "moratorium" or a "cooling off period," and also so as to give a reasonable indication of how long a postponement the Board felt that it needed at this time.

Subsequently, the Board filed a substituted petition containing allegations more or less similar to those of its original pleading and praying that a stay be granted until January, 1961. In that connection, it was alleged: "Petitioners cannot with certainty determine how long operations under the plan should be postponed, but in the light of existing conditions hereinabove mentioned and in the light of conditions as they will probably exist in the foreseeable future, they are of the opinion that a suspension of operations under the plan until January, 1961 is reasonable and advisable. . . ."

It is the theory of the Board, reflected in its pleadings, evidence and briefs, that the plan of integration which it adopted in 1955, upon the assumption that it would be acceptable and workable, has broken down under the pressure of public opposition, which opposition has manifested itself in a number of ways hereinafter mentioned, and that as a result of the educational program at Central High School has been seriously impaired, that there will be no change in conditions between now and the time that school opens again in September, 1958, and that if the prayer for relief is not granted the situation with which the Board will be confronted in September will be as bad as, if not worse than the one under which it has labored during the past school year, and that it is in the public interest that the requested delay be granted. . . .

From the practically undisputed testimony of the Board's witnesses we find that although the continued attendance of the Negro students at Central High School was achieved throughout the 1957–1958 school year by the physical presence of federal troops, including federalized national guardsmen, nevertheless on account of popular opposition to integration the year was marked by repeated incidents of more or less serious violence directed against the Negro students and their property by numerous bomb threats directed at the school, by a number of nuisance fires started inside the school, by desecration of school property, and by the circulation of cards, leaflets and circulars designed to intensify opposition to integration. Mr. J. O. Powell, the vice-principal for boys at the high school, summed the situation up by saying that the first year of operation under the plan was one of "chaos, bedlam and turmoil" from the beginning.

. . . The president of the Board, Mr. Upton, testified that between the spring and fall of 1957 there was a marked change in public attitude towards the plan, that persons who had formerly been willing to accept it had changed their minds and had come to the conclusion "that the local School Board had not done all it could do to prevent integration, and that we didn't have to have integration;" and vice-principal Powell testified that he believed that the white children involved in the incidents "feel that they are morally correct in their attitude and in their opposition," and that such is due to the "cultural patterns and sociological patterns in this community for many years," and that the students who created the incidents felt that it was wrong to integrate the Negro children into Central High School. . . .

Getting back to the effects of the events of the past school year on the educational program at Central High School, we find more specifically that those events have had a serious and adverse impact upon the students themselves, upon the classroom teachers, upon the administrative personnel of the school, and upon the over-all school program. In addition, said events have cast a serious financial burden upon the school district, which it has had to meet at the expense of normal educational and maintenance functions. . . .

The tensions and strain to which the administrative staff were subjected did not terminate with the close of the school day. Mr. Powell stated that on a typically difficult day his phone would commence ringing as soon as he got home from school, the calls coming from people desiring various types of information; that he has spent as much as three hours on certain days "answering the telephone, or in making calls or dodging calls"; that he has had to work long hours during the evenings and nights on many occasions, and that his social life and normal rest had been interfered with to a definite extent during the entire school year.

Looking toward the approaching school term it was the consensus of opinion on the part of the Board's witnesses, and we find, that there has been no softening of the public attitude in Little Rock toward integration, and we further find, as heretofore stated, that unless some relief is granted the Board the conditions that will prevail in Central High School during the 1958–1959 school year will be as bad as they were during 1957–1958, and will probably deteriorate still further. . . .

We further find that if the attendance of Negro students at Central High School is to be maintained during the next school year, the Board will have to have military assistance or its equivalent, and it is financially unable to bear the expense of hiring a sufficient number of guards to control the situation. It cannot be expected that the Little Rock Police Department will be in a position to detail enough men to afford the necessary protection.

. . . There can be no question that the Board made a prompt and reasonable start toward compliance with the principles laid down in the Brown cases; thereafter, it put its plan into operation and has adhered to it in good faith in the face of great difficulties. Now, it has come here seeking relief only after it has been confronted with what is, from an educational standpoint, an intolerable situation, and it does not ask for an abandonment of its plan nor does it attempt to obtain an indefinite postponement. It is simply requesting a tactical delay. We are convinced that in seeking this delay the Board is still acting in good faith, and, upon the showing that has been made, we are satisfied that the Board needs more time to carry out its plan in an "effective manner," and that to grant the instant petition is in the public interest, and is consistent with good faith compliance, at the earliest practicable date, with the principles above mentioned. In reaching this conclusion we are not unmindful of the admonition of the Supreme Court that the vitality of those principles "cannot be allowed to yield simply because of disagreement with them"; here, however, as pointed out by the Board in its final brief, the opposition to integration in Little Rock is more than a mere mental attitude; it has manifested itself in overt acts which have actually damaged educational standards and which will continue to do so if relief is not granted.

. . . The granting of the Board's petition does not, in our estimation, constitute a yielding to unlawful force or violence, but is simply an exercise of our equitable discretion and good judgement so as to allow a breathing spell in Little Rock, while at the same time preserving educational standards at Central High School.

It being in the public interest, including the interest of both White and Negro students at Little Rock, that we have a peaceful interlude for the period mentioned, an order is being entered permitting the Board to suspend the operation of its said plan until mid-semester of the 1960–1961 school year, without the Board, or the individual members thereof, or the Superintendent of Schools being considered in contempt of this Court; and the Court retains jurisdiction of this cause for such other and further proceedings as many hereafter become necessary or appropriate.

THIS the 20th day of June, 1958.
HARRY J. LEMLEY
United States District Judge

The Program of School Desegregation in Little Rock

United States Commission on Civil Rights, *School Desegregation in Little Rock, Arkansas* (Washington, DC: GPO, 1977), 3–17.

The document below is an official report issued by the US Commission on Civil Rights in June 1977. It reviews the progress made at desegregation in all of the Little Rock schools. Parson's Plan was developed by former superintendent of schools Paul Parson. Plans three, four, and five were internal documents prepared by school officials.

A Staff Report of the United States Commission on Civil Rights, June, 1977

Background

Controversy regarding school desegregation in Little Rock has a long history. During the late 1950s, Central High School became one of the Nation's most notorious high schools. It was the example segregationists used to argue that black and white students could never go to school together in peace. Violence in and around the school prompted President Eisenhower to dispatch Federal troops to Little Rock in order to keep the peace. Many of the scars of that desegregation effort are still present in Little Rock, yet many now feel the city has one of the most successfully desegregated school systems in the Nation.

This study examines the history of the school desegregation effort in Little Rock including the factors behind its successes and failures. In addition to the legal battles, the roles of the community and political leaders, the media, the school administration, teachers, parents, and students will be examined. . . .

History of Desegregation

. . . Schools reopened in 1959 under a pupil assignment desegregation plan, in which attendance zone lines were redrawn to enhance desegregation. This arrangement was kept until 1964, when the district instituted a "freedom of choice" plan allowing students in all grades to attend the school of their choice if space was available.

Developing the "Three Year High School Plan"

Because these arrangements did not produce satisfactory high school desegregation, the district considered several other schemes during the period 1968–70.

The first was the "Parson's Plan" of 1968, which provided for complete high school desegregation (primarily through paired schools) as well as for some elementary school desegregation through the creation of special school complexes in the central city. A second plan was prepared in 1969 by a team from the University of Oregon. The "Oregon Plan" was based on the use of "educational parks" where students from wide areas of the city would attend classes at a single campus. Both of these plans, according to school officials, would have been quite expensive to implement because of new school construction. Cost estimates exceeded $10 million for the Parson's Plan and $5 million for the Oregon Plan. Tax increases to finance these plans were soundly defeated in referendums.

A third desegregation proposal appeared in a plan based on geographic attendance zones. This was presented to the Federal Court in early 1970 but was disapproved.

A fourth proposal called the "5–3–2–2 Plan" (five elementary schools, three middle schools, two junior high schools, and two senior high schools) was filed with the court in 1970 by the Little Rock Board of Education and would have required many children from the western part of the district to be assigned to eastern schools for 5 of their final 7 years of school. This plan would have also required approximately 1,300 additional students to be transported; the court found this plan unacceptable also. The administrative staff then prepared and presented to the board yet another proposal.

This fifth proposal, called "The Three Year High School Plan" was acceptable. This plan also produced a racial balance in all the secondary schools and offered certain advantages over the 5–3–2–2 Plan. Under the Three Year Plan fewer students were reassigned. Required teacher reassignments were reduced by about 50 percent. Central High School was retained as a graduating high school adjacent to the eastern section of the city. Athletic programs and all other extracurricular and cocurricular activities were continued without considerable disruption. Also, the conversion of laboratories and other special facilities was minimized.

Desegregating Elementary Schools, 1971–73

While the Three Year High School Plan was being prepared, the board also developed a plan which the court approved for assigning elementary students in grades one to five. The plan was to be put into effect for the 1971–72 school year with the stipulation that the elementary students desiring to transfer from majority to minority schools would have the right to do so.

At the beginning of the 1972–73 school year, the court required that the district pair and group all elementary schools to eliminate the existing dual system of racially identifiable schools. The court had found the then-existing neighborhood arrangement for the primary grades to be unconstitutional because it did not achieve adequate racial balance. The school board was given until January 1, 1973, to submit a plan whereby each of the 17 racially imbalanced elementary schools would be brought within 10 percent of the overall racial composition of the district's elementary school population. There were to be no elementary schools identifiable as intended for the use of students of a particular race. The district was to provide transportation for students, if necessary, to achieve this goal.

It was assumed that the aggregate districtwide racial composition of the elementary schools would not change as a result of this reorganization (that is to say, no white flight was anticipated). On December 21, 1972, the board of directors submitted to the court, as requested, a plan for the further desegregation of the elementary grades, to be implemented at the beginning of the 1973–74 school year.

On May 9, 1973, the school board filed a motion seeking court approval to implement a kindergarten program commencing with the 1973–74 school year. On June 28, 1973, a stipulation was filed by the plaintiffs and defendants in which they announced to the court that all issues raised in the further desegregation of the elementary grades and the introduction of a kindergarten program into the system had been resolved by agreement of the parties. This stipulation was acceptable to the court and was signed on July 12, 1973, by Judge Henley (E.D. Ark.).

The 1973 Accord

By 1973, the responsibility for further desegration [*sic*] in the elementary schools had been accepted by the board of education of the Little Rock district. Also, the NAACP Legal Defense and Educational Fund approved the court-imposed pairing plan. Therefore, both sides decided to implement the pairing plan as expeditiously as possible (as instructed by the court) and jointly to select a biracial committee to assist the school board with the implementation of the plan. The board of directors and the NAACP Legal Defense and Educational Fund also agreed that for a period of 2 years beginning June 28, 1973—and for as long after that as the board adhered to its commitment contained in the plan—no further legal proceeding would be filed by the NAACP Legal Defense and Educational Fund. The fund would also assist the board in any way to implement successfully the plan for the school 1973–74.

Beginning with the 1973–74 school year, all grades in the Little Rock schools were desegregated. Children from the east side were bused to 12 primary schools located in the west side of the city. Pupils in grades four and five in the west were bused to 10 intermediate schools in the east.

One additional change had been made at the high school level: In 1972 the students at Metropolitan High School were reassigned to one of the three present senior high schools so that the school could be converted into a center for vocational education serving all three school districts in Pulaski County. Little Rock students taking courses at this center were provided bus transportation.

The composite result of those actions was that enrollment at every school was almost equally divided between white and black students. Current school enrollment is approximately 52 percent black and 48 percent white.

The desegregation process was not only successful but extremely smooth, according to school and community observers. In comparison with other communities, there was little or no appreciable conflict. . . .

Conclusions

Desegregation efforts in Little Rock span 19 years. Extensive and involved efforts have been carried out by the courts, the school board, the NAACP and the NAACP Legal Defense and Educational Fund, and the citizens of Little Rock to achieve the goal of a unitary public school system open to all the children of the city regardless of race, color, or creed.

Instead of a comprehensive approach to desegregation, a variety of conflicting plans were introduced after the initial court decision. Some were rejected, and those accepted led to desegregation by segments or grades. This piecemeal desegregation was the strategy followed until the acceptance of a more comprehensive approach in 1973. At that time, the school district and the minority community agreed to work together toward bringing about complete desegregation of the schools.

The black community feels that throughout desegregation it has borne the largest share of the burden—for example, all-black rather than all-white schools were closed. White flight in the late 1960s has increased the degree of residential segregation in the city. Black administrators and teachers continue to complain that they receive unequal treatment and opportunity. Black parents dissatisfied with the unequal burden of busing have nonetheless accepted busing because it provides opportunities for their children to attend better schools.

There is a wide variance in community opinion on the merits of desegregation. The range is from open hostility and concern about the quality of schools and education to positive assertions that desegregation has been of benefit to the schools and the city. The white majority gradually accepted desegregation. Many persons interviewed believed that the efforts to facilitate peaceful desegregation were helpful but could have been more extensive.

Despite the many conflicting opinions surrounding school desegregation in Little Rock, both the school administration and the various community organizations exercised positive leadership in bringing about desegregation. Although many problems still remain, the Little Rock School District has made good progress in desegregating its schools.

The Quality Education Act

General Acts of Arkansas, 1969, 67th General Assembly, Regular Session (January 13 –May 8, 1969), vol. 2, bk. 1, 717–21; *Arkansas Gazette (Little Rock),* January 20, 1979.

Beginning with Initiated Act 1, approved by voters in 1948, and continuing with action by the General Assembly in 1969, school officials focused on reducing the number of school districts as the primary way to improve education. However, consolidation was consistently opposed in the less-populated counties and became one of the major points of conflict between rural and urban Arkansas in the Modern Era.

AN ACT to Improve the Quality of Public Elementary and Secondary Education, and Secondary Education, and for Other Purposes.
Be It Enacted by the General Assembly of the State of Arkansas:
SECTION 1. This act shall be known as "The Quality Education Act of 1969."
SECTION 2. All public elementary and secondary schools with a state department of education rating of less than "A" shall be eliminated not later than June 1, 1979, except as hereinafter provided, and districts operating one or more of such schools shall be dissolved and annexed to another district or districts which operate all schools therein with a minimum rating of "A" or above. The County Board of Education shall abolish said districts and shall annex the territory of such districts to the receiving district or districts in a geographically contiguous manner. The receiving district or districts shall be designated by the County Board of Education and said receiving district or districts are hereby mandated to accept such district or parts of districts.

SECTION 3. In the event a County Board of Education fails or refuses to comply with the mandates of this Act, the Commissioner of Education shall notify the Chancery Court having jurisdiction not later than June 10, 1979, and such Court shall, not later than June 20th subsequent to the mandate, issue a Court Order or orders implementing the intent of this Act. Any school district may effect consolidation or annexation under provisions of existing law provided said consolidation or annexation is final prior to the effective date of the mandates of this act.

SECTION 4. Irrespective of other provisions in this Act there shall be at least one senior high school and one or more elementary schools maintained in each county of the State. In the event there is no district with a senior high school and/or elementary school with an "A" rating or higher in any county, the State Board of Education shall have authority to designate which high school and elementary schools in said county. Such designation by the State Board of Education shall be limited to not more than one in each county. In such cases the County Board shall, not later than June 1, 1980, dissolve and annex the remaining districts to the district designated by the State Board of Education to operate the senior high school and elementary schools in the county.

SECTION 5. The State Board of Education shall have authority to designate, on an annual basis, any district, or school within a district, which in its judgment is so isolated as to make its consolidation, or operation if it is a school within a district, with another district, in keeping with this Act, impractical and unwise. If and when such a designation is made the county and local authorities shall be notified. Such notification shall be made at least six months prior to the beginning of the new fiscal year. The State Board of Education may provide supplemental funds from the Minimum Foundation Program or comparable fund to such isolated districts or schools. Such funds as may be provided must be used for the purpose or purposes designated by the State Board of Education and funds therefor shall come from Minimum Foundation Programs Funds. No district or school designated as isolated shall receive additional funds sufficient to pay more than four additional teachers, using the local district salary schedule. The purpose of these funds shall be to improve the quality of the education program in said districts, and the judgment of the State Board of Education shall be final. The Board may not, however, designate more than a total of seven isolated districts and/or schools

in any one year. A district designated as isolated and later not so designated shall become subject to the provisions of this Act.

• • •

Opposition to the Quality Education Act

BATESVILLE (AP)—Local control of school districts will go down
the drain if school consolidation becomes a reality, James O'Dell, director
of the Arkansas Rural Education Association, said Thursday.

"If we go to a large regulated school district, it will effectively wipe
out local control of school districts," O'Dell told about 40 school administrators and school board members while at Batesville trying to recruit
members for the Association. O'Dell is superintendent of Thornton
High School in Calhoun County.

"Society has conditioned us to feel we are less than first class," he
said. "But our air is clean and our water is unpolluted. The neighbors
know each other and there is very close communication between our
schools and our communities."

He said that Governor Clinton is among those that favor consolidation of small school districts and that he had sent Mr. Clinton and the
legislature a list of alternatives to consolidation.

He recommended, among other things, that state-funded resource
cooperatives be established; that rural schools be adequately financed
and the state funds be distributed to school districts on a per teacher
basis. He also said a position should be created in the state Education
Department for a person to direct programs for improving the quality
of rural schools.

O'Dell also said rural schools should be well represented in any study
concerning reorganization of school district. There are no school consolidation proposals in the legislature now, but Governor Clinton said
he would have a bill creating a study commission to produce a consolidation plan.

E. THE NATURAL STATE

Rapid industrialism in the three decades following World War II was not
without its detractors. For many Arkansans, potential industrial waste
and byproducts—often with accompanying soil, air, and water pollution

—could not be offset merely with the promise of more jobs. For those Arkansans, the state's future was best charted by controlling industrial growth and emphasizing the state's natural resources. State agencies took the lead in promoting Arkansas as the "Natural State"—an ironic reversal of efforts by boosters who tried for more than one hundred years to escape this "outdoor" image. Promotion of Arkansas as the Natural State encountered opposition from some landowners and developers with quite different interests in and uses for the state's resources.

Water for Arkansas

United States Geological Survey, *Water for Arkansas*
(Washington, DC: GPO, 1970), 19–24.

This report issued by the Arkansas Geological Commission estimated the water resources in Arkansas in 1966. Below-average rainfall caused the state's political, agricultural, and industrial leaders to reexamine existing water policies. Obviously, any policy tied to resources assumed the availability of those resources. The report raised important questions as to supply and allocation.

We know that our most important source of water in Arkansas comes from an average annual rainfall of about 49 inches. We also know that this will average out to about 120 billion gallons of water per day. However, as we have seen, water is in constant motion in the hydrologic cycle and is not always positioned for convenient interception use. Consequently, not all of the 120 billion gallons of water per day is available for our use.

About 75 billion gallons of the 120 billion is immediately returned to another position in the hydrologic cycle as the precipitation evaporates from water bodies, wet land surfaces, roads, housetops, and grass, trees, and other plants (evapotranspiration, ET). Of the remaining 45 billion gallons, about 40 billion gallons almost immediately becomes surface water runoff. About 5 billion gallons is added to the underground water supply to slowly move toward and into rivers to also eventually become runoff water.

In addition to the foregoing, Arkansas receives over 30 billion gallons of water per day from other states through the Arkansas, White, Red, and St. Francis Rivers and the tributaries to each. The Mississippi River at Memphis has an average flow of about 120 billion gallons per day. Thus Arkansas has access to a large surface water supply "piped" in by natural means.

Surface-water storage in reservoirs in Arkansas has developed at a rapid rate since 1940. Water has been impounded for floods and erosion control, power, navigation, water supply, recreation, or for multiple purposes. Nearly 4,000 billion gallons of storage capacity is presently available in the State for water supply and power.

Many small reservoirs that are used principally for irrigation dot the landscape. The number of these has increased in the last 20 years. The Grand Prairie region in east-central Arkansas is an example of an area of extensive development of surface-water reservoirs where the water is stored for irrigation of rice and soybeans. More than 200 reservoirs have been constructed in the Grand Prairie region since 1910. The capacity of the reservoirs is small and more than half cover only 15 to 40 acres and are shallow.

Many small stock ponds ranging in size from 1 to 10 acres are found throughout Arkansas with new ponds being constructed almost daily. The multitude of ponds and reservoirs dotting the countryside is particularly noticeable from an airplane.

Considering all types and sizes of reservoirs, lakes, and ponds, there is about 6,000 billion gallons of storage capacity presently (1965) available on the land surface in Arkansas, not counting the more than 2,000 billion gallons storage capacity reserved specifically for storage of flood waters.

The amount of water in storage in the ground is many times greater than that coursing the State in rivers and that in impoundments. An estimated average of 5 billion gallons of water per day is available from transient storage in aquifers. An additional estimated 200,000 billion gallons of water occurs as permanent storage beneath the land surfaces.

How much water is there in Arkansas? For all purposes of use from all sources, Arkansas has an estimated 30 billion gallons of water per day available for the future. This is about 20 times more than the State's present requirements, assuming the water is used only one time.

Are we in danger of being short of water? Not when we view our total resources, but the availability of a large quantity of water does not insure an endless supply with no water shortages or problems. We need to know not only how much water we have but also "how do we get it?" and "how do we keep it?"

Preserving the Buffalo River

Orval E. Faubus to William F. Cassidy, December 10, 1965,
Correspondence Files, Ozark Society, Little Rock.

The following letter is from Gov. Orval Faubus to the Little Rock
District of the US Army Corps of Engineers. The Buffalo River
Project was a long and much disputed controversy involving preservationists who wanted to preserve the river's natural beauty and
business interests who wished to dam the stream and promote
development in the region. Governor Faubus's letter is considered
by many to be the critical factor in winning the argument for the
preservationists.

STATEMENT
By Governor Orval Faubus to the Corps of Engineers
On the Disposition of the Buffalo River in Arkansas
Lt. Gen. William F. Cassidy, USA December 10, 1965
Chief of Engineers
Washington, D.C. 20315

Dear General Cassidy:
     Re: ENGCW-PD
     Sometime ago you provided to the Executive Director, Arkansas Soil
and Water Commission, a copy of the proposed report of the Chief of
Engineers, together with the reports of the Board of Engineers for Rivers
and Harbors, and the District and Division Engineers, on an interim
report on Buffalo River Basin, Arkansas (Gilbert Reservoir). This was
done for my review and comment, in accordance with Section 1 of Public
Law 534, 78th Congress, and Public Law 85–624.
     I am also aware of a proposal of the Department of the Interior,
National Park Service, to create what would become known as a National
River in the very same area as the proposed Gilbert Dam. Your agency
is also aware of this proposal, because it is discussed in your report, and
the proposed Gilbert Dam is recommended as a compromise proposal.
I have studied closely both proposals, and my comments are as follows.
     1. The building of a dam (or dams) on the Buffalo River is not essen-
tial for flood control in the White River Valley area, and the creation of
hydroelectric power is not essential.
     2. As an attraction for tourists, or use as a recreational area, the dam

and lake would be only one more attraction, of which there are already five in the White River system, five more in the state (one more under construction), and a half dozen or more now finished or under construction on the Arkansas River. The drawing power of the dam and lake would be limited. A properly developed National River would be a national and international attraction, drawing additional tourists that would number into the tens of thousands annually.

3. Tentative plans for a National River call for the establishment of three major visitor centers. The first would be at Silver Hill on Highway 65 in Searcy County (near the site of proposed Gilbert Dam). Here would be located the National River headquarters, the maintenance area headquarters, and ranger station headquarters. Also a major camping area, a major picnic area, a district ranger station, and boat access points would be established at this point, and last but not least, a museum.

The second visitor center would be at Pruitt in Newton County on Highway 7. Besides the camping and picnic areas, boat access, maintenance, and district ranger headquarters, there would be a residence area. The third center would be at Buffalo River State Park in Marion County on Highway 14, and would be much the same as the second. (A fourth center could be located at Mt. Judea in Newton County on Highway No. 123.)

Three other ranger stations are proposed: the first located at the mouth of the Buffalo River, the second at Woolem, and the third at Ponca.

The proposal calls for nine (9) primitive camps on the river, which would be accessible only by boat. Six (6) others would be accessible by boat and by road, making a total of fifteen (15) primitive camps. There would be six (6) other boat accesses, or crossings of the river, making a total of twelve (12) boat launching areas in addition to the major visitor centers.

A pioneer farm is proposed for Richland Valley, with barns, log cabins, sorghum mills, and water mills.

Nature trails will lead to such areas as Bat Cave, Lost Valley, Big Bluff, Hemmed-In-Hollow, Peter Point, and others. Camp Orr for Boy Scouts would be retained and assisted.

4. There would be twice as many permanent employees to maintain and operate the National River, as would be required for the dam and lake. In addition, large numbers of temporary employees would be

required during the summer season for the National River (as is now the case in all National Parks).

5. With a dam and lake, the land is inundated, with a National River, the land remains, to grow beautiful trees of many kinds, dozens of varieties of wild flowers, and some crops. Many of the present residents would be permitted to remain on the land. The same fields and woods would continue to provide a home for thousands of wild birds, including quail and wild turkey, and continue to produce deer, fox, squirrel, rabbit, raccoon, opposum, mink, and other game. Frogs of every size and kind join with unnumbered katydids to make the summer night musical for the tired camper seeking rest and relief from social and political problems, and the fevered market place.

6. A dam and lake would cover, forever, miles and miles of tree-lined, flower-bedecked river banks; hundreds of the most beautiful holes (pools) of water that have ever been created; numbers of rock-strewn, rippling shoals; the finest sand-bar camp sites to be found anywhere; and dozens of magnificent towering cliffs. All of these are worth retaining as a part of a National River, because of a unique, inspirational, soul-resting beauty which cannot be found in comparable expanse anywhere else.

7. Already created dams and lakes are to be found on every side of the beautiful Buffalo River area within a distance of 30 to 100 miles. The creation of another facility would add little to the attraction of the area as a whole.

On the other hand, the creation of a properly developed National River would complement the attractiveness of the area. It would create a balanced recreational area unlike any to be found in any other region of the United States.

Fishing and skiing are the main, and almost only sport, on the large lakes. There is little, if any, pleasure in boating. The National River would attract the fishermen and the hunters, the boatmen, canoeists, camera bugs, campers, bird watchers, swimmers, and wildlife lovers of all kinds. The area would have accommodations and unusual appeal for family groups. Were there not already dams and lakes for flood control, generation of electric power, and recreation, this would be a different proposition. However, with the present situation, the National River can add far more to the region, and be of far greater benefit in *every way* than can another dam and lake.

It is well to point out also that by a conservative estimate, 90% of the thousands of visitors to Buffalo River State Park favor the National River over the dam and lake. Also, a college-trained businessman, operating a business in the very heart of the area of greatest controversy, became sufficiently interested to make a poll of his visiting customers. He was amazed to find that 95% of the visitors in the area favored the creation of the National River. An awareness of this sentiment probably led to the change in attitude of the members of both the Chambers of Commerce of Mountain Home and Yellville, the county seats of two counties through which the Buffalo River flows. Both groups now support the National River proposal, and have withdrawn their support of the dam. There is no question that both aesthetically and economically, the approval and proper construction of a National River will be far better for the area, the State of Arkansas, and the nation, than would be the construction of the proposed Gilbert Dam and Lake.

Of course, there are other considerations. We cannot place a material value upon the soul, the spirit, and the mind of men. The mind of man must constantly be refreshed, his spirit periodically renewed, and his soul, the greatest force for good is man's capacity to enjoy and be inspired by the unspoiled beauty of God's creation. The Buffalo River area is one of the greatest examples of the majesty of God's creation. The beauty of the region cannot be adequately described in any of the many languages of man.

"The heavens declare the Glory of God, and the firmament sheweth his handiwork." Standing in the Buffalo River State Park, on a point overlooking a stretch of this beautiful river, is a plaque erected in memory of a little boy. The plaque bears the following inscription:

> There are little corners of this earth put aside by nature to be discovered by and to bring joy to little boys. The lands over which you look here, across this beautiful river, are such a corner; and the arrowheads to be found there, the tiny box canyon with its waterfall and the spring above, are set aside forever for all little boys in memory of another little boy who did discover freedom and joy here. . . .
>
> Warren Mallory Johnston

In so many places, the giant power-driven machines of man are flattening the hedges, fence rows, and nooks, where the song birds nested, and the timid rabbits reared their young; draining the swamp where the wild ducks and raccoons once found refuge; leveling the forests where once roamed the wild deer; scarring the mountains and pushing down the lofty crags where perched the eagles; filling up the beautiful pools which furnished a home for the wary bass and the brilliant golden-hued sunfish.

A conscious effort on the part of society must be made to preserve a part of our God-given beauty, or very soon there will no longer be left a sufficient number of these "little corners of this earth put aside by nature to be discovered by . . . little boys," to bring pleasure to their pure fresh minds, and joy to their innocent hearts. Unless this effort is made, under the leadership of the people's government, soon there will no longer be a sufficient number of accessible places where families can have wholesome pleasure and adventure together. This will constitute a loss to society, for which all material wealth cannot compensate. For these and other reasons, your proposed construction of Gilbert Dam is unacceptable. I praise the Corps of Engineers for its fine accomplishments. I have always been in the forefront in supporting your program of the construction of dams as a proper means of conservation, and the building of the nation. For the very first time in my life, I must disapprove one of your proposals. However, it is a unique and exceptional situation, as the facts I have set out prove beyond any doubt. I support the National River proposal.

Sincerely,

Orval E. Faubus, Governor

OEF:dit

Channelization along the Cache

Arkansas Gazette (Little Rock), October 2, 1971.

Another dimension in the controversy over "The Natural State" concerned the Cache River flood plain. This region not only represented some of the state's most fertile farmland but was also a natural habitat for migratory waterfowl and a variety of other wildlife. That the river valley contained an abundant supply of hardwoods and flooded periodically only added to the controversy. Many landowners along the Cache wanted to dredge the channel, drain the surrounding swampland, and control flooding. Sportsmen and wildlife interests argued to preserve the natural habitat.

For almost a quarter century agitation has continued in portions of Northeast Arkansas for full-scale federal implementation of what is known as the Cache River–Bayou DeView drainage project.

Key opposition of channelization along 231 miles of ecologically important, hardwood lowlands has been provided through the years by the state Game and Fish Commission (as well as wildlife and other conservation groups). In mid-summer, however, the commission adopted a position softening its opposition, although it was still "philosophically" opposed. It was a disappointing position, for the passage of time and events have drawn the issue of channelization much more sharply, to the point that it now is indicated that the advantages of a Cache River–Bayou DeView drainage project may be outweighed by the disadvantages.

That is why the Game and Fish Commission's reconsideration of the project is so welcome and why its subsequent hardening decision last week is so gratifying. The commission adopted a statement opposing any further drainage in the project area, because of the ecological and environmental damage that would result. The clear indication was that at least some members of the commission were ready to vigorously oppose the project, placing aside a passive role of opposition. Some sentiment was expressed that the commission should do whatever is necessary, including the filing of a lawsuit, to block construction of the channelization project by the Army Engineers.

Powerful interests have been promoting construction of the big ditch—which is what the project would turn two lowland streams into—for several reasons, and the Army Engineers seem terribly itchy to get on with their part of the multi-million dollar project. Costs in some estimates now have been placed at $60 million, about double the estimated cost when the project was first planned in 1949. The ditches would stretch from the Missouri line to the confluence with the White River near Clarendon. They would touch Monroe, Woodruff, Jackson, Cross, Poinsett, Craighead, Lawrence, Greene and Clay Counties. Originally, the principal reason given in support was that there was a need for flood control in nearby lands used to raise soybeans, cotton and rice. Some land owners in the lower portion, however, have been especially concerned in the past that flooding dangers would actually be increased on the lower reaches.

What the issue really comes down to, however, is economics and the values that are assigned to this very large problem of public land and water management. It is difficult indeed to accept the idea that the public interest dictates support of further drainage and clearing of land along the Cache for agricultural purposes, principally soybean production. It is sometimes argued that clearing and some sort of drainage is going to take place regardless of the federal project, and perhaps this is true, but that does not make channelization consistent with the larger public interest that must take into account values other than crop production.

The issue of implementing the Cache River–Bayou DeView project was actually reopened earlier this year by the Engineers' presentation for public discussion of what has come to be known as a "fish and wildlife mitigation" plan in the project area. It proposes, essentially, to set aside 30,000 acres to preserve and develop the natural habitat. All of it would be in lower portions of the river and bayou.

It was this mitigation plan that led the Game and Fish Commission in July to soften its opposition, the idea being that the plan offered at least some small opportunity to conserve fish and wildlife that would be virtually wiped out without mitigation. Additional thought urged on the commission by individuals and groups has led to the withdrawal of approval and a new policy position that it will oppose any further drainage in the project area, because of the resultant loss of wildlife that was adjusted to the existing habitat, loss of hardwood and commercial fisheries and lowering of the watertable in the area.

It is our own feeling that Arkansas may well have reached the point of diminishing returns on channelization and that the Cache–Bayou DeView project, even with "mitigation" at least for the moment is not justified. It may never be. Preserving fish and wildlife habitat is one important element. Others involve consideration of ecological balance, the question of whether present values can provide a true assessment of the costs and benefits.

There are other considerations as well, but the fact remains that in the context of national policy we really don't know a great deal about the true value of what's left of the country's wetlands, as the Council on Environmental Quality suggests in its most recent report. Sometimes it is argued that land clearing and drainage projects are going to continue regardless of the large federal ditching project. Perhaps that is true, but there are alternatives available for $60 million that could preserve what is left of an ecological system that may be worth far more. Machinery already exists for the federal government to acquire such lands, or even to pay farmers not to drain and clear land—just as some are paid not to plant cotton. There is, we are convinced, a way to serve all interests—especially the basic public interest—by reconsidering the Cache River–Bayou DeView project at whatever level, including the Congress, that is required. Sometimes "progress" can be made by leaving things are [*sic*] they are, letting nature taken its own course.

FOR FURTHER READING

Scholarly publications about Arkansas's Modern Era are both limited and unevenly distributed. Most attention has been focused on the 1957 Little Rock school crisis. Of the multiple titles published on the event, Elizabeth Jacoway, *Turn Away Thy Son: Little Rock, the Crisis that Shocked the Nation* (New York: Simon & Schuster, 2007); Karen Anderson, *Little Rock: Race and Resistance at Central High* (Princeton, NJ: Princeton University Press, 2010); and Sondra Gordy, *Finding the Lost Year: What Happened When Little Rock Closed Its Schools* (Fayetteville: University of Arkansas Press, 2008) provide the best coverage of the crisis. For a broader context of the crisis see John Kirk, *Beyond Little Rock: The Origins and Legacies of the Central High Crisis* (Fayetteville: University of Arkansas Press, 2007). Books by Daisy Bates, *The Long Shadow of Little Rock: A Memoir* (New York: David McKay Co., 1962); Orval Faubus, *Down from the Hills* (Little Rock: Pioneer Press, 1980); Elizabeth Huckaby, *Crisis at Central High, Little Rock, 1957–58* (Baton Rouge: Louisiana State University Press, 1980); Virgil Blossom, *It Has Happened Here* (New York: Harper & Co., 1959); Melba Patrillo Beals, *Warriors Don't Cry* (New York: Simon and Schuster, 1995); Carlotta Walls LaNier, *A Mighty Long Way: My Journey to Justice at Little Rock Central High School* (New York: Random House, 2009); and Terrance J. Roberts, *Lessons from Little Rock* (Little Rock: Butler Center for Arkansas Studies, 2009), present perspectives on the crisis by seven participants.

The best book on politics during this era is by Diane Blair, *Do the People Rule* (Lincoln: University of Nebraska Press, 1988); this volume was revised, updated, and issued as a second edition in 2005 by Jay Barth following Blair's untimely death. Kathy Kunzinger Urwin, *Agenda for Reform:*

Winthrop Rockefeller as Governor, 1967–1971 (Fayetteville: University of Arkansas Press, 1991); Dale Bumpers, *Best Lawyer in a One Lawyer Town* (New York: Random House, 2003); David Pryor, *A Pryor Commitment: The Autobiography of David Pryor* (Little Rock: Butler Center for Arkansas Studies, 2008); and David Maraniss, *First in His Class: The Biography of Bill Clinton* (New York: Simon and Schuster, 1996) provide coverage of the leading politicians in the period. Thomas Murton and Joe Hyams's *Accomplices to the Crime* (New York: Grove Press, 1970) provides an insider's account, somewhat sensational, of the state's prison conditions in the 1960s.

Books of a general nature include Ben F. Johnson III, *Arkansas and Modern America 1930–1999* (Fayetteville: University of Arkansas Press, 2000); Bethany Moreon, *To Serve God and Wal-Mart: The Making of Christian Free Enterprise* (Cambridge, MA: Harvard University Press, 2009); and Robert L. Brown, *Defining Moments: Historic Decisions by Arkansas Governors from McMath through Huckabee* (Fayetteville: University of Arkansas Press, 2010).

CHAPTER X

Contemporary Arkansas, since 1985

INTRODUCTION

The past quarter century of Arkansas history has been dominated by change. In politics the state became one of the last in the Union to abandon its century-long tradition of a two-year term for its executive officers by extending tenure to four years with eligibility for reelection. Many political scientists considered the two-year term as being the single most significant barrier to executive leadership and modernization in the state. Extending the term of office for the executive branch was followed closely by another amendment to the 1874 constitution that limited the length of service for executive and legislative office holders. Executive officers were limited to a total of eight years of service in one office and members of the General Assembly were "term limited" to six years as state representative and eight years as state senator. The same amendment (73) intended to limit terms in office for members of the US Congress, but that provision was declared unconstitutional in federal district court. Further evidence of change came with voters approving a plan for the General Assembly to convene annually, rather than bi-annually, a tradition that also dated to 1874. Perhaps the most dramatic political change in the past twenty-five years was William Jefferson (Bill) Clinton, the state's forty-second governor, being elected, then reelected, as the nation's forty-second president. His eight years in office focused more national attention on the state than any event since the Little Rock school crisis in 1957.

Contemporary Arkansas also received considerable national attention by becoming the only state in the Union to adopt a "creation science" law that required balanced treatment of evolution and creation science. The law was in part a result of a major rift in US society between liberals and conservatives in politics and between modernists and traditionalists in religion—popularly known as the "cultural war." Politics and religion were combined when a religious group known as the Moral Majority actively participated in the 1980 presidential campaign to advance its positions on key issues, including abortion, evolution, and prayer or Bible reading in the public schools. A key component of the Moral Majority's agenda was to offer an alternative to scientific evolution. Variously known as "creation science" or "intelligent design," this alternative was meant to defend the biblical account of creation. The law was declared to be unconstitutional by a federal district judge, but not before the state received extensive national publicity on the matter and for a time became ground zero in the cultural wars.

The election of Arkansas governor Bill Clinton as president of the United States was of tremendous importance to his native state. Arkansans traveling abroad stopped being asked about their racial views and instead answered questions about their most famous and much-admired citizen. The selection of Little Rock as the location for the Clinton Presidential Library made an important contribution to both the cultural life of the city and its tourist industry. Sam Walton, founder of Walmart, also became a national and international figure of importance as his chain of stores gradually grew to be the world's largest retail corporation. Whatever were its past and present problems, Arkansas had demonstrated that it could produce world leaders.

By the 1980s recreational use of illegal drugs and a new form of cocaine, called "crack," reached near epidemic proportions in many regions of the nation. Drug trafficking became a multimillion-dollar business as various youth gangs and their suppliers vied for control of local neighborhoods in most major cities. In 1994, California enacted the single toughest penal statute in state history: "Three Strikes and You're Out." Provisions included increased punishment for repeat offenders convicted of serious or violent felonies. The statute was both lauded and assailed for its stiff penalties and systemic repercussions. Arkansas adopted the "three strikes law"; and that, coupled with a redefinition of cocaine use, and sentencing guidelines mandating that felons serve a minimum of 70 percent of their sentences without parole, led to a huge and rapid increase in the state's prison population. In the first decade of the new millennium, new penal legislation moved the pendulum back toward leniency.

Significant gains in the state's retail and service industries, as well important new developments in the extraction of natural resources, led to an economic boom in the late twentieth and early twenty-first centuries. In addition to Walmart, there was Tyson Foods, Inc., based in Springdale, which used an aggressive business plan featuring mergers and acquisitions and became the world's largest food-processing company. Arkansas Best Freight Company, initially organized to service the transport needs of Walmart, expanded its client base and by 2000 had become one of the nation's largest freight companies, and Little Rock–based Dillard's expanded to become one of the largest department store chains in the nation. These Arkansas-based corporations were greatly aided in their incubation stage with start-up capital and financial services provided by Stephens Inc., also based in Little Rock and until the mid-1990s the largest investment banking company not located in New York's Wall Street district.

In one important way, however, Arkansas still struggled: from the 1970s, in the second decade of the twenty-first century, per capita personal income in the state ranged between 75 and 80 percent of the national average. Public agencies and private citizen groups had long struggled to attract industry to Arkansas, and at the beginning of the new millennium there was a new push to create a "knowledge-based" economic sector. Meanwhile, the development of underground natural gas sources gave a boost to the state's economy but brought potential problems as well.

A. POLITICS

Three amendments to the Arkansas Constitution in the contemporary period had seemingly contradictory goals with regard to state politics. Amendment 63 greatly increased the power and influence of the executive branch by extending the term of office for the state's constitutional officers from a two-year term to a four-year term. A decade later voters, seemingly disturbed by the "professionalization of politics," moved to limit the number of years an individual could serve in the same public office. After a decade of experience, most political observers agree that the term limit amendment has achieved its desired effects. However, those same observers also agree that term limits have contributed to a generation of inexperienced lawmakers and greatly increased the influence of experienced lobbyists. The concept of "citizen-lawmaker" was further confused in the first decade of the twenty-first century when voters agreed to amend the constitution to require annual sessions of the General Assembly. The fourth document below, by then lieutenant governor Win Paul Rockefeller, a member of the Republican Party, offers one perspective on the impact the term limit amendment could have on Arkansas politics.

Four-Year Terms for State Constitutional Officers

State of Arkansas, *Constitution of Arkansas,* Amendment 63.

This amendment, adopted in 1984, greatly increased the power and influence of the executive branch by extending the term of office for the state's constitutional officers from two years to four years. For over one hundred years the executive branch was overshadowed by the legislative branch with respect to policymaking and leadership. By the last quarter of the twentieth century, the cost of campaigning every two years limited the number of candidates seeking executive offices. The four-year term gave the governor more opportunities to exert leadership.

Section: 1. Executive Department—Term of office.

The Executive Department of this State shall consist of a Governor, Lieutenant Governor, Secretary of State, Treasurer of State, Auditor of State, Attorney General and Commissioner of State Lands, all of whom shall keep their offices at the seat of government, and hold their offices for the term of four (4) years, and until their successors are elected and qualified.

Arkansas Term Limitation Amendment

State of Arkansas, *Constitution of Arkansas,* Amendment 73.

Concern that public officials were increasing unresponsive to certain issues in the body politic caused a group of concerned citizens to secure enough signatures to have an initiative petition on term limits placed on the ballot for the general election in 1991. Voters approved the petition and the amendment was added to the Arkansas Constitution in 1993.

Preamble: The people of Arkansas find and declare that this amendment began as an initiated act and was approved by voters in 1992. Originally intended to term limit both state and federal officials, the provision effecting United States Representatives and Senators was ruled unconstitutional in federal district court. It is one of the most restrictive term limit provisions in the nation. Elected officials who remain in office too long become preoccupied with reelection and ignore their duties as representatives of the people. Entrenched incumbency has reduced voter participation and has led to an electoral system that is less free, less competitive, and less representative than the system established by the Founding Fathers. Therefore, the people of Arkansas, exercising their reserved powers, herein limit the terms of elected officials. . . .

1. Executive Branch.

(a) The Executive Department of this State shall consist of a Governor, Lieutenant Governor, Secretary of State, Treasurer of State, Auditor of State, Attorney General, and Commissioner of State Lands, all of whom shall keep their offices at the seat of government, and hold their offices for the term of four years, and until their successors are elected and qualified.

(b) No elected officials of the Executive Department of this State may serve in the same office more than two such four year terms.

2. Legislative Branch.

(a) The Arkansas House of Representatives shall consist of members to be chosen every second year by the qualified electors of the several counties. No member of the Arkansas House of Representatives may serve more than three such two year terms.

(b) The Arkansas Senate shall consist of members to be chosen every four years by the qualified electors of the several districts. No member of the Arkansas Senate may serve more than two such four year terms.

3. Congressional Delegation.

(a) Any person having been elected to three or more terms as a member of the United States House of Representatives from Arkansas shall not be certified as a candidate and shall not be eligible to have his/her name placed on the ballot for election to the United States House of Representatives from Arkansas.

(b) Any person having been elected to two or more terms as a member of the United States Senate from Arkansas shall not be certified as a candidate and shall not be eligible to have his/her name placed on the ballot for election to the United States Senate from Arkansas.

4. Severability.

The provisions of this Amendment are severable, and if any should be held invalid, the remainder shall stand.

5. Provisions Self-executing.

Provisions of this Amendment shall be self-executing.

6. Application.

(a) This Amendment to the Arkansas Constitution shall take effect and be in operation on January 1, 1993, and its provisions shall be applicable to all persons thereafter seeking election to the offices specified in this Amendment.

(b) All laws and constitutional provisions which conflict with this Amendment are hereby repealed to the extent that they conflict with this amendment.

Annual Sessions of the General Assembly

State of Arkansas, *Constitution of Arkansas,* Amendment 84.

Since statehood in 1836, Arkansas has been administered under five constitutions (including the documents adopted by Confederate and Union supporters in the Civil War). Each constitution stipulated bi-annual sessions of the General Assembly. However, as the demands of government became more complex, state leaders were forced to schedule more and more special sessions to effectively deal with legislation. In 2008 voters changed this 150-year tradition by approving this legislatively referred amendment calling for the General Assembly to meet annually.

Amendment No. 86—Providing for annual sessions of the General Assembly
Amended Ark. Const., Art. 5, §§ 5, 17, 29, 34, 39, 40.
Article 5
(a) The General Assembly shall meet at the seat of government every year.

(b) The General Assembly shall meet in regular session on the second Monday in January of each odd-numbered year to consider any bill or resolution. The General Assembly may alter the time at which the regular session begins.

(c)(1) Beginning in 2010, the General Assembly shall meet in fiscal session on the second Monday in February of each even-numbered year to consider only appropriations bills. The General Assembly may alter the time at which the fiscal session begins.

(2) A bill other than an appropriation bill may be considered in a fiscal session if two thirds (2/3) of the members of each house of the General Assembly approve consideration of the bill.

(d) The General Assembly, by a vote of two-thirds (2/3) of the members elected to each house of the General Assembly, may alter the dates of the regular session and the fiscal session so that regular session occur in an even numbered years and the fiscal session occur in odd numbered years.

Approved November 2008

Effects of Term Limits in Arkansas

Win Rockefeller, "Effects of Term Limits in Arkansas: New Faces and New Ideas," *Spectrum: The Journal of State and Local History* (January 1, 2005), 3ff.

Win Paul Rockefeller lived in the governor's mansion while his father, Winthrop Rockefeller, served as governor from 1969 to 1971. The senior Rockefeller spent a large portion of his personal fortune trying to build a two-party political system in the state and reduce the influence of entrenched political leaders. Win Paul Rockefeller later served as lieutenant governor of the state and saw some of his father's efforts succeed as the Arkansas General Assembly became more politically balanced between Democrat and Republican members. Here he argues the benefits of term limits for state legislators.

Imagine that you are an Arkansan in the voting booth on Election Day. As you scan your choices, you can practically hear your legislator whispering, "If you don't reelect me, the district will lose the advantages of my seniority." You know this particular legislator is dishonest and incompetent, but you also know that if you replace him, your district goes to the back of the line for committee assignments and local spending projects. So you vote for the guy—again.

The seniority system left Arkansans little choice but to return their legislators to office year after year, decade after decade. The Arkansas Legislature remained firmly ensconced in the hands of a powerful few who governed uncreatively and occasionally corruptly. Republicans had an especially difficult time crashing the party. There were no more than three or four Republicans in the Legislature when my father was elected governor in 1966. When I was elected lieutenant governor 30 years later, the count wasn't much higher: 14 Republicans in the House and seven in the Senate.

Arkansas voters—and not just Republicans—knew the system needed to be reformed. In 1992, 60 percent of them voted for one of the nation's toughest term limits laws: three two-year terms in the House; two four-year terms in the Senate; and two four-year terms for executive branch officers. They did this despite the opposition of legislators and lobbyists who argued that it was undemocratic (The people democratically decided it wasn't.); that it would increase the power of lobbyists (Then why were they against it?); and that it would lead to bad legislation (That never happened before term limits, did it?). Arkansas' term limits law forced old-guard legislators to give up seats they considered their birthrights and gave other public-spirited Arkansans a chance to serve. In the 2003 session, 35 legislators—34 in the House, one in the Senate—served their first terms. Moreover, the genuine two-party system my father fought to create is finally becoming a reality. In the 2003 session, Republicans were a sizable minority with 30 representatives and eight senators—too small to control either chamber but enough to serve as an effective voice for their constituents.

Opponents argue that term limits rob state government of institutional memory, but Arkansas' law allows elected officials to remain in public service by foregoing the advantages of incumbency and running for new positions every few years. Term-limited House members are allowed to run for the Senate and vice versa, so a legislator can serve up to 14 years. In 2003, 29 of the 35 senators had previously served in the House, and two House members had served in the Senate. Elected officials can move from one branch to another, such as the attorney general and state auditor who are former legislators. Executive branch officers are also allowed to run for other executive branch offices: the term-limited state auditor (a former legislator, by the way) was elected state treasurer while the former land commissioner was elected secretary of state in 2002. Finally, there are no prohibitions on term-limited legislators and executive branch officers running for federal offices. In 2004, two of our congressmen and one of our senators were former state legislators, and three state legislators ran against incumbents in Washington.

As president of the Senate, I have observed pre-term limits and post-term limits legislative bodies. I won't deny that some of today's legislators are as self-serving as some of those in the past, and certainly there is a learning curve for all incoming freshmen. But while new legislators lack experience, most are committed to constituent service, rooted in their communities and less beholden to entrenched interests than the 30-year veterans who once roamed these halls. The Capitol's mid-session social scene has grown much less exciting, as most of today's legislators spend their evenings in their apartments studying bills rather than attending the good-ole-boy parties sponsored by lobbyists that were so common before.

In 2004, Arkansas voters soundly defeated a constitutional amendment that would have weakened the current law by allowing legislators to serve six two-year terms in the House and three four-year terms in the Senate. It was destined to fail. Term limits are popular because they effectively open the process to new faces, new ideas and new leadership. And that's coming from someone serving his term-limited last term.

Arkansas Governors' Poll, 1998

Cal Ledbetter Jr. and C. Fred Williams, "The Arkansas Governors' Poll, 1998," manuscript copy in possession of the authors.

In 1979 an opinion poll of leading historians, political scientists, journalists, and lawyers ranked the state's governors in the twentieth century (see "A Ranking of State Governors in the Twentieth Century" in chapter 9). A follow-up to that poll, taken in 2001, showed somewhat different results. The results of the latest poll are listed below.

ARKANSAS GOVERNORS' POLL, 1998

GOVERNOR	RESPONDENTS	SCORE	CATEGORY	TOTAL POINTS
Dale Bumpers	41	4.54	Great	186
George Donaghey	33	4.21	Good	139
Bill Clinton	41	4.20	Good	172
Sid McMath	35	4.09	Good	143
Winthrop Rockefeller	41	4.04	Good	166
Charles Brough	30	3.95	Good	119
Thomas McRae	27	3.67	Good	99
Carl Bailey	28	3.63	Good	102
David Pryor	41	3.49	Average	143
Francis Cherry	35	3.00	Average	105
John Martineau	21	2.97	Average	62
Ben Laney	31	2.90	Average	90
Harvey Parnell	24	2.60	Average	62
Orval Faubus	39	2.56	Average	100
Jeff Davis	31	2.50	Average	78
J. M. Futrell	25	2.44	Below average	61
George Hays	19	2.39	Below average	45
Homer Adkins	28	2.34	Below average	66
Tom Terral	20	2.33	Below average	47
Frank White	41	1.95	Below average	80

55 Questionnaires mailed
41 Respondents
Ranking Scale: 5.0–4.5 Great; 3.4–2.5 Average; 1.4–0 Poor; 4.4–3.5 Good;
2.4–1.5 Below average

B. SOCIETY

For much of the twentieth century Arkansans had a reputation for being
both hillbillies and racists. The former stereotype was supported by its
mountainous topography and underdeveloped economy and made pop-

ular by a humorous radio show called *Lum and Abner*, which ran from 1931 to 1955. Two years after Lum, Abner, and their Jot'em Down Store left the air, the Little Rock school integration crisis made the city the poster child of segregation. In 1981, when Arkansas passed a law that required the Book of Genesis to be taught as science, many saw it as a step backward intellectually and culturally—although there was also a good deal of support for the measure throughout the nation.

The Creation Science Law

Acts of Arkansas, *Act 580 of 1981*, 73rd General Assembly, Regular Session, 1981

Language for a creation science law was drafted by a West Coast group as a model bill to require a theory of divine creation to also be presented whenever scientific evolution was taught. The template was offered to various state legislators for adoption. Arkansas's General Assembly, with strong support from Gov. Frank White, was the only legislative body among the fifty states to pass such a law. The law was challenged by a group of clergymen and other private citizens, however, and a highly-publicized federal trial in Little Rock resulted in its being declared unconstitutional. The Arkansas law and a portion of the judicial decision that overturned it are given below.

"AN ACT TO REQUIRE BALANCED TREATMENT OF CREATION-SCIENCE AND EVOLUTION-SCIENCE IN PUBLIC SCHOOLS; TO PROTECT ACADEMIC FREEDOM BY PROVIDING STUDENT CHOICE; TO ENSURE FREEDOM OF RELIGIOUS EXERCISE; TO GUARANTEE FREEDOM OF BELIEF AND SPEECH; TO PREVENT ESTABLISHMENT OF RELIGION; TO PROHIBIT RELIGIOUS INSTRUCTION CONCERNING ORIGINS; TO BAR DISCRIMINATION ON THE BASIS OF CREATIONISTS OR EVOLUTIONIST BELIEF; TO PROVIDE DEFINITIONS AND CLARIFICATIONS; TO DECLARE THE LEGISLATIVE PURPOSE AND LEGISLATIVE FINDINGS OF FACT; TO PROVIDE FOR SEVERABILITY OF PROVISIONS; TO PROVIDE FOR REPEAL OF CONTRARY LAWS; AND TO SET FORTH AN EFFECTIVE DATE." BE IT ENACTED BY THE GENERAL ASSEMBLY OF THE STATE OF ARKANSAS:

SECTION 1. Requirement for Balanced Treatment. Public schools within this State shall give balanced treatment to creation-science and to evolution-science. Balanced treatment to these two models shall be given in classroom lectures taken as a whole for each course, in textbook materials taken as a whole for each course, in library materials taken as a whole for the sciences and taken as a whole for the humanities, and in other educational programs in public schools, to the extent that such lectures, textbooks, library materials, or educational programs deal in any way with the subject of the origin of man, life, the earth, or the universe.

SECTION 2. Prohibition against Religious Instruction. Treatment of either evolution-science or creation-science shall be limited to scientific evidences for each model and inferences from those scientific evidences, and must not include any religious instruction or references to religious writings.

SECTION 3. Requirement for Nondiscrimination. Public schools within this State, or their personnel, shall not discriminate, by reducing a grade of a student or by singling out and making public criticism, against any student who demonstrates a satisfactory understanding of both evolution-science and creation-science and who accepts or rejects either model in whole or part.

SECTION 4. Definitions. As used in this Act:

(a) "Creation-science" means the scientific evidences for creation and inferences from those scientific evidences. Creation-science includes the scientific evidences and related inferences that indicate: (1) Sudden creation of the universe, energy, and life from nothing; (2) The insufficiency of mutation and natural selection in bringing about development of all living kinds from a single organism; (3) Changes only within fixed limits of originally created kinds of plants and animals; (4) Separate ancestry for man and apes; (5) Explanation of the earth's geology by catastrophism, including the occurrence of a worldwide flood; and (6) A relatively recent inception of the earth and living kinds.

(b) "Evolution-science" means the scientific evidences for evolution and inferences from those scientific evidences. Evolution-science includes the scientific evidences and related inferences that indicate: (1) Emergence by naturalistic processes of the universe from disordered matter and emergence of life from nonlife; (2) The sufficiency of mutation and natural selection in bringing about development of present living kinds from simple earlier kinds; (3) Emergency [*sic*] by mutation and natural selection of present living kinds from simple earlier kinds; (4) Emergence of man from a common ancestor with apes; (5) Explanation of the earth's geology and the evolutionary sequence by uniformitarianism; and (6) An inception several billion years ago of the earth and somewhat later of life.

(c) "Public schools" mean public secondary and elementary schools.

SECTION 5. Clarifications. This Act does not require or permit instruction in any religious doctrine or materials. This Act does not require any instruction in the subject of origins, but simply requires instruction in both scientific models (of evolution-science and creation-science) if public schools choose to teach either. This Act does not require each individual textbook or library book to give balanced treatment to the models of evolution-science and creation-science; it does not require any school books to be discarded. This Act does not require each individual classroom lecture in a course to give such balanced treatment, but simply requires the lectures as a whole to give balanced treatment; it permits some lectures to present evolution-science and other lectures to present creation-science.

SECTION 6. Legislative Declaration of Purpose. This Legislature enacts this Act for public schools with the purpose of protecting academic freedom for students' differing values and beliefs; ensuring neutrality toward students' diverse religious convictions; ensuring freedom of religious exercise for students and their parents; guaranteeing freedom of belief and speech for students; preventing establishment of Theologically Liberal, Humanist, Nontheist, or Atheist religions; preventing discrimination against students on the basis of their personal beliefs concerning creation and evolution; and assisting students in their search for truth. This Legislature does not have the purpose of causing instruction in religious concepts or making an establishment of religion.

SECTION 7. Legislative Findings of Fact. This Legislature finds that:

(a) The subject of the origin of the universe, earth, life, and man is treated within many public school courses, such as biology, life science, anthropology, sociology, and often also in physics, chemistry, world history, philosophy, and social studies.

(b) Only evolution-science is presented to students in virtually all of those courses that discuss the subject of origins. Public schools generally censor creation-science and evidence contrary to evolution.

(c) Evolution-science is not an unquestionable fact of science, because evolution cannot be experimentally observed, fully verified, or logically falsified, and because evolution-science is not accepted by some scientists.

(d) Evolution-science is contrary to the religious convictions or moral values or philosophical beliefs of many students and parents, including individuals of many different religious faiths and with diverse moral values and philosophical beliefs.

(e) Public school presentation of only evolution-science without any alternative model of origins abridges the United States Constitution's protections of freedom of religious exercise and of freedom of belief and speech for students and parents, because it undermines their religious convictions and moral or philosophical values, compels their unconscionable professions of belief, and hinders religious training and moral training by parents.

(f) Public school presentation of only evolution-science furthermore abridges the Constitution's prohibition against establishment of religion, because it produces hostility toward many Theistic religions and brings preference to Theological Liberalism, Humanism, Nontheistic religions, and Atheism, in that these religious faiths [in] general include a religious belief in evolution.

(g) Public school instruction in only evolution-science also violates the principle of academic freedom, because it denies students a choice between scientific models and instead indoctrinates them in evolution-science alone.

(h) Presentation of only one model rather than alternative scientific models of origins is not required by any compelling interest of the State, and exemption of such students from a course or class presenting only evolution-science does not provide an adequate remedy because of teacher influence and student pressure to remain in that course or class.

(i) Attendance of those students who are at public schools is compelled by law, and school taxes from their parents and other citizens are mandated by law.

(j) Creation-science is an alternative scientific model of origins and can be presented from a strictly scientific standpoint without any religious doctrine just as evolution-science can, because there are scientists who conclude that scientific data best support creation-science and because scientific evidences and inferences have been presented for creation-science.

(k) Public school presentation of both evolution-science and creation-science would not violate the Constitution's prohibition against establishment of religion, because it would involve presentation of the scientific evidences and related inferences for each model rather than any religious instruction.

(l) Most citizens, whatever their religious beliefs about origins, favor balanced treatment in public schools of alternative scientific models of origins for better guiding students in their search for knowledge, and they favor a neutral approach toward subjects affecting the religious and moral and philosophical convictions of students.

SECTION 8. Short Title. This Act shall be known as the "Balanced Treatment for Creation-Science and Evolution-Science Act."

SECTION 9. Severability of Provisions. If any provision of this Act is held invalid, that invalidity shall not affect other provisions that can be applied in the absence of the invalidated provisions, and the provisions of this Act are declared to be severable.

SECTION 10. Repeal of Contrary Laws. All State laws or parts of State laws in conflict with this Act are hereby repealed.

SECTION 11. Effective Date. The requirements of the Act shall be met by and may be met before the beginning of the next school year if that is more than six months from the date of enactment, or otherwise one year after the beginning of the next school year, and in all subsequent school years.

3-19-81 *(signed: Frank White)*
APPROVED   GOVERNOR

Creation Science Declared Unconstitutional

McLean v. Arkansas Board of Education F. Supp 1255
Decision by U.S. District Court Judge William R. Overton.
Dated this January 5, 1982.

In the eyes of those who believed in evolution, Arkansas redeemed itself when a group of clergymen and other citizens sued the state in order to have the Creation Science law declared unconstitutional. The trial, which was held in Little Rock, featured expert witness testimony from many leading national scientists, theologians, and legal experts. Judge William Overton, a Little Rock resident, wrote an opinion that not only overturned the Arkansas law but also effectively ended the Creation Science movement.

In the 1960's and early 1970's, several Fundamentalist organizations were formed to promote the idea that the Book of Genesis was supported by scientific data. The terms "creation science" and "scientific creationism" have been adopted by these Fundamentalists as descriptive of their study of creation and the origins of man. Perhaps the leading creationist organization is the Institute for Creation Research (ICR), which is affiliated with the Christian heritage College and supported by the Scott Memorial Baptist Church in San Diego, California. The ICR, through the Creation-Life Publishing Company, is the leading publisher of creation science material. Other creation science organizations include the Creation Science Research Center (CSRC) of San Diego and the Bible Science Association of Minneapolis, Minnesota. In 1963, the Creation Research Society (CRS) was formed from a schism in the American Scientific Affiliation (ASA). It is an organization of literal Fundamentalists (7) who have the equivalent of a master's degree in some recognized area of science. A purpose of the organization is "to reach all people with the vital message of the scientific and historical truth about creation." Nelkin, The Science Textbook Controversies and the Politics of Equal Time, 66. Similarly, the CSRC was formed in 1970 from a split in the CRS. Its aim has been "to reach the 63 million children of the United States with the scientific teaching of Biblical creationism." Id. at 69.

. . . Creation science as defined in Section 4(a), not only fails to follow the canons of dealing with scientific theory, it also fails to fit the more general descriptions of "what scientists think" and "what scientists do." The scientific community consists of individuals and groups, nationally and internationally, who work independently in such varied fields as biology, paleontology, geology, and astronomy. Their work is published and subject to review and testing by their peers. The journals for publication are both numerous and varied. There is, however, not one recognized scientific journal which has published an article espousing the creation science theory described in Section 4(a). Some of the State's witnesses suggested that the scientific community was "close-minded" on the subject of creationism and that explained the lack of acceptance of the creation science arguments. Yet no witness produced a scientific article for which publication has been refused. Perhaps some members of the scientific community are resistant to new ideas. It is, however, inconceivable that such a loose knit group of independent thinkers in all the varied fields of science could, or would, so effectively censor new scientific thought. . . .

Implementation of Act 590 will have serious and untoward consequences for students, particularly those planning to attend college. Evolution is the cornerstone of modern biology, and many courses in public schools contain subject matter relating to such varied topics as the age of the earth, geology and relationships among living things. Any student who is deprived of instruction as to the prevailing scientific thought on these topics will be denied a significant part of science education. Such a deprivation through the high school level would undoubtedly have an impact upon the quality of education in the State's colleges and universities, especially including the pre-professional and professional programs in the health sciences.

Bill Clinton in Arkansas

Ernest Dumas, ed. and comp., *The Clintons of Arkansas: An Introduction by Those Who Know Them Best* (Fayetteville: University of Arkansas Press), 1993, 99–100, 125–26.

Bill Clinton was born in Arkansas and always remained close to the state and its people. He was elected governor in 1978 but defeated when he ran for re-election two years later. He won the governorship again in 1982 and served in that office until elected president in 1992. In the first selection below, Roy Reed, a journalist who was close to both Bill and Hillary Clinton, discusses those early elections and the future president's response to the first major setback of his career. In the second part, Bobby Roberts, another personal friend and one-time aide, describes some of the characteristics that contributed to Clinton's success.

[Roy Reed writes:]

Clinton was twenty-eight when he first ran for office. He became known at once as a latter-day New Dealer, lashing out at unrestrained corporate power and warning that big business could end up running the country. When he ran for governor four years later, he dropped that issue in favor of local concerns such as economic development, education, and high utility rates. He won the governor's office in 1978. He was thirty-two.

Political problems began in his first term. As state attorney general a year earlier, he had jumped on rising utility rates as a popular issue. As a young governor, he continued to fight the major electric utility, historically a power in Arkansas politics. But the main problem of his first term was one that few people understood until it was too late. The state's highways needed repairs. He raised car license fees to pay for them, and angered thousands of motorists. They turned him out at the 1980 election. The man who beat him was Frank White, an affable, unimaginative Republican with a blustering style and an aversion to syntax.

"I sort of felt sick," Clinton would recall later, with some understatement. "But the next day I resolved that I was going to run for governor again. I knew at some deep-down emotional level that I would have to run again in 1982 in order to live with myself the rest of my life."

He and Hillary went into seclusion for several months. Then he began to travel. He went to almost every county and, in private meetings, asked his old supporters what had done wrong. They told him: He had become uppity; they resented his Ivy League style; his staff had been unresponsive. His ego suffered, and he lost some of his cockiness. But people close to him that said he matured. When it came time to run again, he thrashed White. . . .

[Bobby Roberts writes:]

The 1983 session gave me a chance to observe how Clinton approached the legislative process. It was little different from the way he campaigned. I had learned three things about Clinton when I traveled with him in the 1982 race.

First, his energy is almost limitless. He drove his staff to the point of exhaustion. Our days usually began at dawn and ended at midnight or later. I learned to eat when I could, and my diet consisted of almost wholly of catfish, fried chicken, and spaghetti. We were always over overscheduled, but Clinton loved unplanned detours. He would stop at a remote crossroads store and visit with whomever he found. Every three or four days, his travel aides wore out and were recycled back to Little Rock. But Clinton drew strength from the crowds and continued the relentless schedule seven days a week.

Second, Clinton had an encyclopedic knowledge and a computer memory. He read prodigiously, even during the campaign, and his mind was crammed with minutiae. He would launch into a mind-numbing stream of facts, figures, and conclusions on any subject anyone brought up.

Third, he was willing to talk to anyone he met. "Stop at that grocery store," he would yell as we sped towards our next appointment. "Bill," I would say, "we are already late. We don't have time." He'd say, "Stop anyway." Soon he would be introducing himself to everyone in the store, and would wind up in a long and serious dialogue with a logger who had stopped for some tobacco and who might have a long-held grievance against some level of government. Clinton would often turn to an aide and tell him to follow up on some point. It played havoc with the schedule and made it impossible for Clinton ever to be on time. I at first assumed that Clinton tolerated such long distractions because he disliked being rude or running off even one potential vote. I came eventually to the understanding that these endlessly recurring exchanges about mundane affairs did not have a selfish political motive. Rather, Clinton was genuinely interested in people's problems and what they had to say even if they had ideas that made no practical sense. His concern was rarely lost on the people with whom he spoke. . . .

The Walmart Phenomenon

Walmart, "History Timeline,"
http://corporate.walmart.com/our-story/heritage/history-timeline (accessed January 10, 2013).

In the spring of 2013, as the company celebrated its fiftieth year in business, Walmart's corporate website displayed a chronological history of its development. Some of the dates and accomplishments are listed below, where they outline an astonishing commercial success story. An additional significant event occurred in 2008 when the company changed its name from Wal-Mart to Walmart.

1962	Sam Walton opens his first Wal-Mart in Rogers, Arkansas.
1967	The business has grown to 24 stores.
1969	Wal-Mart goes from a family business to a corporation.
1970	Shares in Wal-Mart are sold at $16.50.
1971	Benton, Arkansas, becomes the companies' headquarters and first distribution center.
1972	Wal-Mart has 51 stores.
1975	Sam Walton introduces the Wal-Mart cheer.
1980	Wal-Mart has 216 stores, 21,000 associates, and $1 billion in sales.
1983	The first Sam's Club is opened. Computers replace cash registers.
1987	Wal-Mart begins to use its own satellite for internal communication.
1988	The first Wal-Mart Supercenter is opened.
1991	A Sam's Club opens in Mexico.
1994	Wal-Mart expands into Canada.
1996	Wal-Mart stores open in China.
1997	Sales reach $100 billion.
1999	Wal-Mart begins operations in the United Kingdom.
2000	Wal-Mart has 3,989 stores.
2002	Wal-Mart is the number one Fortune 500 company. Wal-Mart expands into Japan.
2009	Annual sales are above $400 billion. Walmart enters Chile.
2010	First Walmart opens in India.
2012	Walmart's 2.2 million associates serve 200 million customers at more than 10,000 stores in 27 countries.

C. PENAL REFORM

The documents below illustrate examples of how Arkansas officials attempted to deal with the drug culture. They provide the language for the new approach to crime and punishment while also showing its impact on the state's correction system. In the first decade after the three strikes concept became law, the number of residents in the state prison system increased almost five times and costs grew over 1,000 percent. In 2008 state officials revised the rule requiring inmates convicted of serious felonies including the manufacture of methamphetamine to serve at least 70 percent of their sentences before being eligible for parole and returned to more traditional policies, allowing for a reduction in time served based on good behavior. In 2011 a comprehensive reform law was passed that swung the pendulum further back in the direction of leniency.

Three Strikes Law

Acts of Arkansas, *Act 1011 of 1995,* 80th General Assembly, Regular Session, 1995.

The document below is an opening section from the Arkansas "three strikes law" relating to the sentencing of individuals convicted of felonies. Arkansas law ranks felonies according to the seriousness of the crime. The worst crimes are those in class Y. Class A felonies are just below class Y, with class B, class C, and class D following in order. Many different types are included in each category. Class Y, for example includes crimes related to murder and terrorism but also the distribution of cocaine or methamphetamine cocaine. At the other end of the scale, cruelty to animals is a class D felony, as is damaging telephone, cable, or electricity wires. The distribution of other "controlled substances" is a class A felony, and lesser drug-related crimes are found the other categories.

"AN ACT TO AMEND ARKANSAS CODE § 5-4-501 TO REQUIRE HABITUAL OFFENDERS OF VIOLENT CRIMES IN ARKANSAS TO SERVE MANDATORY SENTENCES OR LIFE FOR COMMITTING TWO (2) SERIOUS VIOLENT FELONIES AND TO SERVE LIFE IN PRISON OR MANDATORY MINIMUM SENTENCES FOR CERTAIN VIOLENT FELONY CRIMES COMMITTED THREE (3) TIMES; TO AMEND ARKANSAS CODE§ 16-93-1302 TO PROVIDE OFFENDERS OF SERIOUS VIOLENT FELONIES WITH PAROLE ELIGIBILITY ONLY AFTER AGE FIFTY-FIVE (55); AND FOR OTHER PURPOSES."

Subtitle

"TO REQUIRE HABITUAL OFFENDERS OF TWO SERIOUS VIOLENT FELONIES TO SERVE MANDATORY SENTENCES OR LIFE AND FOR 3 TIME OFFENDERS OF VIOLENT FELONIES TO SERVE LIFE IN PRISON OR MINIMUM PRISON TERMS."

BE IT ENACTED BY THE GENERAL ASSEMBLY OF THE STATE OF ARKANSAS:

SECTION 1. Arkansas Code § 5-4-501 is amended to read as follows:

31 "5-4-501. Habitual offenders—Sentencing for felony.

(a) A defendant who is convicted of a felony other than those enumerated in subsections (c) and (d) committed after June 30, 1993, and who has previously been convicted of more than one (1) but less than four (4) felonies, or who has been found guilty of more than one (1) but less than four (4) felonies, may be sentenced to an extended term of imprisonment as follows:

(1) For a conviction of a Class Y felony, a term of not less than ten (10) years nor more than sixty (60) years, or life;

(2) For a conviction of a Class A felony, a term of not less than six (6) years nor more than fifty (50) years;

(3) For a conviction of a Class B felony, a term of not less than five (5) years nor more than thirty (30) years;

(4) For a conviction of a Class C felony, a term of not less than three (3) years nor more than twenty (20) years;

(5) For a conviction of a Class D felony, a term of not more than twelve (12) years;

(6) For a conviction of an unclassified felony punishable by less than life imprisonment, not more than five (5) years more than the maximum sentence for the unclassified offense;

(7) For a conviction of an unclassified felony punishable by life imprisonment, not less than ten (10) years nor more than fifty (50) years, or life. (b) A defendant who is convicted of a felony other than those enumerated in subsections (c) and (d) committed after June 30, 1993, and who has previously been convicted of four (4) or more felonies or who has been found guilty of four (4) or more felonies, may be sentenced to an extended term of imprisonment as follows:

(1) For a conviction of a Class Y felony, a term of not less than ten (10) years nor more than life;

(2) For a conviction of a Class A felony, a term of not less than six (6) years nor more than sixty (60) years;

(3) For a conviction of a Class B felony, a term of not less than five (5) years nor more than forty (40) years;

(4) For a conviction of a Class C felony, a term of not less than three (3) years nor more than thirty (30) years;

(5) For a conviction of a Class D felony, a term of not more than fifteen (15) years;

(6) For a conviction of an unclassified felony punishable by less than life imprisonment, not more than twice the maximum sentence for the unclassified offense;

(7) For a conviction of an unclassified felony punishable by life imprisonment, not less than ten (10) years nor more than fifty (50) years, or life.

[Note: There is not a section (b).]

(c)(1) A defendant who is convicted of a serious felony involving violence enumerated below and who has previously been convicted on one (1) or more separate and distinct prior occasions of one (1) or more of the serious felonies involving violence enumerated below shall be sentenced to imprisonment, without eligibility of parole or community punishment transfer, for term of not less than forty (40) years nor more than eighty (80) years, or for life.

(2) For the purposes of this subsection, a serious felony involving violence shall mean any of the following felonies enumerated as follows: Murder in the first degree, § 5-10-102; Murder in the second degree, § 5-10-103; Kidnapping, involving activities making it a Y felony, § 5-11-102; Aggravated robbery, § 5-12-103; Rape, § 5-14-103; Terroristic act, involving activities making it a Y felony, § 5-13-310; causing a catastrophe, § 5-38-202; or a conviction of a comparable serious felony involving violence from another jurisdiction.

Arkansas Sentencing Commission

Acts of Arkansas, *Act 2011 of 1995*, 80th General Assembly,
Regular Session, 1995.

Concerned with the wide discrepancy among sentences handed
down in various courts for the same or similar crimes, Gov. Jim
Guy Tucker led the General Assembly to create a state agency that
would promote standardization in sentencing.

History and Organization

The purpose of the Arkansas Sentencing Commission is to establish,
maintain and revise sentencing guidelines and to monitor and assess the
effect of legislation and policy on correctional resources, and to educate
the criminal justice community and the public regarding sentencing laws
and policy.

As defined in Acts 532 and 550 of 1993, the Arkansas Sentencing
Commission's powers and duties are:

To adopt the initial sentencing standards grid and seriousness reference table within the new sentencing structure and to make any necessary
revisions thereto;

To establish transfer eligibility for the offenses at the seriousness levels with the more serious offenders serving one-half of their sentences
and the less serious serving one-third;

To monitor compliance with standards, assess impact on correctional
resources and determine if the state sentencing policy is furthered;

To make legislative recommendations on revisions to the target
offense group, classifications of crimes, and appropriate changes to sentencing laws, policies and/or practices;

"Strategic planning" with the Board of Correction to further the
goals of equitable sentencing and rational use of correctional resources;

Gather data relative to sentencing in coordination with the
Administrative Office of the Courts, the Arkansas Crime Information
Center, the circuit clerks of the State and the Departments of Correction
and Community Correction;

To develop a research and analysis system to determine the feasibility,
impact on resources and budget consequences of proposed and existing
legislation affecting sentence length.

The Commission is composed of nine voting members: three circuit judges, two prosecuting attorneys, two defense attorneys, and two members of the general public. The Commission currently has five full time staff positions.

Arkansas Prison Population, 1980–2010

Arkansas Department of Corrections, *Annual Report, 1980–2010.*

The impact of the "three strikes law" and the 70 percent rule was reflected in both the number of residents in the Arkansas prison system and the Department of Corrections' annual budget, as shown in the table below.

ARKANSAS PRISON POPULATION, 1980–201

YEAR	POPULATION	% BLACK	% WHITE	% OTHER	CARE/CUSTODY BUDGET
1980	2850	—	—	—	13,000,000
1981	3074	—	—	—	17,000,000
1982	3681	51	49	<1	22,000,000
1983	3935	—	—	—	26,000,000
1984	4373	51	48	1	32,000,000
1985	4527	—	—	—	36,000,000
1986	4682	—	—	—	40,000,000
1987	4891	—	—	—	41,000,000
1988	5365	50	49	1	41,000,000
1989	5759	50	50	<1	43,000,000
1990	6614	52	47	1	54,000,000
1991	7232	54	45	1	65,000,000
1992	7846	57	42	1	75,000,000
1993	8414	57	41	2	83,000,000
1994	8932	57	41	2	90,000,000
1995	8973	57	42	1	101,000,000
1996	9484	55	44	1	105,000,000
1997	9757	54	44	2	117,000,000

YEAR	POPULATION	% BLACK	% WHITE	% OTHER	CARE/CUSTODY BUDGET
1998	10608	54	45	1	135,000,000
1999	11088	53	46	1	144,000,000
2000	11984	51	47	2	155,000,000
2001	11928	50	49	1	175,000,000
2002	12402	49	50	1	183,000,000
2003	13015	47	51	2	180,000,000
2004	13105	45	53	2	199,000,000
2005	13595	43	55	2	209,000,000
2006	13481	45	53	2	239,000,000
2007	13839	46	52	2	253,000,000
2008	14518	46	51	3	272,000,000
2009	14796	46	51	3	280,000,000
2010	15334	45	50	5	288,000,000

The Public Safety Improvement Act: Act 570 of 2011

Arkansas Online, Jeanni Brosius, "Code Changes to Reduce Overcrowding," *Arkansas Democrat-Gazette,* June 6, 2011, http://www.arkansasonline.com/news/2011/jun/26/code-changes-reduce-overcrowding-20110626/?print (accessed January 11, 2013).

After more than a decade of harsher sentences and the increased expenses associated with them, the Arkansas legislature passed Act 570 of 2011, a measure designed to reform the system by lessening the penalties associated with some drug-related offenses and making a clearer distinction between violent and nonviolent crimes. In the following document a news reporter summarizes the law as it was explained in a workshop for law enforcement officials.

BATESVILLE—The way drug and theft charges are handled will drastically change and sentences may be reduced in an attempt to free up space in Arkansas' prisons.

State, county and city law enforcement personnel and others who work in the justice system gathered in Independence Hall at the University of Arkansas Community College at Batesville on Wednesday to learn about changes in the state's criminal code.

When Public Safety Improvement Act 570 was passed by the General Assembly on March 22, the act dramatically changed the criminal code and how criminals are sentenced. The act, which was presented in order to relieve prison overcrowding, will go into effect Wednesday, July 27.

"It is the most drastic change in the criminal code since it was first adopted in 1975, and the drug laws in the state of Arkansas no longer exist as we know them," 16th Judicial Prosecuting Attorney Don McSpadden told the group of law-enforcement officers.

The 164-page act and its changes were explained by Arkansas Prosecutor Coordinator Bob McMahan as a work in progress.

"The projected savings, if it works, is about $875 million," McMahan said. "The savings will trickle down to the county level."

Gov. Mike Beebe said he believes the Public Safety Improvement Act will make Arkansas more safe in a couple of important ways: by reserving prison beds for violent prisoners and by strengthening the state's system of probation and parole.

"When fully implemented, the act will slow the growth of Arkansas' prison population, reserving prison beds for violent and career offenders," Beebe said. "In the past 20 years, Arkansas' prison population has doubled, and the annual prison budget has increased from $45 million to more than $350 million. If left unchecked, the prison population is expected to grow another 43 percent by 2020 at a cost to Arkansas taxpayers of $1.1 billion in new prison construction and operation expenses. Arkansas' budget cannot support these increased costs, so we need a different approach to ensure that we can continue to incarcerate violent and career criminals.

"Additionally, the act strengthens our system of probation and parole, holding offenders accountable through the implementation of evidence-based practices that have been proven to reduce recidivism, such as risk assessment and swift and certain sanctions for violators."

Because drug and theft charges are considered nonviolent crimes, McMahan said, the sentencing has become lighter or shorter for these crimes to save prison space for more violent criminals. The changes that go into effect will not be retroactive.

. . . McMahan said methamphetamine and cocaine offenders will still be treated harshly, but laws regarding marijuana have changed.

Under the previous statute, possessing 1 ounce of marijuana could get someone a class A misdemeanor charge with a sentence of up to a year in prison, and delivering or manufacturing 1 ounce to 10 pounds of marijuana was considered a class C felony with a sentence of three to 10 years in prison.

Under the new statute, possession of less than 4 ounces of marijuana is considered a misdemeanor; and delivery or manufacture of up to 14 grams of marijuana is now considered a class A misdemeanor.

"I think this is something we're going to have to revisit and maybe have help from law enforcement," McMahan said about the lighter sentencing laws for marijuana possession. "Meth and cocaine are still our super drugs, and they will be dealt with more seriously."

A new offense also has been created and added to the drug statutes: trafficking a controlled substance, which in all cases is considered a class Y felony with a sentence of 10 to 40 years or life in prison.

Revisions on theft crimes are also part of the new act. Previously, less than a $500 theft was considered a class A misdemeanor, but that amount has doubled to less than $1,000.

Early-release provisions were also altered.

Probationers and parolees will now be able to gain "day-for-day good-time credit."

"Their sentence could be cut in half," McMahan said.

There is also a 120-day parole eligibility during which a prisoner could be released from incarceration after 120 days, under certain circumstances, and placed on electronic monitoring.

The 120-day parole early release provision doesn't apply if the sentence was a result of a bench or jury trial or if a violent or sex crime was committed, or if crimes resulted in a death or the inmate has previously failed a drug-court program.

There will be a learning curve while law-enforcement personnel evolve into using the new laws, McMahan said.

D. ECONOMICS

Arkansas per capita income was lower than the national level in the last decades of the twentieth century, but it grew at about the same rate. The most noticeable change in the structure of the state's economy was the growth of companies that were able to compete at the national and even international market, Walmart being the outstanding example. Still Arkansas struggled to update its infrastructure of roads and highways and attract new industry to provide jobs for its citizens.

An innovative use of construction bonds allowed the state Highway Department to gain voter approval for the largest bond issue in state history to finance maintenance and improvement on the interstate highway system. Discovery of natural gas sand in the Fayetteville shale region of the Ozark uplift provided a new source of revenue and pointed to the need for greater improvements in the state's rural road network and raised concerns over ground and surface water pollution. Adoption of an initiated amendment to the state constitution legalizing a state-run lottery with revenues dedicated to education also provided an economic boost to some sections of the economy. Even with these gains, Arkansas's overall economy still ranked near the bottom among the fifty states, and state agencies as well as private citizen groups worked to develop programs that would improve that situation.

Highway Construction and Financing

Arkansas Department of Highways and Transportation, *Blue Ribbon Committee on Highway Finance,* final report, December 1, 2010, 2–6, BlueRibbonHighways.com (accessed November 12, 2011).

The distribution revolution in retail marketing that began in the 1970s placed a serious strain on Arkansas's interstate highway system. Increased weight and the number of "big rig" trucks, as well as extreme weather conditions, combined to cause serious damage to key roadways. By the 1990s the damage had become so severe that a national trucking magazine listed Arkansas roads as being among the five worst in the nation. Increased demands on state revenues to finance education, prisons, and social services made it difficult to fund new highway construction or provide maintenance

---

on existing systems. Failing to find sufficient funding among the state's general revenues, highway supporters turned to bonds as a way to finance road construction. The following document explains the strategy used to gain support for a bond program and the economic impact of the project.

HIGHWAY NEEDS—HISTORIC INFORMATION

The modern era in Arkansas highways began in the mid-1950s with reform of the State Highway Commission, the passage of the Interstate Highway System Act and the establishment of the Federal Highway Trust Fund.

During that time, the State Highway System has grown 64% (including 655 miles of Interstate highways), the State population has grown 40%, and the total vehicle miles traveled (VMT) has grown an amazing 590%. By comparison, Arkansas's per gallon motor fuel tax was 6.5¢ in 1955, and today's gasoline tax is 21.8¢ per gallon.

However, Arkansas's gasoline tax would have to be 52.6¢ per gallon today to have the same purchasing power that it had in 1955, yet it is less than half that. The Committee realizes that, as per gallon consumption is trending downward, this discrepancy between Arkansas's motor fuel tax and its purchasing power will only continue to grow. It can therefore be concluded that, by any measure, Arkansans have received a real bargain in mobility over the past five decades.

The Arkansas State Highway and Transportation Department (AHTD) has conducted numerous highway needs studies in the past. The following table shows how the needs have increased over the last several years while anticipated revenue has remained relatively constant.

Two-Thirds of current needs (not including High Priority Corridors) are related to system preservation (reconstruction, rehabilitation, resurfacing, bridge rehabilitation/replacement). One-third of the current needs (not including High Priority Corridors) are related to congestion relief (widening and new location construction). It should be noted that the needs projected in 2009 do not include the damage that has been sustained in the Fayetteville Shale area due to natural gas exploration and production activities. Likewise, the anticipated revenue does not include the projected revenue from the natural gas severance tax. According to recent studies by the AHTD, over $450 million is needed to return the

HISTORY OF STATE HIGHWAY NEEDS VS. REVENUE
(BILLIONS)
NEEDS

YEAR	CAPACITY	SYSTEM PRESERVA- TION	ECONOMIC DEVELOP- MENT CONNEC- TORS	HIGH PRIORITY CORRIDORS	TOTAL NEEDS	FUNDS AVAILABLE	SHORTFALL
1998	—	$7.2	$3.4 *	$3.6	$14.2	$3.9	$10.3
2003	$3.1	$7.0	$1.3	$4.7	$16.1	$4.3	$11.8
2006	$3.4	$8.8	$1.7	$5.2	$19.1	$4.1	$15.0
2009	$3.7	$10.8	$1.6	$7.5	$23.6	$4.1	$19.5

*These were based on public involvement and are not explicitly Economic Development related improvements.

["High priority corridors" are national routes designated by US Congress as vital to the national transportation. There were eighty such corridors in 2010, seven of which ran through Arkansas.]

highways impacted by activities in the Fayetteville Shale to the condition they were in prior to the activity beginning. Approximately $35 million had been received by the AHTD from the Natural Gas Severance Tax through the end of State Fiscal Year 2010, which is far less than original estimates.

It is estimated that an additional $200 million annually (in current dollars—net revenue to AHTD) at a minimum is needed over the next 10 years for highway congestion, pavement and bridge conditions, maintenance, administration and operations to remain at current levels (cost of maintaining "status quo").

In Arkansas, the State Highway System includes 16,443 miles of highways. It is the 12th largest State Highway System in the United States, comprising 16% of Arkansas's public roadways and carrying 76% of our total annual vehicle miles traveled, including 95% of all heavy-truck travel. However, Arkansas ranks 42nd in the ability to fund improvements to the highway system. Being faced with such a formidable discrepancy between responsibility and funding, the AHTD and the Arkansas State Highway Commission developed and adopted the Arkansas Primary Highway Network (APHN).

The APHN is comprised of significant routes that have been identified as important to the State's transportation service on the basis of
their characteristics and performance. The APHN is a system of 7,740
miles (approximately 50% of the total highway mileage) that carries
approximately 90% of all travel on the State Highway System. Priority
for investing the limited amount of funding available is given to projects
on the APHN. With the APHN carrying the vast majority of the traffic
on the State Highway System, this clearly results in "the money following
the cars." The balance of the State Highway System must also be maintained for safe travel, although the scope of work on non-APHN routes
is typically much smaller and much less expensive than improvements
to APHN routes. . . .

As a subset of the APHN, a potential Four-Lane Grid System has
been identified to facilitate the movement of people and goods and economic development among all areas of the State. This system . . . includes
the Interstate System, High Priority Corridors and other routes that have
been identified as regionally significant.

There are 68,811 miles of county roads in Arkansas, making the
county road system the 10th largest in the country, carrying 9% of the
State's traffic.

The balance is comprised of 14,778 miles of city streets, which carry
15% of the total annual traffic volume. The entire public roadway system
in Arkansas includes 100,032 miles and carries 90,854,940 vehicle miles
of travel each day or 3.3 billion vehicle miles of travel in a year.

The . . . State's population of approximately 2.7 million people ranks
32nd in the nation. The result, typical of largely rural states, is that each
Arkansas driver supports a larger number of road miles than in more
populous regions of the country. With highway revenue generated from
current state and federal sources, Arkansas ranks 42nd in the ability to
fund improvements to the highway system. Although the inconsistency
is not uncommon for many rural states, this fact does not make the
Committee's task of defining an equitable and adequate funding formula
any less daunting.

A Strategy for Economic Development

http://www.aralliance.org/__data/assets/file/0015/3138/Battelle Release_11272012_FINAL.pdf (accessed January 22, 2013)

At the beginning of the 21st century it was clear that future economic growth would depend heavily on knowledge, information, and technology, and Arkansas business, government, and educational leaders sought to take advantage of that insight as a means of developing the Arkansas economy. The document below is a press release by the Arkansas Research Council announcing the publication of a strategic plan for that purpose.

Battelle Study Confirms Return on Knowledge-based Initiatives and Underscores Sustainable, Strategic Funding
Knowledge initiatives essential to building a 21st century economy

LITTLE ROCK, Ark., Nov. 26, 2012 – An important and timely economic development study was released today at the Arkansas State Capitol to an audience of state and corporate leaders committed to building a stronger knowledge-based economy. The study was conducted by the Battelle Institute, a nonprofit organization recognized as a global leader in science, technology, education, and commercial innovation.

In 2009, Governor Mike Beebe presented a long-term, statewide economic development plan targeted at increasing the standard of living for Arkansans by developing knowledge-based jobs. Building on that plan, Arkansas organizations have incubated and launched a number of economic development initiatives that advance a knowledge-based economy.

The study, entitled *Arkansas' Knowledge Economy Initiatives: Analysis of Progress and Recommendations for the Future,* was released in cooperation with the Arkansas Economic Development Commission, Arkansas Science and Technology Authority, Arkansas State Chamber of Commerce, Arkansas Research Alliance, and Accelerate Arkansas.

According to Mitch Horowitz, vice president and managing director of the Battelle Technology Partnership Practice, the study evaluates the progress current initiatives are making and measures the return on investment. It also identifies gaps and investment opportunities important to the long-term success of the state. Battelle summarizes a clear and essential need for Arkansas to establish consistent, predictable funding that will sustain and grow a knowledge-based economy.

Economic Progress Defined

The Battelle study shows that Arkansas is now well positioned to take necessary steps to maintain momentum of successful knowledge initiatives including those that create opportunities in the areas of research, commercialization and job creation. The following examples provide a snapshot of progress to date:

• 135 emerging knowledge economy companies, employing 1,259 workers in Arkansas, have participated in the state's knowledge-based economy efforts since 2008. Workers average over $70,000 a year, more than double the $34,014 average annual wage of the private sector in Arkansas.

• Knowledge-based economy initiatives focused on research have received $61.2 million in state funding from 2008 to 2011 and leveraged an additional $191.8 million in non-state sources to further support their research activities.

• Arkansas' economy is being bolstered by growth in high wage, knowledge intensive industries with more than 6,000 direct jobs, which generated a total of 11,800 jobs.

Critical Investment

While Arkansas is making strides and enjoying positive returns from economic initiatives, sustainable funding is vital for continued growth and progress, and without it, knowledge-based initiatives are vulnerable. In order to successfully transition to a knowledge-based economy and bring existing programs up to scale, Arkansas must focus on the following:

• Research
   • Attain a higher level of per capita university research funding.
      • In 2010 the per capita level of university research funding in Arkansas was $87 compared to $189 for the United States.

- Commercialization
  - Accelerate the formation of emerging knowledge-based economy companies and position them for success.
    - From 2008 to 2011, Arkansas supported 135 emerging companies and 1,259 jobs.
- Investment
  - Realize the growth potential from emerging companies that have participated in the existing knowledge-based economy initiatives.
  - Increase newly created jobs from 1,259 to 5,000 or more over the next 5 years.
- Top talent
  - Harness the education, skills and adaptability of a talented workforce and put them to work in Arkansas.

"Achieving success in knowledge-based economic development is complex and challenging but it is imperative for a healthy economy," stated Jeffery R. Gardner, Arkansas Research Alliance board chairman, and CEO and president of Windstream Corporation. "The Battelle study shows us where we are succeeding and demonstrates that strategic funding is essential in moving Arkansas forward."

About the Arkansas Research Alliance

The ARA is a 501(c)(3) nonprofit organization governed by a board of trustees comprised of chancellors from Arkansas research universities and CEOs from across the state. In 2007, the Arkansas legislature approved the appropriation of start-up operational funding for the ARA from the state's general improvement fund. Funding was authorized through the Arkansas Science and Technology Authority. Operating as a public-private partnership, the ARA is committed to strengthening the economic competitiveness of Arkansas by maximizing university-based research and innovation in designated strategic focus areas.

The Natural Gas Severance Tax Issue

Sheffield Nelson to C. Fred Williams, November 2011, letter in possession of author.

Although Arkansas had abundant natural resources, the General Assembly did not tax their extraction until the 1920s, when it adopted a severance tax on petroleum products transported out of state. The "oil boom" collapsed soon after the tax went into effect, and elected officials showed little interest in this source of revenue until a natural gas boom developed in the 1990s. After a lengthy debate between producers, who argued that a severance tax would limit development, and consumer advocates, who countered that the state was in danger of giving away one of its most lucrative sources of revenue, lawmakers adopted a compromise proposal that brought Arkansas in line with the average tax in the region but provided a two-year exemption on "new exploration" in the state. In the document below, a former executive of the natural gas industry discusses the issue and his own efforts to increase state revenue through the severance tax.

Time to Revisit the Natural Gas Severance Tax Issue
By Sheffield Nelson

I filed "The Natural Gas Severance Tax Act of 2008" on January 17, 2008, to prepare to take the matter to the voters of the states as an initiated act. It called for a 7% tax, based on the fair market value of natural gas, on all gas at the point of severance.

Governor Mike Beebe and I discussed the severance tax issue on several occasions, and this resulted in me telling him that I would withdraw my filing if he could reach an agreement with the industry to support a reasonable increase in the amount of severance tax charged, and then get that agreement through the legislature, which would require a super majority or 75% of the votes in both the House and the Senate to succeed. The existing tax of 3/10 cent per thousand cubic feet (mcf) had been set by the Legislature in 1957, and was producing only $550,000 per year, so any acceptable tax in ease would be significant. Governor Beebe worked diligently with all concerned and through a combination of salesmanship, cajoling and raw political power did what most pundits predicted he would not be able to do. He arrived at a pricing structure that was estimated to produce approximately $60 million dollars a year, with sales volumes and sales price of the gas at the well-head to be the factors that determined the actual amount of revenues to be derived by the state. This agreement called for several levels of taxes ranging up to a maximum of 5 [percent] of the sales price, with credits for a number of things, including the cost of treating and transporting the gas. In the last twelve months that income was $47.6 million, which is over 85 times more than would have been received under the old [1957] severance tax structure. . . .

It is important to note that this negotiation was never intended to be the end of consideration of this very important topic, and it is time to revisit the severance tax issue. It is very clear that damage to the roads of the state, with the most damage occurring where the majority of the drilling is occurring[,] is significant. It was recently determined that the cost to repair the roads in the ten counties which have the most drilling taking place would be $219 million, and that amount will increase every day the heavy loads used in drilling for natural gas travel the roads. It is clear that something major has to be done, and the Arkansas Blue Ribbon Committee on Highway Finance is exploring the issue in depth. In June, they announced that their final report with recommendations on how to handle this issue would probably not be ready to present until just prior to the 2011 meeting of the Legislature, and that it may be too late for them to act on their recommendations in that session.

The work that the committee [Arkansas Blue Ribbon Committee on Highway Finance] has done, and the possible means of financing their recommendations, are what make a proposal to give further consideration to another increase in severance tax on natural gas both reasonable and timely. . . . [T]he majority of natural gas that has been discovered and will be discovered in the Fayetteville Shale will be shipped out of Arkansas for consumption in the eastern and northeastern sections of the country, either the gas producers or the consumers of the gas should pay the higher severance tax. They [gas producers] currently pay it for the natural gas they receive from our surrounding states of Louisiana, Texas, and Oklahoma, and there is no reasonable basis for them paying a lesser amount to Arkansas. The severance tax in Louisiana is $.373 per mcf, it's 7% of gross value in Oklahoma and it is 7.5% of market value in Texas.

All three states are receiving significantly more severance tax per mcf than the State of Arkansas. This is simply not right and something needs to be done about it. . . .

My proposed 7% of fair market value, or another fair, significant increase in the natural gas severance tax, should be considered by the committee and the Legislature, and if they decline to adopt such an increase it should be taken to the people for a vote.

Establishing, Operating, and Regulating State Lotteries

State of Arkansas, *Constitution of Arkansas,* Amendment 87.

In 2010 Arkansas voters approved an initiated act to amend the state constitution and legalize a state lottery. The amendment designated the "profits" from sales for academic scholarships in post-secondary education. Amendment 87, listed below, effectively repealed Amendment 15, prohibiting the state from operating a lottery.

Authorizing the General Assembly to establish, operate, and regulate state lotteries

Amendment 87

14. Lotteries.

(a) The General Assembly may enact laws to establish, operate, and regulate State lotteries.

(b) Lottery proceeds shall be used solely to pay the operating expenses of lotteries, including all prizes, and to fund or provide for scholarships and grants to citizens of this State enrolled in public and private non-profit two-year and four-year colleges and universities located within the State that are certified according to criteria established by the General Assembly. The General Assembly shall establish criteria to determine who is eligible to receive the scholarships and grants pursuant to this Amendment.

(c) Lottery proceeds shall not be subject to appropriation by the General Assembly and are specifically declared to be cash funds held in trust separate and apart from the State treasury to be managed and maintained by the General Assembly or an agency or department of the State as determined by the General Assembly.

(d) Lottery proceeds remaining after payment of operating expenses and prizes shall supplement, not supplant, non-lottery educational resources.

(e) This Amendment does not repeal, supersede, amend or otherwise affect Amendment 84 to the Arkansas Constitution or games of bingo and raffles permitted therein.

(f) Except as herein specifically provided, lotteries and the sale of lottery tickets are prohibited.

Lottery Lowdown: Arkansas Family Council

Family Council Action Committee, *Q & A Concerning the Proposed Arkansas Lottery Amendment* (Little Rock, 2007).

The Arkansas Family Council successfully opposed several efforts to create a state-run lottery. Using a widespread network among churches, the council offered multiple reasons for opposing "legalized gambling." Some of those reasons are listed below.

Due to the fact that politicians in Arkansas have repeatedly mounted campaigns to legalize lotteries in Arkansas—the most recent being Lt. Governor Bill Halter's lottery-funded scholarship program—we decided it would be beneficial to devote a portion of our site exclusively to the lottery and its many flaws.

What exactly is wrong with a state lottery? That's the question we hear all the time. *What's the problem? If people want to buy lottery tickets, we should let them buy lottery tickets!* The problem is that a lottery, like any heavy tax, saps money out of the economy. It is a detrimental, inefficient program that never truly lives up to the expectations of the voters.

1. Lotteries are a very bad bet mathematically.

The nerdy flaw. Mathematicians agree that in a standard lottery (as is conducted by most states), the odds of a single ticket winning the jackpot are roughly one in fourteen million (that's 1/14,000,000)! This means that, statistically speaking, only one out of every fourteen million tickets you purchase will have the winning numbers.

As *Arkansas Business* pointed out in a recent editorial, "[In order for the lottery to generate the $100 million per year Lt. Governor Halter promises], Arkansans would have to gamble away almost four times that much, and only a handful of them would win more than they lose." It's bad math, and does nothing to protect the welfare of the citizens who lose money playing the lottery every day.

2. Lotteries constitute a tax.

But lottery ticket-sales are <u>voluntary</u>. No one is required to buy a ticket. That may be true, but the fact of the matter is that while no one is *required* to buy a ticket (they have a choice), those who do purchase tickets have no say over how much of the ticket-price they pay goes to the government; the government just takes whatever profit is left over after the ticket is paid for.

According to a study done in Maryland, the state keeps 32% of lottery ticket sales. . . . That means that if you pay $5 for a lottery ticket, you are, in effect, giving $1.60 directly to the government. If the average lottery player spends $30–$35 each month on lottery tickets, they are giving roughly $10–$11 directly to the government in the form of lottery ticket tax revenue. That's an extremely high sales tax that the state has a monopoly on!

When this practice is applied to tobacco products, we call it a "tobacco tax;" when it's applied to soft drinks, we call it a "soft drink tax;" when applied to alcohol, we call it an "alcoholic beverage tax;" and when we apply it to the cars sitting in our driveways, we call it a "property tax." But when we apply the very same practice to lottery ticket sales, we call it "funding education," or "a voluntary means of collecting revenue." Please. It's a tax, and an extremely high one at that.

3. The lottery tax hurts the poor.

Politicians have called the idea that poor people are more inclined to play the lottery "an urban myth." As *Arkansas Business* recently pointed out, apparently "it's a myth also perpetuated by Duke University researchers working for the National Gambling Impact Study Commission in 1999 and the Federal Reserve Bank at St. Louis, which repeated the findings in a report on lotteries just last year: '[L]ow-income groups spend a larger share of their incomes on the lottery and they also spent more in absolute terms.'"

Poor people are much more inclined to play the lottery than middle- or upper-class citizens are. We know that the lottery has a very hefty sales tax tied to it. Since lottery games are played most heavily by low income individuals and families, it seems fair to say that this program constitutes an unfair, regressive tax on the poor in our state.

Arkansas Business further points out that, "Unfortunately, the share of Arkansans who are living in poverty is significantly higher than the national average (15.8 percent vs. 12.3 percent), so a lottery would be that much more regressive in its effect here than elsewhere." This means that the detrimental effects of the lottery would only be *magnified* here in Arkansas to a degree greater than the states that border us.

The state has a responsibility to enact legislation that does not harm its citizens. A state-sponsored lottery would only hurt its poorest citizens by taking the precious dollars they cannot afford to lose.

4. The lottery is failing in other states, and has not lived up to expectations.

Most states have a lottery. Therefore, Arkansas should have a lottery. That's the logic lottery-proponents espouse. Right now, fewer than ten states do not have at least one state-sponsored lottery in place. Arkansas is one of those states.

A quick lesson in groupthink: The idea is that if the vast majority of the United States has a lottery, it must be a good program. What this doesn't address is why lotteries have consistently struggled to stay in operation in most of those states.

Let's take Tennessee for example. After researching Tennessee's lottery program, our team found that Tennessee's initial lottery game saw a consistent decline in ticket sales during the first few years it operated. How did they offset this decline? First, they increased the cash prizes. This temporary fix helps keep ticket sales on the upswing for a little while, because when more money is on the line, people buy more lottery tickets.

But what about education funding? Remember, the government only takes what is left over *after* cash prizes and administrative costs; some quick 8th grade math tells us that increasing the cash prizes means less money is getting earmarked for education. The lottery is still generating less money for education. So what does the state do? They add another lottery. The truth is that, last we checked, Tennessee has five lottery games designed to benefit education, and the program is still struggling. In fact, this has been the story in virtually every state that has legalized state-run lottery programs. The only thing that seems to keep the lottery illusion alive is its continual expansion—hence why we now have multi-state lotteries with multi-million dollar cash prizes: it's all designed to keep people going back for more lottery tickets.

Regardless of how the state justifies keeping the lottery in place, the only expectations it lives up to are the expectations of those who oppose it.

E. EDUCATION

Education had been an important issue in Arkansas since the Supreme Court outlawed segregation in 1954, and into the second decade of the twenty-first century the Little Rock School District was receiving additional funds from the state in order to carry out desegregation. There were also major differences in the amount of money that school districts spent on the education per pupil in elementary and second schools. And as we have seen, a state lottery was created in order to provide scholarships for Arkansas students who wished to attend college in the state. In addition, as in all other parts of the United States, there were continuing debates over how to improve teaching and ensure that students left school with the knowledge they would need to succeed as adults.

Lake View School District Ruling

Arkansas Supreme Court, *Lake View School, District No 25 of Phillips County, Arkansas, et al. v. Mike Huckabee, Governor of the State of Arkansas, et al.*, March 2, 2000.

Funding for kindergarten through twelfth-grade education became a major issue in the 1990s as smaller rural districts sought to alter the Arkansas General Assembly's funding formula for the common schools. In 1992 the small Lake View School District in rural Phillips County sued the State of Arkansas in an attempt to get a larger share of state funding. Eight years later, after extensive litigation, the Arkansas Supreme Court ruled that the Arkansas Department of Education must develop a method of allocation to ensure "adequate funding" for every student in the public schools.

LAKE VIEW SCHOOL DISTRICT No. 25
of Phillips County, Arkansas, *et al.* v.
Mike HUCKABEE, Governor
of the State of Arkansas, *et al.*
99-28 ___ S.W.3d ___
Supreme Court of Arkansas
Opinion delivered March 2, 2000

I. Procedural History

The history of this case is long and tortured, but reviewing the history is critical to the resolution of the matter. On August 19, 1992, Lake View filed suit against the State of Arkansas, in which it contested the constitutionality of the public school funding system under both the U.S. Constitution and the Arkansas Constitution. Lake View requested that the chancery court declare the school funding system unconstitutional and that the court enjoin implementation of the unconstitutional system. . . .

What was at issue in the Lake View case was the disparity in funds available for education in school districts across the state under the school funding system. In 1994, school districts received approximately thirty percent of their revenue from local funds, sixty percent from state aid, and ten percent from federal funds. Local funds were tied to the local tax base which was tied to property values within the districts. School districts with higher property values necessarily generated higher local taxes and more money available for education. This resulted in significant disparities. As an example, disparities in per pupil expenditures in the 1992/93 school year ranged from $4,064 spent per pupil in the Little Rock School District to $2,270 spent per pupil in the Mountain View School District. One of the purposes of state aid was to equalize per pupil expenditures regardless of the wealth of the school district and to make available equal educational opportunities for all students. . . .

In its November 9, 1994 order, the chancery court concluded that the equal protection provisions of the Arkansas Constitution (Article 2, §§ 2, 3, 18) applied to Arkansas school funding and that there was no rational basis for the disparity in available school funds among poor and wealthy school districts under Arkansas' school funding system. The court further concluded that the school funding system violated Article

14, § 1, of the Arkansas Constitution by failing to provide a "general, suitable and efficient system of free public schools." Two problems were pointed out by the 1994 Order: (1) school districts were allowed to keep excess tax revenues raised locally, thereby producing funding variances; and (2) state aid under Act 1 of 1994 did not cure the disparities in per pupil expenditures.

The chancery court stayed the effect of its decision for two years to give the Arkansas General Assembly time to implement a constitutional system "in conformity with this opinion." . . . [I]n 1995, the General Assembly passed three acts in an attempt to comply with the 1994 Order:

> Act 916—Levied an income tax surcharge of ten percent against residents in a school district which failed to pass the base millage for school funding.
> Act 917—Repealed the old funding system; required the Board of Education to review minimum standards of accreditation and develop a definition for what constitutes an adequate education; and required that all school districts levy the base millage and that the State Treasurer supplement school district revenues to meet the base millage level.
> Act 1194—Appropriated funds for grants and aids to local school districts, special programs, and vocational technical education for the biennium.

Hereinafter in this opinion, the three acts will be referred to as the "1995 legislative acts."

In 1996, Lake View filed its third and fourth amended complaints. In the third . . . complaint, Lake View asked for a declaration that Act 917 of 1995 was unconstitutional under the Arkansas Constitution's equal protection article (Article 2) and its general education article (Article 14). The fourth . . . complaint repeated allegations that Acts 916 and 917 of 1995 were unconstitutional and requested class certification of all generally affected persons in the state. On August 22, 1996, the chancery court certified the class of affected persons as all school districts in the state, students and parents of students in all school districts, school board members of all school districts, and school district taxpayers who have paid taxes to support the public school system.

On August 13, 1996, the chancery court entered a scheduling order which included the setting of a trial "on compliance with this Court's previous orders" to be held over seven days in November 1996.

On November 5, 1996, Amendment 74 to the Arkansas Constitution was passed by a vote of the people. This amendment amended Article 14, § 1, of the Arkansas Constitution and provided a base millage rate of twenty-five mills for all school districts. It further specifically allowed variances in funding among the school districts and authorized school districts to levy additional taxes above the base millage rate for maintenance and operation.

On November 18, 1996, the chancery court entered three orders in which (1) the judge of the chancery court who heard the case in 1994 and entered the 1994 Order recused; and (2) the court postponed the compliance trial because the seven days allotted would not be sufficient time to conduct the trial. In a third order, the chancery court found:

. . . The Arkansas Assembly enacted Acts 916 and 917 in 1995 to establish a new school funding system. A presumption exists that Acts 916 and 917 are constitutional.

. . . Plaintiffs have the burden of going forward with the evidence and the burden of proving that the newly enacted school funding system is unconstitutional.

. . . The enactment of a new school funding system and new statistical data constitute new facts. Therefore, the doctrine of *the law of the case* is not applicable, and the scope of the trial will not be limited to those issues raised at the previous trial of this cause [November 9, 1994]. Nor will the trial be limited to compliance with this Court's previous order [1994 Order]. . . .

In April of 1997, Act 1307 of 1997 and Act 1361 of 1997 (hereinafter the "1997 legislative acts") became law. Act 1307 amended or repealed the former school funding system. It further set out the calculations of what millages may be used to meet the base millage rate of twenty-five mills and set out a system for public school revenues and expenditures, including what a general, suitable, and efficient system of education should include. Act 1361 appropriated funds for grants and aids to local school districts and for special programs for the next biennium.

On May 29, 1997, Lake View . . . contested the constitutionality of the 1995 and 1997 legislative acts under Article 2 (equal protection) and

Article 14 (general education) of the Arkansas Constitution and the Fourteenth Amendment of the U.S. Constitution. . . .

On September 8, 1997, Lake View filed a . . . complaint praying that the 1995 and 1997 legislative acts be declared unconstitutional "under federal and state standards." . . .

On October 30, 1997, the chancery court struck the . . . complaint and noted that there had been no "substantive strides" in the case. . . . The court set a trial for January 27, 1998, through February 8, 1998. . . . On November 3, 1997, the chancery court allowed Lake View until November 21, 1997, to comply with the October 30, 1997 order or to file "some other pleading under which the plaintiffs wish to proceed." On November 21, 1997, Lake View filed an eighteen-page petition to show cause why the State of Arkansas should not be held in contempt of court for failure to comply with the 1994 Order. In that petition, Lake View measured the 1995 and 1997 legislative acts and Amendment 74 against the yardstick of the 1994 Order and asked the chancery court to order the State to provide it with financial information regarding public school funding, after which the court should hold the State in contempt for noncompliance. On December 5, 1997, the State of Arkansas moved to dismiss Lake View's petition to show cause under Rule 8(a) and 12(b)(6) of the Arkansas Rules of Civil Procedure.

On January 29, 1998, counsel for the State of Arkansas and Lake View presented the chancery court with an Agreed Order approved by all counsel, including the Office of the Arkansas Attorney General. The salient parts of the Agreed Order were:

> A pool of money has been created by the efforts of Lake View. Since the 1994 Order, there has been an increase in funding of at least $65 million in each of the fiscal years 1996–97 and 1997–98, totaling approximately $130 million.
>
> The parties agree that upon application of Lake View the chancery court may order reasonable attorneys' fees and costs to be paid.
>
> Upon resolution of the attorneys' fees and cost issue, Lake View shall dismiss this case with prejudice.
>
> Dismissal of the case with prejudice shall act as a bar to all claims by the Lake View class and interveners that the 1995 and

1997 legislative acts violate the federal or state constitutions or federal or state statutes.

On February 2, 1998, Lake View filed a petition for attorneys' fees in which it requested a fee award of $10.25 million or, alternatively, fifteen percent of $130 million.

On February 5, 1998, an order approving notice to class members was signed by the chancery court, calling for a fairness hearing on the proposed Agreed Order. Depositions of two practicing attorneys, Carroll E. Ray and Richard F. Hatfield, who favored payment of the requested attorneys' fees, were taken and filed with the court.

On February 20, 1998, the American Civil Liberties Union filed an objection to the Agreed Order. . . . The Little Rock School District and the Pulaski County Special School District also objected to payment of attorneys' fees from funds allocated to their respective districts. Dr. Winston Simpson of the Bryant School District disagreed that $130 million resulted from Lake View's efforts. On March 25, 1998, the State of Arkansas responded to the various objections and urged the chancery court to sign the Agreed Order. The State pointed out that what was before the court was an Agreed Order by the parties and not a settlement agreement.

The State of Arkansas also filed a prehearing brief which included an argument that the State of Arkansas had complied with the 1994 Order by enacting the 1995 and 1997 legislative acts. Amendment 74 had also passed as well. . . . [T]he Governor [Mike Huckabee] directed the Attorney General [Mark Pryor] to "pursue with the settlement."

On March 20, 1998, and April 1, 1998, hearings were held before the chancery court on matters relating to the Agreed Order. . . . The chancery court . . . refused to approve the Agreed Order [except the sections related to attorneys' fees]. In doing so, the court alluded to its concern about barring future litigation. With respect to Lake View's counsel, the court stated that they had performed a "historic service" and need to be "paid handsomely." It was their efforts, according to the court, that led to the State's "getting a fair school funding formula in place." The court urged the parties to settle the attorneys' fees issue. It concluded that if the court could award fees, it would [make the award]. . . . After the ruling, counsel for the State of Arkansas announced that the State stood by the Agreed

Order and that the case involved whether the State had complied with the 1994 Order by enacting the 1995 and 1997 legislative acts and with the passage of Amendment 74.

On April 3, 1998, Lake View requested the chancery court to determine reasonable attorneys' fees and "adjudicate the matter in its finality." On April 6, 1998, a hearing on attorneys' fees occurred before the chancery court in which the court repeated that Lake View's counsel "need to be rewarded." Counsel for the State of Arkansas contended that the 1994 Order was moot but affirmed the Agreed Order recitation that a $130 million fund was created by Lake View's efforts. Counsel for the Little Rock School District argued that the 1994 Order was moot owing solely to the fact that a new school funding system was now in place. The chancery court announced the figure of $7 million as [payment for] attorneys' fees. . . .

On April 9, 1998, the Attorney General's office for the State of Arkansas raised objections to attorneys' fees for Lake View. [On] April 10, 1998 . . . the chancery court approved an order of . . . award of attorneys' fees in the amount of $7 million. The notice provided that after payment of the fees, the case would be dismissed as moot. . . .

On August 17, 1998, the chancery court entered its final order on the matter. It found that Lake View's . . . complaint and show-cause petition were moot because Amendment 74 had changed the standard for the school funding system and allowed funding variances among the school districts. The court stated that the same analysis applies to the legislation passed by the General Assembly in 1995 and 1997. The court added that the complaint and show-cause petition should be dismissed for failure to state a claim, because the 1995 and 1997 legislative acts are presumed constitutional and no facts were alleged supporting lack of a rational basis for those acts. . . . In this regard, the chancery court noted that Lake View's show-cause petition did assert that findings made in the 1994 Order were violated, but concluded that those findings "*[m]ay* necessarily have changed and *may not be* applicable today." (Emphasis ours.)

With respect to burden of proof, the chancery court stated that the State of Arkansas had the burden of proving that it had complied with the 1994 Order, but that the 1995 and 1997 legislative acts were presumed constitutional. According to the court, this meant that Lake View had the burden of proving that "there is no rational basis for the current legislation." The chancery court added: "Because the new statutes and constitutional amendment could be construed by the Court as a response to the 1994 Orders, the Orders themselves provide a rational response for the new funding formula.". . .

. . . Lake View posits multiple bases for reversing the final order of the chancery court. We believe that two of those points have merit. We do not agree with Lake View, however, that the chancery court was required to sign the Agreed Order. Approval of the court is required for a class action compromise. . . . We do not view court approval as a rubber stamp but rather as action entailing discretion by the trial court. . . .

[Ruling of the Arkansas Supreme Court]

Lake View contends that without a trial on the constitutionality of state initiatives since 1994, there is no basis for the chancery court's finding of mootness and failure to state a claim. We agree. . . .

. . . [T]he issue is whether the 1994 Order has any relevancy in light of the fact that the State's school funding formula has changed since 1994. The chancery court concluded that the mere fact of these legislative and constitutional changes rendered the 1994 findings obsolete.

We cannot subscribe to that conclusion. It would take an extraordinary leap of faith to assume that the mere passage of a new school funding formula resolves all issues relating to disparities in the school funding system set out in the 1994 Order. . . .

This brings us to the Agreed Order. There is no doubt that Lake View agreed to dismiss the case and forego future litigation if its attorneys' fees and costs were paid. But the chancery court refused to sign the order because it barred future contests on the unconstitutionality of the school funding system. The court also refused to approve attorneys' fees of $7 million, following Lake View's agreement that the case was moot. At that point, the agreement among the parties had fallen through, and the parties were back to square one on the compliance issue. . . .

. . . We believe that a compliance trial and decision by the chancery court on whether the disparities in treatment noted in the 1994 order have been corrected so as to pass constitutional muster is the best way to achieve those goals. Without a compliance trial and the chancery court's analysis and decision, we are loathe to conclude that mere changes in the school funding system warrant a dismissal.

We reverse and remand for a trial to take place as soon as is practicable.

Arkansas Lottery Sales and Scholarships

Data for the chart below was collected by the author from the Arkansas Lottery Commission, the Arkansas Department of Higher Education, and the US Census State Data Center for Arkansas at the University of Arkansas at Little Rock.

By 2010 the sale of Arkansas lottery tickets was a producing a large amount of money for college scholarships. The table below shows the amount of money spent by each Arkansas county and the number of scholarships awarded to students in the county. It provides some evidence that, as critics had warned, the poor were buying more lottery tickets than the rich and getting fewer scholarships in return.

ARKANSAS LOTTERY SALES AND SCHOLARSHIPS BY COUNTY, 2010

COUNTY	POPULA-TION	INCOME PER CAPITA ($)	LOTTERY SALES ($)	SCHOLAR-SHIPS AWARDED	SALES PER CAPITA ($)	SCHOLAR-SHIPS PER CAPITA
Arkansas	19,236	33,737	6,643,055	275	345.34	14
Ashley	22,233	23,629	1,615,421	176	72.66	8
Baxter	42,115	28,944	4,237,274	425	100.61	10
Benton	209,791	33,908	11,301,719	1,863	53.87	9
Boone	36,881	23,893	4,169,731	460	113.06	12
Bradley	11,906	26,049	1,277,199	93	107.27	8
Calhoun	5,435	22,814	854,833	58	157.28	11
Carroll	27,557	24,786	2,841,370	155	103.11	6
Chicot	11,993	23,522	2,387,663	82	199.09	7
Clark	23,888	25,534	5,513,440	347	230.80	15
Clay	15,845	24,099	1,028,583	146	64.92	9
Cleburne	25,397	28,676	4,680,849	273	184.31	11
Cleveland	8,665	22,177	1,537,856	123	177.48	14
Columbia	24,146	22,335	2,609,529	—	108.07	—
Conway	20,755	27,748	5,642,880	302	271.88	15
Craighead	92,640	27,873	13,906,142	1,186	150.11	13
Crawford	59,682	25,029	6,058,690	701	101.52	12

COUNTY	POPULA-TION	INCOME PER CAPITA ($)	LOTTERY SALES ($)	SCHOLAR-SHIPS AWARDED	SALES PER CAPITA ($)	SCHOLAR-SHIPS PER CAPITA
Crittenden	52,554	29,119	7,259,450	447	138.13	9
Cross	18,808	22,589	2,741,690	217	145.77	12
Dallas	8,144	23,565	3,235,972	85	397.34	10
Desha	13,538	27,321	2,921,454	129	215.80	10
Drew	18,670	25,069	2,779,878	218	148.90	12
Faulkner	106,823	30,149	17,448,701	1,864	163.34	17
Franklin	18,185	21,944	2,720,501	217	149.60	12
Fulton	11,688	22,454	796,848	139	68.18	12
Garland	97,465	28,678	13,464,235	1,025	138.14	11
Grant	17,690	29,420	3,272,191	234	184.97	13
Greene	40,684	21,818	6,215,142	507	152.77	12
Hempstead	22,900	24,150	5,087,678	197	222.17	9
Hot Spring	31,909	27,990	4,436,541	390	139.04	12
Howard	14,143	26,391	2,130,033	189	150.61	13
Independence	34,641	27,199	7,569,578	460	218.51	13
Izard	12,992	21,098	1,122,826	173	86.42	13
Jackson	16,936	25,280	4,392,515	170	259.36	10
Jefferson	78,373	26,484	21,671,778	889	276.52	11
Johnson	24,851	23,565	3,457,085	300	139.11	12
Lafayette	7,705	22,806	914,642	60	118.71	8
Lawrence	16,861	30,803	3,414,259	214	202.49	13
Lee	10,782	20,488	1,302,449	63	120.80	6
Lincoln	13,609	22,409	1,772,271	116	130.23	9
Little River	12,807	23,028	915,300	88	71.47	7
Logan	22,567	23,970	3,624,905	255	160.63	11
Lonoke	65,233	31,770	15,026,922	877	230.36	13
Madison	15,651	27,456	1,698,795	162	108.54	10
Marion	16,774	23,272	2,401,837	152	143.19	9
Miller	43,226	24,158	4,118,381	145	95.28	3
Mississippi	46,808	24,411	7,959,997	305	170.06	7
Monroe	8,518	26,246	2,067,126	84	242.68	10

COUNTY	POPULA-TION	INCOME PER CAPITA ($)	LOTTERY SALES ($)	SCHOLAR-SHIPS AWARDED	SALES PER CAPITA ($)	SCHOLAR-SHIPS PER CAPITA
Montgomery	9,047	20,587	417,454	117	46.14	13
Nevada	9,157	21,006	3,377,046	86	368.79	9
Newton	8,298	23,280	613,627	113	73.95	14
Ouachita	25,770	38,157	6,464,950	268	250.87	10
Perry	10,317	29,211	1,423,112	127	137.94	12
Phillips	21,603	23,091	2,974,025	170	137.67	8
Pike	10,616	27,552	1,737,459	136	163.66	13
Poinsett	24,721	24,703	6,871,804	238	277.97	10
Polk	20,257	23,862	1,841,566	281	90.91	14
Pope	59,952	23,850	11,068,288	900	184.62	15
Prairie	8,580	25,109	2,019,143	107	235.33	12
Pulaski	376,797	43,092	93,399,321	4,620	247.88	12
Randolph	18,134	22,533	1,961,770	244	108.18	13
Saint Francis	26,336	32,165	3,499,395	195	132.87	7
Saline	98,209	22,976	18,019,061	1,333	183.48	14
Scott	11,248	26,053	1,411,137	142	125.46	14
Searcy	8,048	35,112	1,363,347	105	169.40	13
Sebastian	122,274	26,663	11,796,699	1,468	96.48	12
Sevier	16,519	26,178	1,703,361	169	103.12	10
Sharp	17,866	24,015	2,479,745	187	138.80	10
Stone	12,090	23,419	1,374,064	141	113.65	12
Union	43,213	26,547	7,568,315	425	175.14	10
Van Buren	16,575	26,357	2,684,954	153	161.99	9
Washington	195,803	24,286	18,894,036	2,233	96.50	11
White	74,845	30,845	15,172,348	918	202.72	12
Woodruff	7,439	22,941	2,282,768	66	306.86	9
Yell	21,976	29,463	3,250,414	211	147.91	10
TOTAL	2,855,390		$459,916,256	32189		

Arkansas Adopts National Educational Standards

Department of Education, Common Core Standards Initiative, http://www.commoncorearkansas.org/what/ (accessed January 17, 2013).

Seeking to improve the quality of education, in 2012 the Arkansas Department of Education adopted a set of national standards for courses in the state's kindergarten through high school curriculum.

The Common Core State Standards initiative is a state-led effort coordinated by the National Governors Association Center for Best Practices (NGA Center) and the Council of Chief State School Officers (CCSSO). The standards were developed in collaboration with teachers, school administrators and other experts to provide a clear and consistent framework to prepare our students for college and the workforce.

These standards define the knowledge and skills students should have within their K-12 education so they will graduate high school able to succeed in entry-level, credit- bearing academic college courses and in the workforce. They are designed to be robust and relevant to the real world. The new learning standards stress conceptual understanding and application. They are internationally benchmarked to guarantee our students are competitive in the emerging global marketplace.

The Arkansas State Board of Education adopted the Common Core State Standards in July 2010. With our students fully prepared for the future, our state will be best positioned to compete successfully in the global economy.

The Common Core State Standards provide opportunity to ensure all students, no matter where they live, are prepared for success in post-secondary education and the workforce. The standards are designed to be robust and relevant to the real world, reflecting the knowledge and skills our young people need to experience success in college and the workforce.

Currently, each state has its own set of standards. Consequently, what students are expected to learn varies state to state. The new standards articulate the same expectations for all students and ensure they are receiving a high quality education consistently, no matter where they live.

The Common Core State Standards represent a coherent progression of learning expectations in English language arts and mathematics designed to prepare students for college and career success.

A significant piece of the initiative is the adoption of a common assessment system. Along with 23 other states, Arkansas is a member of the Partnership for Assessment of Readiness for College and Careers (PARCC) which has formed to create a next generation assessment system to provide more services and supports to students and teachers than are currently available. The common assessment is a natural continuation of the work already underway in Arkansas and builds on our current assessment system. By partnering with other states, we will be able to leverage resources, share expertise and produce a system that will meet the needs and expectations of Arkansas students and teachers.

The new assessment system will be in place in the 2014–2015 school year. Until then, the ADE will continue using the Benchmark and End of Course exams to assess students in mathematics, English language arts, and science.

In Arkansas, the implementation of the new standards, including training for teachers, is ongoing. Our goal is to be ready when the new assessments arrive in 2014–2015.

F. NATURAL GAS AND THE ENVIRONMENT

The contemporary "green revolution," with its concern for the physical environment and natural resources, began as an organized movement in the 1970s and gained additional support in Arkansas in the 1980s when the General Assembly adopted "The Natural State" as the state's official nickname. Concern for environmental issues focused attention on water quality, wildlife habitat, and forest management. Ironically, discovery of natural gas deposits in the Ozark hill country presented a serious challenge to environmentalists. Concerns over how developing the gas resources would affect surface and ground water and the county and state road system, as well as how fluids would be used to extract the gas, became some of the most divisive issues in the first decade of the twenty-first century. Most of the raw natural gas was transported out of state for refining and preparation for retail sales.

The Fayetteville Shale

"Fayetteville Shale: Reducing Environmental Impacts,"
http://lingo.cast.uark.edu/LINGOPUBLIC/index.htm (accessed
January 18, 2013).

A website maintained by the University of Arkansas in cooperation
with Argonne National Laboratories provided information on the
natural gas exploration and extraction going on in the Fayetteville
Shale natural gas exploration. The selection below comes from an
introductory section.

An introduction to the Fayetteville Shale including its location and geographic extent, economic importance, and physical characteristics.

The Fayetteville Shale is an unconventional natural gas reservoir
located on the Arkansas side of the Arkoma Basin, ranging in thickness
from 50 to 550 feet and ranging in depth from 1,500 to 6,500 feet. The
shale is a Mississippian-age shale that is the geologic equivalent of the
Caney Shale found on the Oklahoma side of the Arkoma Basin and the
Barnett Shale found in north Texas.

The Fayetteville Shale play stretches across Arkansas from approximately Fort Smith east to beyond Little Rock, Arkansas. It is approximately 50 miles wide from north to south. The most active area of natural
gas development is from western Conway County through eastern White
County. Development further to the east is anticipated to proceed very
slowly because the shale is considerably deeper, making gas extraction
less economical.

The Fayetteville Shale is important to Arkansas because it holds large
quantities of natural gas. Unlike more traditional oil and gas fields that
contain hydrocarbons in porous rock formations, shale holds natural gas
in a fine-grained rock matrix. Until recent years, most shale formations
were not considered profitable areas for gas production. With new technology and elevated natural gas prices, companies have made the Barnett
Shale play in north Texas one of the hottest production fields in the country. Encouraged by the success in the Barnett Shale formation, operators
looked at other large shale formations, including the Fayetteville Shale.

Geologists describe the Fayetteville Shale formation as tight, which
means it requires fracturing to produce economic quantities of gas. The
most prolific gas production from the Fayetteville Shale is associated with

---

horizontal wells that have been completed with multi-stage fracture jobs in the middle to lower portions of the formation. At the end of 2007, there were approximately two million acres under lease to production companies in the play. It is anticipated that thousands of wells will be drilled during the next several years. This activity will include construction and installation of roads and pipelines, as well as drilling fluid disposal pits and infrastructure to handle hundreds of millions of gallons of fracturing fluids.

Natural Gas Drilling in the Fayetteville Shale Region

Arkansas Geological Commission, *Report on Fayetteville Shale Deposits* (Little Rock, AR: Arkansas Geological Survey, 2009).

Beginning in 2004, the extraction of natural gas quickly became a big business in Arkansas.

The Fayetteville Shale Formation (Upper Mississippi) is the current focus of a regional shale-gas exploration and development program within the eastern Arkoma Basin of Arkansas. Approximately 2.5 million acres have been leased in the Fayetteville Shale gas play with a cumulative production of 106 BCF [billion cubic feet] since drilling began in 2004. Annual 2007 production from the Fayetteville Shale B-43 producing region is reported as 89,138,371 Mcf [million cubic feet] by the Arkansas Oil and Gas Commission. The thickness of the producing zone ranges from 50 to 550 feet and wells range from 1,500 to 6,500 feet deep.

As of September 17, 2007, approximately 436 wells have been drilled and completed in the Fayetteville Shale and petroleum services companies are relocating to Arkansas in order to capitalize on the economic boon that is occurring in the state. Southwestern Energy and Chesapeake Energy are the major players in this emerging gas play and the two companies report a combined expenditure of > $1.5 billion on Fayetteville Shale development for 2007. As of February 19, 2008 there are 561 producing gas wells; however, many additional wells have been drilled and completed and operators await construction of gas gathering systems before these wells begin production. Southwestern Energy reports that average completed well costs for horizontal wells with multistage slick water fracture completions is approximately $2.9 Million. The average horizontal lateral length for Southwestern wells drilled in 2007 is 3,120 feet and average time to drill to total depth is 15 days. Estimated ultimate recoveries (EUR) for horizontal wells with laterals greater than 3,000 feet range from 2.0 to 2.5 Bcf per well. Approximately 1700 governmental sections are available for Fayetteville Shale development within the core region of the gas play. Schlumberger has built a 31,000 sq ft facility in Conway, Arkansas to provide operators with well services for Fayetteville Shale development and currently touts a staff of 202 employees. Southwestern Energy and Chesapeake Energy have opened offices in Conway County and White County respectively to facilitate Fayetteville development. Texas Gas Transmission plans to build a 167-mile gas transmission line from Conway County, Arkansas to Coahoma County, Mississippi to transport Fayetteville Shale gas. This proposed pipeline is referred to as the "Fayetteville Lateral" and has an estimated ultimate capacity of 1.1 BCF/day. Other industry partners involved with Fayetteville Shale exploration and development ventures include: Hallwood Energy, KCS Resources, Tepee Petroleum, Edge Petroleum, Alta Operating, Aspect Energy, XTO Energy and 14 other companies.

Environmentalist Criticism

Earthjustice, "Fact Sheet on Fracking," http://earthjustice.org/features/campaigns/fact-sheet-on-fracking (accessed January 10, 2013).

Supporters of natural gas saw fracking as the answer to America's energy problems, but many environmental groups did not agree.

"Fracking" is a term used to refer to oil and gas development, generally. Technically, "fracking" is short for "hydraulic fracturing," a process used in 90 percent of the wells, whereby fluid is injected underground at high pressure to fracture rock and release oil or gas trapped inside the formation.

Fracking fluid—which is laced with toxic chemicals that have not been fully tested or disclosed to the public—may be released into the environment through inadequate waste disposal, leaks, spills, and other accidents, presenting serious risks to public health and the environment.

. . . The United States is experiencing a natural gas rush. Natural gas development in the Rocky Mountains region, in the Northeast's Marcellus Shale deposit, and in other parts of the country is skyrocketing.

With an increase in domestic production and massive corporate investment backing the industry, natural gas is quickly becoming a larger component of America's energy portfolio.

The champions of natural gas promote it as a clean energy alternative, but natural gas development leaves extensive environmental degradation in its wake. From well site preparation, to drilling and production, and finally to the disposal of wastes, the industry pollutes soil, air, and water, and leaves scars on the landscape that last for decades.

Natural gas is not a permanent solution to our energy crisis and brings with it the same baggage as other fossil fuels: pollution and environmental destruction. That's why Earthjustice promotes clean, renewable energy sources—such as wind and solar—that can eventually replace fossil fuels. We are working at the state level to guide public utility commissions along a path to a clean energy future. This work entails prioritizing alternative energy sources, removing barriers to clean energy, and investing in energy storage infrastructure.

Water Use in Fayetteville Deep Shale Gas Exploration

Chesapeake Energy Corp., "FACT SHEET, JULY 2010," © 2010 Chesapeake Energy, www.chk.com (accessed November 15, 2011).

The process of fracking used to extract natural gas from underground deposits raised major concerns about its effect on the quality of nearby water. In the following document, the Chesapeake Energy Corporation provides information on its own use of water in the development of natural gas resources in Arkansas.

How much water is used in Fayetteville deep shale gas development? Water is an essential component of Chesapeake Energy's (Chesapeake) deep shale gas development. Chesapeake uses water for drilling, where a mixture of clay and water is used to carry rock cuttings to the surface, as well as to cool and lubricate the drill bit. Drilling a typical Chesapeake Fayetteville deep shale gas well requires approximately 65,000 gallons of water. Water is also used in hydraulic fracturing, where a mixture of water and sand is injected into the deep shale at a high pressure to create small cracks in the rock which allows gas to flow. Hydraulically fracturing a typical Chesapeake Fayetteville horizontal deep shale gas well requires an average of 4.9 million gallons per well. How does Fayetteville deep shale gas water use compare to regional uses?

The volume of water necessary to drill and fracture Fayetteville deep shale gas wells represents a very small percentage of the total water resources used in the Fayetteville geographic area. This area includes 19 counties in East-central, central and West-central Arkansas. The total water use in the Fayetteville Shale area in 2005 was approximately 1.3 trillion gallons. The natural gas industry is expected to increase the amount used by less than 0.2%, and is well within available resources in the region. Again, this volume is very small in terms of the overall water budget for the area. The largest water users in the Fayetteville Shale area are irrigation (approximately 63%), power generation (approximately 33%), municipal/public water supply (approximately 2%), industrial and mining (approximately 1%), and livestock (less than 0.5%). Water used in Chesapeake Fayetteville deep shale gas wells differs most notably from all other uses because it is temporary, occurring only once during the drilling and completion phases of each well. Use of this water does not represent a long-term commitment of the resource in the Fayetteville Shale geographic area. How much water is used in Fayetteville deep shale gas development compared with other energy sources?

Water and energy are interdependent. Water is essential to energy resource development. Conversely, energy resources are needed for producing, processing, distributing and using water resources. A typical Fayetteville deep shale gas well will produce approximately 2.4 Bcf (billion cubic feet) of gas over its lifetime, the amount of water used to produce the gas equates to about two gallons for every one million British thermal units (MMBTU—one MMBTU equals about a thousand cubic feet of gas). To put this in perspective, this is approximately 20% of the water needed to produce one MMBTU of coal that is ready to burn in a power plant, or 0.08% of the water needed to produce the same energy equivalent of ethanol for fuel. The table on the following page compares water use per unit of energy for several energy sources.

ENERGY SOURCE	GALLONS OF WATER USED PER MMBTU OF ENERGY
Fayetteville Shale Natural Gas[1]	2.02
Coal (no slurry transport)	2–8
Coal (with slurry transport)	13–32
Nuclear (uranium ready to use in a power plant)	8–14
Conventional Oil	8–20
Synfuel-Coal Gasification	11–26
Oil Shale	22–56
Tar Sands	27–68
Synfuel–Fisher Tropsch (from coal)	41–60
Enhanced Oil Recovery (EOR)	21–2,500
Biofuels (Irrigated Corn Ethanol, Irrigated Soy Biodiesel)	> 2,500

[1]*Source:* GWPC Report

While these represent continuing consumption, the water used for a shale gas well is a one-time use[;] where does the water come from?

Chesapeake utilizes several sources of water in Fayetteville deep shale gas exploration including rivers, ponds, lakes and to a limited extent, groundwater wells. Due to the abundance of surface water in the Fayetteville Shale area, it is preferred by the state for non-domestic use. As a result, Chesapeake has committed to using surface water with the construction of a 500-acre-foot capacity reservoir filled with surplus diverted water from the Little Red River. This reservoir can supply water during the drilling and fracturing of 1,200 to 2,000 wells. Chesapeake is also reviewing the use of a variety of other water resources, such as discharge water from industrial or city wastewater treatment plants, power plant cooling water and the reuse of fracturing water. In addition, Chesapeake is looking into working with local officials to arrange water purchases from municipalities and rural water systems when drilling in their areas. Water is typically transported by temporary pipelines to drilling locations for storage in tanks or impoundments prior to use. In some cases, Chesapeake also uses trucks to transport water supplies. Due to the diverse geographic area overlying the Fayetteville Shale, the overall mix of water sources used depends on the region and the availability of sources near drilling sites.

Are water resources protected and regulated?

Regardless of the source, water used in the drilling and fracturing process by Chesapeake is purchased and, as required, properly permitted. This permitting ensures that water used for drilling and hydraulic fracturing does not interfere with the available supply for other users.

Chesapeake works collaboratively with federal, state and local agencies to ensure that water used for deep shale gas development is consistent with water use plans and does not adversely affect other users. In the Fayetteville Shale area, Chesapeake coordinates closely with entities such as the U.S. Army Corps of Engineers, Arkansas Natural Resources Commission, Arkansas Department of Environmental Quality and others on its water use. Chesapeake's deep shale gas development, with its comparatively small water use per unit of energy, is consistent with the nation's energy/water strategy by making a positive energy and economic contribution at a relatively low cost to the overall water supply. Chesapeake's deep shale gas has the potential to supply decades of natural gas for the U.S., while using less water than other currently available viable energy sources. About Chesapeake[:]

Chesapeake Energy Corporation is one of the largest producers of natural gas and the most active driller of new wells in the U.S. Headquartered in Oklahoma City, the company's operations are focused on discovering and developing unconventional natural gas and oil fields onshore in the U.S. Chesapeake owns leading positions in the Barnett, Fayetteville, Haynesville, Marcellus and Bossier natural gas shale plays and in the Eagle Ford, Granite Wash and various other unconventional oil plays. The company has also vertically integrated its operations and owns substantial midstream, compression, drilling and field service assets. Further information available at www.chk.com.

Government Studies Find Water OK

T. M. Kresse, N. R. Warner, P. D. Hays, A. Down, A. Vengosh, and R. B. Jackson, "Shallow Groundwater Quality and Geochemistry in the Fayetteville Shale Gas-Production Area, North-Central Arkansas," US Geological Survey Scientific

Investigations Report 2012–5273, 2011, http://pubs.usgs.gov/sir/2012/5273/ (accessed January 15, 2013).

In 2011 the Arkansas Department of Environmental Quality did a small study that found no deterioration of the water supply and in 2012 the United States Geological Survey released a much larger study that found the same result. The summary portions of the USGA report are given below.

The Arkansas Department of Environmental Quality (ADEQ) operates a water-quality laboratory in North Little Rock, Arkansas, and analyzes samples using U.S. Environmental Protection Agency approved methods, in addition to participating in the biannual USGS SRS program. The ADEQ sampled 51 domestic wells (unpublished data) distributed throughout the Fayetteville Shale production area in 2011 for a suite of volatile organic compounds, including benzene, toluene, ethylbenzene, and xylene, using U.S. Environmental Protection Agency method 8260C, Volatile Organics by Gas Chromatography/Mass Spectrometry (U.S. Environmental Protection Agency, 2012a). No organic compounds used as additives by the gas industry were detected in any of the samples.

. . . The findings from this study were based on the sampling of 127 domestic wells in the western part of the shale-gas production area, representing approximately one-third of the entire gas-production area. These findings are similar to those of Nottmeier (2012), who sampled 100 wells distributed across the entire shale-gas production area in north-central Arkansas. Nottmeier (2012) also made comparisons to historical analyses and similarly attributed primary control of groundwater geochemistry to natural rock-water interaction. A review of groundwater inorganic chemistry with particular emphasis on chloride concentration was used for this study and that of Nottmeier (2012) to indicate that no regional effects on groundwater are apparent from activities related to gas production in the Fayetteville Shale in north-central Arkansas. [A. M. Nottmeier, "Groundwater Quality Assessment in Domestic Water Wells within the Fayetteville Shale Gas Play in Central Arkansas" (Masters of Science thesis, University of Arkansas, Fayetteville, 2012), 124.]

. . . The Mississippian Fayetteville Shale serves as an unconventional gas reservoir across north-central Arkansas, ranges in thickness from approximately 1,500 to 6,500 feet below the ground surface. Primary permeability in the Fayetteville Shale is severely limited, and successful extraction of the gas reservoir is the result of advances in horizontal drilling techniques and hydraulic fracturing that enhance and develop secondary fracture porosity and permeability. Drilling and production of gas wells began in 2004, with a steady increase in production thereafter. As of April 2012, approximately 4,000 producing gas wells had been completed in the Fayetteville Shale in Arkansas.

Gas-well drilling and completion activities in the Fayetteville Shale have the potential to affect water quality in shallow aquifers. Potential sources of contamination include fluids associated with the drilling operation and spent water from the fracturing process. Contaminant transport pathways include potential leakage from earthen pits used to store drilling mud and other process waters including hydraulic fracturing and flowback fluids, leakage from pipes, and losses from overflows, spills, and other unexpected releases. The process of fracture propagation during hydraulic fracturing adds a lesser but additional threat to shallow aquifer systems by creation of new fracture sets, enlargement of existing vertical fractures, and upward migration of pressurized fluids through poorly cemented annulus sections of the gas well. The potential for migration of gas-production fluids is greater where the gas-production zone is shallow or where deep faulting intersects the vertical or horizontal well bore.

. . . Although preproduction water-quality data were lacking for the wells sampled for this study, geochemical data presented a well-defined pattern of geochemical evolution based on natural rock-water and microbially mediated processes, strongly suggesting that the resulting water quality is derived from these natural processes with no effects from gas-production activities. Results from the groundwater-quality monitoring activities for this study provide a baseline range and variation of geochemistry for the shallow groundwater in the study area, which can be used to assess future potential changes to groundwater quality in the area of gas production from the Fayetteville Shale.

FOR FURTHER READING

For general coverage of contemporary Arkansas, see Ben F. Johnson III, *Modern Arkansas, 1930–1999* (Fayetteville: University of Arkansas Press, 2000); David Maraniss, *First in His Class: A Biography of Bill Clinton*

(New York: Simon and Schuster, 1995); Jeannie Whayne, Thomas A. DeBlack, George Sabo III, and Morris S. Arnold, *A Narrative History of Arkansas* (Fayetteville: University of Arkansas Press, 2002); Grif Stockley, *Ruled by Race: Black/White Relations in Arkansas from Slavery to the Present* (Fayetteville: University of Arkansas Press, 2009).

INDEX